*R*EADING
*D*IFFICULTIES

INSTRUCTION
AND
ASSESSMENT

READING DIFFICULTIES

INSTRUCTION
AND
ASSESSMENT

Barbara Taylor
Larry A. Harris
P. David Pearson

McGRAW-HILL PUBLISHING COMPANY
New York St. Louis San Francisco Auckland Bogotá
Caracas Hamburg Lisbon London Madrid Mexico
Milan Montreal New Delhi Oklahoma City Paris
San Juan São Paulo Singapore Sydney Tokyo Toronto

READING DIFFICULTIES

First Edition
987654

Copyright © 1988 by McGraw-Hill, Inc. All rights reserved.

Library of Congress Cataloging-in-Publication Data

Taylor, Barbara (Barbara M.)
   Reading difficulties: instruction and assessment/Barbara Taylor,
Larry A. Harris, P. David Pearson.
     p.   cm.
   "Developed for Random House by Lane Akers, Inc."
   Bibliography: p.
   Includes index.
   ISBN 0-07-555546-8
   1. Reading disability.   2. Reading—Remedial teaching.
I. Harris, Larry Allen, 1940–   . II. Pearson, P. David.   III. Lane Akers,
Inc.   IV. Title.
LB1050.5.T34 1988
428.4'2—dc19   87-20739
                                             CIP

Cover photo: Rae Russel

Preface

This book is intended for classroom teachers who want to learn about providing sound instruction and assessment for their students who are low-achieving readers. The focus of the book is on instruction and assessment in the regular classroom. Therefore, we see the book as useful for elementary and secondary teachers who are participating in a course or series of in-service sessions on reading difficulties or for teachers who simply want to learn about this field of study on their own. We believe that the suggestions provided for instruction and assessment will also be useful for reading specialists working with small groups of students in schools and for reading tutors working with students on an individual basis in reading clinics.

A contemporary view of the reading process with an emphasis on metacognition and reader and text interaction is employed throughout the text. Part I, The Fundamentals of Reading Difficulties, discusses the reading process as well as difficulties in reading experienced by low-achieving readers (Chapter 1) and factors contributing to low-achieving readers' reading problems (Chapter 2). Two chapters are devoted to motivation (Chapters 3 and 4) because we believe that this topic is of utmost importance when working with low-achieving readers. The book gives specific suggestions for assessing motivation, and it develops a conceptual understanding of how motivation can be rekindled in students who have experienced difficulty with learning to read.

Part II, Instruction and Assessment for Low-Achieving Readers, provides an overview of remedial reading instruction and assessment (Chapter 5). This book was written in response to the perceived need for a reading difficulties textbook that focuses on classroom instruction and assessment in word recognition, comprehension, and vocabulary based on students' reading of actual text. Since low-achieving readers typically receive most of their reading instruction in the regular classroom, classroom teachers need guidance on how to effectively help low-achieving readers learn to read better. We believe that teachers can maximize low-achieving readers' reading growth by focusing on instruction and assessment based on the reading of actual text and on regular classroom reading tasks instead of on instruction and assessment based on reading skills performed in isolation.

The book places a heavy emphasis on instruction. Assessment is necessary, but only insofar as it helps teachers make decisions about initial and ongoing remedial instruction in reading. For this reason, we have placed the chapters on instruction (Chapters 6, 8, and 10) before the chapters on assessment (Chapters 7, 9, and 11) in the areas of word recognition, comprehension, and vocabulary. There are detailed descriptions of instructional techniques that have been found to be effective in improving students' abilities in these three areas. In most cases, we follow a model of explicit instruction in which we explain *what* a particular skill or strategy consists of, *why* the skill or strategy is important, and *when* students would use the skill or strategy as they are reading on their own. We also discuss ways in which a teacher can model *how* to perform a particular skill or strategy and provide suggestions for guided and independent practice. Throughout the chapters on instruction in word recognition, comprehension, and vocabulary there are concrete examples of the instructional strategies we recommend.

The book emphasizes informal assessment (Chapters 7, 9, and 11). It provides detailed explanations of how to assess students' word recognition, comprehension, and vocabulary skills while they are reading instructional level classroom material. Ways in which the teacher can use frequent measurement, careful record keeping, and analysis of collected data to determine students' relatived strengths and weaknesses in these areas are discussed.

Part III, Traditional Approaches to Reading Difficulties, discusses assessment principles applied to remedial reading (Chapter 12). To illustrate what typically has been done in the past in terms of assessment and instruction in the area of remedial reading, we have included chapters on formal diagnostic reading tests and special remedial techniques. We also point out some of the problems with existing commercial diagnostic reading tests and with conventional remedial techniques.

Part IV, Remedial Programs, provides suggestions for implementing a program of remedial instruction and informal assessment for low-achieving readers in the regular classroom (Chapter 15). It also discusses remedial reading programs that might be implemented by reading specialists within elementary buildings or by reading clinicians.

To help the reader comprehend the content of the book, a number of learning aids have been included. Each chapter begins with a list of *main ideas* and ends with a *summary*. *Suggested activities* at the end of most chapters recommend activities the reader can engage in to enhance his or her learning of important concepts and techniques provided in the book. Also, annotated *selected readings* at the end of most chapters provide recommendations for additional reading.

Contents

Part 3   Traditional Approaches to Reading Difficulties   293

READING DIFFICULTIES

INSTRUCTION
AND
ASSESSMENT

Part 1

The Fundamentals
of Reading Difficulties

The first part of this book sets the stage for what is to follow. In this part we make a statement about our views on the nature of the reading process and how children normally come to be literate. Against this backdrop we examine a number of factors that can interfere with learning to read. Various explanations concerning the cause(s) of reading difficulty are discussed and some of the evidence believed to support these explanations examined. However, regardless of the causes for reading difficulties, classroom teachers are confronted with the task of addressing and overcoming the symptoms of the problem. Because a child's willingness to continue trying to learn to read in the face of repeated failures is often the initial problem to be tackled by the teacher, we first devote our attention to the topic of motivation—what it is, how it relates to reading, how it can be rekindled, and how it can be assessed— before we turn to remedial instruction and assessment in Part 2.

Chapter 1

Reading and Reading Difficulties

OVERVIEW

As you read this chapter, use the following list of main ideas to guide your understanding and reflection.

Reading is very closely allied to other language processes such as listening, speaking, and writing. It is better understood when it is regarded as a language process.

Reading is a cognitive process, very much reliant on other basic processes such as attention and memory.

When reading is viewed from these perspectives, we can develop a consistent way of understanding how normal reading occurs and what we do when reading does not develop normally.

Perspective is an important aspect of our lives, for it determines how we view and understand the world around us. As authors of a book about reading difficulty, we are affected by our perspective; the recommendations we give for the assessment and instruction of students who have reading difficulties are a direct function of our view of the processes of reading and learning to read.

When we say that Amy Smith has a reading difficulty, we imply that something is wrong, that somewhere in her reading skill development something that ought to have happened did not happen. Our judgment about the source of Amy's problem is therefore directly affected by our view of what *normally occurs,* how reading skill *normally develops.* And our recommendations for an instructional program for Amy will be similarly biased. We will undoubtedly want to get Amy back on "the right track." Our conception of "the right track" is, again, nothing more or less than a view of the normal reading process.

So, in order to reveal our underlying views of normal reading, we begin our journey into the world of mind, eye, and print with an overview of our perspective about the processes of reading and learning to read. In so doing, we hope that what we say later about assessment and instruction will be clearer, and we hope that you will be able to recognize our biases for what they are—the natural consequences of our point of view about how children learn to read.

Reading is a language process. It is closely linked to other language processes that children acquire: speaking, writing, and listening. Reading, like the other language processes, is a cognitive process. It is centered in the brain, and it involves all the processes that the brain uses in the normal course of mental activity: we pay attention, we perceive, we remember, we forget, and so on.

This chapter has been organized to make these two points as vividly and as convincingly as possible. First it will describe the components of the reading process that characterize it as a language process—its bases in the phonology, syntax, and semantics of oral language. Then it will discuss reading as a cognitive process, using the framework of schema theory to describe how reading works. Finally, it will try to convince you that understanding reading activities and reading difficulties becomes easier and more natural when they are examined from this linguistic and cognitive perspective.

READING AS LANGUAGE

What Children Learn When They Learn Spoken Language

Children learn language. They do it on their own (as long as they can hear others talk), sometimes, it seems, almost in spite of our efforts to perpetuate "charming" baby talk. When they learn language they learn three systems: phonological, semantic, and syntactic.

Phonological Knowledge   The phonological system includes knowledge of the different phonemes (individual sounds) in the language, knowledge of how they are blended together to create words, as well as knowledge of less obvious aspects of the sound system—things like stress, juncture, and pitch. Stress is exemplified by the difference between "I *found* a red bandana" (I did not buy

Language abilities are fundamental to reading. Children can improve their language facility through interactions with people and objects they encounter daily. *(James Silliman)*

it) and "I found a *red* bandana" (not a blue one). Juncture is characterized by the difference between "I *scream*" and *"ice cream,"* in short, word boundaries. Pitch enters the picture in terms of the intonation pattern differences between:

1. You went downtown.

2. You went downtown!

3. You went downtown?

Since the focus of this book is reading rather than listening, it will not dwell on the phonological system. Although phonological knowledge is prerequisite to listening comprehension (if you do not have it, you cannot understand auditory messages), once developed, it seems not to play as major a role in listening comprehension as do the syntactic and semantic systems. In other words, just because a person can discriminate the basic sounds of the language from one another is no guarantee that he or she will understand what anyone says. On the other hand, factors like juncture, stress, and pitch are important in comprehending written and spoken messages.

Syntactic Knowledge   The syntactic system refers to the orderly arrangement among words in sentences. A child's knowledge of snytax is remarkably sophisticated by the time he or she enters school. A six-year-old has probably spoken and/or understood some 80 to 90 percent of the basic sentence patterns he or she will encounter or use as an adult.[1]

Syntactic knowledge is what is at work when we recognize that (4) and (5) but not (6) and (7) are grammatically acceptable English sentences. It is also syntax that accounts for our ability to recognize that (4) and (5) are equivalent in meaning.

4. The boy thanked the girl.

5. The girl was thanked by the boy.

6. Girl was the by thanked boy the.

7. Thanked girl boy was by the the.

It is snytax that is at work when we are able to read (8) and answer questions (9), (10), and (11).

8. The argle zoolked the bordiddy in the ershent because the bordiddy larped the argle.

9. Who zoolked the bordiddy?

10. Why did the argle zoolk the bordiddy in the ershent?

11. What did the bordiddy do to the argle?

Of course, there is no real meaning in (8). Yet we are able to answer (9), (10), and (11) because of our syntactic knowledge and our ability to recognize the syntactic similarities between (8) and the questions (9), (10), and (11). Our ability to answer questions (9), (10) and (11) is evidence that we have actually understood (8); or is it?

Think about what you did when you answered (9), (10), and (11). Then compare it to what you did when you were a student and you were asked that infamous question in your geography classes: What are the major products of X (where X is the name of some country)? If you were clever, you probably searched the text for a sentence beginning with: "The major products of X are. . ..." But did you really understand what you read? Did the fact that you could answer the question prove anything except that you could visually match a question with a similar segment of text? For example, close your eyes and try to paraphrase (8). Chances are that you cannot do it. The reason you cannot paraphrase (8) is that there is no way you can integrate those meaningless nonsense words with anything that you already know about—anything that is already "in your head."

Semantic Knowledge   Your inability to paraphrase (8) leads to a discussion of the importance of the semantic system. Semantic knowledge refers to our knowledge of word meanings (the concepts that underly the labels we call words). But it is more than that. It also includes our knowledge of the

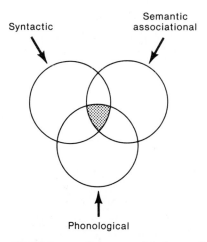

FIGURE 1.1   Sources of Information Used in Listening

relationships among words. Dogs *are* mammals; dogs *have* ears; dogs *do* bark; dogs *are* loyal; dogs and cats are *both* pets.

It is semantic knowledge that accounts for our surprise when we encounter the words *whale* in the same context as the words *horse, farm,* and *plow,* as well as our smugness when we encounter it in the same context as shark, dolphin, or harpoon. It is semantic knowledge that accounts for the fact that most of you will order the random array of words in (12) as they are ordered in (13). You cannot order (12) like (13) by using syntactic knowledge alone.

12. Cows dog barn into the the the chased.

13. The dog chased the cows into the barn.

14. The cows chased the dog into the barn.

15. The barn chased the cows into the dog.

If you use just syntactic knowledge, both (14) and (15) would be acceptable. But knowledge about the world tells you that (13) is the most probable order.

The whole process can be pictured schematically as in Figure 1.1. Comprehension of spoken language occurs when all three systems—phonological, syntactic, and semantic—operate interactively. That is, Matthew Jones understands your spoken message, "Come over to my desk because I want to speak with you," when he is able to match the phonological, syntactic, and semantic elements of your utterance with similar elements that are part of his linguistic knowledge—elements he literally carries around in his head. We will deal with the issue of how we, as human information processors, organize those elements in memory shortly. For now however, let us see how all of what we have said about oral language is related to written language comprehension, or reading, if you will.

What Children Learn When They Learn Written Language

About the only thing that changes when one moves from spoken to written language comprehension is the phonological component. While we would not want to argue that spoken and written language are the same, we believe that our general knowledge of semantic and syntactic relations applies equally to comprehension of spoken and written messages.[2] What differs in the case of comprehending written language is that a new code is introduced—the conventions of our writing system. We *see letters* instead of *hearing sounds*. We *see punctuation* instead of *hearing intonation contours*. We *see underlining* or *italics* or *special print* instead of *hearing* the *stress* a speaker gives to various words in a sentence (or more often, we are forced to use the context of the passage, paragraph, or sentence or infer stress). We *see* the *white spaces* between words instead of *hearing* the *juncture breaks* between words. Table 1.1 compares the phonological features of spoken language with graphemic counterparts in written language. In all cases, except for juncture, the advantage is clearly in favor of listening to a message over reading it, especially for stress and pitch.

We believe in the primacy of speech over writing as the more natural mode of language communication. First, speech was a much earlier development in the natural history of mankind.[3] Second, speech is universal but writing is not; all human societies have a spoken language but not all have a written language. Third, with the exception of deaf children, all children learn their spoken language earlier than their written language. Fourth, spoken language is *learned* naturally and seemingly with little conscious effort whereas written language is usually *taught*, often with torturous effort and great

TABLE 1.1   Written and Spoken Language Counterparts

	Spoken	Written
Organization:	**Auditory Patterns in Temporal Sequence**	**Graphic Marks in a Two-Dimensional Directional Sequence**
	Phonemic Units	Graphemic Units
	1. Significant sounds	1. Letters
	2. Stress	2. Italics, boldface, quotes, other special emphasis features
	3. Pitch (intonation contours)	3. Punctuation
	4. Juncture	4. White space between words

SOURCE: From R. Schreiner (1970), Useful linguistic principles in teaching reading. Paper presented at the annual meeting of the International Reading Association, Anaheim, CA. Used with permission.

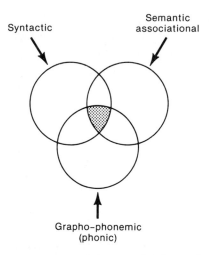

Syntactic

Semantic
associational

Grapho-phonemic
(phonic)

FIGURE 1.2   Sources of Information Used in Reading

frustration on the part of both teacher and learner. Fifth, if a child has a speech or hearing problem, we immediately look for a neurological, medical, or intellectual cause; on the other hand, even the most avid neurological advocates admit that such "organic" causes account for but a small portion of the "reading failures" in our schools. Environmental and emotional causes are more commonly cited for reading difficulties.[4]

The reading process, in the model in Figure 1.2, is similar to that for listening (Figure 1.1). Figure 1.2 depicts the sources of information used by readers in understanding written messages. The only difference between Figures 1.1 and 1.2 is that graphemic information (the right-hand column of Table 1.1) has replaced phonological information (the left-hand column of Table 1.1) as the third source of information in the model. We contend that in comparing listening and reading there is no difference in the role played by syntactic and semantic information. What is added to the reading model is a new "code," a code in which graphic symbols represent certain phonological (sound) features of the spoken language: letters represent sounds (more accurately, graphemes represent phonemes), punctuation represents intonation contours, and spaces represent juncture breaks. It is tempting to oversimplify the model by suggesting that this new code, especially letters that represent sounds, be called *phonic* information. Phonic information is defined as a set of rules that tell a reader how to translate (or recode) printed squiggles into sounds. It includes most of what novice readers learn in the phonics component of their early reading programs. It includes the knowledge that the letter *b* translates as the sound /buh/ or the first sound in the word, /b rd/ (*bird*). It also includes knowledge, be it implicit or explicit to the reader, about phonics generalizations (when two vowels go walking, the first one does the talking: *ai* → /a/), silent letters (*kn* → /n/ or *gh* → /g/) and certain predictable word patterns (*oll* usually → /ol/ as in *toll*).

This model of reading suggests that real reading occurs when all three kinds of information are used in concert (see Figure 1.2). Some theorists, like Ken Goodman and Frank Smith, argue that efficient readers maximize their reliance on syntactic and semantic information in order to minimize the amount of *print to speech* processing (call this decoding, recoding, phonic, or graphemic analysis) they have to do. They literally predict what is coming and get enough graphemic information to verify their predictions. A single letter of a single syllable may be enough information to verify their predictions. For example, it does not take much graphemic information to confirm the hypothesis that *telescope* fits into the sentence, "The astronomer looked through the _____."

Other theorists, most notably Keith Stanovich, argue that efficient readers rarely use contextual information to "short circuit" the word identification process. Since they are so good at word identification processes, including recoding print symbols into speech sounds, they simply do it. Then, argues Stanovich, they reserve their contextual (semantic and syntactic) processing for the more difficult and important process of comprehending the written message.

The final word is not in on this debate, so we have taken the position that good word identification instruction is permissible, even advisable, as long as it is not done in an isolated fashion with little resemblance to the kind of word identification processes that real readers engage in when they are reading.

Regardless of which side of this debate one favors, the basic model in Figure 1.2 still applies to *the whole of the reading process*. And almost all theorists would agree on a few principles. For example, readers must vary the amount of attention they pay to the textual information according to their familiarity with the content: One can read *Time* magazine much more rapidly than a philosophical treatise. In terms of the model, *familiarity* with text can be translated into the degree of congruence between the syntactic and semantic information in the text and the syntactic and semantic relations stored in readers' heads. In simpler terms, familiarity implies *knowing* more about what is in text; hence, processing is simpler and more efficient. Another principle that both groups would agree on is that novice readers allocate more attention to *recoding* print symbols into a speech code than do more expert readers (although the first group would argue that they have not yet realized just how helpful context can be while the second would argue that their decoding skills are not yet adequately developed).

In all these examples of the model at work, a common thread appears: the highly active interactive nature of processing during reading. By interactive, we mean that the reader *varies* the relative amount of emphasis on the various sources of information in the head or in the text, depending on the situation. Such a model is to be contrasted with views of reading which, even in the case of efficient readers, assign an invariant set of steps to processing during reading (for example, that all decoding must be completed before the reader can attend to comprehension processes). The present model will allow for situations in which decoding processes become the primary target of the reader's attention. But whenever possible the model demands that the reader's attention focus on semantic/syntactic (meaning) processes.

READING AS COGNITION

A Schema Theoretic Perspective on the Reading Process

To illustrate reading as a cognitive process, imagine a reader, Dan, thinking out loud about his understanding of a text right after he reads each segment. In the example, the text is presented in boldface, and Dan's think-alouds are presented in quotation marks.[5]

Business had been slow since the oil crisis.

"Oil crisis, hmm, must be some business related to oil. Let's see—service stations? (no, they boom in crises) cars? (could be cars) could be anything affected by inflation! I'll wait and see."

Nobody seemed to want anything elegant anymore.

"Aha! Expensive cars!. . . or recreational vehicles . . . probably Cadillacs, though."

Suddenly the door flew open and a well-dressed man burst onto the showroom floor.

"This must be a salesman? But, it could be the potential buyer? . . . I'll wait and see."

John Stevens looked up from the want-ad section of the morning paper, adjusted his now loose-fitting coat to hide the frayed sleeves of his shirt and rose to meet the man . . .

"Now this is the salesman, right? Times are hard; therefore the want ads, frayed shirt, and weight loss. So the other guy must be the customer, the well-dressed one, I mean."

. . . whose hand-painted tie and rhinestone stickpin seemed incongruous amidst the array of steel-gray and black . . .

"That guy is the customer. And he's one of those got-rich-quick kind of guys. And I bet he's going to buy either a Mercedes or a Rolls Royce, probably a Mercedes. He'll probably pay cash too."

. . . Mercedes sedans. "I'll take it, cash on the line," the man asserted, pointing to the most expensive model on the floor.

"I knew it. He is *nouveau-riche*."

Later, as he completed the paperwork, John muttered to himself, "I'm glad I didn't blow that one." Then he added, "What does he know about elegance,

anyway? What does anyone know about elegance anymore?" With that, he smiled and returned to his newfound pastime.

"Aha! We have an existential cynic. He probably remembers better times and, definitely, better customers. He seems resigned to his new fate in life, though."

Each of our protocols for this text would be different from Dan's, but we would all experience certain similarities. For example, although a second reader may not have hypothesized after the first segment that the business was cars, he or she would have chosen *some* other plausible candidate for the type of business. But after the second or third segment, it is likely that almost any reader would think of expensive cars. Readers will sometimes jump to a conclusion, and sometimes they will decide to wait and see, letting the text dictate the flow of hypotheses. Sometimes, readers will make correct predictions; sometimes they will be wrong. When they realize they are wrong, they will probably correct their predictions.

This journey through a hypothetical reader's mind illustrates, at an intuitive level, a number of the processes and hypothesized mental structures that cognitive psychologists and reading researchers use to explain how people process, store, and retrieve information during the act of reading. Although several of the different theories that have arisen, such as Roger Schank's *scripts,* Marvin Minsky's *frames,* and several researchers' *schemata,* share the goal of describing how information is stored in human memory, they do not claim to be theories of reading. Many reading researchers, however, have adopted these theories of cognition to explain how people read.[6]

By analyzing several of the subject's reactions to the "Oil Crisis" text, we can show how each illustrates a facet of schema theory.

To begin with, the subject could never have understood the text without prior knowledge about business, oil crises, automobiles, sales transactions, hard times, and resigned cynicism. In the language of schema theory, the subject had to select a number of already existing *schemata,* or knowledge frameworks, as repositories for the information contained in this specific text.[7] Schema selection, then, is a critical step in comprehension. Two questions about selection must be answered: (1) What is the nature of schemata that readers select? (2) How do readers select them?

What Is the Nature of Schemata?

A basic premise of schema theory is that human memory is organized semantically (as opposed, say, to phonologically or alphabetically). In other words, memory is organized like a thesaurus rather than a dictionary. Presumably, one can possess schemata for all manner of things, ranging from simple objects (chair, boat), to abstract entities (love, hope, fear), to actions (buy, dive, run), to complex events (attending a conference or a football game), to very complex entities (story, novel, world affairs).

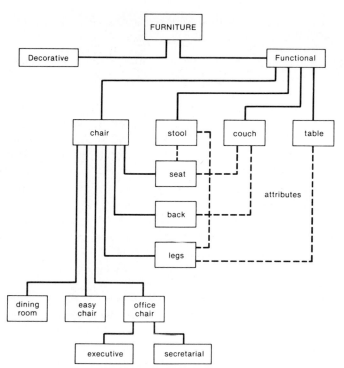

FIGURE 1.3   Partial Semantic Network for "Chair"

SOURCE: From P. D. Pearson (1982), A primer for schema theory, *Volta Review 84*, p. 27.

A schema for *chair* might be organized as Figure 1.3. This schema, referred to as a semantic network,[8] gives a picture of the semantic interrelationships among different schemata; that is, *chair* is a schema, but it also belongs to other classes (for example, *functional furniture*) that are themselves schemata and members of other classes of schemata (*furniture*). Chairs also have certain other attributes, or *slots*, that must be present, or filled, in order to be recognized as chairs. That is, a chair must have some sort of seat, will likely have a back, and will probably have a set of legs of some sort. In addition to the upward organization (*chair* to *functional furniture*), the system also has a downward organization that requires examples (*dining room chair, easy chair*). Schemata are *abstract* by definition and hence correspond not to any particular chair but to some idealized chair that may not even exist.[9]

Schemata for objects and for abstract entities such as *love, hate,* or *fear* appear to be very much like concepts. But schemata for actions and events have a dimension that is not typically associated with concepts—an episodic or sequential dimension. Figure 1.4 depicts a schema that is more like a play than a concept.[10] *Slots*, or *variable slots*, since they can be filled by a variety of specific elements, are akin to the roles in a play. The particular characters

Readers draw on their prior knowledge as they attempt to construct meaning for the written text they encounter in books. *(Peter Vadnai)*

who are selected to fill these slots are akin to the actors one might call on to play the roles. The particular entity that fills a variable slot is called a *value*.

In addition to the cast of characters, the *buy* schema has a set of episodes (more slots) that typically take place when a buying activity occurs, as represented in the dotted box in Figure 1.4. They correspond to the scenes in a play.

Along with hierarchical organization there is a great deal of cross-referencing among schemata.[11] For example, if a *buy* schema is selected and the buyer is a criminal, then the separate schema for *criminal* is called up and added to the *buy* schema. The values (actors) that fill variable slots (roles) in one schema are themselves schemata in other parts of a person's semantically organized memory.

How Are Schemata Selected?

How does a reader decide what schema or schemata to select in order to comprehend and remember a particular text? The author may be informative, as in: "This is a story about a man who wanted to buy a car." Usually, however, a reader has to rely on more subtle clues and form hypotheses.

One of the common ways for a reader to select a schema is to recognize a specific value (for example, a character) as the kind that usually fills a particular variable slot in a schema. He or she then guesses that that schema

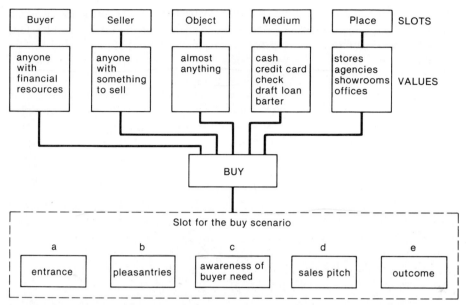

FIGURE 1.4   Partial Representation of What Might Exist in a Person's "Buy" Schema

SOURCE: From P. D. Pearson (1982), A primer for schema theory, *Volta Review 84*, p. 28.

is appropriate. In other words, inferential leaps on the part of the reader are often necessary just to decide what the text is about.

How Do Slots Get Filled?

The process of filling slots is usually called *instantiation*, from the word *instance* (that is, a specific instance is bound to a variable slot). Once a schema is selected, filling slots is usually simple. Having decided that the story was about buying, it was fairly easy for the subject in the opening example to decide who or what should fill the *buyer, seller, object, medium,* and *place* slots. But again, slots are sometimes filled before schemata are selected; in fact, slot-filling can lead to schema selection.

Slots can also be filled (at least temporarily) before a reader actually finds a likely candidate (value) to fill a slot. In the example, the subject suspected that the buyer would pay cash before he came across the information in the text; he also thought that Cadillacs were a likely object early on in his interpretation of the story.

Much slot-filling takes place through inference. In fact, readers are constantly filling slots for which authors specify no values. The reader's "best guess" or "most likely candidate" to fill a slot not specified by the author is termed a *default value*.

Inferences are also necessary even where the text provides a likely candidate to fill a variable slot. When our hypothetical reader Dan said, "This must be the customer," there was nothing in the text that compelled him to this conclusion. Indeed, inferences are very often necessary just to decide who or what fills what slots in a working schema. This stems from the fact that authors do not provide explicit information when they believe that readers can easily infer values for themselves. And, in fact, as readers we would be upset and bored to death with authors who told us everything. In taking out some of the guesswork they would be taking much of the fun out of reading.

A Word About Inference

Schema theory has shown that reading is only incidentally literal. *Product* measures can tap recognition or recall of explicitly stated information; however, in the *process* of working one's way through a text, tens, hundreds, even thousands of inferences are necessary. Inference is an essential part of schema selection and instantiation (in deciding who or what in the text fills what slot *and* in filling slots with default values).

Inference arises in another way: The value that fills one slot will affect the choice of a default value for a second slot. When the subject of the sample predicted that the buyer would pay cash for his Mercedes, he assigned cash as a default value for the medium slot because the buyer slot has been filled by a *nouveau-riche* character. In fact, a bank loan would have been his default value for almost any other type of character. Similarly, in a story of a woman who takes 18 friends to dinner and picks up the tab, the default value for *medium* would be credit card, not cash or check. Slot-filling is an interactive process: How one slot gets filled influences how other slots can get filled.

How Do People Change Their Schemata?

Unfortunately, schema theory has been more helpful in explaining comprehension than it has in explaining learning. However, schema theory does include mechanisms for learning.[12] The most common kind of learning within schema theory is what Rumelhart calls *accretion*. The notion of accretion is similar to Piaget's notion of assimilation and Smith's notion of comprehension. Accretion occurs each time an individual experiences an example of a schema and records in long-term memory its particular insantiation. Accretion is what allows a person to recall the specific circumstances involved, for example, in a particular trip to a restaurant. Unlike other forms of learning, accretion does not alter the structure of the schema.

A second kind of learning is *fine tuning*. Although fine tuning has no exact counterparts in Piaget's or Smith's views of information processing, it would be included in what Piaget calls *accommodation* and what Smith calls *learning*. Through fine tuning, the components of schemata are modified in important ways. New variable slots are added, variable slots are changed, or default values are altered. For example, a person who has encountered male automobile salespersons only might have a variable constraint that such salespersons must be male. When a female salesperson is encountered, this variable slot must be modified to include females.

The third kind of learning, *restructuring*, occurs when old schemata must be discarded in favor of new schemata necessary to accommodate existing and incoming data. Old theories or paradigms are replaced by new ones. The Copernican revolution, the advent of Newtonian physics, and Einstein's notions of relativity are extreme examples of restructuring.[13] Restructuring occurs continually at a more modest level in daily life: a four-year-old child learns that not all four-legged creatures are cats and is forced to develop specialized schemata for horses, cats, cows, and goats; a teacher learns that different teaching routines are suited to children of differing abilities; or a student discovers that the laws of commutativity generalize from addition to multiplication but not to subtraction or division.

There are two aspects of restructuring. Schema *specialization* occurs when several new schemata are needed to replace a single one: four subcategories of dogs where one sufficed before. Schema *generalization* occurs when several subschemata are seen to share some common variable slots, and the learner realizes that they can be seen as variations on the same theme: fables and myths are both stories.

How Are Schemata Controlled During Reading?

Sometimes readers engage in what has been variously called top-down processing, schema-based processing, inside-out processing, reader-based processing, or conceptually driven processing. This is a very active mode of processing in which the reader generates hypotheses, using his or her store of schemata, about the text to be read. These hypotheses guide the processing of the upcoming text and hypotheses are either confirmed or negated, in which case they need to be modified. Dan, the subject in the example, revealed several instances in which he engaged in this sort of processing.

Other times, readers are more passive. They engage in what has been variously called bottom-up processing, outside-in processing, text-based processing, or data-driven processing. In this particular mode, the reader decides to suspend judgment, waiting instead for more information from the text before drawing any conclusions. This kind of processing often occurs when a reader initially encounters a text, when a hypothesis has been negated, or when the reader simply cannot understand the sequence of events. Dan gave several such examples.

An interesting way to think about these two control modes is that in top-down processing, a reader is operating within his or her own schema, but in bottom-up processing, he or she is trying to operate within the author's schema. And, of course, any competent reader will shift back and forth constantly between the modes in the process of negotiating an interpretation of the text with the author.

Of What Conceivable Benefit Is Schema Theory?

The critical question is: How can teachers and clinicians use schema theory to help them make better diagnostic and instructional decisions about students? Pearson and Spiro (1980) found that five kinds of problems that students exhibit can be explained in a schema-theory framework, with some implications for assessment and instruction. These can be thought of as five reasons for students' failure to comprehend what they read.

Schema Availability   Put simply, if students do not have well-developed schemata for a topic, they will not understand selections about that topic. This phenomenon has been amply demonstrated in the research about prior knowledge. Indeed, Johnston and Pearson (1982) and Johnston (1981) have found that prior knowledge explains individual differences in comprehension better than measured reading ability does.

Regarding assessment of prior knowledge, Langer (1980) and Pearson and Johnson (1978; Johnson & Pearson, 1984) have found that simple free-association techniques with key concepts in a passage provide a quick diagnostic picture of where a student stands with respect to these concepts. For remediation, Hagen (1979) and Thoms (1982) have found that approaches that follow Pearson and Johnson's (1978) semantic mapping paradigm are most beneficial to students with meager backgrounds.

Schema Selection   Some students have the prior knowledge but neglect to call it into focus at the appropriate time. These students quite often rely too much on bottom-up processing, failing to realize which of their schemata can be used to comprehend and intercept the text at hand. In this case, remediation is relatively straightforward: Any prereading teaching strategy that brings appropriate schemata into focus will help.[14]

Schema Maintenance   Just because a reader has available and selects a schema for comprehending a passage does not mean that he or she will maintain that schema throughout the reading. Readers can literally forget what they are reading about. This is a schema maintenance problem. One reason for this problem is that readers may rely too heavily on bottom-up processing, directing all their attention to processing low-level text units (letters, syllables, words), thus leaving no cognitive capacity for the integrative thinking that is necessary for comprehension. Another reason is what some researchers have come to call *inconsiderate text*—text that does not make clear how different ideas in the text should be tied together—which has been found to be more of a problem for poor than good readers. Good readers seem more able to create ties where none are offered by the author.[15]

None of the instructional advice about this problem has been tested. However, clinical experience and a few experimental studies suggest the importance of helping students develop schemata for the ways in which stories and expository texts are organized. This can be accomplished either through systematic questioning techniques or the use of visual representations of the way texts are organized.[16]

Overreliance on Bottom-Up Processing   Overreliance on bottom-up processing is a case of failing to see the forest for the trees. Such readers will make oral reading errors because of attention to graphic features rather than to semantic concerns. In addition, they give verbatim answers from the text when inferences to prior knowledge are called for.

Helping students who have acquired this habit is not easy. Basically, they need to learn two things: that reading should make as much sense as listening, and that comprehension sometimes requires going beyond the text. To help them learn the first principle, there has been some success with anomaly detection techniques. Students are given texts that contain anomalous words, phrases, or sentences, and asked to delete things that do not fit the passages. Obviously, they cannot perform this task unless they have a good idea of what the text is about, that is, unless they operate top-down. For the second principle, the students are given questions followed by several answers; then they are asked to determine which came from the text and which did not. Finally, they are asked to judge which answers are appropriate, in an attempt to demonstrate that sometimes nontextual answers are as good as textual answers.

Overreliance on Top-Down Processing   It is possible for students to rely too much on schema-based (or top-down) processing. Such students make semantically appropriate oral reading errors. Their answers to questions, while sensible, often reveal a cursory or careless reading, or no reading of the text. Although getting the "gist" may serve a student well in most situations, it is a serious disadvantage when careful reading is required (such as in experiments, following directions, poetry, evaluative reading). Sometimes it is essential to work within the author's schema!

Several approaches are used to counter these tendencies. To help with question-answering behavior, students are engaged in precisely the same task as bottom-up overreliers (finding good answers within and outside the text), but the goal is different. These students need to understand that it is all right to give answers from the text. For the careful reading problem, students are given complex directions and fill-in-the-blank exercises in which all answers *denote* a semantically appropriate response (for example, *walked, skipped, trudged*), but only one carries the appropriate connotation (for example, "Susan felt so happy that she _____ through the park").

A LOOK AHEAD

As suggested earlier, we have taken you on this journey through the mind, eye, and printed page in order to establish a context for the remainder of our book. The remainder of Part 1 will embellish the context. Chapter 2 introduces the concept of reading difficulties and explains it in terms of the framework established in Chapter 1. Chapters 3 and 4 turn to a very crucial and often underrepresented topic, motivation. If you are or have been a classroom teacher, you do not have to be convinced of the importance of this topic. It permeates the daily life and decision making of classrooms everywhere.

Part 2 turns to our main course. It offers you an introduction to the whole issue of remedial instruction and assessment, followed by paired chapters on instruction and assessment for three crucial facets of reading and reading instruction: word recognition (Chapters 6 and 7), comprehension (Chapters 8 and 9), and vocabulary (10 and 11).

We have adopted what some might regard as an unconventional approach in Part 2. Paired chapters begin with a chapter on instruction and follow with a chapter on assessment. The more traditional approach is first to diagnose, then to remediate. We have violated convention intentionally for three reasons. We begin with instruction because we think that, in the final analysis, it is far more important than assessment. Second, the order implies that instruction drives assessment and not vice versa; we think that a major problem in American schools is that all too often assessment does, indeed, drive instruction. Third, we hope that staging instruction up front will begin to blur the distinction between instruction and assessment. If we could accomplish that goal, we will have made a contribution to the field.

Part 3 turns to issues of convention and implementation. Chapter 12 introduces principles of assessment as they apply to students with reading difficulties. Then two chapters follow on conventional aspects of assessment and instruction; Chapter 13 reviews many of the still popular diagnostic reading tests, and Chapter 14 discusses many of the standard approaches to working with students with reading problems. We do not necessarily endorse all of the concepts introduced in these three chapters; indeed, we are often quite critical and take delight in contrasting them with what we endorse in Part 2. Yet we feel obligated to inform readers of the existence, rationale, and good and not-so-good features of practices that have stood the test of time. Finally, we present our *pièce de résistance:* how to help students with problems in both classroom and clinic settings.

Those who are familiar with a more traditional and popular clinical view of reading difficulties may, at first blush, find this approach discomforting. We hope you will stay with us, however, until the "last act," for we hope to convince you that the distinction between classroom and clinic treatment of students who have problems should, like the distinction between assessment and instruction, *go away*.

SUMMARY

This chapter pointed out that reading is at once a linguistic and a cognitive process. As a linguistic process, it is closely allied to the other language processes—listening, speaking, and writing. With those processes, it shares a concern for and reliance upon the phonological (sound), graphemic (written representations of oral language), semantic (word meanings and interrelationships among word meanings), and syntactic (the arrangement of words into meaningful strings) subsystems of language. Of particular interest in this day and age is a changing view of the active (no longer passive) role played by a reader in comprehending written messages.

As a cognitive process, reading relies on those mental operations that comprise most kinds of thinking—attention, perception, encoding, memory, and retrieval. Modern versions of schema theory provide the most convincing and useful account of reading as a cognitive process. Of special interest to one who wishes to understand reading difficulties are the processing problems that schema theory helps to explain. Specifically, schema theory explains problems due to schema availability (no appropriate prior knowledge), schema selection (failure to call up appropriate available schemata), schema maintenance (calling up but then losing the appropriate schema), overreliance on bottom-up processing (paying too close attention to text), and overreliance on top-down processing (paying too much attention to what is already in prior knowledge and not enough to the text).

As suggested in the preview of upcoming chapters, when dealing with reading and reading difficulties in more detail, we will encounter these problems in different disguises again and again.

NOTES

1. Space does not permit a decent treatment of the complexities of the syntactic systems of language. They are far more complex and intricate than we pretend in this chapter.
2. We are indebted to our colleague, Robert Schreiner, for this idea of contrasts between oral and written linguistic representations.
3. See Gelb (1966).
4. Others might take issue with us on this distinction in the attribution of cause of oral versus written language problems. There are, unfortunately, few data to evaluate the veracity of claims by either side.
5. We are indebted to David Rumelhart (1980) for the germ of the idea for this extended passage. The following discussion of schema theory previously appeared in *The Volta Review 84*, no. 5 (September 1982): 25–34.
6. The following references, consulted in chronological order, would provide a good overview of the development of schema theory in the last twenty years: Collins

and Quillian (1969), Lindsay and Normal (1972), Anderson (1977), Rumelhart and Ortony (1977), Collins, Brown, and Larkin (1980), Pearson and Spiro (1980), Rumelhart (1980), and Anderson and Pearson (1984).

7. See Anderson, Reynolds, Schallert, and Goetz (1977); Pearson, Hansen, and Gordon (1978); Pearson and Spiro (1980).

8. See Collins and Quillian (1969).

9. See Shoben (1980).

10. For a fuller treatment, see Rumelhart (1980), or Pearson and Spiro (1980).

11. See Pearson and Spiro (1980).

12. See Piaget (1952), Rumelhart (1979), and Smith (1975) for their respective discussions of comprehension and learning mechanisms.

13. See Kuhn (1962).

14. Specifically, the experimental work of Hansen (1981) and Hansen and Pearson (1983) as well as the advice of Stauffer (1969), Pearson and Johnson (1978), Herber (1970), or Hanf (1971) all contain techniques that will help such students become more active processors of text.

15. The considerate text issue, to our knowledge, was first raised and coined by Anderson, Armbruster, and Kantor (1980). Marshall and Glock (1978–1979) and Irwin (1980) have both examined the effect of considerateness on the comprehension of readers of different abilities.

16. For some examples of techniques to sensitize students to the structure of different types of text, see Gordon (1980), Singer and Donlan (1982), or Bartlett (1978).

Chapter 2

Explaining Reading Difficulties

OVERVIEW

As you read this chapter, use the following list of main ideas to guide your understanding and reflection.

The search for causes of reading difficulty may be somewhat useful, but not nearly so useful as the search for solutions to whatever problems exist.

There are many types of purported causes of reading disability: neurological, psycho-emotional, and environmental (home and school).

Of the three, the greatest emphasis is placed on the last since it is the one area that teachers stand the best chance of changing for the better.

Chapter 1 devoted considerable explanation to the processes of normal reading development, only twice hinting at issues related to reading difficulties. It did so as a way of introducing this book's treatment of reading difficulties; that is, so that you would better understand this book's explanation of as well as plans for instruction and assessment of reading difficulties. This chapter turns to a discussion of the explanations that are typically offered for the reading difficulties that so many children seem to exhibit in today's schools. Although it is difficult to develop clear-cut categories, it is convenient to divide the explanations into three categories: neurological, emotional, and environmental (both school and home factors). The logic of this order is that it presents you with explanations that come *increasingly under your influence* as a teacher; that is, you can do little about the way a child comes "wired" into the world, but you can do more to influence his or her emotional state through motivational techniques, and you can do even more to influence the environment in which he or she learns. Before discussing causal explanations, however, let us deal with the troublesome aspects of searching for causes.

THE SEARCH FOR CAUSES: A DOUBLE-EDGED SWORD

We approach the task cautiously. The term *causes* should be avoided in preference to the more modest term *explanation*. As it is difficult to fix the precise cause of a reading difficulty, dealing with some explanatory factors is a more attainable goal than listing the definitive causes of reading difficulty.

Furthermore, it is not certain that effective instruction for students who exhibit reading difficulty depends on such a precise determination of causes. Like a medical doctor who treats the symptoms of a cold or influenza without great concern for what caused the ailment, educators are well-advised to focus on treating the symptoms of reading difficulty exhibited by students rather than trying to eradicate its causes.

We advocate this more modest approach because it is practical and possible. Eradicating causes is desirable, however probably not feasible. First, it is rare that there is a single causal factor for a student who has difficulty learning to read. Second, even if a teacher were able to discover definitive causes for a particular student, chances are that the teacher would not be able to eradicate them. Causes may derive from the home environment and be totally beyond the control of a teacher. Or they may stem from a psychological trauma so deeply rooted in the student's psyche as to be visible only to a psychiatrist. Third, and most important, a teacher who can make the reading experience successful for a student—irrespective of the sources of difficulty—does a great deal to minimize the effect of any causes.

Some may argue that this position discourages teachers from examining a child's educational, medical, or family history. Although it is important for a teacher to be aware of a child's history at a certain point in time, sometimes a little knowledge can be as damaging as it is helpful. Sometimes a teacher may become unduly biased toward a new student because of a remark casually recorded in a student's cumulative folder or noted on a diagnostic workup. As a result, the teacher's expectations for that student may also become biased. The dreadful Pygmalion effect, documented by Rosenthal and Jacobson (1968) in the 1960s, should give us all pause to refrain from quick judgments about students.

The best advice regarding a child's educational history is for the teacher to postpone that look through the folder (especially value-laden comments) for a month or so after the beginning of the year. Let the teacher's relationship with each student develop naturally. This advice is based on a belief that all human interactions are, to a certain degree, unique to the individuals involved in any particular interaction. You may possess exactly the type of personality that a particular student feels comfortable with, you may be just the teacher the student needs, just the one to succeed where the others have failed. So let time and nature take their course, at least for a while, and then check the records. You may be surprised—even shocked—when you do.

The search for explanation (and hence the checking of educational records) is a double-edged sword, and we encourage restraint in your search; but it would be unprofessional to suggest that teachers postpone examining certain kinds of information. For example, if a child has a visual, auditory, physical, or medical handicap, a teacher needs to be aware of it in order to properly adapt the instructional environment. A child who comes from a troubled home may need (and deserves) extra emotional support; a child without a stimulating language environment at home may have some direct instructional needs in vocabulary development.

The potential value (or potential damage) of prior knowledge hinges on what a teacher makes of it, both cognitively and affectively. Damage is done when existing knowledge is used to label a child: "Oh, he can't learn to read; he's retarded (or dyslexic, or a troublemaker, or Jeff's little brother)." The labeling can be used as a rationalization for a teacher's inability to help the student. There is an analogue in medicine. Some doctors discuss a professional malady called "diagnosis by labeling." Apparently some patients, and some doctors, feel better when they can attach a label to a set of symptoms, even though the labeling will not help one iota with treatment.

Prior knowledge is valuable when it helps to do two things: to obtain a clearer grasp of what to do with a particular student, and to bolster a teacher's conviction that he or she can help that student.

The following anecdote serves to illustrate the point. The faculty of all the elementary schools in a district had been invited to hear a child neurologist discuss the neurological bases of dyslexia. After hearing the presentation, one of the first-grade teachers was overheard to say, "I've been teaching first grade for 15 years. Each year I helped most of the children learn to read, but I always failed with some. And it used to bother me so when I failed. Now I know what was wrong: They all had dyslexia." This is a clear example of the danger of "diagnosis by labeling." Her conviction that she could help was tainted; she now had a convenient excuse to explain away a frustration, and it may have caused her to try a little less hard with her next group of first-grade students.

Much space has been devoted to this disclaimer about the value of searching for causes and attending too much to prior information about students. This was done in the hope not that teachers will avoid the search for causes or prior information, but rather that they will approach the task cautiously, with a proper perspective and a healthy dose of common sense.

NEUROLOGICAL EXPLANATIONS

Neurological explanations of reading difficulties tend to focus on "how kids are wired." That is, within the central (or sometimes, peripheral) nervous system, are there inherited or acquired malfunctions that explain why a student is failing to learn to read? Neurological explanations have a long, varied, and controversial history. In general, the rather obvious problems, such as poor vision and poor hearing, have widespread acceptance in the field among physicians, psychologists, and educators. The less obvious problems, dealing with theories of nervous system organization, have been emphasized by medical doctors and others concerned with neurological development, but they have been deemphasized by educators and psychologists. First, the less controversial issues of vision and hearing are discussed. Then the issues of neurological organization are presented; these explanations tend to fall into two categories: laterality and minimal brain damage.

Visual Problems

Although the relationship of visual problems to reading ability has been studied extensively, the degree to which reading problems are caused by visual problems remains unclear.[1]

Myopia (nearsightedness) and astigmatism have not been found to occur more frequently in low-achieving readers than in better readers. On the other hand, hyperopia (farsightedness) has been found to occur more frequently in low-achieving readers. In any case, hyperopia, myopia, and astigmatism are correctible with lenses. Visual problems may be a contributing factor but are probably not a major cause of reading disability in most instances.[2] However, if a teacher suspects a student has a visual problem, it is prudent to recommend that he or she be screened and referred to a vision specialist if necessary. A bibliography by Weintraub and Cowan (1982) offers more information on the relationship between vision and reading.

Auditory Problems

As with visual problems, mild auditory problems may be a contributing factor but not a major cause of reading disability in most instances.[3] Students with severe auditory problems (for example, deafness, severe hearing loss), on the other hand, do have difficulties with reading.[4] Students with suspected hearing loss should be referred to the school nurse for auditory screening and to a hearing specialist if necessary. A bibliography by Weintraub (1972) contains more information on the relationship between hearing problems and reading.

Lateral Dominance

Human beings tend toward physical symmetry: two each of feet, legs, arms, hands, eyes, ears, and even cerebral hemispheres in the brain. But the physical symmetry does not extend into functional symmetry. People tend to have a dominant hand, leg, eye, and cerebral hemisphere. They prefer to use one side of their bodies, and that side usually functions in a superior manner.

It is interesting to note how long this perception of sidedness has been with us. The word "dextrous," with its positive connotation, stems from the latin root for "right," whereas the word "sinister" originally meant "left." You probably have heard stories from your parents or grandparents about teachers who tried to change a naturally left-handed person into a right-handed writer or eater. Sports such as baseball and tennis with their numerous "south paws" have done wonders to enhance the image of left-handed people. Eye dominance is almost as common as hand dominance. Most people have a preferred eye, the one they use to zero in on something or look through a telescope. However the dominant hand and eye are not always on the same side of the body.

People whose dominant eye is on the opposite side of the body from their dominant hand have *crossed dominance*. People who show no particular hand preference (ambidextrous persons, for example) exhibit *mixed handedness* while people who have no particular eye preference have *mixed eyedness*.[5]

Some time ago, theorists[6] thought that the dominant side of the cerebral hemisphere, the side controlling most language and other cognitive functions, was opposite the dominant side of the body (that is, the left cerebral hemisphere for right-sided persons and the right hemisphere for left-sided persons). When one side of the brain failed to achieve its appropriate dominance over the other, they reasoned, the hemispheres competed in processing visual information, for example. Hence alternative and competing interpretations of the printed message were being processed, resulting in cognitive confusion. The outward symptom of such confusion, they reasoned, was what is commonly called *reversals*, such as *p* for *b*, *was* for *saw*, or *Rover fed John* for *John fed Rover*. Orton even coined the term *strephosymbolia* (meaning, literally, twisted symbols) to describe the symptoms.

Historically, there have been enough reading disability cases exhibiting both ambiguity in handedness or eyedness and "strephosymbolic" symptoms to tempt concerned professionals into inferring that the one was the cause of the other. The logic is appealing: Lack of body sidedness yields lack of hemispheric dominance, which in turn yields perceptual confusions in reading.

Research Evidence   Mysterious labyrinth that it is, the brain is still the object of formative research by neurologists and allied scientists. In fact, there has been a renaissance of hemispheric research in the last decade. The point is that the final verdict on the relationship between lateral dominance of body or brain and reading disorder is a long way from settled. However, a great deal more is known now than when Orton expounded his theory in 1937.

For example, the relationship between body sidedness and hemispheric dominance is not what Orton reasoned it to be. Several studies[7] indicate that (1) about 80 percent of the population is right-handed, of which about 38 percent are left-eye dominant (indicating widespread crossed dominance), (2) all but a small percentage of the right-handed population is left-hemisphere dominant with respect to language functions, (3) the remaining 20 percent are split among left-handed (about 12 percent) and ambidextrous (about 8 percent) persons, (4) hemispheric dominance for language among that 20 percent is widely distributed with some right, some left, and some both hemisphere dominant persons (eye dominance is equally as heterogeneous). Hence the convenient and intuitively appealing notion of a crossover from dominant body (hand plus eye) side to the other hemisphere for language functions is not supported.

Moreover, as Kershner (1983) points out, the hemisphere not associated with language functions plays a major role in reading: spatial relations, form discrimination, and right-left orientation usually have locus of control in the right hemisphere. According to Kershner, the issue is not so much hemispheric dominance as it is hemispheric specialization (hemispheric asymmetry).

Research completed on populations of disabled readers[8] has tended to find a relationship between laterality confusions (particularly mixed-handed-ness) and reading, with some notable exceptions.[9]

Research completed on normally distributed populations, including read-ing disability cases,[10] tends to find no relationship between reading ability and laterality confusions; that is, the incidence of poor readers is just as great among appropriately lateralized students as it is among students exhibiting crossed dominance, mixed-handedness or mixed-eyedness. We subscribe to a point of view similar to the vulnerability argument often given to explain the relationship between low birth weight and subsequent medical or psychological problems. Low birth weight is thought to make infants more vulnerable to their environment. Hence babies of low birth weight born into medically and psychologically nurturing environments stand a good chance of becoming normal toddlers, while the incidence of abnormality is great for low birth weight babies born to a less nurturing environment. By analogy, children who fail to achieve appropriate hemispheric specialization are more vulnerable to their academic environment. If it is supportive and academically nurturing, normal reading growth can be expected. If not, reading difficulties are likely to occur. Such an explanation could conceivably account for the discrepant results between laterality and reading studies among normal versus reading disabled populations.

Treatment   Among those who have subscribed to the laterality argument, there has been wide disparity in recommendations for treatment. Orton (1937), for example, advocated hard-core remedial reading instruction. In fact, the Orton-Gillingham[11] approach was developed by June Orton and Anna Gil-lingham specifically to help strephosymbolic students. By concentrating on synthetic blending of letters in a left-right fashion ($c + a + t$ says /cuh/ + /ah/ + /tuh/ says /kat/), they hoped to avoid possible reversals. That is, you can reverse *was* for *saw* only if you examine the whole word. Letter reversals, such as *d* for *b* or *p* for *g*, were handled by using tactile and kinesthetic reinforcement (sand trays for finger tracing or sandpaper letters) along with symbol-sound instruction. Above all, the instruction was (and is) characterized by a great deal of systematicness and order, with heavy cuing to minimize the likelihood of letter (*b* for *d*) or word (*was* for *saw*) reversals.

By contrast, Delacato (1966) has recommended perceptual-motor treatment as a first step in eradicating the reading disorder. Believing, as Orton did, that incomplete hemispheric dominance was the source of the problem, Delacato was convinced that a student must achieve complete subcortical (before the spinal cord hits the cortex at the base of the brain) integration before hemispheric dominance could occur. Hence, students attending a Delacato clinic went through a set of creeping, crawling, walking, and sleeping exercises to establish subcortical integration (complete right-side or left-side dominance). In addition, special glasses were used to help the would-be dominant eye play its role.

If problems persisted after sidedness was firmly established, Delacato recommended other procedures to help achieve hemispheric dominance. For example, since music perception usually has its locus in the hemisphere opposite the language locus, music was eliminated from the lives of students receiving the Delacato treatment. Or special glasses were used to insure dominant eyedness usage.

The profession has not been kind to the Delacato point of view, either in its opinion or its research. Robbins (1966) and O'Donnell (1970) tried the Delacato procedure on large groups of normal and retarded subjects, respectively. In neither experiment was there any advantage for the Delacato procedure over normal—and sometimes diametrically opposite—teaching procedures. Glass and Robbins (1967) took Delacato to task for what can euphemistically be called sloppy statistics in reporting successful cases.

Laterality in Perspective   Where do we stand on this controversial issue? First, we look forward to further research by both neurologists and educators in sorting out the complex relationship between laterality and reading. Second, we agree with Orton's advice to treat students exhibiting laterality confusions with the best available instructional techniques. When all is said and done, once the labeling has occurred, you still have a student who cannot read. And your job as a teacher is to do as much as you possibly can to help. What should be added here is that you should use as much as possible, materials and techniques that minimize potential reversal problems. Do not conclude, therefore, that we advocate a strict synthetic blending approach. As Smith, Goodman, and Meredith (1970) point out, context can be used to minimize reversals. For example, contrast sentences (1) and (2). The *saw/was* reversal makes sense in (1) but not in (2).

1. Mary saw a girl.

2. Mary saw a boy.

In fact, unlike Orton, we recommend that all reading instruction, including instruction for unlocking unknown words, occur in settings where real texts are read for real purposes.

Minimal Brain Damage

Perhaps even more controversial than laterality is the minimal brain damage explanation of reading disability. It has a variety of synonyms that go back more than a century: congenital word blindness, alexia, dyslexia, subclinical insult. The symptoms of the malady is that earnest teachers have done their very best to teach students to read with little or no success. It is an explanation by default: If teachers have tried so hard for so long with so little success, there must have been some neurological malfunction all along. Balow (1971) has summarized the issue succinctly:

> Historically, people with problems of this sort were seen as being quite rare, but in recent years there has been a great tendency to attribute special learning disabilities to a number of youngsters whose difficulties are not very special, not very specific, and not very clearly related to neurological deficiencies. The common acceptance of skill deficiency itself as *prima facie* evidence of neurological disorder can be interpreted as reflecting wishful thinking. If the problem can be defined out of education into the realm of medicine, educators can then remain relatively complacent about their efforts to correct the problem. With such a medical excuse, it is possible to ignore the educational limbo to which most such children are consigned. (pp. 514–515)

Implicit in this argument is the assumption that if we had better devices for measuring neurological defect, we would find insult in these students, hence, the genesis of the terms *subclinical* (below our capacity to diagnose) insult or *minimal* (not enough to really measure) brain damage.

The Evidence   As was the case for laterality, the evidence supporting the minimal brain damage explanation of reading disability is, on the whole, more negative than positive. In fact, what research exists even brings into question the relationship between frank (obvious) brain damage and reading disability.[12]

For example, Ackerly and Benton (1947) reported a case study in which a boy with average intelligence and good reading skills was diagnosed as emotionally disturbed with associated behavior problems. Subsequent medical diagnosis and surgery revealed that he had a large part of his brain missing (in spite of the fact that his EEG tracings were normal). Somehow he had overcome massive brain damage and was able to read well.

Byers and Lord (1943) traced the development of fifteen cases of lead-poisoned children (frank brain damage can develop from lead poisoning). The students were not doing well in school, exhibiting symptoms such as visual perception and visual-motor skill problems, fatigue, poor attention, and poor reasoning. However, over half of these children were reading in the normal range for their age.

Yacorzynsky and Tucker (1960) followed the progress of thirty anoxic (low blood and cellular oxygen supply) infants who had been hospitalized up to 150 days after birth. They were compared with the same sex sibling nearest to them in age. The anoxic group had six children with IQ scores below 70, but the control group of siblings had only one. On the other hand, the anoxic group had several students with extremely high IQ scores but the control group had only one such child. In short, the anoxia (a malady commonly associated with frank brain damage) resulted in more deviant, not just lower, IQ scores.

The data from these studies make it difficult for us to accept the argument offered by Clements (1966), for example, that certain behavioral patterns of children in school lead one toward a diagnosis of minimal brain dysfunctions.

Special Treatments for Minimal Brain Damage   Special remedial treatments for allegedly brain-damaged children are not common. However, if so-called dyslexic children as well as those diagnosed as having perceptual or perceptual-motor deficits are considered as a group, there are many programs that purport to serve such students. Rather than attack reading problems directly, these programs tend to focus on treating what their advocates describe as prerequisites to reading. These prerequisites tend to be perceptual or perceptual-motor skills: visual discrimination, hand-eye coordination, left-right scanning, awareness of directionality and laterality, fine motor control. Remedial activities often include shape discrimination, shape tracing and drawing, games involving finger dexterity, careful visual scanning (for example, following the line of descent of a ball in a vertical maze).

Although such programs often come with the endorsement of highly qualified specialists,[13] there is little evidence to support their positive contribution to the education of reading disabled students. In fact, those experimental studies that have evaluated the effectiveness of various perceptual-motor training programs[14] consistently show no advantage over control programs with no perceptual motor emphasis.[15]

Brain Damage in Perspective   Like laterality, brain damage explanations of reading disability are both popular and controversial. There is no doubt that a small proportion of reading disability cases exist whose etiology (causal explanation) can be traced to major or minor brain damage, yet we remain "doubting Thomases" when confronted with admonitions to treat reading disability with perceptual motor programs or claims that most children who have difficulty learning to read must, therefore, have neurological deficits. What evidence exists just does not support such beliefs. As Balow (1971) points out, the demography (geographic distribution) of reading disability flies in the face of such an argument. The problem is that the preponderance of reading disability cases come from geographic areas in which all aspects of the environment (home, school, and community) are hostile to academic learning; hence it is difficult to believe that reading disability is primarily a medical problem. It is likely that the culprit is the educational environment.

Neurological Explanations: How Should We Regard Them?

It should come as no surprise that we are skeptical of the widespread application of neurological etiology for reading disabled children. Previous discussion in this chapter has built a strong case to diminish their importance as both explanatory factors and treatment variables.

That skepticism is not total, however. We agree with Harris (1970a) that a small proportion of all reading disability cases (perhaps 5 percent to 10 percent) will be the result of some neurological problem. And in *some* of those cases, the student will need to be referred to a neurologist or a residential treatment center. The emphasis is on *some*, as it is not certain to what degree differences in instruction are dictated by a diagnosis of neurological difficulty; that is, what will a classroom, or remedial reading teacher, or for that matter, a special treatment center, do differently for a child classified as neurologically handicapped than a child classified as educationally handicapped? The answer is not clear, as the previous review of special treatment programs indicates. When all is said and done, the task of teaching the child to read remains. Again, we echo the sentiments of Balow (1971):

> Despite evidence that standard frontal assaults on the academic deficiencies of learning disabled pupils are successful (Balow, 1965; Fernald, 1939), such a "stodgy and unglamorous" prescription has seldom ever been followed, quickly giving way in favor of the more seductive dosages of the ever present patent medicine peddler. Some of those patent medicines may well be useful; the problem is that a careful review of the literature on such "cures" as those focusing on motor learning leaves the reader confused at best. This reader is dismayed over the amount of faith necessary and the egregious absence of evidence supporting motor activities for the development of reading, arithmetic, or spelling skills. . . . (pp. 518–519)

PSYCHO-EMOTIONAL EXPLANATIONS OF READING DIFFICULTY

It is hard to imagine a child with reading difficulties who has no emotional scars. Human beings seem to regard failure in any endeavor with great disdain. All of us avoid one or another physical or mental activity because at some point we experienced failure when attempting the task. How many people have given up a complex motor activity such as golf, tennis, or skiing because early endeavors were simply too frustrating? "It's not worth the hassle," is an expression many use to rationalize their withdrawal from such situations.

School children rarely have some prerogatives, however, when it comes to school subjects that have proven to be frustrating to them. They cannot adopt the total avoidance strategy typical of adults who find themselves in a frustrating situation. They must remain within the instructional setting, like it or not. Hence, they must resort to avoidance strategies that operate within the instructional setting that serve the goal of escaping or avoiding as much anxiety or frustration as possible.

In short, children with reading difficulties are likely to have emotional scars because they are forced to face the reality of their failures whether they want to or not. And, once failure occurs, it begins its own self-perpetuating course.

The key to dealing with psycho-emotional problems is motivation. When motivation is low, for whatever reasons, students have little enthusiasm for efforts to help them help themselves. Conversely, nothing will help a teacher get off to a better start with an individual child than finding a high level of motivation and enthusiasm. Chapters 3 and 4 offer an extensive discussion of motivational explanations of reading difficulty.

ENVIRONMENTAL EXPLANATIONS OF READING DIFFICULTY

The explanations of reading difficulty discussed so far, although related to the environment in which students find themselves, have focused primarily on characteristics of students themselves; that is, what occurs in their minds and in their hearts. The focus in this section is on external factors. First, factors arising from the home environment are presented and then those related to the school environment are discussed. It is not possible to neatly separate explanations of reading disability that exist within students from those that arise outside; the relationship is interactive, with internal and external factors shaping one another. So the distinction between this section and previous sections is a manner of emphasis and focus only. Further, environmental factors, especially those arising from the school environment, are probably the most important for educators to consider. After all, these are the factors over which teachers exercise some control. Although they have less influence on the home environment, teachers talk to parents, parents talk to teachers, and it is possible that together they can change a situation that is preventing a student from learning in school.

Factors Related to the Home Environment

Nearly everything that occurs in a child's home environment has an effect on everything that happens to the child at school. However, in terms of the child's progress in reading, certain factors are more salient than others. The most important home environmental factors influencing a child's progress in reading are the language environment of the home and the types of values that a child extracts from his home environment.

A child's success with learning to read is very much related to the values learned from the home environment. *(James Silliman)*

Language Environment   Because we are committed to a view of the reading process as a language process, it should not be surprising that we place much importance on a student's language environment: Reading involves decoding and comprehending concepts that appear in the form of words strung together in sentences, and the child's acquisition of language occurs at home. Specifically, the focus is on two populations for whom the whole language of environment is of special concern; namely, bilingual and bidialectial students.

It has been less than two decades since reading educators have devoted much attention to the "linguistically unique child," the child who comes to school speaking a language or a dialect different from the language or dialect spoken in school and used in reading materials. Previously there was an implicit assumption in our instruction that a language difference was the child's problem and not the school's problem. Hence, if a child spoke a language or a dialect that was different, it was his or her responsibility to acquire the dialect of school. At the urging of linguists and educators alike, the emphasis began to shift toward a more responsible view in the early 1960s. There exists a rich literature[16] dealing with possible accommodations teachers can make to aid the linguistically unique child. Each of these accommodations is related to and derived from *assumptions* about the nature of the discrepancy between a child's language and the school's language.

Some have viewed the discrepancy as a deficit. A child who speaks a different dialect speaks a deficient dialect, one that is inferior to the standard dialect. Hence, if this child is to make progress in reading standard dialect then the teacher must first teach the child to speak the standard dialect. If this is not done the child will continually be disadvantaged compared to the child who speaks standard English. From a deficit viewpoint, then, the teacher's first task is to teach the child to speak standard English, after which reading instruction may ensue.

Others view the discrepancy as a difference, making no value judgments regarding which dialect—standard or nonstandard—is superior. If a teacher views a language or a dialect discrepancy as a difference rather than a deficiency he or she will take different actions to accommodate the student's needs. For example, some educators[17] wrote special books for readers who speak Black English. In these books words are spelled the way a speaker of Black English pronounces them (*post* might be spelled *pos*), special vocabulary terms are used (*bad* meaning really *good*), and accommodations are made in syntax (*he be goin'* instead of *he is going*).

A second accommodation consistent with a difference assumption allows speakers of a special dialect to read materials written in standard English and to pronounce them in their dialect without penalty. For example, when a child who speaks Black English says *pos* for *post*, the teacher simply accepts that pronunciation as consistent with the child's dialect, making no attempt to remediate the pronunciation as though it were a reading error. In other words, the teacher recognizes the fact that the child sees the *t* in *post* but simply does not say it because in his or her dialect the appropriate pronunciation for *post* is /pos/ (see Chapter 1).

A third accommodation consistent with a difference assumption is the recent emphasis in bidialectical and bilingual reading programs. For example, in the southwestern United States there is a growing number of bilingual reading programs in which children are taught to read both Spanish (their first language) and English (the acquired language). By allowing children to read in both languages their equal status is maintained. Unfortunately, recent legislative trends do not provide much optimism about the continuation of bilingual reading programs.

The degree to which these language and dialect differences interfere with learning to read standard English is not clear. For example, Melmed (1973) found that nine-year-old speakers of Black English have difficulty distinguishing between pairs like *past* and *pass* when they hear these word pairs and when they try to pronounce them in isolation, but they have no difficulty recognizing the difference in meaning between those words when they are used in sentences. In a sense a child who speaks Black English as a first dialect has a larger set of homophones (words that sound alike but have different meanings and are spelled differently) than does the speaker of standard English. But when the child is reading, the extra orthographic cues provided by letters like *t* and *s* in *past* and *pass* help the child determine the meaning of the words.

Simons and Johnson (1974) found that second-grade students who spoke

Black English as the first dialect made many translations of standard English into Black English when they read orally. Conversely, they also found that these same children made many translations of Black English spellings into standard English (for example, reading *past* and *pass*). What seems to happen to the child who is learning a second language or dialect is that he or she makes confusions in both directions. These findings substantiate the earlier work of Lambert[18] in which he found that French Canadians who were reading in English or in French tended to make oral reading errors from one language to the other.

On the issue of dialect and reading, we offer three recommendations. First, we believe that the most sensible position on materials is this: Let the students read materials written in standard English (hopefully, they might be culturally interesting) but use your knowledge of predictable dialect differences to help distinguish between a reading miscue and a child who is performing the remarkable feat of translating from one dialect to another.

Second, make certain that you treat all children's dialects with respect. After all, they have devoted many years to learning to speak the way they do. The last thing they need is a teacher who continually tells them, directly or indirectly, that they talk funny.

Third, go ahead and teach standard English but do so in a way that lets children know that they are learning a second dialect and not a superior dialect. Some educators[19] have recommended that a good time to teach standard English is in the secondary years when children recognize the importance of being able to get a job in "the white man's society." There is probably no conclusive evidence regarding the optimal time to teach standard English to a dialect speaker. When it is undertaken, however, it should be with respect. Do not fall into the trap of generating low expectations for a child simply because he or she speaks a different dialect. The negative effects of unduly low teacher expectations are frightening.

Home, Values, and Reading Achievement   Success in a school environment is facilitated when there is a match between the values a child learns at home and the values that exist in the school environment. Failure, on the other hand, is more likely when these two sets of values do not match. Such a point of view hardly seems controversial. Sociologists and anthropologists have studied value conflict for decades, and have confirmed these views. Yet, how well schools are able to accommodate to differences in value orientation among students is not clear. What seems more likely among students who face a value conflict is that those students succeed who are able to change their values or to accept the school's values *within the context of the school environment.*

We make no judgment regarding the appropriateness or inappropriateness of the school's values. We simply recognize their existence. Similarly, we make no judgment about the validity of values students bring to school but simply point out that value conflict is likely to create problems for students.

It is hoped that schools can find ways to accommodate the conflicts that will inevitably arise.

What are the values that underlie the school experience? Any answer to that question is risky and likely to be inaccurate. First, the values may differ slightly from one district or region to another, from one school to another, even from one classroom to another. Second, within a given region, district, school, or classroom, values can change, or there may be some values that conflict with others. Nonetheless, a surprising commonality is found across classrooms, schools, districts, and regions, especially, when it comes to values that affect reading growth. Among them are the following:

1. *Achievement is a good thing.* Doing well on assignments, scoring high on tests, reading accurately, and so on all bring the *official* praise of the school and all the benefits that go with that praise.

2. *A competitive spirit is useful and desirable.* It is not too difficult to deduce this value from the instructional environment. All one has to do is to observe the fervor of students playing a word identification game, correcting one another's oral reading in the reading circle, or playing in the school yard to realize that schools both promote and capitalize on the competetive spirit.

3. *An appropriate combination of aggressive and passive behavior goes a long way.* This is a subtle combination. Students in school are encouraged to be aggressive in academic pursuits but passive in their "behavior." Hence a student should be quiet and keep to himself or herself when doing assignments or when others are the center of attention. However, when called upon to perform an academic task, the student is expected to act vigorously to complete the assignment. Such a philosophy is an extension of the aphorism, "Don't speak unless spoken to (but when spoken to, speak loudly)."

4. *Literacy is central to the school experience.* First, language arts and reading activities dominate the early curriculum of schools. Second, reading and writing are important prerequisite tools to learning in content area instruction (for example, science, social studies, or health). Implicitly as well as explicitly, literacy skills are valued in our schools.

By implication, any child whose personal values conflict with those mentioned is likely to experience difficulty accepting and adjusting to the schooling experience.

Academic achievement is clearly not valued by some students. That is not to say that *achievement* is unimportant; most often such students substitute one kind of achievement (often athletic, sometimes delinquent) for another (academic). Whether they come to school with this disdain for academic achievement or acquire it because of failure is difficult to determine. And when such children are in your classroom, the source of the problem does not seem to matter. But the symptoms are clear; they will not be motivated by, will not work for, the traditional incentives of good grades, high marks, or teacher praise.

Clearly, also, the peer group has an important role in helping to shape students' values. A conversation was overheard among some American Indian students returning to their reservation from the "white man's" high school in a nearby town. One young man climbed aboard the bus with two textbooks under one arm. Before he could find a seat he was besieged with catcalls from his peers: "Hey man, you playin' the white man's game?" "You wanna become one of them?" Value conflict can assume a stark reality.

Horatio Alger and the dream of American capitalism notwithstanding, competition is not universally valued by all subcultures in our society. It is said that there exist Indian cultures in the Southwest in which the goal in a foot race is that all the entrants cross the finish line at precisely the same time, emphasizing the solidarity of the tribe and equality of its members. Imagine a child from that culture placed in a predominately Anglo classroom playing an allegedly motivating game of phonics rummy in which the goal is to collect the greatest number of cards with similar vowel sounds, and thereby beat the rest of the players. And there is substantial evidence that some minority cultures do not respond well to competitive incentives.[20]

EDUCATIONAL EXPLANATIONS OF READING DIFFICULTY

Fortunately, there are factors operating in the school environment that promote reading failure. We say "fortunately" because if these factors can account for failure, then their removal or opposition can account for success. Maybe every cloud has a silver lining. Purposely, this set of explanations was saved for last because this is the one area of causal explanations, the one set of factors under the control of teachers.

Student Time on Task

Some children fail to learn a given skill, master a set of vocabulary words, or accurately read a passage simply because they have not been allowed to engage in the process often enough.

Rosenshine and Stevens (1984), after reviewing several studies on teaching effectiveness, concluded that student *engaged* time on task was one of the single most powerful instructional variables affecting student achievement. The key word in their conclusions is "engaged." For them it means time when the student is actively working on a reading task (e.g., reading orally or silently, completing a work sheet, writing an answer to a question). Just sitting in the

Reading performance seems to improve when teacher and pupil are actively engaged in tasks that involve actual reading. *(Elizabeth Hamlin/Stock, Boston)*

classroom does not count. Furthermore, engagement rates are highest when students are working in small groups, next highest in whole class configurations, and lowest when students are working independently on work sheets.[21]

The key issue for the time on task factor is what it is students will spend their time doing. After reviewing substantial literature on the topic Anderson et al.[22] concluded that time spent engaged in oral and silent reading activities was substantially more rewarding, in terms of growth on reading tests, than completing work sheets. What this means is that although we know that additional time on task doing anything will probably make someone better at that thing, the question for teachers is, What do we want students to become more skilled at? There is at least one choice—completing workbook pages or reading text.

Teacher Time on Task

If only it were that simple—just providing extra independent practice. Unfortunately, many students cannot or do not get that extra practice independently. They seem to need more guidance if they are to reach a satisfactory level of achievement. In short, it is not just increased time on task that they need, it is increased *teacher* time on task.

One of the great contradictions of the classroom is that the best readers seem to be able to engage a teacher in a thoughtful discussion of a story for what seems a painlessly endless period of time whereas the poorest readers get, in place of a teacher, a well-structured phonics workbook. The irony is, of course, that the best readers probably need the teacher least, and the poorest readers need the teacher most (and the workbook least).

Teachers should be on guard about how they spend their instructional time. It is easy to be seduced by the better readers. The time a teacher spends with them seems so productive, when in fact they might have done just as well—learned just as much—without the teacher's guidance. On the other hand, a teacher cannot forsake the better students simply because the poorer students need his or her presence.

A compromise of sorts has been reached on this issue, which is, at heart, as much a matter of ethics as efficiency. There is a trade-off between preparation time and instructional time, on the one hand, and better and poorer readers, on the other. That is, better readers may not demand as much of a teacher's instructional time since they are more self-sufficient, but they probably demand more of a teacher's preparation time. It takes more time and creativity to organize appropriate independent activities for them. Poorer readers, in contrast, may not demand as many creative or elaborate instructional materials, but they do need considerable on-the-spot guidance and feedback. In short, teachers must learn to balance the ethical and efficiency issues related to students who differ in reading ability by taking into account all aspects of their teaching act—curriculum preparation as well as instruction.

Why is it that low-achieving readers demand more of a teacher's time? There are several reasons. First, because they are not likely to be familiar with success, they feel less sure about their performance. Hence they need systematic, frequent reinforcement concerning the quality of their work. Because they are not sure, they need to be told that they are doing well, are on the right track.

Second, low-achieving readers need more task monitoring and substantive feedback. Because they are poor readers, they are likely to make errors. If unmonitored and uncorrected, these errors get practiced more often than do the appropriate responses. With extensive error-laden practice, they build up strong habit strengths for the errors. To take a simple example, a student who practices saying /this/ for *that* soon becomes more inclined to say /this/ than to say /that/ when he sees *that*. Those who have tried to remediate habitual function word errors will readily recognize the difficulty involved in trying to reverse error responses that have such a great habit strength. The most important part of frequent task monitoring is substantive feedback.

By substantive feedback we mean feedback that tells students what they should be doing as well as what they should *not* be doing. A teacher who says, "No, the word is not 'that'; try again," is probably less helpful than the one who says, "No, the word is not 'that,' even though I know it looks like 'that,' it is really 'this.' " Similarly, a student who learns that he missed three of five on a comprehension work sheet has not been helped to the same degree as one who has had the benefit of a three-minute discussion with a teacher about why certain answers to the question are more plausible than others, or one who has been provided with a model or a strategy for solving these puzzles we call questions. In the next section of this chapter and throughout the instructional chapters, many examples of teacher modeling and guided strategy development are provided.

Perhaps the best conclusion to this section on teacher time on task is that good students need good materials to the same degree that poor students need live bodies.

Alternative Teaching Strategies

For years, teachers have professed what must be the "holy grail" of reading instruction: The task is not to find the "best" method of teaching reading but to find the best method for a particular student. What research there is on such aptitude by treatment interactions[23] suggests that such a search is futile when it comes to broad distinctions between methods, such as whole word versus phonic instruction. However, there are no data to suggest that short-term changes in approach do not make a difference for particular skills or particular students or kinds of students.

Operating on the principle that change is sometimes good simply to get out of a rut, it is advisable to alter an approach to teaching a given skill when it becomes obvious that the approach in use is not working. Too often teachers do not alter their approach. This reluctance to change is sometimes bred by lack of knowledge and experience; a teacher knows only one way to teach a sound-symbol correspondence, for example. Sometimes it is bred by the unwarranted fear that a change in method will confuse the student. It should be noted that the child who is experiencing the difficulty was originally taught by *that* method. Furthermore, there is enough similarity in methods of teaching a given skill to encourage doubt that change will cause confusion. The teacher is, after all, dealing with the same skill. Who knows, a slight modification in method may be just the key to reach that student.

We recognize—and freely admit—that this proposal assumes that teachers have at their disposal a variety of techniques for teaching a given skill. There is one particular alternative teaching strategy that has been quite successful in both classroom experiments with groups of students and clinical settings with individuals or very small groups. It has been labeled "Explicit Instruction" by Pearson.[24] The model is described here in some detail since it will support many of the teaching sections in later chapters.

The key components in explicit instructional activities appear to be these:[25]

1. *Modeling.* The teacher begins instruction in a new skill by modeling for the students how he or she goes about applying it. Often this is a sort of think aloud about what he or she does to perform the skill, a "sharing of the cognitive secrets of the teacher's success," if you will. Usually in this step, the teacher emphasizes the *what* and *how* of the skill.

2. *Guided practice*. In this step the teacher and the students work cooperatively on new instances of the skill. Students can share with their peers *how* they went about solving the task, why they rejected some answers and settled on others, or what they found difficult or confusing and why. The teacher's role in this step is to provide feedback and encouragement for students' taking the risk of "sharing publicly their cognitive secrets." Also, the teacher must intervene when students are stumped or unresponsive; he or she must reassume some of the responsibility for completing the task that ceded when he or she moved from the modeling to the guided practice step.

3. *Consolidation*. At this point the teacher consolidates, helping the students see what they have learned so far about *what* this skill is and *how* to apply it. The teacher might conduct some "what if" sessions, in which he or she tries to get students thinking about *when* and *why* they might apply the skill. In the process the teacher begins, without any conscious effort to do so, to deal with what is called the metacognitive aspects of reading instruction—students' awareness of and control over the processes they go through to understand a text.

4. *Practice*. Here is where the old reliable work sheet or workbook page, if it has any role, enters the instructional cycle. In this step students must assume near-total responsibility for completing instances of the skill on their own. Feedback is especially important as a part of the first few independent practices, especially for students who experience difficulty completing the tasks on their own. When students share responses and the reasons for creating or selecting these responses, the greatest benefit accrues to students who appear to have no approach to applying comprehension skills and strategies other than to guess and pray. As a part of the discussion following practice, it is often necessary to review the *what* and *how* of the skill.

5. *Application*. Application is a critical step, one often omitted from instructional cycles. In this step teachers ask students to apply the skill in basal readers, content area textbooks, and trade books, moving them from the unreal world of workbook pages to the real world of text. In the application step, students look for examples of the skills in the selections they read from week to week, finding paragraphs that do or do not have main ideas, or examples of statements of fact or opinion, or instances of clear or unclear sequences of events. Another important feature of application is to show how the skill or strategy works across modalities—in writing or listening, for example. Again in the application step teachers need to emphasize the *when* and *why* of the skills, for it is to real texts that students must apply the skills they practice with the teacher and on their own. It is in this informal application that, it is hoped, students come to "own" the skills.

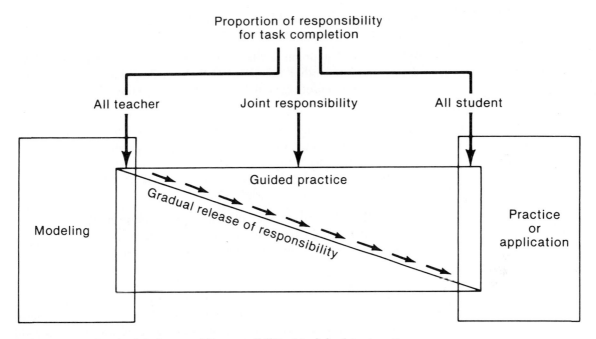

FIGURE 2.1   Gradual Release of Responsibility Model of Instruction

SOURCE: From P. D. Pearson and M. C. Gallagher (1983), The instruction of reading comprehension, *Contemporary Educational Psychology, 8,* 317–344 Used with permission.

Think of these steps as representing an optimal instructional cycle. Notice that instruction varies across the steps in terms of the amount of teacher guidance or the amount of "responsibility" teachers take for completing the task. The whole process can be depicted graphically, as in Figure 2.1. Instruction, Figure 2.1 suggests, should proceed from a maximum to a minimum of teacher responsibility, and, conversely, from a minimum to a maximum of student responsibility. Responsibility, Figure 2.1 argues, should be released gradually from teacher to student.

The explicit instruction model shares some features and some terminology with the direct instruction model associated with the work of Carnine, Becker, and Engelman,[26] but it differs on a number of counts. In explicit instruction:

1. There is no presumption that the teacher is the person in the learning community who possesses the "right" answers. No one may have that knowledge, or anyone may have it.

2. There is no need to break down a strategy into component skills, each of which has to be mastered. The members of the learning community, instead, can get together and say, "Okay, here is what we need to do; now who is going to do what so that we can complete the task?" There

may be some division of labor among individuals in the group, but the entire strategy always gets carried out.

3. What is explicit about explicit instruction is the willingness of the teacher and the other members of the learning community to share their strategic secrets in sufficient detail to give a novice a sense of how to do it.

4. There is no assumption that there is a single right way to complete any particular task; there are only the ways that the teacher and the students within the learning community actually use. Now, some may be more effective or more efficient or more fun than others; but that does not make them better or more right.

5. Progress is indexed by the amount of support, or scaffolding a student requires to solve a particular problem. It is not indexed by a score on a test or by passing some mythical mastery threshold.

We believe that the best hope for any teacher is to concentrate on the area of educational explanations of reading difficulty. In those educational explanations come the resources for helping children overcome the problems they have developed. As you read the chapters in Part 2 of this book, you will encounter a model of explicit instruction with emphasis on modeling, guided practice, consolidation, practice, and application. However, when this model is applied to different skills, slightly different facets of the model will be emphasized. What the chapters in Part 2 try do, when they focus on specific strategies that students should develop, is to present suggestions for helping students understand the *what, how, why,* and *when* of each strategy. But it is through the processes of modeling, guided practice, consolidation, practice, and application that teachers can help students develop an appreciation for:

What the strategy is

How you go about applying it while reading

Why you would ever want to try to apply it

When you would try to use it

SUMMARY   This chapter took you on a journey of the etiology, the study of causes or explanations, of reading difficulty—neurological, emotional, and environmental. It focused on environmental explanations, and within that subset, on educational explanations, precisely because these are the areas in which teachers can help students the most. Furthermore, it did not just study explanations of difficulty. Especially in the case of educational explanations, every explanation of reading difficulty, if turned on its head, is an explanation of reading success. Consequently, we hope that we have set the stage for the remainder of this book by convincing you that changes in instruction represent the key to helping students achieve their greatest aspirations for literacy.

NOTES

1. See Harris and Sipay (1985); Hartlage, 1976; Suchoff (1981).
2. See Harris and Sipay (1985).
3. See Ekwall and Shanker (1983).
4. See Bond, Tinker, and Wasson (1984).
5. The term *mixed dominance*, according to Harris (1970a), is no longer in vogue since it fails to distinguish between eyedness and handedness. Harris offers evidence to support a relationship between mixed handedness and reading disability but no relationship between mixed eyedness or crossed dominance and reading disability.
6. See Orton (1937), for example.
7. See Annett (1972), Groden (1969), and O'Donnell (1970).
8. See Harris (1970) and Harris and Sipay (1985).
9. See Belmont and Birch (1965), Capobianco (1966), and Capobianco (1967).
10. See Balow (1963), Balow and Balow (1964), and Robbins (1966).
11. See Orton (1966).
12. See Balow (1971) for a readable critique of this evidence.
13. See Cruickshank (1966), for example.
14. See Frostig and Home (1964) and Kephart (1960), for example.
15. See Cohen (1966), Jacobs (1968), McBeath (1966), Olson (1966), and Rosen (1965).
16. See Simmons (1979) or Natalicio (1979).
17. See Baratz and Shuy (1968).
18. See Lambert (1978) and Lambert and Tucker (1972).
19. See Sledd (1969), for example.
20. See Au and Mason (1982), Erickson and Mohatt (1982), Philips (1972), and Tharp (1983).
21. See Fisher, Filby, Marliave, Cohen, Dishaw, Moore, and Berliner (1978).
22. See Anderson, Hiebert, Scott, and Wilkinson (1985).
23. See Bateman (1968) and Robinson (1972), for example.
24. See Pearson and Gallagher (1983) and Pearson (1985).
25. This conceptualization of an *Explicit Model of Instruction* first appeared in an article by Pearson and Dole (in press).
26. See Becker and Carnine (1976), Becker, Engelmann, and Carnine, Carnine and Silbert (1979), and Gersten and Carnine (1986).

Chapter 3

Motivation and Reading

OVERVIEW

As you read this chapter use the following list of main ideas to guide your understanding and reflection.

In literate societies children are motivated to learn to read because it is an important part of mastering their environment.

Learner-oriented views of motivation hold that a child's natural curiosity and desire to succeed with important tasks provide the teacher with the necessary base for motivation, whereas other views emphasize external rewards that the teacher manipulates to shape behavior.

Human behavior is typically motivated in complex ways often involving intrinsic as well as extrinsic factors.

Attitudes, interests, and self-concept all play important roles in motivating children to read.

Children who encounter difficulty in learning to read often develop low self-concepts and feelings of helplessness leading to counterproductive behaviors that interfere with subsequent attempts to provide remediation.

Good readers seem to attribute any difficulties they encounter in learning to read to factors they can control (such as effort), whereas low-achieving readers are more likely to believe they are powerless to prevent their own failures.

Teachers can help children who have developed feelings of helplessness by redirecting their attention to factors over which the children have some control.

Informal assessment devices and techniques such as questionnaires and interviews can be helpful to the teacher in identifying factors that contribute to insufficient motivation.

In 1976 the film *Rocky* set box office records throughout the United States and abroad. Since then *Rocky II*, *Rocky III*, and *Rocky IV* have elevated the main character to a folk hero of sorts. In the first film the reigning heavyweight boxing champion of the world, Apollo Creed, decided to give an unknown boxer the chance to fight for his title in Philadelphia to mark the nation's bicentennial. Rocky Balboa, a local club fighter who, during the day, collected payments from dock workers for a loan shark and spent most evenings bumming around his neighborhood, was chosen. Rocky went into training for the fight under the most difficult of circumstances. After weeks of hard work and sacrifice, he nearly upset Creed in a hard-fought match. Rocky lost the fight but gained great status among his neighbors, a good amount of money, and a lovely girl friend. His life was transformed, virtually overnight, from poverty and anonymity to fame and fortune. Although not written by Horatio Alger, the story fits into a popular theme in literature exemplified by the Alger stories: Through hard work and strength of character even the lowliest person can leave behind his miserable existence and rise to the top.

What was it that propelled Rocky to success? The word *motivation* comes to mind. Rocky wanted to be somebody. He wanted to improve his situation and his prospects for the future. Opportunity knocked and Rocky was motivated to put enormous physical and emotional energy into getting ready for the fight.

Each of us can remember times when we have been highly motivated just as Rocky was. We can also remember times when we let something slide that we knew should be done. We just could not get motivated. We all know something about motivation and recognize the critical role it plays in human behavior. That is, we seem to know until we encounter a case of low motivation that defies explanation, then we discover we may not know as much as we thought. Classroom teachers seem to encounter more than their share of inexplicable cases of low motivation.

This chapter looks first at motivation as a psychological construct in order to understand its origins, how it operates, and what teachers can do to develop and nurture it. It also looks at how motivation influences reading and how teachers can assess students' level of motivation in order to develop a plan for improving it. The next chapter will then offer several case studies involving low motivation and a number of specific activities for motivating low-achieving readers.

WHAT IS MOTIVATION?

In order for humans to survive, certain needs have to be met. Obviously food and water satisfy the basic needs of hunger and thirst. Without these necessities a person would die. The satisfaction of these needs gives rise to *primary drives.* These drives are unlearned in the sense that no one teaches an infant to become hungry or thirsty or to engage in sucking as a means of statisfying these drives. Other primary needs that seem to be fundamental to human survival include sleep, shelter, and procreation.

With respect to motivation, needs activate or energize the individual. This "inner push" that stems from the need to satisfy a drive is probably the most fundamental form of motivation. Is it fair to say that Rocky was motivated to train for the heavyweight title fight by the need for food? In an indirect way the answer is "yes." Rocky had to eat. He earned his money by fighting. In order to fight he had to train. Thus, through a series of links, he was training to eat. But Rocky was not starving when the opportunity to fight for the title came up. He earned a subsistence living by collecting debts for a loan shark. He also earned an occasional dollar or two by boxing in a local club. In this he was not fighting to satisfy a basic need as much as he was fighting for recognition and a feeling of importance. Are these needs the same as hunger or thirst?

Here it is helpful to introduce the notion of *secondary* needs. Primary needs are unlearned, that is, they occur instinctively, but secondary needs are learned. For example, infants growing up in one culture learn to eat at particular times and to eat particular types of food. Over time their basic need for food develops certain habits. In our own culture it is fairly predictable that they will eat three times a day and that hamburgers or hot dogs will form part of their diet. As much as our acculturation tempts us to deny it, there is no instinctive basis for either of these patterns of behavior. Other cultures eat only twice a day and favor insects, for example. Who is to say which set of behaviors is most basic?

The point is that even though secondary needs are learned or acquired, they have the same capacity as basic needs to energize or activate behavior. Exactly what needs children acquire as they mature reflects the culture they live in as well as their own values and tastes.

To return to Rocky Balboa for a moment: If we agree that Rocky was not fighting to satisfy a basic need (for example, he was not starving), was he fighting to satisfy an acquired need? If we conclude that the cash he would receive for the fight was the primary source of motivation for Rocky, this is clearly an acquired need. Money has no inherent value, but it can be used to satisfy various primary and secondary needs, including hunger.

Food and water satisfy basic or primary needs that are unlearned and fundamental to survival. In different cultures people meet these needs in different ways that are learned from society. *(Peter Vadnai)*

Sources of Motivation

In a literate society schools have the responsibility for teaching children how to read. Clearly this is not a primary need like eating or sleeping. If it were, teachers would have a relatively easy task. All children would learn to read in order to survive. Although reading does not qualify as a primary (survival) need, children have other needs that can serve as the basis for teaching them to read. Whether these needs are primary or acquired, unlearned or learned, is an interesting philosophical question that bears directly on the matter of motivation.

According to one school of thought[1] human beings have a basic need to achieve "competence" or to become "self-actualized." Despite some differences in the detail of their theories, White and Maslow both posit an energizing force within humans that causes them to strive for mastery of their environment. Weiner (1974) might logically be grouped with these theorists on the basis of his research on need achievement as a motivating force in human behavior. Piaget's notions about cognitive development are also quite consistent with this school of thought. In essence, these experts would agree that children are constantly striving to make sense of their world and to structure their interactions with the world so that they can be "in charge" of their own destiny.

This learner-oriented view of motivation has immediate and far-reaching implications for the way in which teachers approach reading instruction. A central premise of this view is that external rewards are less effective motivators than a child's own feelings of satisfaction when a goal has been achieved. Also basic to this view is the notion that personal interest in a topic or task is a critical part of establishing sustained motivation. The teacher's role is to create an environment that stimulates the child's natural curiosity and desire to succeed. In short, meaningfulness of what is learned is vitally important to the learner.

A second school of thought, represented by Skinner (1953) or Hull (1952), emphasizes the importance of external rewards as motivating devices. Teachers are placed in the role of selecting which goals to pursue and establishing a reward system that will motivate learners toward those goals. Personal interest is a factor only to the extent that the rewards offered must be attractive to the child. It is the teacher who motivates and the child who responds. Meaningfulness of what is to be learned is less important than the appropriateness of the rewards offered.

Extrinsic and Intrinsic Motivation

One's beliefs about the nature of motivation influence how they view the relative importance of internal and external sources of reward. Motivation occurring for reasons that lie within a task and within the person, such as feelings of satisfaction or competence, is usually called *intrinsic* motivation. For example, Rocky Balboa proved to himself that he was nearly the equal of the heavyweight champion of the world. Rocky also gained status in the eyes of the sports world and enhanced his reputation with his friends by fighting. These social rewards appear to have an extrinsic basis—that is, they lie outside the person. This leads us to external motivation, which is discussed next.

Motivation that occurs for reasons that lie outside the individual or the task (for instance, for an external reward) is called extrinsic motivation. In Rocky's case the money he could earn for fighting is a clearcut example of an extrinsic reward that could generate extrinsic motivation. Other possible extrinsic motivators for Rocky were the chance to have a personal manager-trainer, and the chance to get back his locker at the local gym (something he had recently lost because he seemed to be going nowhere as a boxer), and his increased status.

Although the intrinsic-extrinsic concepts are useful, they should not be taken as mutually exclusive. Some motivators have both internal and external elements. For example, had Rocky won the fight he would have received a belt that accompanies the title. Although valuable in its own right, at a hock shop for example, the belt is symbolic of high achievement. How did Rocky view the belt? Was he interested in this tangible reward worth several hundred dollars? Probably not, at least not when he was doing well financially. Later, had he won the belt but become destitute, the extrinsic value of the belt might have outweighed its intrinsic value and been sold for cash to buy a sack of groceries. It is important to realize that individuals will often pursue a given task for both internal and external rewards.

In a classroom setting the value of extrinsic rewards is often hard to calculate. Where does symbolism begin and end for Paul? When does a good grade give him a sense of satisfaction or feeling of competence and when does it literally earn him a ticket to the circus or save him a swat on the posterior at home? Motivators that may look straightforward and simple to the teacher may become distorted and complex from a child's perspective.

From the standpoint of learning, the most powerful motivator seems to be that of self-actualization. Humans seek to master what they believe to be important. They want to control their own destiny. Such motivation is internal. Teachers can and must seek to build, nurture, and capitalize on the intrinsic need to improve oneself.

At the same time, extrinsic rewards are often effective, and sometimes the only recourse, with children who have learned to dislike reading. By rewarding Paul for his achievement the teacher attempts to encourage (or motivate) subsequent attempts. Extrinsic rewards can take the form of symbols (grades, gold stars), treats (candy), substitutes for treats (tokens, money), and praise. The teacher's goal is usually to employ extrinsic motivation until sufficient success has been achieved by Paul for his own intrinsic motivation to replace the need for external rewards. In providing tangible incentives for particular behaviors like reading a page without errors or answering ten questions correctly, teachers hope to associate the tangible reward with a sense of accomplishment and self-worth. When that bond becomes strong enough, so the theory goes, the tangible incentive can be removed because the child's internal sense of self-worth that accompanies achievement will have become strong enough to motivate further attempts to achieve.

Human Behavior Is Motivated in Complex Ways

The case of Rocky Balboa has been used to examine the principle of motivation. The primary question has been: What motivated Rocky to fight Apollo Creed? We have considered a variety of possible motives, ranging from pride to hunger. In actuality it is fairly easy to see that Rocky, like most people, is seldom motivated by a single factor. Rocky probably had five or six competing, perhaps even conflicting, motivations. Beyond the cradle, the complexities of life probably make this the rule rather than the exception.

To help Paul learn to read, we need to recognize the complexity of what motivates Paul and adjust our approach accordingly. We need to know something about his general disposition toward reading, his areas of personal interest, and his concept of himself as a person and as a reader. If he dislikes reading and has a backlog of negative experiences associated with learning to read, motivation will be much more difficult. We will not be able to approach him from the standpoint of mastering his environment. For reasons we will explore later, he has probably abandoned trying to learn to read and may even deny that reading is important. With effort, intrinsic motivation can be rekindled, but probably will not provide the most effective starting point. Extrinsic motivation will have a better chance of succeeding with Paul at the outset. Just which rewards he will value must be discovered as well as how they should be provided. Only by getting to know Paul better as an individual will we gain a sense of what motivates him. The key can be found in the information we gather using several assessment instruments.

THE RELATIONSHIP OF MOTIVATION TO ATTITUDES, INTERESTS, AND SELF-CONCEPT

Thus far we have looked closely at the internal and external sources that can give rise to the energizing force we call motivation. Several other factors must also be examined to understand fully the topic of motivation. First, we must look at *attitudes* and how attitudes about reading affect motivation. Next, we should consider how *interests* are related to motivation. Finally, the topic of *self-concept* must be examined with respect to its impact on motivation.

Attitudes

The term *attitude* is often used to refer to a person's predisposition toward a topic.[2] People are said to have a positive or favorable attitude toward nuclear power, for example, meaning they generally favor the generation of power by nuclear reactors and probably support the construction of additional reactors. Positive feelings about a topic almost always emanate from previous pleasant experiences with that topic. Thus, we would not expect residents of Chernobyl to have positive feelings about nuclear power because of the personally disruptive and life-threatening experiences they went through in 1986.

Attitudes are often a matter of degree rather than kind; that is, we are less likely to be totally negative or positive than we are to be "sort of" positive or negative. Thus, in an opinion poll (which basically measures attitudes), respondents are often given an opportunity to strongly agree or disagree with a statement, agree or disagree mildly, or even to indicate neutral feelings. Some opponents of nuclear power feel strongly enough to attend hearings, stage protests, and even go to jail to express their resistance. Others write letters and contribute money to the cause, but keep their resistance at a lower level. Some talk about their opposition at cocktail parties. All have negative attitudes about nuclear power, but the degree or intensity of their negative feelings varies considerably.

These illustrations suggest that at least three factors are critical with respect to attitudes. First, an attitude has a focus; that is, we do not speak of attitudes in general, but about attitudes on specific topics or issues. Second, attitudes grow from experience with a topic, either direct or indirect. And third, attitudes typically fall somewhere on a continuum ranging from absolutely

This woman's attitude toward running causes her to jog for conditioning purposes just as her attitude toward reading for information might encourage her to read the daily newspaper. *(Peter Vadnai)*

favorable on one extreme to absolutely unfavorable on the other extreme. Let us consider the implications of these principles for attitudes toward reading.

Attitudes Toward Reading   One's attitude toward reading is most meaningful when discussed in terms of a particular type or use of reading. It is impractical to assess attitude toward reading in general, but possible to examine attitudes toward different types of reading and attitudes toward various uses of reading. A physical education teacher might use different teaching approaches to a running task with two children whose attitudes toward competitive long distance running are different. In the same way, a teacher will want to approach the motivation of the avid book reader differently than the child who generally avoids reading for recreation. Attitude toward a particular type of reading can and should be assessed to make instructional plans.

Interests

The question still remains: How is attitude toward reading, even in an applied sense, related to motivation? Mathewson (1976) addressed this question by stating that motivation is the energizing force that actually causes reading to occur when a favorable attitude toward reading exists. He uses the term *interest* to describe the action orientation that occurs when positive attitude and motivation are both present. Mathewson believes that a favorable attitude toward reading by itself does not cause an individual to read. Interest becomes the factor that triggers actual reading. Thus, interest is another element that should be included in an assessment of motivation.

It is important to note, however, that high motivation can work in the absence of a positive attitude toward reading. This can occur in two ways. First, the topic may be of such personal importance to readers that they will read something related to that interest even though reading is not a favored activity (for example, when adolescents need to read the state vehicle code in order to pass a test to obtain their driver's license). Here internal motivation is at work. On the other hand, rewards can be offered that provide external motivation for readers who would not normally read a selection. These observations about motivating reading in the absence of positive attitudes will be especially important in a later section on instruction.

Self-Concept

A person's self-concept is defined by Quandt and Selznick (1984) as "all the perceptions that an individual has of himself; especially emphasized are the individual's perceptions of his value and his ability" (p. 1). Restated, we might say that self-concept relates to what a person thinks of himself or herself.

Realistically speaking, rational people rarely think of themselves in totally positive terms because it is human nature to recognize one's faults and weaknesses. Nevertheless, a good or positive self-concept usually accompanies feelings of competence and importance. One aspect of self-perception relates to one's success with reading (learning to read and using reading in real life settings). A person could have a good self-concept and not be able to read, of course, but in a literate, print-oriented society, reading difficulty is likely to have a strong negative impact on self-concept.

Self-concept develops largely in response to interactions with others. A *self-perception* develops as we compare ourselves with others. Schools often unwittingly underscore negative self-comparisons by using a graded measuring device (i.e., the basal series), and arranging a race of sorts through the various levels of the series.

Self-concept also has a *self-other* dimension involving children's views of how others view them. Constantly told, directly or indirectly, that they are doing poorly with reading, children can soon accept their fate and begin performing down to these expectations. A self-fulfilling prophecy begins to operate as such children become problem readers because they think they are. The real tragedy in all this is that too often the well-meaning teacher has contributed to this demise through efforts to "motivate" with comments such as, "You're falling behind. You're not doing well. You aren't trying hard enough." Though we do not wish to advocate a simplistic, Pollyanna approach to reading instruction, it is clear that the *self-other* perceptions of children can be critical in their development of a reading self-concept which may in turn affect their future reading performance.

A third dimension of self-concept is the *self-ideal*. This relates to what individuals wish they could do. As with self-perceptions and self-other perceptions, the development of self-ideals is heavily dependent upon interactions with people who are important to children (significant others). This normally includes teachers, peers, and of course, parents. If the people who are important to children regard reading as important and give evidence of this belief, children will develop a positive disposition toward reading. Furthermore, if these significant others help children monitor their own progress rather than compare them with other children, reading self-concept will be enhanced. With a healthy self-concept children are better able to withstand the temporary setbacks and frustrations that invariably accompany the acquisition of any new ability.[3]

Children with poor reading self-concepts, whether justified by their progress or not, will gravitate toward what Quandt and Selznick call "counteractions." Counteractions are defense mechanisms that anyone employs in the face of repeated failure with an important task. One counteraction is to deny the importance of the activity—in this case, reading. Does the child really believe reading is unimportant? Probably not at first, but over time the child may actually begin to accept this defense as true. The solution may or may not be to attack the defense mechanism and *prove* the child is wrong. A better solution is probably to tackle the negative self-concept by giving the child success experiences, by praising and documenting progress, and by indicating you think the child is worthy and capable. If this can be done in reading situations, all the better, but remediation may have to begin with something else, such as puzzles or games, and gradually lead into reading.

A second counteraction unsuccessful readers often employ is to hide or disguise their lack of ability.[4] Illiterate adults, and older children in particular, become very adept at hiding their reading disability. A skilled teacher will make allowances for the individuals' fragile egos by not publicly displaying the disability, and will privately support them with an understanding attitude. Trust and rapport must be established before remediation can proceed and, again, improvement of the individual's self-concept is the best starting point. Several specific strategies for approaching this problem are offered in the following chapter.

Another counteraction that we have all used at one time or another is simply to make it clear that we really did not try to succeed at an activity. This works fine if the activity is an optional one such as riding a bicycle or playing softball. We may suffer temporarily for lacking a skill of this type, but life rolls on. This is not so true with a skill as important as reading. Children may attempt to protect their egos by not trying, but the problem of illiteracy will not go away.

A fairly extensive body of literature has developed in recent years in which children who have experienced repeated failures with reading or some other task are portrayed as "passive failures." Such children are easily discouraged and do not persist with tasks as do children who have developed positive self-concepts.

The classroom teacher who wants to help low-achieving children do better in reading confronts a genuine problem when it comes to motivation. Because of the low self-concept that many of these children develop over time, they are often unwilling to try and, consequently, they develop an attitude of helplessness. If these feelings of helplessness were better understood, it would be much easier to plan instructional activities.

Weiner (1974) has theorized that in the process of trying to accomplish a task people typically develop explanations for their successes or failures. According to Weiner, they attribute success or failure to both internal and external factors. Internal factors include the amount of effort expended and one's ability to perform a particular task. External factors include the difficulty of a task and luck. To illustrate, suppose you wanted to hit a golf ball from the tee to a green that is 150 yards away. What determines how well you succeed in accomplishing that feat? Different people give different explanations. One person may do poorly and attribute the outcome to the difficulty of the task saying, "Even a pro finds it hard to hit the ball on the green." Another person might attribute the outcome to ability, saying, "I'm not a very good golfer." A third person might say, "I didn't concentrate on that shot," thereby implying, "I could do better if I tried harder." In most situations people recognize that each of these factors plays a role in the final outcome. Though Weiner's attribution theory is far more complex than the above example indicates, it is sufficient here to note that people differ in how they account for their success on a task.

Returning to the notion of learned helplessness, there is evidence to suggest that low-achieving readers often attribute their reading failure to factors beyond their control.[5] Low-achieving readers usually believe it is lack of ability that accounts for their reading failure whereas good readers attribute their occasional failures to lack of effort. The implications of this difference are monumental. Lack of certain abilities is something everyone must face and is something that cannot be rectified. Someone lacking good hand-eye coordination will simply never play golf as well as someone who is blessed with outstanding coordination. Hard work is simply no substitute for ability.

Similarly low-achieving readers who attribute their failure to low ability naturally feel helpless and passive about reading. If they continue to fail when extra effort is expended, it convinces them that success is unrelated to effort. "I tried hard and still failed. I just can't do it because I'm stupid." Motivating such a reader is challenging, to say the least.

Better readers, on the other hand, seem to believe their failures are due to lack of effort.[6] Assuming a task is within one's reach, this explanation for failure can lead to corrective efforts. In fact, any corrective efforts on the teacher's part will probably have positive effects because it implies that the student has the ability needed to correct the failure.

Bristow (1985) suggests that despite having good intentions, teachers often unwittingly reinforce the beliefs of low-achieving children concerning the cause of their difficulty (lack of ability) by expressing sympathy for their failure. In contrast, these same teachers often become angry when better readers fail, thus conveying the impression that their failure is due to lack of effort, not lack of ability.[7] Later we will explore various means for helping low-achieving readers overcome the passive behavior that seems to accompany their learned helplessness. But first, let us look at how motivation can be assessed.

ASSESSING MOTIVATION TO READ

It would be convenient if there were a single test instrument that collected all the needed information about reading motivation. Unfortunately, none exists. Some useful data can be collected by commercially produced instruments; other information can be gathered informally by teachers. However, no formula exists for putting all the pieces together to arrive at the "truth" about Harry's or Hilda's motivation for reading. Ultimately, as with all assessments, it will be the task of the teacher to weigh and interpret all the information available, to seek additional information where needed, and to develop a working hypothesis that guides instructional efforts. A teacher's conceptualization of motivation determines what information should be gathered and how it should be interpreted. It makes sense that information in the following areas is useful:

Attitudes toward reading

Areas of personal interest

Records of reading undertaken—what was and was not liked

Self-concept

We now propose to examine how each of these topics can be assessed.

Assessing Attitudes Toward Reading

Educational measurement is not an exact science. Any assessment is subject to some error and this is particularly true concerning affective topics such as the motivation to read. Later, once a variety of devices and procedures for gathering such information have been described, certain cautions will be discussed in using and interpreting the results of such measures.

It is sufficient to say, as an introduction to this topic, that people's feelings are elusive and ever-changing. This probably explains why very few formal measures of reading attitude are available. Alexander and Filler (1976) identify eighteen attitude assessment instruments or procedures reported in the published literature, but properly refrain from calling them formal tests. Rather, they suggest that these instruments may be useful in helping classroom teachers devise their own instruments. We agree that few such devices can be used without adaptation to the local setting. Attitudes toward reading can be assessed through a variety of informal techniques, including questionnaires, incomplete sentences, teacher observation, interviews and conferences, and reading attitude scales, which will be examined.

FIGURE 3.1   Reading Attitude Questionnaire

Name   Age   Date

DIRECTIONS: Read each of the statements given below. Respond by circling *Yes* or *No* to indicate if the statement applies to you.

Yes   No   1. Reading is my favorite subject in school.

Yes   No   2. I would rather read a good book than watch TV.

Yes   No   3. I usually understand what I read in books.

Yes   No   4. I have gotten to know some interesting people in books.

Yes   No   5. Sharing books in school is fun.

Yes   No   6. Reading out loud to a parent or friend is fun.

Yes   No   7. I would like to hear my teacher read a story out loud every
                  day.

Yes   No   8. I like to receive books as gifts.

Yes   No   9. Members of my family borrow books from the library.

Questionnaires   Nearly every adult has had experience with a questionnaire. Given a particular topic, questions are asked that reveal the respondent's position on that topic. With respect to attitudes about reading, the questions seek to ascertain *if* you read, *when* you read, *what* you read, and perhaps even *why* you read. Typically, questionnaires present a forced choice between *yes* and *no* as a response, though some may provide for a response of *undecided* or *I don't know.*

Questionnaires are relatively easy to construct and may readily be adjusted to fit the reading level of the group and even the local situation. A sample questionnaire developed for upper-grade children is presented in Figure 3.1. Notice that the questions are constructed so that a response of *yes* suggests a positive disposition toward reading. By totaling the number of yeses for each child and ranking the scores from high to low, a teacher can quickly see which children are least likely to spend time reading. It requires a leap of faith to conclude that either the score or the rank of a child is an accurate index of the child's attitude toward reading, however. Such a leap is not advisable.

What is justified, however, is a search for further information about each child using the other devices described here. Patterns of behavior gathered over time give rise to a working hypothesis that, "Alice avoids reading whenever possible perhaps because of a negative attitude." Causes for this tentative conclusion and possible solutions can then be explored.

Questionnaires Using More Sensitive Scales   As stated earlier, an assessment device will be more useful if it allows for a range of responses (not just *yes-no*) and if it specifies reading of a particular type or topic rather than reading in general. Instead of asking children to answer *yes* or *no* to a question such as, "Do you like to read?" a range of responses (Likert-type scale) such as, *Always—Usually—Sometimes—Seldom—Never*, can be provided. It is also possible to offer children an opportunity to indicate the quality and intensity of their feelings regarding a concept. Thus, the following scale is employed to measure quality:

Where on the following scale would you rate reading?

Good   ____ ____ ____ ____ Bad
Happy ____ ____ ____ ____ Sad (Alexander & Filler, 1976)

Intensity is measured with a scale using adjectives such as *strong-weak*, *big-little*, and so forth.

The sample question above may also be framed differently so that it is more applied. For example, the question might ask, "Do you like to read before going to bed at night?" Or the question may give several alternatives: "Before going to bed at night I like to: (a) read, (b) listen to the radio, (c) watch TV, (d) play with a game or toy." Alexander and Filler (1976) call devices of this sort "paired choices." Pairings may be presented with two or more choices. With older children a *yes-no* questionnaire can be modified with a scale that asks students to rate their level of agreement with each statement: "I like to read before going to bed: strongly agree—agree—disagree—strongly disagree."

Any questionnaire, regardless of the scale used or type of response made, should sample enough behaviors (that is, have enough questions) to provide a reliable assessment. At least 20 items are needed to yield a useful picture of the child's disposition toward reading. Even then, we must recognize that questionnaires, as well as other paper-and-pencil devices to be described later, ask students to report what they believe or prefer. Inaccuracy can creep in if they really do not know their own mind on a question.

Incomplete Sentences   Another relatively simple-to-make device that can provide useful insights about children's attitudes toward reading consists of short phrases or stems that elicit a response (a word or phrase) that completes the sentence. For example, a stem could state, "I would rather read than _____." The respondents reveal something about their disposition toward reading in their responses. As with a questionnaire,

FIGURE 3.2   Sentence Completion

Name   Age   Date

DIRECTIONS: Complete each sentence in whatever way describes you best.

1. Reading books at home is _____

_____ .

2. The best book I ever read was _____

_____ .

3. Reading is hard when _____ .

4. Most books are _____ .

5. When I see a library I _____

_____ .

6. Reading class is _____ .

7. I think reading _____ .

8. When my teacher reads a book to us I _____

_____ .

9. I think the newspaper is _____ .

10. My favorite magazine is _____ .

incomplete sentences can be developed to reflect local concerns and conditions. A sample of assessment using incomplete sentences is presented in Figure 3.2.

The value of incomplete sentences depends on the teacher's ability to combine this information with other information about attitude toward books and reading. No simple scoring scheme is available for summarizing or interpreting the responses. Some teachers gain further insight into children's feelings about reading by discussing some of their more revealing responses in a one-to-one conference. For example, it would be important to discuss Hector's response to the following stem: "I think reading *a book is a waste of time.*" A pattern of negative responses such as this one signals a serious problem that needs immediate and individual attention. An isolated response of this sort may mean Hector is merely having a bad day or is struggling with a difficult book right now. Here the problem is much less serious, but still worth a few minutes of conversation between teacher and pupil.

Teacher Observation   Teachers have countless opportunities during the course of a day to gain a sense of their pupils' attitudes toward reading. Some clues are obvious while others are more subtle. The teacher who makes it a point to watch for the quick frown or the eager volunteer when a reading activity first begins can gain valuable information that confirms or belies a working hypothesis about Hector's attitude toward reading. Simple anecdotal records provide a way to document fleeting incidents that may eventually add up to a significant insight. Some teachers use 3 × 5 index cards to quickly jot down notations like, "Pete became so engrossed in a Hardy Boys Mystery that he was last in line for lunch today." Other teachers use a notebook with a page for comments on each child; some have checklists that help them focus on behaviors they find revealing.

Figure 3.3 presents a sample checklist that could be used to record a student's behavior over an entire day. Although it would not be practical to complete such a checklist every day, a teacher could pay attention to the types of behavior noted on the checklist several times a semester. One strategy is to watch one or two children each day noting their behavior on the checklist. Another strategy is to watch for a particular type of behavior among all the pupils in a class one day, then focus on another type another day. In either case, systematic observation is taking place. Over time this builds a useful data base that enables a teacher to go beyond general impressions in drawing conclusions or planning instruction.

Teacher observation should also note the incidental happenings that occur in a classroom every day. Some events are visible to everyone (for example, Mary cries out of frustration with the difficulty of the science textbook), others are seen only by the alert teacher (Scott participates actively in a discussion about rodeos). Such observations belong in an anecdotal record to be used later when planning a science lesson or locating books for the classroom library.

Interviews and Conferences   Of the various approaches suggested here for assessing attitudes toward reading, perhaps the most difficult to arrange is the personal interview. It is a very time-consuming activity to meet periodically with each child in a classroom. In addition, the problem of keeping the other children in a classroom productive while a teacher sits with one child may seem overwhelming.

Even though there is no magic solution to these issues, a one-to-one session has the greatest potential from an assessment standpoint. Surrounded by the information gathered from questionnaires, incomplete sentences, or observations, a teacher can explore what all the indirect information means. Straightforward questions can be asked: "Do you enjoy reading, Henry? What kind of books do you prefer? Do you read at home? Does anyone ever read to you?" Reasons for a negative attitude can be sought: "What do you dislike most about reading? What causes you trouble when you read? What do you think would make reading class more enjoyable? Why?"

Questions such as these can be asked on a written questionnaire, of course,

FIGURE 3.3   Teacher's Observation Checklist

_____   _____   _____
Name   Date   Teacher's Name

                                            _____   _____
                                            Class   Period

DIRECTIONS: Indicate which behaviors are observed during the period of observation by making a check in the margin.

The student was observed:

_____ 1. Carrying a library or paperback book not assigned by the teacher.

_____ 2. Reading for recreation.

_____ 3. Discussing a book he or she had read independently.

_____ 4. Participating in a discussion about a topic of personal interest.

_____ 5. Describing an article he or she read in the daily newspaper.

_____ 6. Browsing in the classroom library.

During reading class the student:

_____ 7. Volunteered to read a passage aloud.

_____ 8. Participated in a discussion of the assigned reading.

_____ 9. Looked up the meaning of an unknown word in the dictionary or glossary.

_____10. Expressed an interest in reading further about the topic.

_____11. Identified an application of an idea from the assigned reading to his or her own life.

_____12. Appeared confused or unsure about the assigned reading.

During an oral reading activity the student:

_____13. Listened attentively.

_____14. Answered or asked questions about the material shared.

_____15. Volunteered to take a turn reading aloud.

but children may be hampered by their ability to express themselves in writing. The personal attention they receive in a conference or interview should encourage the child to "open up." The sensitive teacher is able to read nonverbal cues in a face-to-face meeting that may provide insight not possible otherwise.

Some may believe that all this is well and good but irrelevant, because interviews are virtually impossible to arrange. Several suggestions should make it clear that interviews can be managed. First, not everyone has to be interviewed. Although it is desirable to organize an instructional program around conferences, a teacher may choose to interview only children whose attitudes are a cause for concern. This plan should reduce a teacher's interview load by half or even two-thirds.

A second suggestion is described in greater detail by Harris and Smith (1986). They suggest that conferences be made a part of the weekly schedule with time set aside for perhaps two or three short conferences per week. Other children are given time to read silently a book of their choice for the twenty or thirty minutes this involves.

Other possibilities exist, of course (such as using aides to free the teacher for conference time, holding conferences before or after school or during library period), if the idea of meeting with children one-to-one is a priority.

Alexander and Filler (1976) suggest that interviews be structured to some extent. This can be accomplished by completing a questionnaire or a complete-sentence device orally with the child, or by using a set of prepared questions.

Published Reading Attitude Scales   An advantage can sometimes be gained by using assessment instruments that have been developed by specialists and subjected to reliability and validity studies. Alexander and Filler (1976) summarize a number of published attitude assessment instruments. Among the better known questionnaires they describe is a twenty-five-item inventory designed for use in grades 1 through 6 developed by the Department of Education, San Diego County, San Diego, California. Known as the *San Diego County Inventory of Reading Attitude* (no date), the instrument has been examined for validity through item analysis procedures and has an established .79 split-half reliability. The inventory is not unlike the questionnaire presented in Figure 3.1. The child is asked to answer *yes* or *no* to questions such as "Do you think that reading is the best part of the school day?" and "Do you like to read catalogues?"

Another well-known instrument designed for grades 3 through 12 and having a five-point scale (strongly agree to strongly disagree) was developed by Thomas H. Estes (1971). The *Estes Reading Attitude Scale* is a twenty-item instrument consisting of statements such as, "Most books are too long and dull." The scale was developed through tryout and selection of items having demonstrated validity. Reliability estimates on a split-half basis were reported to be satisfactory.

A more extensive inventory having seventy items was developed by

Kennedy and Halinski (1975). Although designed for secondary grades only, the extraordinarily high reliability reported for this survey (.94) makes it a good model for teachers at all levels by suggesting a broad range of item types. Kennedy and Halinski use a 4-point Likert-type scale.

Alexander and Filler (1976) presented two attitude scales by Betty S. Heathington that are designed for use with elementary-age children. The Heathington Primary Scale uses a unique answer format that appears to have special value with young children. As the teacher reads a question (for example, "How do you feel when you go to the library?"), children select a face that represents their response.

The Heathington Intermediate Scale uses a strongly agree–strongly disagree type scale with 5 points. The Primary Scale includes twenty items and the Intermediate Scale twenty-four items.

Another published inventory by Askov (1973) designed for primary-age children does not require reading or writing ability and reports high validity and reliability.[8] We believe published instruments of the type described here can be of value, but prefer to see teachers develop their own instruments whenever possible. With experience, teachers will probably feel more comfortable using devices they have made.

Assessing Children's Interests

Reader interest is of primary importance in considering motivation to read. With respect to intrinsic factors, probably no other variable energizes a person to act in so strong a way as interest does. High personal interest in seeing a National Football League playoff game will cause people to stand in line for hours or even days to get a ticket. Interest in seeing one's offspring perform explains the unusually large crowds at those PTA/PTO meetings that feature children performing, as in a music festival. Personal interest accounts for the popularity among ten-, eleven-, and twelve-year-old girls for Judy Blume's books dealing with the approach and onset of puberty.

If further support is needed, consider how you spent your leisure time last weekend. There is a very good chance that personal interest accounted for a fair share of that time. If you are an avid golfer, you probably played golf (weather permitting). If you enjoy gardening, hiking, jogging, sewing, playing backgammon, or strumming guitar, one of these activities may have occupied your time.

Children behave very much as adults when it comes to what they like to read. The boy scout who is working on a merit badge for woodworking will be attracted to a magazine article on how to select the correct sandpaper (if

High personal interest in a subject often accounts for a child's willingness to read about that topic. *(Peter Vadnai)*

he has faced that dilemma). Another child with different interests would lack the motivation to read the same article, and if forced to do so, would probably find it irrelevant and maybe even meaningless.

To motivate the second child to read the article on sandpaper, an external motivation would be required. Personal interest becomes important even in this case, however. Offer Hank a chance to earn tokens that can be exchanged for free time building a model race car as a reward for reading the article on sandpaper and it may elicit a positive response—motivation. Make the reward a chance to earn a gold star or even a good grade in reading for the day and motivation may go by the boards (on the assumption that these are not meaningful rewards to Hank). Personal interest—or personal payoff—is a major factor in motivation at all levels. The classroom teacher needs to know how to identify topics that interest each child and how to capitalize on those interests in planning instructional activities.

An Interest Inventory   Teachers often use interest inventories to collect valuable information that can be used to locate reading material geared to individual student interests. The incomplete sentence approach described in the previous section is readily adaptable to surveying interest. Items can be constructed that probe many aspects of the child's life for possible interests.

Use of leisure time is often an index of personal interests, for example. A sample interest inventory based on incomplete sentences is presented in Figure 3.4.

Interest can also be surveyed through the use of a questionnaire. We recommend the use of a five-point scale on an interest questionnaire to provide students with an opportunity to express the strength of their interests. A sample interest inventory using a questionnaire format is presented in Figure 3.5.

Records of Recreational Reading Habits

One particularly good source of information about student reading preference is a record of books they have read previously. Such information can be gathered in a number of ways, the simplest being a log or journal kept by students showing the title, author, and date on which a book was started and/ or completed. A record of this sort can easily be passed from teacher to teacher as students progress through school. Sometimes children can be enticed into writing a brief "reaction" to the book by each bibliographic entry. These reactions serve to focus on a child's level of interest in the topic and provide an indication of his or her willingness to read more along the same line. For example, a teacher can then see at a glance that Cheryl preferred romantic novels and historical fiction set in pre-Civil War days. Science Fiction, on the other hand, received a less-than-enthusiastic reception.

Another approach to tracking reading habits is to first develop a list of topics then record titles of books read by a student under the appropriate category. As titles accumulate in one area, a teacher gains a sense of the student's reading preferences. Possible categories might include sports, humor, adventure, romance, travel, biography, nonfiction, hobbies, and so forth.

A unique record-keeping form might show a floor plan of the school library. Students could indicate where in the library they found each book they have read by pasting a gold star on the form in the appropriate spot. Stars clustering in the reference section would indicate a student is interested in books of world records perhaps, or how-to books.

These examples only suggest the types of record-keeping devices a teacher can employ to identify what a child is reading. Although the focus here has been on records of books read, personal interests may be reflected even more directly by the types of magazines, brochures, and other nonbook materials that students read. Here, too, a log of what has been read recently would be useful to the teacher in understanding a child's interests.

Teacher Interviews and Observations   Whether structured as an interview or left more open to general observation, a teacher's interactions with students offers many opportunities to gain a feel for their personal interests. In an interview a teacher may get an idea of students' interests by asking a general question about what hobbies they enjoy, or what television shows they have

FIGURE 3.4   Interest Inventory Using Incomplete Sentences

_____   _____ _____
Name   Age   Date

DIRECTIONS: Complete each sentence in whichever way describes you best.

1. My favorite television show is _____.

2. My favorite kind of music is _____.

3. If I could get one person's autograph, I would most prefer _____

   _____.

4. On the weekend I like to _____

   _____.

5. My favorite sport is _____.

6. I like to read about _____.

7. My favorite magazine is _____.

8. The part of the newspaper I read first is _____

   _____.

9. The best book I ever read was _____.

10. I like to collect _____.

11. I enjoy movies about _____.

12. Most evenings I _____

    _____.

13. If I had three wishes they would be:

    a. _____.

    b. _____.

    c. _____.

FIGURE 3.5   Interest Inventory

Name _____   Age _____   Date _____

DIRECTIONS: Place a check in the column that indicates how the statement applies to you.

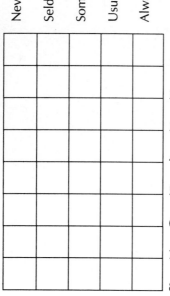

Never	Seldom	Sometimes	Usually	Always	
					1. Each week I borrow books from the library.
					2. I watch TV in the evening.
					3. I read before going to bed.
					4. I play a musical instrument.
					5. My mother or father reads to me each day.
					6. I read the newspaper each day.
					7. I work with my hobby each day.
					8. I enjoy reading class

watched lately. Even a friendly invitation to, "Tell me about yourself, Ann. What are some of your interests?" will be sufficient to gain insights about an individual not ordinarily available in a group instructional setting.

Teachers can also identify topics that interest students by watching their reaction during a lesson (that is, their reaction to a book or story that is being discussed or their level of involvement in a discussion of upcoming school and community events, such as an athletic event, an election, a circus, or a band concert). Before and after class teachers can often detect interests by merely observing students interacting informally with their peers. Teachers who themselves participate in such conversations and reveal some of their own interests and activities to students often find a greater willingness by class members to share information about their out-of-school lives.

Assessing Self-Concept

Self-concept can be assessed in exactly the same ways as attitudes and interests. Incomplete sentences are especially useful and can be constructed to focus primarily on reading self-concept or on self-concept in general. Some sample stems are given below:

1. People usually think I'm _____.
2. When I read out loud my classmates _____.
3. I'm good at _____.
4. I'm not good at _____.
5. Learning to read is _____.
6. When I fail at something I _____.
7. When I try something new I _____.
8. My teachers think I'm _____.
9. My parents get upset when _____.
10. The thing I do best is _____.

Teacher observation is probably the best assessment strategy with respect to self-concept. Quandt and Selznick (1984) suggest that teachers pay particular attention to comments children make about themselves and watch for children's reactions to daily interactions. Apparent lack of interest and concern must be viewed as possible indications of poor self-concept. Children's reactions to a disappointment or failure can be a particularly revealing event for the watchful teacher as can the willingness to volunteer answers. Obviously, level of confidence is directly related to self-concept. Reluctant risk takers who seem unsure of themselves often have poor self-concepts as do children who ask excessive questions about an assignment.

CAUTIONS ABOUT ASSESSMENT IN THE AFFECTIVE DOMAIN

Any kind of assessment is subject to a certain amount of error. Assessment conducted with human subjects is particularly difficult. Some important principles of assessing reading are offered in Chapter 12, "Assessment Principles Applied to Remedial Reading." In the present chapter there is an even greater concern with respect to errors in assessment. That is to say, the attempt to assess human feelings is even more difficult than the assessment of human cognition. The fact that it is difficult makes it no less important, however.

Teachers must resist the temptation to ignore the affective domain on the grounds that error can creep into the assessment. Rather, the possible sources of errors must be recognized and special pains taken to keep them to a minimum. Teachers must also interpret affective assessments with special caution in recognition of the limitations described here.

Possible Sources of Assessment Error

To be helpful, information that will be used in planning classroom activities must be reliable. As will be discussed in Chapter 12, that reliability is concerned with consistency. In addition to the usual factors that affect the reliability of test results, the affective domain presents another consideration: Human feelings change or can vacillate over relatively short periods of time. This means that information gathered from a well-designed questionnaire on personal interests may be out-of-date soon after it is collected. The very act of responding to the questionnaire may cause introspection that triggers a resolution by respondents to broaden their interests. It is also likely that they are unsure of their own mind on some matters. One day they might be feeling expansive and cite several interests; the next day, in a different frame of mind, they might respond more selectively. Attitudes and self-concept are probably more stable than interests but are nevertheless subject to the same fluctuations.

One way to deal with reliability considerations is to use recent information only, thereby acknowledging the likelihood of change over time. Another solution is to use information from several sources so the teacher is not depending on a single questionnaire or interview to give an accurate picture. Finally, the length of any data collection device should be sufficient to gather an adequate sample of responses. For example, Alexander and Filler (1976) recommend no fewer than twenty items on a questionnaire.

Reliability is one of several important considerations with respect to accuracy in assessment. A second factor of equal importance is the concern for validity, for whether an instrument measures what it claims to measure and, from an application standpoint, whether that measure is of practical value. Because of the scarcity of well-developed instruments of established validity, there is no simple way of studying the validity of new instruments. Statistical validity established by correlating the results of a teacher-made device with some widely accepted measure is not possible, for example.

In assessing affective factors, care should be taken to avoid getting socially acceptable responses from students. What may be called a measure of student attitude toward reading, for example, may actually measure students' ability to figure out what the teacher wants to hear ("I like books"; "I enjoy reading"; "I read a lot"). Validity is highest when students understand that the results will be used in their own best interests and when trust between student and teacher is high.

Another consideration when paper and pencil instruments are used is the students' ability to read and write. Inability to read the items on a questionnaire obviously prevents children from giving valid responses, as does the inability to express honest thoughts in writing when confronted with an incomplete-sentence task. Obviously, shyness or suspicion can affect what children share even in an interview. Again, student trust is critical. Validity can also be increased if provisions are made to help poor readers and/or writers respond to the task without prejudice. The questions can be read aloud by the teacher, for example, and responses can be dictated to an aide or volunteer parent.

Validity will be improved if the teacher has a clear notion of what an attitude is and how it is reflected in children's actions, verbal and nonverbal. The same is true of interests and self-concept. Beyond that, the best assurance of validity is the corroboration gained by comparing results across a variety of sources and the emergence of patterns over time. Teachers should be diagnosticians seeking to put information together for the purpose of formulating a hypothesis about Otto, Olav, and Olive.

SUMMARY

This chapter looked briefly at theories concerned with how motivation occurs. It distinguished between external and internal motivation, and it suggested that success is the key to internal motivation. When constant failure is experienced, children become passive, feeling helpless about their ability to control the factors that cause their failure. In such cases internal motivation dwindles and the teacher is faced with manipulating external rewards to encourage a child to respond.

The assessment of motivation is best pursued on many fronts, using both published and teacher-made devices. Although difficulties exist in measuring elusive often-changing factors related to motivation, the teacher can gather information on attitudes, interests, and self-concept that is useful in determining how to approach the child who seems unmotivated.

SUGGESTED ACTIVITIES

1. Select a character such as Rocky Balboa from a popular book or movie. Analyze the character from the standpoint of motivation. Identify what goal or goals the character seems to be pursuing in the story. Make a list of internal or intrinsic and external or extrinsic rewards that you believe motivate the character.

2. Develop a questionnaire that asks respondents to reveal their attitudes about some topic of current interest, such as types of music, political preference, career opportunities, physical fitness activities, or other topics where opinion can vary. Ask several acquaintances to complete the questionnaire. Ask for feedback on how the questionnaire could be improved by being more comprehensive, less obtrusive, longer or shorter, and so forth. Revise in accordance with these suggestions and ask several more people to complete

the revised version. Summarize what this experiment has taught you about the development of attitude surveys.

3. Arrange to interview a colleague concerning his or her recollections of learning to read. Focus your questions on the extent to which success or failure with classroom reading instruction affected his or her self-concept as a child. Relate those feelings to the person's current attitude toward reading for enjoyment.

NOTES
1. See Maslow (1970) and White (1959).
2. See Klausmeier and Ripple (1971).
3. See Bristow (1985).
4. See Johnston (1985).
5. See Butkowsky and Willows (1980).
6. See Butkowsky and Willows (1980).
7. See Graham (1984) and Johnston and Winograd (1985).
8. Other published instruments of note include those by Sartain (1970), Gallian (Cooper et al., 1972), and Greenberg et al. (1965).

SUGGESTED READINGS

JOHNSTON, PETER H., AND WINOGRAD, PETER N. (1985). Passive failure in reading. *Journal of Reading Behavior, 17,* 279–301.
This article presents a conceptual framework for understanding how children who have difficulty with reading react to repeated failure. The authors draw on the notion of learned helplessness as a way of explaining the self-defeating behaviors such children exhibit. Suggestions are given for preventing and remediating what the authors refer to as passive failure in reading.

QUANDT, IVAN, AND SELZNICK, RICHARD (1984). *Self-concept and reading.* Newark, DE: International Reading Association.
Discusses the relationships between reading and self-concept. Techniques and strategies that an elementary school teacher can employ to improve self-concepts while teaching children to read are described. Tests and informal observation procedures that can be used to diagnose self-concepts are presented.

WIGFIELD, ALLAN, AND ASHER, STEVEN R. (1984). Social and motivational influences on reading. In P. David Pearson (Ed.), *Handbook of reading research* (pp. 423–452). New York: Longman.
Summarizes and synthesizes research concerning how motivation and socialization are related to learning to read. Reviews achievement motivation theory as it relates to reading and discusses the influence of home and school on motivating performance in school. Examines the effects of repeated failure on children's willingness to strive and offers suggestions for the classroom teacher in coping with learned helplessness.

Chapter 4

Increasing Motivation

OVERVIEW

As you read this chapter use the following list of main ideas to guide your study and reflection.

Most children are motivated in learning to read by the success they experience with the school reading program. Brian Bussell is a typical example.

The motivation that normally accompanies success can go astray when repeated failure is encountered, as in the case of Debbie Howard.

Some children who have experienced success with reading may still need special attention in the area of motivation, as in the case of Sam Brady.

Behavior modification is an approach to motivation that uses external rewards in a systematic fashion to shape desired behaviors.

Specific ideas worth trying as motivational devices include some described in this chapter, such as the teacher reading aloud, cross-aged tutoring, using games in the classroom, and using the daily newspaper.

Letter grades have very limited value in motivating children, especially remedial readers.

This chapter considers how a teacher of reading can approach the challenge of motivation. The previous chapter made the point that many children are largely self-motivated; that is, they approach learning to read with confidence and a desire to achieve competence. An approach to reading instruction that recognizes and capitalizes on that predisposition seems advisable in those cases. The teacher will want to help self-motivated students see how their personal needs and interests can be realized through reading (for example, recreation, problem solving, gathering information). The teacher will also want to nurture the positive feelings self-motivated students have about themselves as competent readers through praise and the maintenance of record-keeping devices that document growth and progress. In this way the self-satisfaction that motivates such students continues. Their history of successful experiences with reading will enable them to persist in the face of occasional disappointment and difficulty.

BRIAN BUSSELL: A SELF-MOTIVATED READER

Brian Bussell represents a case of self-motivation. As a ten-year-old, Brian entered fourth grade having had a series of success experiences with reading. He learned to read without trauma beginning in first grade, but even prior to entering school he had happy, reinforcing experiences with books in the company of a parent or grandparent who enjoyed holding Brian and sharing a story with him. He took naturally to the basal reader, workbook, and other written assignments given by his teacher each day to help him acquire and practice certain skills. He found such tasks relatively easy, in fact, and almost always completed them on time and with accuracy.

Brian also enjoyed reading aloud and received praise consistently for having good "expression." He joined in discussions about the stories his reading group completed every day, giving evidence through his comments that he readily understood the characters and events. During free time in school and in the evenings at home it was not unusual for Brian to read a book for recreation. In fact, he had a collection of paperback books he had purchased over the years with money given to him by his mother for that purpose.

When Brian first experienced difficulty reading the fourth-grade science textbook used in his school, it was surprising and somewhat frustrating to him. He found the vocabulary to be difficult and the concepts rather foreign. The science book also had diagrams and charts unlike anything he had seen in books before. He was tempted to give up at first and wanted to avoid science. But with the teacher's help he discovered that he was not alone in his difficulty; several other good readers were also struggling. Brian's teacher seemed supportive and understanding concerning the problem he was having and offered help in the form of study guides that gave Brian direction in reading the book. With the teacher's guidance he gradually grew more confident. A breakthrough of sorts occurred when the class began studying fossils and Brian remembered a rock he had found during a hike on vacation the previous summer. He brought the rock to school and learned that it was truly a fossil. Science took on a new meaning and the information found in books took on new importance for Brian.

This anecdote illustrates several important points. First, it suggests that many children succeed with a rather routine, conventional approach to beginning reading instruction. It is, in fact, the exceptional child who does not succeed. A second implication is that motivation is not a special problem for many children. Their readiness for reading and the importance attached to learning to read will dispose most children to attend to assigned tasks so long as they continue to be successful. (This is not to suggest that a teacher may not have to spend time occasionally explaining the nature and importance of a task to get a student to put forth effort, nor to deny the value of the teacher providing feedback on daily work as an incentive for students to complete it. We are not in any way suggesting that teachers can ignore or take for granted the motivation of children like Brian. We *are* suggesting that external rewards such as gold stars, tokens, and treats are not essential.)

Third, the anecdote suggests that even "successful" readers have occasions when they experience difficulty. On such occasions their history of successes encourages them to persist in the face of failure.

Finally, the teacher's attitude and skill at providing the necessary assistance are critical in helping even the self-motivated. Here Brian's teacher was patiently supportive and evidenced confidence that the problem would be surmounted. It can be inferred that Brian's teacher reminded him that he had solved such problems before and that with time and effort he would again succeed. If this response is one of acting as a "cheerleader" of sorts, it is also significant that Brian's teacher did more than cheer. The teacher also developed study guides and related the topic under study to something Brian had experienced firsthand (fossils). In other words, Brian's teacher did not manipulate the student, but respected his need to master a task. The teacher concentrated on what could be done to support Brian's efforts from both an attitudinal and instructional standpoint.

When Self-Motivation Is Lost

Some children have lost the self-motivation to read that characterizes children like Brian. A number of explanations for this loss were examined earlier. An approach to reading that depends on self-motivation will be unlikely to succeed in these cases. Rather, the teacher will need to play a much more dominant role by consciously establishing specific goals to be achieved and identifying rewards to be earned for reaching those goals. Extrinsic motivation becomes the *modus operandi* until the child begins to see intrinsic value in reading and reading-related matters.

Two types of children can be identified among those who lack self-motivation: those who *cannot* read and do not, and those who *can* read and do not. Though the reasons for their behavior are probably very similar, in both cases the challenge is to make reading relevant to the daily lives of the students. When reading becomes a tool that helps the student solve personal problems and needs or pursue personal interests, motivation to read becomes intrinsic.

DEBBIE HOWARD: A REMEDIAL READER

Unlike her older brother who had difficulty with reading from the beginning, Debbie was moderately successful with reading in first grade. Although not a member of the top reading group, Debbie held her own in first grade until March. Then, like her brother before her, she began to experience repeated failures; by the end of second grade, she was a *bona fide* remedial reader who claimed to hate reading. And the claim was legitimate. The frustration, anger, and shame she felt during attempts to read were real. Actual physical manifestations of her dislike were evident in her appearance and manner. She frowned constantly, clinched her fists, gritted her teeth, and fidgeted in her seat. A physician examining Debbie would have found a racing pulse, increased blood pressure, and shortness of breath during reading. Debbie was clearly not a candidate for motivation techniques that appealed to her now-defunct desire to master an important task: reading.

The best avenue open to Debbie's teacher is to identify specific tasks that can be achieved quickly and successfully for the attainment of a specific reward. As much as possible, the tasks should not obviously be connected to reading, at least not to reading as she has come to know it. And, most important of all, the teacher should identify topics and activities that reflect Debbie's personal interests as a means of gaining her attention and participation. It is important to remember that Debbie is not without motivation. Although she has failed at reading, she likes to engage in other activities such as roller skating or bird watching, for example. It is through these areas of interest that the teacher can approach Debbie, gain her trust, establish rapport, and rebuild what is bound to be a shaky self-concept. Gradually the planned activities can be brought around to recording events and ideas in writing, listening to information the teacher shares from a book, and finding ideas in magazines relevant to Debbie's interests.

The teacher still has one additional problem even after she has gained Debbie's trust and nurtured her self-concept: Debbie does not read successfully. For some reason(s), toward the end of first grade, Debbie experienced repeated failures with reading. Until Debbie learns to construct meaning from the printed page, the activities described above will only work on the symptoms of the deeper problem. In reality, motivation and instruction cannot be separated as is commonly done in texts like this one. Restoring Debbie's intrinsic motivation to read necessarily involves dealing with problem(s) that caused her to stop trying in the first place.

In Debbie's case, she was doing reasonably well in first grade reading until March. Was something introduced to her group at that time that explains her difficulty? Was there a new skill or set of skills she could not learn? Or was there a change at home that distracted Debbie and caused her to fail? Could the problem be related to a vision or hearing defect that flared in March? These questions probe for a possible cause of Debbie's failure. In most cases there are a number of causes that interact. Taken singly, each factor is probably insufficient to cause a major breakdown but combined, they exacerbate the problem and can defeat a child. That is exactly what happened in Debbie's case.

An analysis of the situation reveals that by early March Debbie's reading group had reached the heavy word identification phase of the first grade skills program. What had been a whole word approach shifted to synthetic word analysis with emphasis on identifying isolated sounds. Debbie found this to be a difficult task that confused and frustrated her.

At the same time Debbie's parents began a difficult marital breakup. Her father moved out of the house and visited with Debbie and her brother only on weekends. The trauma associated with this separation and divorce worked directly on Debbie's feelings of security, distracting her with thoughts of home.

Unfortunately, Debbie also experienced a low-grade ear infection in March that went undetected altogether. The immediate result was difficulty hearing and a feeling of listlessness. A mild hearing loss in one ear was the long-term result of the infection.

A special reading teacher began working with Debbie early in third grade. By piecing together the available evidence, the teacher developed a general picture of what led to Debbie's difficulties with reading. What confronted her was a child who read well below her peers, disliked reading intensely, and resisted putting forth any effort related to learning to read.

At first, the teacher concentrated on getting to know Debbie better, learning about her personal interests, her attitudes toward school and reading, and her self-concept. Debbie's interest in roller skating became the key to establishing a point of contact. The teacher arranged to take Debbie roller skating at a local rink one Saturday afternoon. There she learned that Debbie wanted very much to have her own pair of skates. The teacher suggested that they gather some information on the cost of various brands and types of skates from sales brochures and catalogs available at the rink and at a local sporting goods store. They developed a chart that displayed information about each skate according to categories such as cost, color, and features (type of eyelets for lacing, height of boot, etc.). The teacher suggested that Debbie dictate a letter to her parents explaining why she wanted a pair of skates, which ones she preferred, and why. The letter was written, read, and revised, and reread a number of times. Certain words were taken from the letter and written on index cards in short phrases, such as *white roller skates* and *steel ball bearings*. The teacher helped Debbie appreciate how many words she could recognize by developing a chart that recorded how many cards Debbie had learned.

The letter was shared with Debbie's parents and a suggestion made that Debbie be permitted to earn the skates by earning points for completing certain reading tasks. Reading an entire (easy) book, for example, earned ten points, completing a work sheet two points, and so forth. Debbie's parents agreed to support the idea, and over a two-month period Debbie earned enough points to get the skates. She also made significant progress on a number of reading and reading-related tasks that improved her ability to read independently. By documenting her progress with charts and checklists, Debbie's teacher helped her see that she could be successful with reading. By finding reading materials that related to Debbie's interest in roller skating, the teacher also sought to cultivate an intrinsic source of motivation to read. Once the cycle of failure was turned around, Debbie began to think of reading and of herself as a reader in more positive terms.

In contrast to Brian Bussell's teacher, Debbie's teacher found it necessary to manage the student and the reward system. Although she respected Debbie as an individual and sought to work through personal interests, she played a much more overt role in deciding what should be done and in energizing Debbie toward those ends. She did this in a humane way, to be sure, but still made the instruction teacher-directed.

SAM BRADY: A RELUCTANT READER

"You won't get away with that when you're in school next year," was a threat Sam Brady heard from his mother dozens of times before starting first grade. As a result, he entered school full of resentment and apprehension concerning what he would encounter there. As fate would have it, Sam's first teacher was a no-nonsense type who assumed all children were guilty until proven innocent. She approached reading instruction strictly from a standpoint of drill and memorization.

Over the years she had evolved a fairly intricate system of rewards and punishments that enabled her to gain and hold a pupil's attention. The child who could accommodate her approach would learn to associate spoken words and their printed counterparts, to mark long and short vowels, to divide words into syllables, to find main ideas, and so forth.

Sam learned to read partly from sheer repetition and partly from working to receive good grades. The good grades kept his parents and his teacher off his back. He understood the system of doing Job A to earn Reward X because he faced it at school and at home. "Do this homework page correctly and earn a chance to play outside at recess." "Dry the dinner dishes every night and earn a week's allowance that could buy candy and a ticket to a movie." It was not very long before Sam approached nearly every situation with a "What's the payoff for me?" attitude.

In second grade Sam's teacher quickly saw that he had become dependent upon extrinsic rewards. She set up a contract system involving various treats and privileges that could be earned by Sam for completing certain work. He thrived in that environment, reading many stories and completing many modules of work to receive his payoff.

All of this seemed quite innocent and functional because Sam was learning to read nicely, if recognizing words and gaining an author's message were all that one considered. What Sam was not gaining was any intrinsic appreciation of reading. Reading was simply a means to an end for Sam; unfortunately the end was not self-satisfaction or self-improvement, but some concrete reward.

All of this began to come apart when Sam entered third grade. His teacher was in her second year of teaching and full of fresh concern for individualizing reading instruction. The teacher implemented a free-choice reading program involving self-selection, self-pacing, and teacher-pupil conferencing, as described by Veatch (1959), Barbe and Abbott (1975), and Brogan and Fox (1961). For many of Sam's classmates this approach proved to be optimal. Freed to pick books on topics they enjoyed, previously "unmotivated" pupils began to read more regularly and with greater understanding. But for Sam the method was a disaster. With no extrinsic payoff for reading, Sam saw no reason to participate. His teacher exhibited patience based on her belief that some children took longer to find themselves with this approach than others. By Christmas Sam still had not finished reading a single book in its entirety. Concerned that perhaps he was unable to read, the teacher asked a special reading teacher to test Sam. The results indicated that Sam could read, of course, but that he saw no need to since there was no reward to be gained by doing so.

Satisfied that Sam could read, the teacher then established a system of incentives to cause him to read. For reading a short book Sam could earn two points. Reading a magazine article or a short story was worth one point. Points were accumulated and could be used to "buy" time at one of the interest centers the teacher had created in several classroom locations. One center housed games such as Monopoly, Clue, chess, checkers, and the like. Another center contained art supplies that could be borrowed to make a special project. Other centers were designed to appeal to a variety of interests: handicrafts, model buildings, and even an animal center with gerbils and an aquarium, for example.

Sam began to read again for the chance to earn one of these rewards. But the teacher realized this short-term solution failed to address the problem of getting Sam to read for his own purposes. So along with the program designed to award points, the teacher instituted two additional ideas. First, she created interest groups that periodically brought together pupils who were reading about similar topics for the purpose of book sharing. Here the aim was to promote discussion about books read that would cause others in the group to become interested in something someone else had enjoyed.

The teacher also used interest inventories and pupil-teacher conferences to discover how Sam spent his out-of-school time. This, in turn, suggested school activities that would capitalize on Sam's established interests. Those activities initially focused on exploring the topic through various means (such as viewing films and video tapes), and later turned to reading and reading-related activities.

You will recognize this strategy as the one used in the previous case by Debbie Howard's teacher with the topic of roller skating. Finding a way to connect school work with the child's world is basic to cultivating intrinsic motivation. In Sam's case, short-term goals could be reached by providing extrinsic rewards. He was willing to read a book to earn a reward, just as Debbie was willing to do workbook pages to earn points that could be exchanged for a pair of roller skates. But Sam and Debbie both needed to value reading personally, for their own ends, not because their teachers thought reading was important.

Teachers are sometimes fooled by some pupils' apparent lack of involvement in school activities. "Sam isn't interested in anything . . ." is sometimes heard. What is missing from that statement is ". . . I try to get him to do in school." All children have personal interests. The unresponsive child in the classroom is often an active participant in playground conversations and out-of-school activities such as 4-H, scouts, or sports. It is a mistake to conclude that disinterest in reading, math, social studies, science, health, and so forth, *in school* indicates a lazy or uninquisitive mind, however. If those subjects can be made relevant to the child's daily life and leisure time pursuits, interest can be created.

Returning to Sam Brady, his teacher discovered that Sam enjoyed sketching and painting in his free time. This insight gave the teacher a way to make a mural that could be displayed with poems the class had written during the winter. She specifically asked Sam to include birds and animals in the mural. When he expressed concern about his ability to do this, she suggested they go to the library to find a book about how to draw animals. A useful reference was found and perhaps for the first time in his life Sam's own interests and needs provided the impetus for reading. The teacher seized this opportunity to introduce Sam to other books related to his interest in art. She suggested that Sam's parents take him to an art museum where brochures, pamphlets, and even a printed program of activities and exhibits could be obtained. These items provided information about different types of art, the lives of various artists, and the like. This, in turn, opened up a host of topics that Sam was willing to read about in books ranging from biographics to encyclopedias. Sam's personal interests had been used to create motivation to read.

The approach taken with both Sam and Debbie illustrates a favorite method for dealing with reluctant readers: temporary use of extrinsic rewards for the purpose of gaining positive experiences with reading. Those positive experiences gradually cultivate the intrinsic motivation that normally grows from personal interests and the self-satisfaction gained from learning to read.

USING BEHAVIOR MODIFICATION

The use of extrinsic rewards can be an effective way to encourage students to engage in particular behaviors. Certain cautions have been expressed about the effectiveness of extrinsic rewards in reshaping long-term behavioral patterns. Evidently behavior changes that are motivated by intrinsic factors

When using the behavior modification approach, the rewards offered must be ones that have value to the child. Tokens awarded for meeting goals might be used to "buy" time on a woodworking project, for example. *(James Silliman)*

are more likely to be lasting. Children who read a book to earn a treat, for example, will acquire a commitment to reading only if the prospect of the external reward causes behavior that comes to be valued for its own sake. Otherwise, once the treat is no longer offered, they will stop reading.

Extrinsic rewards can be offered under any number of circumstances, some of which seem to have a better chance than others of causing the individual to internalize the motivation and effect lasting change. One approach to the use of external rewards that has proven effective in making the important transition to internal motivation has been labeled *behavior modification*.

Behavior modification is a strategy designed to eliminate undesired behaviors and reinforce desired ones. Reinforcement is provided on a systematic basis to shape an individual's behavior. A typical program involves:

1. The behavior to be modified is identified. Inappropriate behavior is targeted for reduction and desirable behavior is targeted for development.

2. The nature of the goal toward which the teacher is working is described in terms of the child's behavior.

3. The level of behavior is observed and recorded for frequency to provide a baseline against which progress can be assessed.

4. The conditions under which the target behavior occurs are identified and recorded.

5. The consequences of the target behavior are identified and recorded.

6. An intervention program designed to increase or decrease the target behavior is developed. The contingencies, that is, the reinforcers (rewards) and the conditions for receiving reinforcers are specified.

7. The program is implemented and records kept of the target behavior.[1]

This approach takes various forms, but has several basic principles that are described below.

The first principle is critical to the subsequent internalization of motivation: The individual whose behavior is to be modified must help establish the need for change. Ideally the individual initiates this step himself (for example, the student says, "I'd like to stop wasting time during reading class."), but in actuality the teacher often identifies the problem and raises it for the student's consideration ("You don't seem to be getting your daily assignments done. I've observed that you spend a lot of your work time doing other things such as straightening your desk, sharpening your pencil, and the like. I think you need to stop activities that are not related to your assignment. What do you think?"). Unless the student recognizes a need for change, helps develop a plan to alter his or her behavior, and agrees to the conditions of that plan, there is very little chance that long-term changes in behavior will be effected. Once the program is over, an unwilling participant can easily slip back into old behavior patterns. (Even *willing* participants in a program to change behavior often find it difficult to resist backsliding once the program is completed.)

A second principle underlying behavior modification programs is that changes in behavior are sought on a gradual schedule. Typically, a final behavior is approached in stages. For example, a boy who needlessly gets out of his seat twenty times a day is first asked to reduce that behavior to fifteen times a day. Next, the goal is reduced to ten times a day, and so on. Rewards are earned for meeting each intermediate goal, and steady progress is made toward the final goal (only getting out of his seat when necessary).

A third principle basic to behavior modification is establishing or selecting meaningful rewards. The child who dislikes and, therefore, avoids reading will probably not be willing to work for the reward of a book. What rewards will work varies from case to case, of course, and is limited to some extent by philosophical as well as cost and nutrition factors. Candy treats may motivate behavior, for example, but their use may be unacceptable due to health and expense considerations. Some programs with older students have gone as far as to use trading stamps and portable radios for rewards. What motivates one child may not work with another. What one teacher uses may offend another. The advice to teachers in this respect is that extrinsic rewards must be attractive to the learners involved.

MOTIVATION STRATEGIES

In the folklore of teaching there are probably as many ways to motivate children to read as there are ways to cure hiccoughs. Popular teaching magazines such as *Grade Teacher, Instructor,* and *Learning* often feature articles in which practicing teachers share a variety of ideas that work for them. Reading conferences invariably include sessions on motivating the disadvantaged, motivating remedial readers, and so forth. Publishers of instructional materials often tout their wares on the basis of their high motivational value. Needless to say, this widespread concern for and attention to motivation is well-deserved. Despite the emphasis given in this chapter to intrinsic motivation, there is much to be said for using techniques and materials that make reading attractive, enjoyable, and stimulating.

What follows here is a sample of various strategies a teacher can use to encourage students to read. The teacher must keep in mind, however, that ultimately motivation has to come from the learners themselves if they are to become habitual readers outside of a school setting. The activities presented here can contribute to the students' habit formation by providing success experiences in reading, by making reading personally meaningful and useful, and by capitalizing on the tendency of many children to prefer active, participatory learning.

Reading Aloud

A simple activity that has the effect of arousing student interest in a particular book or author is oral reading by the teacher (or by students who have rehearsed ahead of time what they will read). Primary grade teachers seem to be most prone to engage in this activity, but teachers at intermediate, middle, and secondary levels have employed this approach effectively. Students of all ages seem to enjoy listening to a skillful presentation of good literature. By choosing carefully what to share, a teacher can expose children of various reading abilities to literature they might not select on their own. Through discussion and explanation student attention can be focused on the subtleties of characterization, plot development, use of language, and so forth.

Teachers who regularly read aloud attest to the power of this activity for creating interest in a book. Even students who do not read much on their own often ask if they can have a book when the teacher is finished sharing it with the class. Other books by the same author or on the same topic can also be introduced to a class while the teacher is sharing a particular book.

Some schools have parent volunteers share a favorite book over the span

Teachers who read regularly to their students often arouse interest in a topic and demonstrate that reading can be enjoyable. *(James Silliman)*

of several weeks or a month. This approach introduces variety into the read-aloud program, demonstrates that nonteachers enjoy reading, too, and creates the opportunity for the parent of a reluctant reader to demonstrate the value he or she places on reading. If the teacher still wants to read aloud during this period, children can be given a choice as to which group they will join, the teacher's or the parent's.

See the Movie: Read the Book

Most of us have had the experience of seeing a film at a local theater or on television and then are spurred on to read the book on which the film was based. Just why this happens probably varies among people, but the responses may spring from curiosity about how the book and film compare, interest created by an actor's portrayal of a character, or the desire to relive an entertaining experience at our own pace. In any event, motivation to read occurs.

Children and adolescents often react in much the same way. Whether the film is a full-length Disney cartoon feature such as "Dumbo," or an adventure such as "Jaws," students seem to be interested in reading the book on which a film was based (or a book that is related in some way to the story and characters met in the film). Marketing experts have long known about this fact and have reaped the commercial benefits of products based on films. Thirty years ago it was "Davy Crockett" and more recently it was "Star Wars."

Whereas films used to grow from books, nowadays books often grow from films or more commonly, from television programs. While teachers may have legitimate concerns about the literary quality of many books that grow from film or television scripts, children are highly motivated to read them and this provides an opportunity to cultivate the reading habit. Critical reading skills and personal standards of taste can also be developed through skillful analysis and discussion of "junk books" that capitalize on the popularity of some films and television programs. The teacher can also encourage children to see an upcoming film or television program as an interest builder in high-quality literature. Stevenson's *Treasure Island* or Wilder's *Little House on the Prairie* could be promoted in this fashion, for example.

One way of promoting greater interest in a book is to have several students who have seen a film such as Disney's "That Darn Cat" and have also read the book by the same title participate in a panel discussion. The teacher or an able student can serve as a moderator who asks questions and moves the discussion forward. This activity also promotes careful analysis and review of a book by students who are members of the panel.

Displaying Evidence of Book Reading

In an extremely useful brochure titled *50 Ways to Raise Bookworms*, Hillerich (no date) describes a multitude of ways to encourage children to read. The title of the brochure refers to one type of activity that provides visible evidence of the reading going on in a classroom. A bookworm, cut out of sections of colored paper, is formed on the classroom walls and on each section the title of a book and the name of the child who read it is written. The bookworm grows as books are completed and recorded on new sections that are added to the bookworm's body by members of the class. The body of the bookworm curves over and around bulletin boards, windows, doors, and chalkboards.

Variations of the bookworm idea can range from paper footprints on the walls that carry out a "Bigfoot" theme to paper leaves on a branch of a tree or decorations on the silhouette of a bulletin board Christmas tree. Inventive teachers create numerous ways to highlight the fact that Peter read *Madeline*, Alice read *A Snowy Day*, and Alex read *Peter Rabbit*. Basic to all these ideas is the fact that every child can contribute to the class project. Charts showing number of books read are not used because they make someone a winner and everyone else a loser. Competition should be deemphasized as a motivational device because it discourages the very children who are most in need of recognition for the reading they complete. We seriously doubt that contests of any sort have long-term beneficial effects insofar as encouraging the reading habit. Each child can be encouraged to do better than he or she has done in the past (read more books, read on a greater variety of topics), but reading to outdo a classmate has no redeeming value.

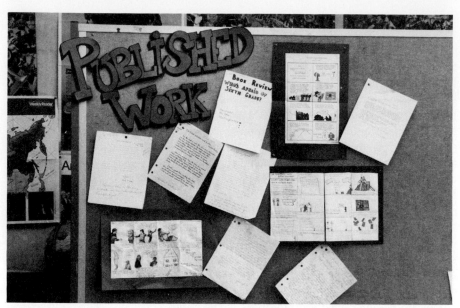

Classroom displays that show children as reading often encourage others to read as well. *(Peter Vadnai)*

Develop an Advertising Campaign

One of the most important values of book sharing is that students develop an interest in reading a selection one of their peers recommends. Students can share their reactions to a book in a number of ways—dramatization, art work, oral or written reports, and so forth. One means that students seem to enjoy is developing an advertising campaign designed to entice others to read a particular book. A broadly based campaign can include designing and creating an attractive dust cover for the book, writing and producing 30- or 60-second mock commercials for television and radio, writing a book review that highlights the good features of the book, dressing in the costume of a character in the book, creating a billboard display, posing as the author on a mock television talk show, and so forth. This activity can be even more fruitful if several students who read the same book cooperate on the development of the advertising campaign.

Of course, time and space should be set aside for the students to present the advertising they develop to their classmates. This gives the students a goal to work toward and exposes other members of the class to the book. The result will often be an eagerness to get and read a copy of the featured book.

Using Comic Books

At first blush it might seem odd, even self-defeating, to encourage the use of comic books in school. Comic books often compete directly with trade books for the child's time. Why, then, include a discussion on using comic books and comic strips in a chapter on motivating children to read?

First, comic books are included because "they are there." To ignore comic books or to write them off as unworthy is to deny their existence. Students will continue to read them despite the contempt teachers may hold for them. Wright (1979) reported that millions of comic books are distributed and purchased annually. Primary, intermediate, and junior high school students all read comic books, with peak interest existing among 12 to 14 year olds. Consequently, it seems better to recognize the popularity of comic books and take advantage of the interest they engender.

A second reason for using comic books in school is that many of them are extremely easy to read and, consequently, can be used to help some remedial and reluctant readers feel successful. Using several readability estimates Wright (1979) calculated that just over 50 percent of the comic books included in his sample fell below a 3.0 grade level; a number were below a 2.0 grade level. This does not mean all comic books are easy to read, of course, but suggests that children who have difficulty reading a textbook may be able to succeed with materials the teacher helps them select. Arlin and Roth (1978) caution that low-achieving readers spend most of their time looking at the illustrations in comic books so a strategy that leads to text processing must be adopted (students could act out a story reading the text as a script, for example).

Wright (1979) also reports that publishers are making use of the appeal of comic books. Holt, Rinehart and Winston, for example, has published a beginners' dictionary (*The Super Dictionary*) that includes heroes such as Superman, Batman, and Wonder Woman. The Macmillan Series r basal program includes several stories that are presented in comic book form. A program published by Harr Wagner uses a comic book format to present stories of high interest that are accompanied by audio tapes with narration and sound effects. Many similar items are available from other publishers as well.

Comic strips in the daily newspaper also have high appeal to students. Some comic strips form a continuous story (*Dick Tracy, Gasoline Alley*), but others are primarily self-contained (*Peanuts, Hi and Lois*). Students can be asked to collect installments over a period of time, turning them into a book of sorts. Collections of comic strips are available in book form, of course, and these too, can be useful tools in getting students to read. Comic strips for more sophisticated audiences (*Doonesberry, Gil Thorp*) can stimulate discussions of current events and problem solving of a true-to-life nature.

The transition from comic book to trade book reading is not as abrupt as it may first appear. Students who have been reading comic books can read short, high-interest, low-vocabulary books such as those published by the Field Enterprise Company, for example. Topics of personal interest preferred in comic book reading (for example, humor, romance) can be reflected in the types of books offered as an alternative to comics. Words learned in comic books can be used to create a pool of known words for vocabulary study. Students can even try their hand at rewriting a comic book as a piece of non-illustrated prose. Details of setting, characterization, and plot would be added by the student as an exercise in creative writing. The books produced in this manner would be a transition reader of sorts, having greater meaning to a student who has previously read the comic book version.

Reading to Younger Children

Another strategy that seems to be very effective as a way of encouraging some students to read is having them read aloud to younger children. For example, a reluctant ten-year-old reader who will not willingly sit down with a book for his or her own recreation or improvement may find attractive the idea of reading to a small group of first-grade children. The opportunity to be the "person in charge," so to speak, motivates some children. Others may simply enjoy working with and helping younger children. Still others may see this as a way to break away from the normal routine of the classroom. For whatever reason, students of all ages are usually willing to spend a considerable amount of time selecting a book to be shared, rehearsing their oral reading to achieve fluency, and reading aloud to younger students. Each of these activities has potential value as a learning experience for the student, particularly if a teacher supervises each step, offers suggestions, and gives feedback on strengths and weaknesses of the student's performance.

The advantages of a program that features youth reading to youth are manifold. First, the older students often spend more time reading under these circumstances than they would otherwise. Second, the success they experience and the recognition they receive reinforce them for reading. Third, the practice students get in reading silently and orally contributes to the improvement of their own reading even if the material is quite easy for them. They are still meeting words and phrases in various contexts, and trying to convey an author's meaning through good oral interpretation. If the older students are low-achieving readers, the "easy" material they read may even be at or close to their own recreational reading level (this is especially good for their growth). Fourth, the younger children receive individual attention in a small group situation and are exposed to more good-book-level language than they would be otherwise. Finally, the teacher of the younger children has more time to work with individuals or small groups who are not participating in the read-aloud activity at the time.

More detail suggestions on how to establish and maintain a youth-reading-to-youth program are offered by Smith and Fay (1973) and Harris and Smith (1986).

Motivating with Letter Grades and Teachers' Comments

The use of letter grades and teachers' comments as motivational devices is a highly complex matter. There is no denying that some students do put forth greater effort when they know a grade will be given on an assignment. The

American system of schooling makes heavy use of letter grades and most parents and teachers regard them as a means for motivating students. Indeed, college admission and real-life employment often depend to some extent on the grades a student has earned in school. It seems reasonable to assume, then, that those who recognize the importance of grades in their lives will be motivated by them. Grades become the academic equivalent of the monetary reward system used in the job market.

Space does not permit us a thorough analysis of the many issues surrounding the topic of grading.[2] For our purposes here several conclusions from Kirschenbaum, Simon, and Napier (1971) are relevant. Generally speaking, the students who earn good grades would probably do well in school without the prospects of grades. However, low-achieving students, the kind we might expect to be remedial readers, are rarely motivated by the threat of grades. The word *threat* is used advisedly because poor students hold very little hope for achieving the good grades which some students see as an extrinsic reward for a job well done. Even when they do try hard in school, low-achieving students generally expect to receive low grades because the quality of the work they produce is usually poorer than that of the better students. Low grades, consequently, become a type of punishment.

The question of low-achieving students then becomes, Is learning enhanced by the threat of punishment? For students who fail in school more often then they succeed, the answer is probably *no*. The threat of poor grades often embitters these students and causes them to put forth less effort because even their best will not be A work.

Teachers who work with low-achieving readers are in a special bind when it comes to grading. The low-achieving student who works especially hard and makes extraordinary gains deserves an A by all reasonable standards. Yet the unreasonable standard that requires grades to be assigned on a comparative basis is typically invoked. Put in the form of a question the community might ask, the issue becomes, "How can a fifth grader (or an eighth grader, or a twelfth grader) get an A in reading when he or she is struggling to complete a second-grade book?"

The teacher who responds to this question by citing the progress students have made is reminded that employers, other teachers, and parents will interpret the A as a measure of their ability. "That's unfair to the students who really earned an A," the teachers hears. Following is an observation about what is at fault in this situation and several suggestions concerning how to maximize the motivational effects of grades for all students. Also described is how teachers' comments can be employed to have special motivational value.

Grading becomes a shorthand method of communicating information about a student's progress and level of achievement. The problem is that it communicates very little. What should be described in considerable detail gets reduced to a single symbol. Instead of describing what Susie has learned to do, what she is working on now, and what she has not yet learned in reading, science, math, and so forth, the student's performance is reduced to a simple code that has come to have a simplistic meaning in American society. The grade C designates average, B means good, and A means excellent. If Susie gets an A in math, everyone is elated and the school mill grinds onward. But what does that grade *really* represent? Is Susie performing well given her ability in math? What progress has she made on fractions, and has she learned the material that she did not know last grading period when she got a B in math? How was the grade determined? Does it represent the quality of daily work (including the insightfulness of her comments and questions in discussions), or is it based strictly on written work? Does neatness affect the grade received on daily written work? Should it in math? Or is the grade based solely on test performance? If so, what type of test was used? Were math concepts tested or just calculation ability? Were problem-solving abilities tested?

This line of questioning could go on, but the questions raised above serve to illustrate the point: Grades obscure more than they reveal. Too many students are satisfied if they get a good grade on an assignment whether they learned anything or stretched themselves or not. Too many teachers are satisfied if they "graded" the papers and made an entry for each student in the grade book. The problem with grading in general and with grading as a motivational device in particular is that form is victorious over substance. Students can earn good grades by figuring out what the teacher expects. Teachers can award good grades on the basis of who parrots back the expected facts. Standards can be fixed arbitrarily and those who fall short are labeled "slow" or "lazy." The club of grades can be wielded over students' heads. Some students respond and that seems to give the system validity; others do not or cannot fit and the blame is theirs.

Why have schools settled for a letter grade system as a means for communicating information about a student's progress? For a variety of reasons to be sure, but primarily because it is efficient and it makes educators think they understand its meaning. By using a system that reduces all the details down to one grand generalization (A, B, C, D) the teacher need not bother looking carefully at each response and deciding what it tells about the student's growth. The parent need not bother with the details either so long as good grades are received (this is relative of course—A's are good in some homes, C's in others). When poor grades are received the focus is often on "getting those grades up," not on getting at the cause of the learning failure. In effect, the grades become an end in themselves.

A proposed solution to this unhappy state of affairs is to do away with grades altogether in the interest of forcing all parties involved to talk about Susie's progress as an individual learner. The concerned parties include Susie, her parents, and her teacher. The means for communicating include face-to-face conferences, the telephone, and the postal service. What greater motivational device is there than for Susie to realize that the people she cares about are interested in her progress?

Is this proposal realistic? Not altogether. Unfortunately, society is not willing to pay the price that such a personalized educational system would cost. Teachers who face dozens of students each day simply cannot invest hours communicating with each student and parent. Nevertheless, direct contact should be valued and sought whenever possible. Descriptions of progress can be employed in place of, or to supplement, report cards and letter grades. This can certainly be the case with students having difficulty in a subject. It is these students who are most vulnerable to the damage an impersonal grading system can inflict.

Another proposal for making grades a more useful motivational device for all students is to give grades on several bases. A teacher may grade students against a fixed standard and against each other, but also against themselves. In other words, if Walter is a sixth grader reading at first-grade level, he may receive a D or F in reading on a comparative scale, but if he is making strides and trying hard, he should receive an A on a second, personalized scale. It is preferable that no child get less than a C if he or she is making satisfactory progress regardless of his or her level of performance. In those situations in which school policy requires a low grade, a teacher can furnish additional information to help both student and parents get a more complete picture.

Some teachers supplement letter grades on report cards with checklists and written comments giving greater detail with respect to gains being made and areas needing improvement. This approach is preferred, which leads into the upcoming discussion.

Can you as a student recall the last time a professor made written comments in the margin and at the end of your paper? How did you react? Even if the comments were not entirely positive and your letter grade disappointing, you probably appreciated the fact that written comments were provided. That is how students typically react and it is amazing to learn how seldom professors give that type of feedback.

Children are no different in this respect. A teacher should write comments throughout when reading and correcting written work. It is better to read every other assignment carefully and make comments than to read every assignment and make no comments. The tone of the comments should be supportive, emphasizing things the student did well, with criticisms held to a manageable number. This approach gives students something to work on for improvement without overwhelming them. A study by Page (1958) reported that students who received written comments from teachers that were "relevant and helpful" performed better on a subsequent task than students who got no comment, or a standard comment such as "A—excellent paper."

Finally, teachers' comments should focus on how the student is doing as an individual. It is much more encouraging to a student to be told, "This is your best effort in a month. Next time check your spelling more carefully," than "Your spelling is terrible." Comments on written work should instruct and encourage the child on a daily basis. They should be used generously and regularly as motivational devices. They communicate far more to students concerning their progress than do letter grades.

Using Games to Motivate Reading

Children of all ages are attracted to games. Evidence of this is plentiful at Christmas and Hanukkah time when games of various types are given. Electronic games have been especially popular in recent years. Teachers have long appreciated the high interest games have for children. Authors such as Daniels (1971), Cleary (1978), Wagner and Hosier (1970), and Spache (1976) have described ways in which games can be incorporated into the reading curriculum in a substantial, not superfluous, way.

Games can contribute to the development of reading ability in several ways. First, many games call for some limited amount of reading, such as reading the directions for the game (this is usually an exacting kind of reading requiring careful attention to detail), reading labels on a playing board, reading cards that the player "draws" during his turn, and the like. Games that fall in this category are *Monopoly, Password, Stop Thief,* and *The Alumni Game,* for example. One might reason that the amount of time spent playing a game could better be spent reading a book if practice with reading is the goal. But children enjoy variety and a well-rounded reading program ought to have room in it for various types of activities. The kind of reading students engage in while playing a game does illustrate directly the value of reading in a way they should find personally meaningful. The importance this insight may have for students and their attitude toward reading should not be discounted.

A second way games can contribute to the development of reading ability is through games that are designed specifically for reading practice. Word identification is sometimes practiced through a rummy-type card game that involves drawing word cards and matching pairs of words, for example. Or a dominoes-type game can be played with tiles that display high-frequency words that are matched. Many other examples could be given. In all cases such games focus directly on reading (usually phonics and word identification). Companies such as Milton Bradley and Ideal develop and distribute hundreds of reading games. However, it is easy to develop "homemade" reading games of this type. From the standpoint of motivation, students are often willing to apply themselves in a game situation when practice on the same skill through a work sheet would meet with apathy.

To the teacher who protests that school cannot always be fun (and games), the response is in the affirmative. Neither should school always be a drag. Games have their place in the overall program as a way of adding variety, but constant use of games lessens their novelty and and thereby their motivational value. Games provide practice but they are ill-suited to the task of introducing or teaching a skill. That would be akin to learning through trial and error. One final note in the same vein: When using reading games teachers should make sure that students practice skills correctly. For example, it makes little sense in a rummy game described earlier to have students match cards incorrectly but get credit because none of the players knows the difference. One of the players, or an observer who is fully competent at the skill being practiced, should monitor the progress of the game. Otherwise the game provides practice in performing a skill incorrectly.

A third way games can contribute to a reading program is by allowing students to associate enjoyment with school and with reading class in particular. This encourages a more positive disposition toward reading. Interviews with children reveal that doing workbooks and reading aloud often describes their strongest perceptions of what constitutes reading. If all we can add to this perception is that reading includes playing games, we have accomplished little. If the *application* of reading to uses such as playing games, following directions, and the like can be added to other healthy perceptions of reading, the results will be worthwhile.

One other matter related to the topic of games concerns how best to use them to gain optimum motivation. Stated as a question, a teacher might ask, "Should games be a reward for students who get their work done, or should all students get to participate?" The answer is "yes" to both. Sometimes the opportunity to play games is effectively used to promote completion of assigned work. Daniels (1971) gives a detailed description of how a program can be established in which points are earned during the week that can be used to "buy" free time on Friday. Free time can be spent playing games. Some students will respond positively to a system of this sort.

We caution, however, that under such a plan some students may never get to play games. These may be the very students who most need a change of pace and a chance to enjoy school and reading. For this reason it may be wise to have some occasions on which everyone gets to play games (particularly games that involve planned rather than incidental reading). This can be accomplished by purchasing, making, or borrowing games that relate to the instructional needs of the students. Those who need practice on phonics can play "consonant rummy" or "fish for vowels." Those who need help with affixes can play "prefix concentration." After playing a reading game or two for a set period of time, a brief free-choice period can follow, one that allows students to play any of the games (reading games or games involving reading only incidentally).

Cleary (1978) describes a variety of game and gamelike activities that could be employed in classrooms where variety is sought. The activities she describes are obviously appropriate for all learners, but some could be used to reward students who complete assigned work. No conflict is seen in using both approaches at the same time.

The Language Experience Approach

Most people have probably had the experience of coming across an old term paper, letter, or report they wrote, which they reread with much interest. That same type of interest seems to be generated by the use of the language experience approach to reading.

The language experience approach has been described in considerable detail in a variety of places.[3] It is an approach to reading and writing instruction that involves story dictation, chart development, and group oral reading (see Chapters 6 and 8). The fact that students write (or dictate) their own stories makes this approach highly motivating.

The Newspaper as a Motivational Device

In this day of tight school budgets, it is increasingly difficult to find the funds to purchase books, games, and many other attractive materials that publishers have developed for reluctant readers. This is unfortunate because in recent years a nice array of items has become available on topics that interest children (such as motocross racing, hang gliding, deep sea diving, and the like).

Though not as colorful, the daily newspaper is used by many creative teachers to capitalize on students' awareness of trends and fads in contemporary society. No textbook begins to approach the range of topics covered in the daily newspaper. Furthermore, the newspaper is relatively inexpensive (even free if a day-old copy is brought from home by students or if unsold copies are donated by a distributor), and constantly changing. Studies have shown that the overall reading level of daily newspapers is relatively low (often averaging about sixth-grade level) with a range of levels being represented within the same issue (Burton, 1974). This means nearly any student in a classroom can find an article, feature, or even a section that he or she can read. Given a high level of interest in a specific topic, students may even manage articles that would normally be difficult for them.

From a motivational standpoint, the appeal of using the newspaper is that each student's personal interest can be served. Whether it be sports, the horoscope, TV schedules, or advice to the lovelorn, the newspaper contains such a broad range of features that personally meaningful material can be found for nearly everyone.

It is beyond our means here to explore in detail the various ways a newspaper can be used to teach reading; a number of excellent sources address that need. Cheyney (1984), Criscuolo (1981), Rupley (1979), and Gitelman (1983) are examples of resources available to help teachers use the newspaper as an instructional device. Many newspapers sponsor local programs that provide specific suggestions for using the newspaper as part of the curriculum. The American Newspaper Publishers Association Foundation, The Newspaper Center, Box 17407, Dulles International Airport, Washington, D.C. 10041, publishes a regular newsletter "Teaching with Newspapers." Also check your local newspaper—many of them have programs you can employ in your classroom.

Using Contracting to Motivate

Contracting is a not-so-new teaching idea that seems to have a positive motivational effect on some students. As the name suggests, the teacher and student jointly develop an agreement concerning what work will be accomplished over a set period of time. The agreement is summarized in writing and signed by both parties. Typically the contract states that an agreed-upon grade will be awarded for completing the work specified in the contract. Students who contract for an A normally complete more work of a more difficult or complex nature than do students who contract for a lesser grade.

The rationale for contracting is based on a belief that students will be more willing to engage in activities that they help select and design. It is fundamental that contracts be truly negotiated with provision being made for the preferences and special abilities of the student. Thus, in a social studies setting the student with an artistic flair might arrange to complete a particular unit of study such as Lincoln's presidency with a mural, a collection of sketches, or a collage. The significance of these materials could be explained in a written paper or audio tape. Students sometimes work together to complete a contract, each one contributing according to his or her special talents.

The most obvious application to a remedial reading situation is for student and teacher to contract for the completion of certain books and practice exercises. With a little imagination, this meager beginning can be broadened to include more active and potentially rewarding experiences. The student could agree to read aloud to a parent, sibling, or younger child for a specified number of minutes per week. The contract could include making several trips to the library, developing a bibliography of books on a particular topic, reading at least two of those books, and sharing one of them with peers in some creative manner. It is evident that contracting creates an opportunity for the student to personalize and expand the normal classroom routine. This often proves stimulating to students and has the advantage of making them responsible for their own learning within a framework approved by the teacher. A successful beginning contract can provide a foundation from which longer and more involved contracts may be built. This is particularly good for older remedial readers who need to feel that they are making progress and controlling their own destinies.

SUMMARY

This chapter provided several case studies to illustrate how motivation operates in different situations. Brian Bussell's case was described as typical of the normal motivation that grows from success in learning to read. Two cases in which self-motivation had been lost were also presented: Debbie Howard, a child who experienced difficulty with learning to read in second grade, and Sam Brady, a capable, but unwilling reader. The approach used by each of these children's teachers in the matter of motivation is described. A special approach to motivation known as behavior modification was described as were a number of other strategies, such as reading aloud to children, making connections between movies and books, and using comic books in the reading program (to name a few). Letter grades were discussed with respect to their capacity to motivate, especially low-achieving readers.

SUGGESTED ACTIVITIES

1. Using the *Reader's Guide to Periodical Literature, Current Index to Journals in Education*, or other reference index, identify articles appearing in professional journals during the past two years that are listed under the heading, "motivation." Locate and read several articles that strike you as interesting and helpful.

2. Experiment with the behavior modification strategy described in this chapter to see whether you can reduce or even eliminate a behavior you would like to avoid or increase a behavior you would like to build up. Remember to gather base line data as a first step then set an intermediate target that can be reached within a reasonable period of time. See how long it takes you to achieve the final objective. You may want to maintain a chart that shows progress toward your goal. If no other behavior occurs to you, consider using this strategy to increase the amount of time you devote to recreational reading.

3. Suppose that Sam Brady, the third case study reported in this chapter, had not been interested in sketching and painting, but preferred to spend his leisure time fishing. How might you approach the challenge of motivating Sam to read using the principles suggested in this and the previous chapter? Compare your approach to the approach one of your colleagues suggests. Identify the advantages and disadvantages of each approach.

NOTES

1. See MacMillan (1973) and Ringness (1975).
2. For those who are interested, an excellent book by Kirschenbaum, Simon, and Napier (1971), titled *Wad-Ja-Get?: The Grading Game in American Education*, presents a penetrating look at grading as a whole, the advantages and disadvantages of various grading systems, and a review of the relevant professional literature on the topic.
3. See Hall (1981), Van Allen (1976), Stauffer (1970), Veatch et al. (1979), and Harris and Smith (1986).

SUGGESTED READINGS

BRISTOW, PAGE SIMPSON. (1985). Are poor readers passive readers? Some evidence, possible explanations, and potential solutions. *The Reading Teacher* 39:318–325.
Presents evidence that suggests low-achieving readers are passive because of repeated failures. Offers specific suggestions the classroom teacher can follow to help such children develop active reading behaviors, thereby enhancing comprehension.

CIANI, ALFRED J. (ED.). (1981). *Motivating reluctant readers.* Newark, DE: International Reading Association.
Included in this booklet are ten essays written by participants in an institute on motivating reluctant readers. Specific strategies are described to help

classroom teachers, reading clinicians, and parents with the task of motivation. Special attention is given to finding and developing materials that arouse and maintain interest and in using methods that cause student involvement.

MATHEWSON, GROVER C. (1985). Toward a comprehensive model of affect in the reading process. In Harry Singer and Robert B. Ruddell (Eds.), *Theoretical models and processes of reading* (pp. 841–856). Newark, DE: International Reading Association.
Examines the role of affect in reading behavior and suggests a model that can be used to guide research in this domain. Major components of the model include attitude, motivation, affect, and physical feelings.

SPIEGEL, DIXIE LEE. (1981). *Reading for pleasure: Guidelines.* Newark, DE: International Reading Association.
Discusses the importance of a recreational reading program as a way of enhancing the regular instructional program. Emphasizes the motivational aspects of reading for pleasure and describes ways to expand reading interests through recreational reading. Provides specific suggestions for initiating a recreational reading program, and for managing time and materials.

Part 2

Instruction and Assessment for Low-Achieving Readers

Part II expounds the main theme of this book: The classroom teacher is in the best position to identify where difficulties are being experienced by low-achieving readers. Daily instructional activities provide an ongoing opportunity to assess needs, adjust instruction to those needs, and evaluate the effectiveness of those adjustments. Instruction is most effective when it is provided in an explicit fashion that emphasizes *what* a particular skill or strategy entails, *why* the skill or strategy is important, and *when* readers would use the skill or strategy as they are reading on their own. The teacher must also model *how* a particular skill or strategy can be performed, then provide opportunities for learners to practice in guided and independent activities. By collecting and recording information on a regular basis, the classroom teacher is in a position to determine the relative strengths and weaknesses of each child. Part II discusses in detail how these themes are carried out in the fundamental areas of word recognition, comprehension, and vocabulary.

Chapter 5

Overview of Remedial Reading Instruction and Assessment

OVERVIEW

As you read this chapter use the following list of main ideas to guide your understanding and reflection.

Classroom teachers can effectively assess low-achieving readers based on classroom reading tasks.

Remediation should focus on explicit instruction in word recognition, comprehension, and vocabulary strategies that students can apply to actual reading.

Independent reading is an important part of a remedial reading program.

Students need to read material at an appropriate level of difficulty for optimal reading growth.

Rosie is a fifth-grade student reading approximately a year and a half below grade level. She "knows her phonics" and can decode fairly well. For the most part, she is fluent but stumbles over some multisyllabic words. However, her biggest problem seems to be in the area of comprehension. Rosie cannot answer comprehension questions very well after reading in her basal. She does not seem to be aware of when she does and does not understand; she always says she has understood what she has read even when she does poorly on comprehension questions following a reading assignment in the basal reader. Needless to say, Rosie does very poorly when it comes to reading her content textbooks.

Rosie may seem like a typical low-achieving reader to many classroom teachers. However, it may be relatively easy for a teacher to neglect Rosie in terms of remedial reading instruction because it appears that Rosie is decoding fairly well. She generally does not do well in comprehension, but many would say there is not much that can be done about this. Besides, some would argue, there just is not enough time in the regular classroom to help someone like Rosie with remedial reading.

We disagree. Even from the brief description above, it becomes apparent that several of Rosie's reading problems can and should be addressed in the regular classroom. Rosie has learned to decode, but she has not learned to comprehend well, the real goal of reading. She appears to need some help in attacking multisyllabic words and could be grouped for special instruction with other students in the class having a similar difficulty. Working with the teacher, the students can learn how to attack multisyllabic words in actual text.

However, Rosie's greatest problem appears to be in the area of comprehension where she does not appear to be monitoring for meaning (noticing when she is and is not comprehending) very well and is not using fix-up strategies when her comprehension has failed. She could be grouped for special instruction with other students having difficulty in comprehension monitoring. Also, Rosie would benefit from instruction in comprehension-building strategies which, in turn, would help her do a better job answering questions. Additional assessment of her comprehension performance on classroom reading tasks would be needed before the classroom teacher could determine which comprehension strategies Rosie should be taught. Students with similar needs in comprehension might again be grouped together for special instruction.

Classroom teachers can effectively assess the strengths and weaknesses of low-achieving readers like Rosie on the basis of their classroom reading tasks. They can provide them with effective remedial instruction in word recognition, comprehension, and vocabulary when the students are grouped together, based on similar needs. The term *low-achieving readers* refers to students who are reading below grade level and whose reading difficulties are interfering with their school achievement. Part 2 of this book provides suggestions for assessing and remediating low-achieving readers in word recognition, comprehension, and vocabulary. Although many of the strategies discussed are learned by better readers with minimal instruction, low-achieving readers will often need explicit instruction.

The strategies contained in this text are also applicable to reading specialists, reading tutors, and special education teachers, as well as classroom teachers. Furthermore, these suggestions apply to all low-achieving readers,

A classroom teacher works with a group of low-achieving readers. *(Elizabeth Crews)*

be they regular students or special education students. It may even be the case that some average and above average students may not have learned some of these strategies and, consequently, will also benefit from such instruction.

THE IDEAL RELATIONSHIP BETWEEN READING PROCESSES, READING INSTRUCTION, AND READING ASSESSMENT

If teachers worked in an ideal educational world with unlimited resources and talent, they would have no need to differentiate among these activities: asking students to engage in a reading comprehension activity, instructing students about how to perform a comprehension strategy, and assessing students' ability to use such a strategy. A skilled teacher armed with a strong background in learning and literacy development and a range of texts varying in topic and difficulty can do all three tasks—engagement, instruction, or assessment— more or less simultaneously with a student. It would only be necessary to sit down with a student reading a passage and ask him or her to engage in some comprehension task, for example, summarizing the passage.

Then, depending upon the student's initial success at the task, the teacher can decide how much extra instructional support (what some people call scaffolding) the student will need in order to complete the task successfully. This instructional support can take the form of extra clues, as in (1).

1. My guess is that a good summary would have to say something about how the Pilgrims got to this country and about how they survived their first winter.

Or it can take the form of turning an open-ended task into a multiple-choice task, as in (2).

2. Well, let me give you two possible summaries and you tell me which one you think is the best.

   • It is about the Pilgrims' voyage across the ocean to this country, their first winter in America, and their joy when Spring came.
   • It is about what the Pilgrims learned from the dual hardship they experienced—a difficult voyage and a tough winter—during their first year in America and how their appreciation of the successful harvest led to the first Thanksgiving.

Or, it could take the form of directing the students to another resource (for example, the text or their own prior knowledge), to help them with the task, as in (3) and (4).

3. I bet if you look at the first sentence in each paragraph on pages 63 and 64, it would help you to come up with a good summary.

4. Hey, wait a minute, all you have to do is to think about this for a minute and you will realize that you already know a lot about the Pilgrims and what they learned that first year. And if you can say that in a sentence or two, it might be a good summary for this passage.

Or it might take the form of offering the student some advice about who to consult, as in (5).

5. I bet if you got together with George and the two of you put your heads together on this (you know, you both know quite a bit about the Pilgrims), you could work out a real helpful summary.

Or it might offer a different task perspective, as in (6).

6. Think of it this way. Suppose your friend George walked into class right before you were going to take a test on this passage and announced that he had not read it. What could you say to him in just a few sentences that would at least give him a clue about what was important in the passage?

In what sense can such interactions permit engagement, instruction, and assessment simultaneously? The engagement is transparent, that is, the student is asked to perform the comprehension task. The extra support, or scaffolding, illustrated in each example can be thought of as "instruction," or at the very least, "instructive." In fact, much of what is included in the recently popularized direct and explicit instruction routines is very much like examples (1) through (6). Assessment enters the picture in at least two senses. First, the teacher has to judge whether or not the student's initial attempt is successful or unsuccessful (notice that on-line assessment of success results in an immediate instructional decision). Second, the amount and degree of teacher support the student needs in order to complete the task becomes an index of the degree of independence the student has developed for this comprehension task. And such a judgment is likely to be extremely useful in planning future instructional activities.

Alas! This ideal world is all too remote from the reality that teachers face in schools. Few teachers have the time to work extensively in the kind of tutorial situation implied in our examples. Furthermore, not all teachers are familiar enough with the learning and literacy acquisition processes for them to do such "on-line" diagnosis and instruction. Realities demand compromise with this integrated engagement-instruction-assessment model. Wherever possible, however, techniques that permit or even encourage such integration (for example, the instructional technique of reciprocal teaching in Chapter 8) are presented. Although such integration is always an ultimate goal, textbook analysis forces us to discuss instruction and assessment as separate, but interrelated, endeavors.

APPLYING EXPLICIT INSTRUCTION

Chapters 6, 8, and 10 emphasize explicit instruction in reading strategies. By explicit instruction we mean the following steps: (1) teacher explanation of *what* a strategy consists of, (2) teacher explanation of *why* this strategy is important, (3) teacher modeling of *how* to perform the strategy, (4) teacher explanation of *when* to use the strategy in actual reading, (5) guided practice, in which the teacher and students work through several examples of the strategy together using actual text, and (6) independent practice, in which students continue to use the strategy on their own using actual text. Too often, instruction in reading consists of steps (1) and (6), with the key activities in (2) through (5) being omitted. Consequently, students may not fully understand specific strategies and may not learn how to apply them when actually reading.

Teacher modeling of reading strategies is important because many students need to see a clear demonstration of how to perform a specific strategy before it means anything to them. By modeling, we mean the teacher talking aloud as he or she performs the strategy for a group of students. Modeling is not easy. It is difficult for skilled readers to be explicit about mental processes which they perform rather automatically. Chapters 6, 8, and 10 provide numerous *examples* of teachers modeling specific strategies. Although modeling will vary from teacher to teacher, it is important that the teacher always try to be explicit about how to perform a particular reading strategy.[1]

Guided practice is the logical follow-up to modeling. In guided practice the teacher and students attempt to talk aloud as they perform the just-modeled strategy with *actual text*. "Actual text" is stressed here because work sheets are of limited usefulness. There is no guarantee that students will learn to transfer the strategies practiced on work sheets to actual text.[2]

In addition to modeling and guided practice, it is important for teachers to be explicit about *why* a particular strategy is important to learn and about *when* students should consciously use the strategy during actual reading. We do not propose that students consciously use specific word recognition, comprehension, and vocabulary strategies whenever they read. It is only when decoding and comprehension are not progressing smoothly (common problems of low-achieving readers) that students should think about specific strategies they can apply to facilitate their reading. Teachers should help students by being explicit about *when* specific strategies might be used.[3]

In Chapters 6, 8, and 10 suggestions for instruction in word recognition, comprehension, and vocabulary will focus on strategies which students can apply to actual reading instead of on skills which they practice in isolation on work sheets. As mentioned above, the classroom teacher or special reading teacher can effectively provide instruction in specific strategies to groups of low-achieving readers based on diagnosed needs. Suggestions for actually implementing remedial reading programs in the classroom and clinic are presented in Chapter 15.

INFORMAL ASSESSMENT

Chapters 6, 8, and 10 discuss teaching and learning strategies that students must acquire if they are to become fluent, thoughtful readers. However, in order to provide beneficial instruction, teachers need to know which strategies students already possess and which ones they need to develop. Teachers also need to evaluate student progress after instruction in order to decide whether instruction has been sufficient, should continue, or should be changed.

Chapters 7, 9, and 11 discuss reading-based approaches to assessment which are informal, direct, and frequent. Teachers can use these assessment techniques to identify deficiencies in reading strategies for the purpose of planning appropriate instruction and to evaluate students' progress in using these strategies. Informal, direct, and frequent reading-based assessment means weekly or biweekly assessment of students' performance on specific strategies while they are actually reading connected text. These informal assessment techniques provide the most valid data possible pertaining to the specific instructional strategies identified in Chapters 6, 8, and 10.

Formal reading measures typically do not provide the kind of information teachers need in order to determine the instructional needs of individual students. For example, group achievement tests provide little diagnostic information and are of questionable content validity, thus limiting their usefulness for instructional planning.[4] Individual diagnostic reading tests (such as those reviewed in Chapter 13) and criterion-referenced reading tests (the type commonly built into basal reader programs) generally assess reading skills in isolation or in short, unnatural passages. Also, these tests provide only a small number of items and are often based on a small sample of reading material. Consequently, these tests do not directly or adequately assess students' performance on the specific strategies contained in this text. For example, because commercially prepared diagnostic and criterion-referenced tests assess word recognition skills in isolated lists as opposed to real text, they are not useful for directly assessing students' ability to *apply* phonics knowledge to reading.

Informal, frequent, reading-based assessment of students' reading performance has a number of important features.[5] First, it has high content validity and is instructionally relevant. Students' performance on strategies they are learning to use with actual text can be measured directly and interpreted easily for purposes of instruction. Second, it can be very reliable.[6] When students' performance on specific strategies is measured repeatedly with real materials, stable patterns of errors and persistent problems can be identified. Third, frequent, reading-based assessment is useful for monitoring students' progress and for making instructional changes on a regular basis. This approach to evaluation and instructional change has been found to facilitate student achievement.[7] Fourth, frequent, reading-based assessment can be relatively easy for teachers to develop and use if it is based on data taken from regular classroom reading tasks.

General Approach to Assessment

In Chapters 7, 9, and 11 we will focus on informal, direct, frequent reading-based measures of students' performance on word recognition, comprehension, and vocabulary strategies used when reading actual text. These measures are informal in that they are teacher-developed, yet these informal measures can be used to gather systematic, relevant, interpretable, and reliable data. The measures are direct in that they are designed to assess precisely what students need to learn or have been learning to use when reading. The measures are frequent in that they are collected at least several times for initial assessment and at least once per week as soon as instruction has occurred. The measures are reading-based in that they are based on students' performance when reading actual text.

In some instances, such as assessment of basic sight word knowledge or knowledge of symbol-sound correspondences, we violate our own basic principles by presenting informal assessment procedures for tasks in isolation, such as students reading lists of basic sight words or giving sounds for symbols in isolation. In these instances, we see the isolated tasks as quick, straightforward ways to obtain initial information about students' basic sight word and phonics knowledge. In all such cases, however, additional suggestions are provided for assessing this knowledge when students are reading connected text. For example, in addition to assessing students' knowledge of symbol-sound correspondences in isolation on an informal phonics inventory, we discuss looking for patterns of errors in weekly samples of students' oral reading, which indicates symbol-sound correspondences not known.

The interpretation of the informal assessments must be left up to the teacher. "Acceptable" levels of performance cannot be recommended because such levels would be arbitrary. Even the conventional mastery levels (80 percent correct) on criterion-referenced skills tests such as those found in basal programs are arbitrary. What the teacher must do to interpret informal assessment data is what good teachers do naturally in the classroom on a regular basis. The teacher must form reasonable expectations for individuals on various decoding, comprehension, and vocabulary tasks and then use the assessment data to determine if a student's performance and overall progress are acceptable given those expectations.

Completing a Reading Difficulties Record Sheet

Chapters 7, 9, and 11 discuss many aspects of word recognition, comprehension, and vocabulary knowledge that may be important to assess for low-achieving readers. In word recognition the majority of the recommended assessment can be achieved through oral reading analysis (discussed in Chapter 7) made in regular reading groups. In comprehension, students' ability to comprehend and answer questions on narrative and expository text and their ability to answer literal and inferential questions can be assessed through oral or written questions following regular reading assignments. In vocabulary, students' ability to use contextual and structural analysis and the dictionary can often be assessed through already prepared basal reader material or, if necessary, through teacher-made materials that are based on regular reading assignments. Students' knowledge of specific words taught for specific reading assignments can also frequently be assessed through basal reader or teacher-made materials.

In short, classroom teachers can produce most of the assessment needed for low-achieving readers by using regular classroom activities and materials. The only modifications to the regular teaching routine will involve taking notes during oral reading, categorizing questions asked, keeping additional records on various aspects of the reading performance of low-achieving readers (as explained in Chapters 7, 9, and 11), and then analyzing this data to plan for special instruction where needed. Figure 5.1 provides a reading difficulties record sheet which teachers may find useful in their assessment of low-achieving readers. Various aspects of this summary sheet are explained in Chapters 7, 9, and 11.

Since these additional activities will be time-consuming, we recommend

FIGURE 5.1   Reading Difficulties Record Sheet

Student's Name _____

Age _____   Grade_____

I. Instructional Level

   A. IRI

      Comments:

   B. Ongoing assessment of instructional level (from oral reading analysis sheet and comprehension questions)

      Comments:

II. Word Recognition

   A. Basic sight words not known/frequently missed (from informal test and/or oral reading analysis)

      Comments:

   B. General word recognition strategy

     1. Student's comments:

(Cont.)

FIGURE 5.1   Reading Difficulties Record Sheet (*Cont.*)

2. Degree to which unfamiliar words deliberately and successfully decoded (from oral reading analysis sheets)

Comments:

C. Phonic analysis
    1. Informal phonics inventory   Date _____

Results:

2. Consistent errors in symbol-sound correspondence knowledge and/or ability to analyze 1 and 2+ syllable words (from oral reading analysis sheets)

Comments:

D. Structural analysis—inflectional endings and/or knowledge of affixes
    1. Informal testing

Date   % Correct/Comments

FIGURE 5.1   Reading Difficulties Record Sheet (*Cont.*)

2. Consistent errors (from oral reading analysis sheets)

Comments:

E. Contextual analysis
   1. Self-correction of nonsemantic substitutions (from oral reading analysis sheets)

Comments:

F. Fluency
   1. Rate
      Date   Pages/Book   Words per Min.   Comp.

Comments:

2. Automaticity/phrasing

Comments:

III. Comprehension
   A. Comprehension monitoring   (*Cont.*)

FIGURE 5.1   Reading Difficulties Record Sheet (*Cont.*)

1. Knowing when do/don't understand

Comments:

2. Locating sources of comprehension difficulty

Comments:

3. Using fix-up strategies

    a. Student's comments:

    b. Comments:

4. General comments

B. General comprehension

Comments:

FIGURE 5.1   Reading Difficulties Record Sheet (*Cont.*)

C. Drawing inferences

Comments:

D. Reading for important ideas

Comments:

IV. Vocabulary
   A. General knowledge (from formal test)

B. Using context

Comments:

C. Using the dictionary

Comments:

(*Cont.*)

FIGURE 5.1   Reading Difficulties Record Sheet (*Cont.*)

D. Structural analysis

Comments:

E. Secondary meanings/homographs

Comments:

F. Learning of specific words

Comments:

G. Interest in unfamiliar words

Comments:

V. Recommendations for Special Instruction

A reading specialist provides word recognition instruction to two low-achieving readers with similar needs. *(James Silliman)*

that no classroom teacher have more than six to eight low-achieving readers, and that a building reading specialist assist with the initial and ongoing assessment and with special instruction. If a teacher has more than six or eight low-achieving readers in his classroom, our recommendations for assessment and instruction are still viable. Record keeping, however, will be more difficult and probably less complete. Chapter 15 will have more to say about providing for low-achieving readers in the regular classroom.

INDEPENDENT READING

Although Part 2 of this book focuses on instruction and assessment of specific reading skills and strategies, independent reading should be an integral part of a remedial reading program. People learn to read by reading and, consequently, low-achieving readers need to spend as much time as possible reading materials of their own choosing.[8] Techniques to motivate students to read were presented in Chapter 4. Chapter 15 presents two plans that schedule time for all students, including low-achieving readers, to engage in independent reading in the classroom.

INSTRUCTIONAL READING LEVEL

For optimal reading growth, it is important that all reading material be at an appropriate level of difficulty; that is, it must be neither too difficult for students to decode and understand nor too easy to provide challenging practice.[9] If readers have to struggle too much with decoding and err on too many words, their comprehension will be impaired. Low-achieving readers also must not have to struggle excessively with comprehension. Even if they can decode material accurately but are not comprehending well, they are achieving little because the purpose of reading is to understand the written message.

The term *instructional reading level* is used by reading educators to refer to the most difficult level of material that a student can handle given assistance from a teacher. Word recognition errors are few at this level and comprehension is reasonably high.[10] Students should be placed in instructional level material for reading instruction.

It is important to point out that identifying instructional reading level is an inexact procedure. Students' ability to read material at a particular level will vary depending on their interest and background knowledge for particular reading selections. For example, a student who is generally reading on fourth-grade level may be able to read a story written on sixth-grade level if he or she is very interested in or knowledgeable about the topic. Consequently, using readability formulas to determine reading levels of materials will yield only estimates at best.[11]

Although instructional reading level is an inexact yet important term, the best way it can be determined is by using materials which students will actually be reading. Initial placement can be approximated by using the popular informal reading inventory procedure and basal reading materials. To check the reliability of initial placements, teachers need to apply the logic and procedures of the informal reading inventory to samples of the students' weekly reading. These samples should be taken and analyzed at least weekly. In short, students' ability to decode and comprehend their reading material should be closely monitored. If material is too easy or too difficult, appropriate changes in terms of reading level/reading group should be made.

Grade-equivalent reading scores from standardized achievement tests are often readily available and they might present a quick, easy way to determine instructional reading level. However, the score does not really reflect reading level but compares students to peers in terms of reading achievement.[12] If Amy, for example, gets a grade norm score of 6.1, it does not necessarily mean that she can handle sixth-grade material; all it means is that she got the same number of items correct as was the mean for all those students who were in the first month of sixth grade when they took the test. Because of widespread misuse, the International Reading Association passed a resolution requesting publishers of norm-referenced tests to discontinue grade-equivalent scores (see *Journal of Reading*, 1981). Grade-equivalent scores are further discussed in Chapter 11.

Administering and Interpreting an Informal Reading Inventory

Informal Reading Inventories (IRIs) are collections of short reading passages written at different reading levels. Usually, there are at least two passages at each reading level, pre-primer through sixth grade, one of which is to be read orally by a student and one to be read silently. A student reads passages of increasing difficulty until a frustration level is reached. Frustration level is that level at which a student has to struggle considerably with word recognition or comprehension. Based on the student's word recognition accuracy and comprehension accuracy at various reading levels, an instructional reading level is determined. (IRIs are discussed fully in Chapter 13.)

Directions for administering and interpreting IRIs vary from one inventory to another (Jongsma & Jongsma, 1981). We recommend following whatever directions accompany the IRI for a particular basal series. However, the following set of general guidelines could be followed to administer an IRI and to interpret students' performance on it.

Instead of using a graded word list (words in isolation) to determine beginning reading passages, a procedure that has not been found to be particularly accurate or informative,[13] teachers can simply have students begin reading at a level which is two years below their actual grade placement. Passages at this level should be relatively easy for most students to read. If this is not the case, however, students should read passages at an easier level.

The conventional procedure for an IRI involves having a student first orally read one of the two passages at a given level, as the teacher records word recognition errors. The student then answers the comprehension questions, which the teacher asks aloud, without looking back at the passage. Next, the student silently reads the other passage at that level and answers the questions. If the student is not at the frustration level in either word recognition or comprehension, the same procedure is continued with the passages at the next level.

There is some disagreement among reading experts and across IRIs as to what should be counted as a word recognition error.[14] The following should be counted (see Figure 5.2 for definitions): substitutions, omissions, insertions, and unknown words pronounced by the teacher (the student just could not say anything). The following should *not* be counted as word recognition errors: repetitions, self-corrections, hesitations, "mispronunciations" due to dialect, missed punctuation marks. Repetitions and self-corrections, in particular, are often counted as errors on IRIs. However, both repetitions and self-corrections are usually positive signs, indicating that a student is attempting to read for meaning and can self-correct a word which does not make sense.[15] For this reason, repetitions and self-corrections should not be counted as errors. And, of course, dialect-motivated "mispronunciations" are not mispronunciations at all; they are simply the appropriate application of a different set of pronunciation rules.

There is also some disagreement as to what criteria levels should be used

FIGURE 5.2   Definitions of Word Recognition Errors and Nonerrors

Counted as Errors

Substitution   Any word (*exiting* for *exciting, was* for *saw, dog* for *dogs*) or nonsense
    word (*relatisting* for *relaxing*) that is substituted for an actual word in the text.
Omission   Any complete word that is omitted by the reader.
Insertion   Any word or string of words that do not occur in the text but are inserted
    by the reader. An inserted string of words should be counted as one error.
Teacher pronunciation   Any word that the teacher pronounces for a student after
    waiting at least five seconds. Only difficult, important words should be
    pronounced for students to encourage them to try words on their own.

Not Counted as Errors

Hesitation   Any word on which a student hesitates before pronouncing, mispro-
    nouncing, or receiving teacher assistance.
Self-correction   Any word that is originally mispronounced but is spontaneously
    self-corrected by the reader.
Repetition   Any word or words that are repeated entirely or partially by the reader.
"Mispronunciation" due to dialect   Any word that is "mispronounced" due to
    dialect.
Omission of punctuation mark   Any punctuation mark that is omitted by the
    reader.

to determine instructional and frustration levels.[16] Although there are problems
with IRIs, they are better than no assessment at all in terms of instructional
placement. Students, particularly low-achieving readers, cannot grow optimally
in reading if they are frequently confronted with material that is difficult to
decode or comprehend. Therefore, for better or worse, the existing convention
is acceptable: that instructional reading level be defined as the level at which
a student can read with approximately 95 percent accuracy in word recognition
and approximately 75 percent accuracy in comprehension, averaged across
silent and oral passages. It is also recommended, with reservation, that
frustration level be defined as the level at which a student is reading with less
than 90 percent accuracy in word recognition and less than 70 percent accuracy
in comprehension.

Because these criteria are actually quite arbitrary, the teacher should
regard them as guidelines needing "generous" interpretation. If a real discrepancy occurs between word recognition and comprehension accuracy, it is
recommended that more faith be put in the word recognition scores. This is
because comprehension accuracy scores are generally based on a small number
of questions, typically between four and ten questions per passage. If a teacher
is unsure about a student's basal placement level, the lower level should be
used because it is less frustrating and it is always more encouraging to later
move up to a higher level than to move down to a lower one.

Since informal reading inventories are administered on a one-to-one basis, teachers will not be able to use the procedure very often due to time constraints. Teachers should administer IRIs at the beginning of the school year to their low-achieving readers in order to place them at the appropriate level in the basal and to obtain initial information on their strengths and weaknesses as readers. During the remainder of the year, teachers should continue to assess these low-achieving readers based on their oral reading performance on daily reading tasks and, when justified, should adjust their reading groups and reading materials.

The techniques used with an informal reading inventory to assess word recognition ability are valuable. However, the techniques, when applied to daily reading tasks in what is called oral reading analysis (discussed in Chapter 7), actually provide better data about a student's instructional reading level and word recognition difficulties than when used with a single administration of an informal reading inventory.

SUMMARY

This chapter provided an overview of an approach to remedial intervention, based on explicit instruction, which will be elaborated in Chapters 6, 8, and 10. An overview of an approach to assessment was provided, based on frequent measures of daily performance in reading, which will be elaborated in Chapters 7, 9, and 11. The reading difficulties summary, presented in this chapter as a way to systematically record assessment data, will also be elaborated in Chapters 7, 9, and 11. This chapter concludes with a discussion of instructional reading level determined through use of an informal reading inventory and ongoing assessment of students' oral reading.

SUGGESTED ACTIVITIES

1. Administer either a commercial IRI or an IRI in a basal reader to several children. Determine their instructional reading level.

2. On three different occasions listen to several children read (50–200 words) aloud from the basal in which they have been placed for instruction. Take notes on their oral readings. Have them finish reading the story. Ask them to answer (orally or in writing) approximately ten questions about the story. Determine whether or not the students are reading at their instructional level based on three samples. If students are not available, your instructor may be able to provide you with an audio tape on which one or more children are orally reading and answering questions on three occasions from their basal reader.

NOTES

1. See Roehler and Duffy (1984).
2. See Taylor, Olson, Prenn, Rybczynski, and Zakaluk (1985).

3. See Baumann and Schmitt (1986) for a discussion of explicit instruction in reading.
4. See Salvia and Ysseldyke, 1981, Johnston (1984b), and Zigmond and Silverman (1984).
5. See Zigmond and Silverman (1984).
6. See Tindal, Marston, and Deno (1983).
7. See Fuchs, Deno, and Mirkin (1984).
8. See Anderson et al. (1985) and Fielding, Wilson, and Anderson (1986) for discussions on the importance of independent reading to reading growth.
9. See Bristow, Pikulski, and Pelosi (1983).
10. See Harris and Sipay (1985).
11. See Klare (1984) for a review on readability.
12. See Baumann and Stevenson (1982).
13. See Jongsma and Jongsma, 1981, Marzano, Greenlaw, Tish, and Vodehnal (1978), and McKenna (1983).
14. See Jongsma and Jongsma (1981); McKenna (1983).
15. See Leu (1982).
16. See Jongsma and Jongsma (1981); McKenna (1983).

SUGGESTED READINGS

BAUMANN, J. F., AND SCHMITT, M. B. (1986). The what, why, how, and when of comprehension instruction. *The Reading Teacher* 39:640–647.
The authors explain how to provide direct instruction in the area of reading comprehension.

FIELDING, L. G., WILSON, P. T., AND ANDERSON, R. C. (1986). A new focus on free reading: The role of trade books in reading instruction. In T. E. Raphael (Ed.), *The contexts of school-based literacy*. New York: Random House.
The importance of independent reading is stressed in this book chapter.

KLARE, G. R. (1984). Readability. In P. D. Pearson (Ed.), *Handbook of reading research* (pp. 681–744). New York: Longman.
The issues pertaining to readability are reviewed.

MCKENNA, M. C. (1983). Informal inventories. A review of the issues. *The Reading Teacher* 36:670–679.
The author reviews the issues related to use of informal reading inventories.

ZIGMOND, N., AND SILVERMAN, R. (1984). Informal assessment for program planning and evaluation in special education. *Educational Psychologist* 19:163–171.
The advantages of informal assessment in schools are discussed.

Chapter 6

Word Recognition Instruction

OVERVIEW

As you read this chapter use the following list of main ideas to guide your understanding and reflection.

Decoding is an important part of the reading process, but the ultimate goal of reading is comprehension.

Word recognition instruction should focus as much as possible on words found in actual texts.

Explicit instruction in a word recognition skill will explain to students *what* the skill is, *why* the skill is important, *how* to perform the skill, and *when* to use the skill in the reading of connected text.

Students experiencing difficulty with word recognition typically need to be shown how to use phonic and contextual analysis to attack unfamiliar words when actually reading.

In addition to developing word recognition accuracy, emerging readers need to develop word recognition fluency.

Since comprehension is the ultimate goal of the reading process, reading involves more than decoding or accurately identifying words on a page. A reader who is simply identifying words, but not comprehending, is not really reading.

All readers (especially low-achieving ones) must realize that learning to read well involves more than learning to decode well. Decoding is necessary, but not sufficient, for good comprehension. Consequently, decoding instruction should emphasize meaning, not just correct pronunciation. This approach to decoding instruction will help low-achieving readers to develop the ability to read for meaning. Reading instruction that focuses exclusively on decoding may be detrimental to students' reading comprehension. To illustrate, Anderson, Mason and Shirey (1984) found superior reading comprehension among young readers who received instruction with a meaning emphasis as opposed to instruction with an emphasis on accurate oral reading.

Nevertheless, decoding is a necessary part of the reading process, and poor decoding skills are characteristically one of the factors that differentiate poor readers from good ones.[1] This chapter examines those aspects of word recognition accuracy and fluency that may cause problems for low-achieving readers.

WORD RECOGNITION PROBLEMS OF LOW-ACHIEVING READERS

Word Recognition Accuracy

One important strategy that readers use to decode, or recognize words, is phonic analysis. Low-achieving readers often have less knowledge than good readers about symbol-sound correspondences, particularly as pertains to vowels, and how to use this knowledge flexibly in reading.[2] Low-achieving readers may have difficulty with segmentation (the segmenting of words into phonemes or syllables) and blending of phonemes or syllables.[3] In addition to poor knowledge of symbol-sound correspondences and poor ability to sound and blend word parts, low-achieving readers may also have difficulty applying these word recognition skills to the reading of connected text.[4]

Another important aspect of decoding involves contextual analysis. Readers, especially good readers, appear to use context only when they have to, as in the case of mediated, or noninstantaneous, word recognition.[5] Good readers, for the most part, have reached a more or less automatic stage in word recognition whereas low-achieving readers, who are not so automatic, have to depend more on contexual analysis.[6] Interestingly, however, good readers appear to apply their contextual analysis skills not to decoding but to comprehension. Hence, when good readers make an oral reading substitution, they are more likely than low-achieving readers to make one that is congruent with the meaning of the text. This is because they are constantly monitoring their reading for meaning. Ironically, low-achieving readers, who appear to devote their contextual analysis energies to identifying unknown words rather than to comprehension, tend to make more oral reading substitutions that are not congruent with the meaning of the text. Moreover, regardless of how they attempt to allocate their energies, low-achieving readers do not use context as effectively as they should, even in mediated word recognition.[7]

Fluency

In addition to word recognition accuracy, fluency (an index of the degree to which a reader's oral reading resembles everyday spoken language) is an important aspect of skilled reading.[8] Since skilled readers' word recognition is both automatic and quick, they can use their freed-up cognitive capacity for comprehension processes. In short, readers who are automatic in word recognition can think more about what they are reading. In addition to being less automatic in word recognition than good readers, low-achieving readers generally have been found to be slower at decoding.[9]

This chapter will focus on instructional strategies that develop students' word recognition accuracy and fluency. In the area of word recognition accuracy strategies are discussed that are designed to develop: (1) basic sight word knowledge; (2) knowledge of symbol-sound correspondences and ability to use this knowledge flexibly (for example, variant vowel sounds); (3) ability to break words into parts, sound out parts, and blend parts back together; (4) use of context clues; (5) use of structural analysis; and (6) ability to apply word recognition skills to actual reading. In the area of fluency strategies are discussed that are designed to develop fast, automatic word recognition leading to smooth and speechlike oral reading.

GENERAL MODEL OF
WORD RECOGNITION INSTRUCTION

As mentioned at the beginning of the chapter, instruction in word recognition should not focus on decoding to the exclusion of comprehension. Decoding is a necessary, but not sufficient, part of the reading comprehension process. Therefore, isolated word recognition instruction and practice are discouraged. Occasionally, to make a particular point about a symbol-sound correspondence or a process, an excursion into isolated instruction can be justified if it is immediately recontextualized (that is, put back into a real reading context). We are all too familiar with low-achieving readers who can perform word recognition skills in isolation but cannot use them when actually reading.

Unfortunately, text-related reading instruction occurs too infrequently in our classrooms.[10] Teachers tend to be "givers" and "helpers" with written skill assignments in both word recognition and comprehension; that is, teachers spend too much time helping students complete written assignments.[11] Direct, explicit instruction in word recognition skills is frequently lacking.[12] Explicit instruction in word recognition skills includes the following steps:

1. An explanation of *what* the skill is

2. An explanation of *why* the skill is important

3. An explanation/modeling of *how* to perform the skill

4. An explanation of *when* to use the skill in the reading of connected text

5. Guided and independent practice using the skill, in which connected text is used as much as possible

Most of the word recognition strategies in this chapter will be covered using the above steps.

WORD RECOGNITION ACCURACY

Developing a Basic Sight Vocabulary

Skilled readers automatically identify most words as sight words. That is, they use immediate, as opposed to mediated, word identification. They are able to do this because they have seen most words they come across in print many times before. However, we do not recommend that emerging readers be drilled in new words until they have memorized them as sight words. This "whole word" approach to identifying new words is too slow and inefficient a technique, especially for learning how to identify unfamiliar words on one's own. The simultaneous use of contextual and phonic analysis to decode unfamiliar words is a much more efficient and realistic approach to word recognition for an emerging reader.

Nevertheless, there are some instances in which the whole word approach should be used, in which students should receive repeated, meaningful exposures to words until they learn them as sight words. For example, students reading at a preprimer or primer level essentially have no word recognition skills, and if they are taught some sight words, they can begin to read simple text as they are developing their word recognition skills. Examples of words that might be learned this way are *Pat, Ken, play, ball,* and *good* (that is, high-interest, emotional, and high-frequency words).

Also, primary grade readers who lack sufficient basic sight words will benefit from meaningful drill on certain high-frequency words until they know them instantaneously as sight words. These words (for example, *is, an, the, said, was, there, they*) occur so frequently in primary level reading materials that students should learn to recognize them instantly as sight words in order to maximize their reading fluency.[13]

Many basic sight vocabulary lists have been developed.[14] One list developed by Johnson (1976) is presented in Figure 6.1. In an investigation designed to validate this list, it was found that the 180 first-grade words were known by at least 70 percent of the first-grade subjects and the 126 second-grade

FIGURE 6.1 Johnson's Basic Sight Word List

Johnson's First-Grade Words

a	end	in	off	they
above		into	old	think
across	feet	is	one	this
after	find	it	open	those
again	first	its	or	three
air	five	it's	out	time
all	for		over	to
am	four	just		today
American			past	too
and	gave	keep		took
are	get	kind	play	top
art	girl		point	two
as	give	let	put	
ask	go	like		under
at	God	little	really	up
	going	look	red	
back	gone	love	right	very
be	good		room	
before	got	make	run	
behind		making		want
big		man	said	wanted
black	had	may	saw	was
book	hand	me	school	way
boy	hard	men	see	we
but	has	miss	seen	well
	have	money	she	went
came	he	more	short	what
can	help	most	six	when
car	her	mother	so	where
children	here	Mr.	some	which
come	high	must	something	who
could	him	my	soon	why
	his		still	will
day	home			with
days	house	name	table	work
did	how	never	than	
didn't		new	that	year
do		night	the	years
don't	I	no	then	yet
door	if	not	there	you
down	I'm	now	these	your
			these	

(Cont.)

FIGURE 6.1   Johnson's Basic Sight Word List (*Cont.*)

Johnson's Second-Grade Words

able	close	head	on	take
about	company	heard	only	tell
almost	cut		other	their
alone		idea	our	them
already	different		outside	thing
always	does	knew	own	things
America	done	know		thought
an		last	part	through
another	each	leave	party	together
any	early	left	people	told
around	enough	light	place	town
away	even	long	plan	turn
	ever		present	
because	every	made		until
been	eyes	many	real	us
believe		mean	road	use
best	face	might		used
better	far	morning	same	
between	feel	Mrs.	say	water
board	found	much	says	were
both	from	music	set	west
brought	front		should	while
by	full	need	show	whole
		next	small	whose
called	great	nothing	sometimes	wife
change	group	number	sound	women
church	hands	of	started	world
city	having	office	street	would
			sure	

SOURCE: From *Teaching Reading Vocabulary*, 2/e, by Dale D. Johnson & P. David Pearson. Copyright © 1984 by CBS College Publishing. Reprinted by permission of CBS College Publishing.

words were known by at least 65 percent of the second-grade subjects. Furthermore, 93 percent of the first-grade words and 87 percent of the second-grade words occurred in the first- and second-grade books of all five of the basal reading series that were studied. Thus, these words were known by a majority of beginning readers and are commonly found in beginning reading materials.

In general, students learn to recognize instantly these basic sight words without receiving special drill, simply through repeated contact when reading. However, some of these words are difficult to learn for low-achieving readers. Many of the words in Figure 6.1 are verbs and function words (prepositions, conjunctions, auxiliary and past tense verbs, relative pronouns) that do not carry a great deal of meaning by themselves. Many are not "high imagery" words. Low-achieving readers may need extra help in learning some of these high-frequency words as sight words.

General Method for Teaching Basic Sight Words

There has been a fair amount of controversy about whether it is best for beginning readers to learn sight words in context or isolation.[15] Ehri and Wilce (1980) concluded that there are benefits to both approaches. Students evidently learn more about the semantic features of words when they are exposed to them in context but learn more about their orthographic features when they are exposed to them in isolation. Consequently, Ehri and Wilce recommend that instruction in sight words include work with words in isolation and in meaningful contexts.

McNinch (1981) has developed a method for instructing low-achieving readers in sight words that includes teaching the word in both context and isolation. Teachers using this approach has reported it to be effective. This approach is particularly useful for low-achieving readers who have had difficulty learning high-frequency sight words, such as those on the Johnson Basic Sight Word list. Explicit instruction using McNinch's approach might look something like this.

How. First, the teacher presents the word to be learned in context, in an *oral* sentence. Then, the teacher reads the word to the students as they *see* it (on the chalkboard, overhead, or sentence strip) in the *written* context of one or more sentences or phrases. If possible, the other words in the sentences or phrases should also be in the students' sight reading vocabulary. (Initially, the "other" words might come from group language experience stories. See the section on language experience, later in this chapter.) The basic sight word being taught in each sentence or phrase should be highlighted by the teacher, such as by underlining or other methods.

Second, the word is written by the teacher in isolation on the board, the overhead, or the back of the sentence strip. The teacher then asks the students questions about it to focus their attention. For example:

What is the first letter?

What is the last letter?

How many letters are in the word?

Please spell the word.

Please trace the word.

Third, students practice reading the word in sentences or phrases. Again, as much as possible, all other words should already be a part of the students' reading vocabulary.

Fourth, students practice reading the word in actual text, such as in a book or a language experience chart or story. The teacher asks questions that require students to use the word in order to answer the questions. The teacher may also ask students to reread a sentence in the text containing the word.

Fifth, students engage in independent practice involving the word under study. Independent practice activities may include trying to find the word in other books or language experience stories or playing games using the word. Examples of activities that may be used for independent practice are provided below.

What, Why, and *When.* In addition to following the steps of the McNinch procedure, it is important for the teacher to explain to students *what* they will be learning; they will be learning how to read a word that they will often come across in text. The teacher should also explain *why* this is important; it is important to learn this word because it seems to be a difficult word for students to remember and because it shows up a lot in books. Finally, the teacher should explain *when* this will be helpful; for example, after practicing this word, students will be able to remember it and read it as they come across it again in their reading.

Activities to Provide Practice in Basic Sight Words

Once instruction has occurred using the approach just outlined, a teacher can engage students in practice activities such as these:

1. Direct the students to find additional examples of the word in books or language experience stories and to try to read the sentence that the word is in. Students may also want to look in magazines and newspapers. If the material is consumable, let the students underline the word with multicolored pens or make a collage of the word. Let the students make charts indicating the number of times they find a particular word.

2. Direct the students to read into a tape recorder a number of basic sight words they have been working on. The words should be written in isolation and in sentences on cards. Students can listen to what they have read while looking at the cards.

3. Direct the students to write basic sight words they have been working on in a manner that is somewhat engaging, such as typing them on the computer or writing them on the chalkboard. In this situation words should be written in the context of sentences or at least in phrases.

4. Allow the students to play games using a number of the basic sight words they have been working on. Games such as concentration, checkers, and bingo can be developed in ways that incorporate word recognition practice. Also, board games can be used in which a player goes x number of steps forward on a track if the player knows a basic sight word he or she has been practicing. With games, however, it is important that students be directed to actually read aloud the words they are trying to learn as they come across them in a game. In this way they actually are receiving practice in reading the words. Otherwise,

a student may be able to make a match in a concentration game, for example, by turning up "there" and "there" without being able to read the word. Also, in a game it is important that students practice basic sight words that they need to learn as opposed to ones that they already know.

5. Give the students a number of these "sight words" plus a number of other high imagery words. Let them write individual, partner, or small-group language experience stories using these words. Then they can share their stories with one another to provide added practice in reading these words in natural contexts.

Using Predictable Materials to Develop Students' Basic Sight Vocabulary

Bridge, Winograd, and Haley (1983) have developed a program for teaching basic sight words to beginning readers that makes use of predictable books and group language experience stories. Predictable books are stories with repetitive and/or predictable structures. A list of predictable books is presented in Figure 6.2. The pattern in this type of book provides good opportunities for students to practice reading high-frequency words. Students reading at a beginning primer level have been found to learn more basic sight words through this program than students in regular basal primer material. An example of instruction using predictable books follows.

First, the teacher reads a predictable book aloud to the students, then rereads it, encouraging them to join in as much as possible. The students take turns chorally reading the book with the teacher. The next day they again read the story which has now been reproduced on a chart. The purpose of this is to practice reading the story without the aid of pictures. The students are given sentence strips to place under the appropriate lines of the story on the chart. They are also given, in order, individual word cards which they place under the matching words on the chart. On the third day, the students read the story chorally from the chart. Word cards are placed in random order at the bottom of the chart, and students match the word cards with the words on the chart.

Group language experience stories can be used in the same manner except that on the first day, the teacher begins with a discussion of a particular topic. Next, students dictate a group language experience story on the topic, then the teacher and students reread the story together. A more detailed discussion of the language experience approach is presented later in this section.

Using Children's Literature to Develop Students' Basic Sight Vocabulary

Eeds (1985) developed a basic sight vocabulary list of 227 words based on 400 storybooks for beginning readers. The list, called Bookwords, consists of the

FIGURE 6.2   Predictable Books

Asch, Frank, *Just Like Daddy*. Prentice-Hall, 1981.
Barrett, Judi. *Animals Should Definitely Not Wear Clothing*. Atheneum, 1970.
Bayer, Jane. *A. My Name Is Alice*. Dial Books for Young Readers, 1984.
Brown, Margaret Wise. *The Friendly Book*. Western, 1954.
Brown, Margaret Wise. *Good Night Moon*. Harper and Row, 1947.
Burningham, John. *Mr. Gumpy's Outing*. Scholastic, 1970.
Cameron, Polly. *I Can't Said the Ant*. Coward, McCann, & Geoghehan, 1961.
Carl, Eric. *The Very Hungry Caterpillar*. Hamion Hamilton, 1970.
Charlip, Remy. *Fortunately*. Parents Magazine Press, 1971.
Crews, Donald. *Freight Train*. Greenwillow Books, 1978.
Crews, Donald. *School Bus*. Greenwillow Books, 1984.
DePaolo, Tomi. *The Comic Adventures of Old Mother Hubbard*. Harcourt Brace
    Jovanovich, 1981.
Emberly, Barbara. *Drummer Hoff*. Prentice-Hall, 1967.
Emberly, Barbara, and Emberly Ed. *One Wide River to Cross*. Scholastic, 1966.
Galdone, Paul. *The Three Billy Goats Gruff*. Seabury Press, 1973.
Ginsburg, Mirra. *The Chick and the Duckling*. Macmillan, 1972.
Graham, John. *I Love You Mouse*. Harcourt Brace Jovanovich, 1976.
Guilfoile, Elizabeth. *Nobody Listens to Andrew*. Scholastic, 1957.
Hoban, Tana. *Count and See*. Macmillan, 1972.
Krauss, Ruth. *A Hole Is to Dig*. Harper and Row, 1952.
Langstaff, John. *Over in the Meadow*. Harcourt Brace Jovanovich, 1957.
Martin Jr., Bill. *Brown Bear, Brown Bear*. Holt, Rinehart and Winston, 1967.
Mayer, Mercer. *Just for You*. Western, 1975.
Nodset, Joan. *Who Took the Farmer's Hat*. Scholastic, 1963.
O'Neill, Mary. *Hailstones and Halibut Bones*. Doubleday, 1961.
Patrick, Gloria. *A Bug in a Jug*. Scholastic, 1970.
Pearson, Tracey Campbell. *Old MacDonald Had a Farm*. Dial Books for Young
    Readers, 1984.
Peppe, Rodney. *The House That Jack Built*. Delacorte, 1970.
Shaw, Charles. *It Looked Like Spilt Milk*. Harper and Row, 1947.
Tolstoy, Alexei. *The Great Big Enormous Turnip*. Franklin Watts, 1968.
Zemach, Margot. *The Teeny Tiny Women*. Scholastic, 1965.

most frequently occurring words in the 400 books. The 227 words account for 73 percent of all running words in the 400-book sample. The Bookwords list is presented in Figure 6.3.

Eeds recommends that these high-frequency basic sight words be taught by reading and rereading children's books with students. A list of fifty recommended books from the 400-book sample is presented in Table 6.1. A number of the stories might be put on tape so students can listen and follow along. In addition, a small group of students can sit with the teacher and together read one of these books. The teacher can focus on a particular Bookword by leaving a blank for the word while reading aloud, pointing to the word, and asking the students to predict from context the missing word.

These students are sharing a predictable book. *(James Silliman)*

For independent practice, students can look through the book they have just read with the teacher to see how many times they can find one of the targeted Bookwords. They might also do this with other books that have been read earlier.

Reading and rereading children's books is an excellent way to teach basic sight words to low-achieving readers since the material, generally, will be more appealing to students than basal reader material. There is also the possibility that low-achieving readers, students who have already "failed" to some extent with traditional materials, will be motivated to learn through this approach.

Using Language Experience Stories to Develop Students' Basic Sight Vocabulary

The language experience approach to teaching reading involves an individual student or group of students dictating stories about topics of interest and then rereading the stories many times as practice reading material.[16] The language experience approach is a particularly effective way of helping low-achieving readers to develop a basic sight vocabulary for a number of reasons. First, the reading material is interesting to the students because they have created the stories themselves. Second, the stories provide material that low-achieving readers who are older can and will read because, unlike much of the basal

FIGURE 6.3   Bookwords: Final core 227-word list based on 400 storybooks for beginning readers

the	1334	good	90	think	47	next	28
and	985	this	90	new	46	only	28
a	831	don't	89	know	46	*am	27
I	757	little	89	help	46	began	27
to	746	if	87	grand	46	head	27
said	688	just	87	boy	46	keep	27
you	638	*baby	86	take	45	*teacher	27
he	488	way	85	eat	44	*sure	27
it	345	there	83	*body	43	*says	27
in	311	every	83	school	43	*ride	27
was	294	went	82	house	42	*pet	27
she	250	father	80	morning	42	*hurry	26
for	235	had	79	*yes	41	hand	26
that	232	see	79	after	41	hard	26
is	230	dog	78	never	41	*push	26
his	226	home	77	or	40	our	26
but	224	down	76	*self	40	their	26
they	218	got	73	try	40	*watch	26
my	214	would	73	has	38	*because	25
of	204	time	71	*always	38	door	25
on	192	*love	70	over	38	us	25
me	187	walk	70	again	37	*should	25
all	179	came	69	side	37	*room	25
be	176	were	68	*thank	37	*put	25
go	171	ask	67	why	37	*great	24
can	162	back	67	who	36	gave	24
with	158	now	66	saw	36	*does	24
one	157	friend	65	*mom	35	*car	24
her	156	cry	64	*kid	35	*ball	24
what	152	oh	64	give	35	*sat	24
we	151	Mc	63	around	34	*stay	24
him	144	*bed	63	by	34	*each	23
no	143	an	62	Mrs.	34	*ever	23
so	141	very	62	off	33	*until	23
out	140	where	60	*sister	33	*shout	23
up	137	play	59	find	32	*mama	22
are	133	let	59	*fun	32	*use	22
will	127	long	58	more	32	turn	22
look	126	here	58	while	32	thought	22
some	123	how	57	tell	32	*papa	22
day	123	make	57	*sleep	32	*lot	21
at	122	big	56	made	131	*blue	21
have	121	from	55	first	31	*bath	21
your	121	put	55	say	31	*mean	21
mother	119	*read	55	took	31	*sit	21
come	118	them	55	*dad	30	*together	21

FIGURE 6.3 Bookwords: Final core 227-word list based on 400 storybooks for beginning readers (*Cont.*)

not	115	as	54	found	30	*best	20
like	112	*Miss	53	*lady	30	*brother	20
then	108	any	52	soon	30	*feel	20
get	103	right	52	ran	30	*floor	20
when	101	*nice	50	*dear	29	wait	20
thing	100	other	50	man	29	*tomorrow	20
do	99	well	48	*better	29	*surprise	20
too	91	old	48	*through	29	*shop	20
want	91	*night	48	stop	29	run	20
did	91	may	48	still	29	*own	20
could	90	about	47	*fast	28		

*Indicates words not on Durr list.
SOURCE: From Bookwords: Using a Beginning Word List of High Frequency Words from Children's Literature K–3, by Maryann Eeds, *The Reading Teacher*, January 1985. Reprinted with permission of Maryann Eeds and the International Reading Association.

primer material, it is not too immature for them. Third, students feel good about using this material because they are generally proud of their stories and usually can reread them fairly successfully. Fourth, the use of language experience stories is often perceived as "something different" by older low-achieving readers and therefore novel enough to motivate them.

Language experience stories may be dictated by a group of students or by an individual. We have found that individual dictations are particularly motivating to students because they are extremely proud of and interested in their "very own" stories.

In using the language experience approach, the teacher first engages the student or group in a brief discussion about a topic for a story, such as "How I spend my free time" or "My favorite TV show." Second, the teacher takes down the story exactly as it is dictated, since it is important for the students to feel successful, which may not be the case if the teacher alters or corrects a story as it is being dictated. It is also important to keep the dictated story short at first. If students are nonreaders, two or three sentences are enough. If the story gets very long, the children will not be able to "reread" the story and consequently will not feel successful. Third, the teacher rereads the story orally, tracking or running her hand under the words as they are read. Fourth, the teacher helps the individual or group reread the story orally several times. Finally, each story is put into a collection of language experience stories which students continue to reread both orally and silently as practice reading material. This is an important part of the approach that is often neglected. Beginning readers need to practice rereading familiar, manageable material, and their language experience stories provide an enjoyable source of such material.

TABLE 6.1   Fifty Books for a Good Beginning

Author and Title	Total Words	Total Number of Different Words	Percentage of Running Words Relative to Bookwords	Percentage of Different Words Relative to Bookwords
Bancheck, Linda. *Snake In, Snake Out*	38	8	100	100
Barton, Byron. *Where's Al?*	34	18	82	89
Ginsberg, Mirra. *The Chick and the Duckling*	112	30	75	67
Burningham, John. *The Blanket*	66	33	86	85
Burningham, John. *The Friend*	51	34	86	88
Asch, Frank. *Yellow, Yellow*	97	47	70	62
Burningham, John. *The Dog*	69	48	77	69
Browne, Anthony. *Bear Hunt*	83	52	62	75
Kraus, Robert. *Whose Mouse Are You?*	108	54	77	76
Ets, Marie Hall. *Elephant in a Well*	286	56	71	64
Alexander, Martha. *Blackboard Bear*	128	62	78	70
de Paola, Tomie. *The Knight and the Dragon*	129	65	70	66
Kraus, Robert. *Leo the Late Bloomer*	166	70	68	67
Breinburg, Petronella. *Shawn Goes to School*	132	75	83	77

TABLE 6.1   Fifty Books for a Good Beginning (*Cont.*)

Author and Title	Total Words	Total Number of Different Words	Percentage of Running Words Relative to Bookwords	Percentage of Different Words Relative to Bookwords
Mayer, Mercer. *There's a Nightmare in My Closet*	142	76	76	68
Buckley, Helen. *Grandfather and I*	291	79	90	70
Bornstein, Ruth. *Little Gorilla*	173	80	72	63
Brown, Margaret Wise. *The Runaway Bunny*	441	83	81	57
Burningham, John. *Come Away from the Water, Shirley*	129	86	74	65
Asch, Frank. *Rebecka*	203	88	87	80
Asch, Frank. *Elvira Everything*	183	92	81	73
Burningham, John. *Mr. Gumpy's Outing*	289	95	73	62
Wells, Rosemary. *Noisy Nora*	206	101	68	55
Hutchins, Pat. *The Surprise Party*	336	101	76	68
Udry, Janice. *Let's Be Enemies*	229	102	73	68
Clifton, Lucille. *Everett Anderson's Goodbye*	200	104	76	64
Bradenburg, Fritz. *I Wish I Was Sick Too*	327	107	68	63

(Cont.)

TABLE 6.1   Fifty Books for a Good Beginning (*Cont.*)

Author and Title	Total Words	Total Number of Different Words	Percentage of Running Words Relative to Bookwords	Percentage of Different Words Relative to Bookwords
de Paola, Tomie. *Watch Out for Chicken Feet in Your Soup*	254	107	68	63
Alexander, Martha. *Move Over, Twerp*	245	111	78	72
LaFontaine (Wildsmith). *The North Wind and the Sun*	210	113	70	59
Kellogg, Steven. *Pinkerton Behave*	233	116	65	56
Barton, Byron. *Jack and Fred*	263	118	80	72
Flack, Marjorie. *Ask Mr. Bear*	632	119	77	68
Asch, Frank. *MacGoose's Grocery*	322	123	76	70
Lionni, Leo. *Little Blue and Little Yellow*	284	123	81	71
Griffith, Helen. *Mine Will Said John*	506	124	70	69
Boynton, Sandra. *Hester in the Wild*	283	124	75	61
Sendak, Maurice. *Where the Wild Things Are*	350	129	70	57
Allard, Harry. *The Stupids Die*	296	140	55	61
Keats, Ezra Jack. *Googles*	336	139	66	62

TABLE 6.1   Fifty Books for a Good Beginning (*Cont.*)

Author and Title	Total Words	Total Number of Different Words	Percentage of Running Words Relative to Bookwords	Percentage of Different Words Relative to Bookwords
Hoban, Russell. *The Stone Doll of Sister Brute.*	494	143	73	65
Sharmat, Marjorie. *I Don't Care*	451	147	74	65
Keats, Ezra Jack. *Whistle for Willie*	391	149	78	69
Asch, Frank. *Sand Cake*	443	153	71	63
Delton, Judy. *New Girl in School*	379	158	80	60
Burningham, John. *Avocado Baby*	373	160	73	60
Allard, Harry. *The Stupids Step Out*	413	176	68	59
Cohen, Miriam. *Will I Have a Friend?*	464	177	74	63
Dauer, Rosamond. *Bullfrog Grows Up*	627	204	75	61
Marshall, James. *George and Martha*	645	210	75	68

SOURCE: From Bookwords: Using a Beginning Word List of High Frequency Words from Children's Literature K–3, by Maryann Eeds, *The Reading Teacher,* January 1985. Reprinted with permission of Maryann Eeds and the International Reading Association.

An individual's collection of language experience stories can be used to reinforce basic sight words upon which the teacher has been focusing. For example, if the teacher has been helping students learn the basic sight word *there*, students can read through their language experience stories to see how many times they can find examples of this word. The word can be underlined each time it is found and the number of times a word is found can be entered on a chart.

It is inevitable that language experience stories will include many of the basic sight words precisely because these words are such an important part of any communication act, be it oral or written. To demonstrate how many basic

FIGURE 6.4   Language Experience Stories by a Third-Grade Student

My Summer Vacation

I went for a ride. I rode my new bike.
I went to church. I played a game.
Me and my mom went to the beach.
I played ball. I got hot.

Yellow

Yellow makes me feel like I am by the
sun. Yellow smells like trees blowing
in the wind. Yellow smells like a field
of flowers.

Air Pollution

Some days it is a nice fresh day or it
can be one of the pollution days. It
can get in your lungs and make you sick.
It can sting your eyes. Pollution is a
very bad thing for people.

sight words can be found in just a few short language experience stories, Figure 6.4 shows three stories created by a third-grade student reading on a first-grade level. Out of a total of 103 words, these three stories contain 35 different basic sight words and 70 basic sight words in all from the 306 words on the Johnson Basic Sight Vocabulary List.[17]

Using Phonic Analysis

Phonic analysis is an essential decoding tool. Segmenting a word into parts, attaching appropriate sounds to these parts, and blending the parts together is one of the primary strategies a reader should use to attack a word not instantly known at sight. Furthermore, research has demonstrated consistently that systematic, intensive phonics instruction is beneficial.[18]

Although phonic analysis is extremely useful, it also can be confusing to a beginning reader for a number of reasons. The English language has fifty-two symbols, approximately forty-four sounds, and several hundred symbol-sound relationships (Mazurkiewicz, 1976). These numbers point out a major problem with phonic analysis, that there is considerable irregularity or unpredictability in symbol-sound correspondences. For example, the symbol *a* has a different sound in each of these words: *bad, aloud, take, want, ball, park.* Students may become overwhelmed and confused if they are taught too many symbol-sound correspondences. They simply cannot remember several hundred of them. Later in this section a list of symbol-sound correspondences is presented which are most beneficial to teach because they are the most common and useful.

Another problem with phonic analysis is that there are very few phonics rules that occur with enough regularity to warrant teaching as rules. Clymer (1963) carried out a study on the utility of phonic rules in primary grade reading material. Bailey (1967) Burmeister (1968), and Emans (1967) performed similar studies. These studies all suggest that some phonics rules that are frequently taught to students are misleading if taught as hard-and-fast rules because there are so many exceptions. For example, Clymer found that the double vowel rule (when two vowels are together, the first one is long and the second is silent) held only 45 percent of the time. He found that the silent *e* rule (when there are two vowels, one of which is a final *e*, the first vowel is long and the *e* is silent) held only 63 percent of the time.

Therefore, symbol-sound correspondences involving vowels should not be taught as infallible rules. Instead, children should be taught to be flexible when trying to come up with the appropriate sound for a vowel or vowel pair. For example, students may be taught that a good sound to try first when decoding a word with the CVCE (consonant, vowel, consonant, silent *e* pattern) pattern is the long sound of the vowel. However, if students do not come up with a word that makes sense, they should be flexible and try another sound for the vowel, such as the short sound (for example, *live*).

There are two basic approaches to teaching phonics, an explicit approach and an implicit approach, sometimes called synthetic and analytic approaches.[19] In an explicit approach, the sounds of individual letters in words are identified and blended together (/c/, /a/, /t/, *cat*). In an implicit approach, sounds of letters are never pronounced in isolation and consequently, blending is not stressed (for example, *c* makes the sound that is heard at the beginning of *cut*, *a* makes the sound that is heard at the beginning of *at*, and *t* makes the sound that is heard at the beginning of *toy*, *cat*). Research suggests that an explicit approach to phonics instruction may be superior to an implicit approach.[20] As pointed out earlier in this chapter, skill in phonemic segmentation and blending have been found to differentiate good and poor readers. Also, students receiving extra instruction in blending have been found to make superior gains on beginning reading achievement tests.[21]

Based on this research, we cautiously support an approach to phonics instruction that focuses on segmenting and sounding word parts and then blending the parts together. It is important that sounds of individual letters not be distorted, such as /cuh/ /ah/ /tuh/ for *cat*. One way to minimize this problem is to say individual sounds as quickly as possible as opposed to drawing them out. Another approach is to include in blending instruction and practice only that subset of consonants whose sounds can be "continued" as they are pronounced. For example, the sounds of *s*, *z*, *sh*, *f*, *v*, *m*, *n*, and *r* can be continued indefinitely. By contrast, the consonant stops in our language can only be pronounced if some vowel sound is added to them. Common stops are *b*, *p*, *d*, *g*, *t*, *k*, and *c*. After sounding and blending instruction with the continuants occurring in initial consonant positions, as in CVC patterns, the teacher hopes that the sounding and blending strategy transfers to stops without specific instruction and practice.

In spite of the problems with sounding out word parts and blending the sounds together, instruction in sounding and blending is useful if applied to the decoding of words that are causing students problems in actual text. Many low-achieving readers may have learned the basic symbol-sound correspondences in isolation but may need help in applying this knowledge to the reading of connected text. In other words, they need to learn how to break a word into parts, sound out the parts, and blend the parts together to come up with a word that makes sense in context. But there is one thing a teacher always needs to remember about "heavy duty" decoding instruction, such as blending: Once you get the children into it, you have got to get them out of it. Children need to become rapid, automatic decoders. Blending, like other decoding skills and strategies, is only a means to an end, not an end in itself. The real "end" to decoding instruction is comprehension. In the remainder of this section, strategies are discussed that help students learn symbol-sound correspondences and help them apply this knowledge to the decoding of unfamiliar words in text.

General Method for Teaching Symbol-Sound Correspondences   A problem with many of the teaching suggestions and materials currently available for teaching symbol-sound correspondences is that they direct students to move from sound to symbol instead of from symbol to sound. For example, students are often presented with a set of pictures and instructed to write down the letter representing the beginning sound of each picture. Skill in activities such as this, however, provides no assurance that students are also skilled in coming up with the appropriate sound when they see a particular symbol. Therefore, instruction and practice in phonics should proceed as much as possible from symbol to sound instead of from sound to symbol. Examples of this type of instruction and practice will be provided in the following pages.

As mentioned earlier, it is important to limit the number of symbol-sound correspondences that are emphasized in instruction to avoid overwhelming and frustrating students. Some correspondences are so confusing and complex that they are best avoided altogether. For example, attempting to teach students all of the different sounds for the symbol *ou* will not be fruitful (for example, *ounce, cousin, ought, soup, would, though*); readers are not going to take the time to recall all of these different sounds when trying to decode an unfamiliar word containing *ou*. Other correspondences may be highly predictable, but they apply to so few words that instruction in them seems pointless. There simply are not enough examples to which they apply (for example, *o* followed by *ld* has the long sound). Time and effort should be directed to a relatively small number of symbol-sound correspondences that are most common. A recommended list is presented in Figure 6.5.

FIGURE 6.5   Common Symbol-Sound Correspondences

Consonants   b, d, f, h, j, k, l, m, n, p, qu, r, s, t, v, w, x, y, z
    c as in can, come, cut
    c as in cent, city, cycle
    g as in game, gone, gum
    g as in gem, ginger, gym

Blends   bl, br, cl, cr, dr, dw, fl, fr, gl, gr, ld, mp, nd, ng, nk, nt, pl, pr, rk, sc, sk, sl, sm, sn, sp, st, sw, tr, tw, wr, sch, shr, spl, spr, squ, str, thr

Digraphs   ch, ph, sh, th (think, then), wh (which, who)

Vowels
    Short sounds: a (hat), e (bed), i (sit), o (not), u (run)

    Long sounds: a (cake), e (here), i (bite), o (hope), u (cute)

    R-controlled: ar (far), er (her), ir (fir), or (for), ur (fur)

    L-controlled: al (ball)

    Vowel pairs: ai (rain), ay (day), au (author), aw (law), ea (meat), ea (head), ee (feet), ei (weight), ei (receive), ew (few), oa (boat), oi (boil), oo (book), oo (food), ou (cloud), ow (slow), ow (now), oy (toy)

To teach the symbol-sound correspondence for a consonant, blend, or digraph, follow the steps listed below:

1. *What.* Explain what the students will be learning. They will be learning what sound to try when they come across a difficult word, or word not known instantly, containing a particular consonant, blend, or digraph.

2. *Why.* Explain why this is important. This is important because if students have to decode a difficult word that contains this letter or letters, they will need to know what sound to try out for the letter.

3. *How.* Provide instruction in the symbol-sound correspondence. Write two or three examples of words containing the consonant, blend, or digraph on the board (for example, *sun, sing, sad*). If possible, these initial examples should come from words that the students already know or from familiar reading material, like language experience stories. Ask the students to tell you what letter or letters the words have in common, then read the words or ask the students to read them. Ask the students if the letter under study (*s*) has the same sound in all of

the words. Identify the letter sound (/s/) and explain that this is the usual sound for this letter or cluster of letters. Have the students write the two or three examples on a piece of paper. Do not worry about their spelling of other parts of the word; monitor to see if the target correspondence is spelled correctly.

4. *Provide guided practice.* Ask the students if they can think of any more words beginning with the same sound as the letter under study (*s*) to add to the list (*Susan, summer*). Write these words on the board and have the students add them to their list. Also, accept words that have the same sound but are not spelled with that letter. For example, when teaching the sound of *s*, students might suggest words such as *cent* and *cider*. When this occurs, congratulate the one student for getting the right sound, show the students how to spell the word, and tell them that you will study that sound later. To give the students practice going from symbol to sound, write a few more words on the board (*silly, song, soap*). Pronounce all but the initial letter for them (*illy, ong, oap*), and ask them to blend the initial sound and the rest of the word together to come up with each whole word. Have students add these new words to their list. To provide students with practice in reading all of the words on their list, make up oral sentences in which a word is missing. Ask the students to point to the correct word from their list that would fit in the blank in the sentence ("The _____ is shining." "I will _____ a _____." "That is a _____ thing to do." "The boy felt _____.").

5. *When.* Explain when students should use what they have learned as they are reading on their own. If they are trying to decode a word that contains this letter (*s*), they should remember the sound of the letter (/s/), and use this sound when trying to sound out the word. Illustrate this by sounding out several words beginning with *s* in actual text. The text might be a language experience story, a story recently read by the students, or a short paragraph containing a number of *s* words.

6. *Provide for independent practice.* Students should try to apply their new symbol-sound correspondence knowledge to the reading of connected text or engage in a gamelike activity using this knowledge. Suggestions for independent practice are presented later in this section.

The steps for teaching the symbol-sound correspondences for vowels or vowel pairs are similar to the steps described above. However, a few modifications should be made. To teach the symbol-sound correspondences for vowels or vowel pairs, follow this sequence of activities:

1. *What.* Explain what the students will be learning. They will be learning

what sound or sounds to try when they come across a difficult word containing a particular vowel or vowel pair.

2. *Why.* Explain why this is important: This is important because if students have to figure out a difficult word which contains this vowel or vowel pair, they will need to know what sound or sounds to try out.

3. *How.* Provide instruction in the symbol-sound correspondence. Write two or three examples of words containing the vowel or vowel pair (*fat, sad, band*) on the board. Read the words to the students or ask them to read the words. Have them copy the words on a piece of paper. Ask students to tell you what letter or letters the words have in common and ask them if the letter being studied (*a*) has the same sound in all of the words. Identify the sound of the vowel or vowel pair (/a/). Explain that this is one common sound they might try to use when they have to decode a difficult word containing the letter being studied (*a*), particularly when the word has a particular spelling pattern (for example, a CVC or CVCC pattern).

4. *Provide guided practice.* Write several more examples on the board (*tap, black, fast*). Ask students to decode these and then add them to their list. It is best to give students more examples here instead of asking them to come up with examples because a particular vowel sound can be spelled in different ways (*laugh* has the "short *a*" sound). Provide the students with oral sentences in which a word is missing and ask them to point to the correct word from their list that would fit in the blank.

   The teacher may want to work with phonograms to generate more words with the vowel sound under study. A phonogram is a common spelling pattern consisting of a vowel followed by one or more consonants (*-at, -ike, -and, -ight*). After discussing one symbol-sound correspondence for the letter *a*, the teacher might work with the *-at* phonogram. He or she might show students the word *cat*, write *fat* below it, and ask the students the word. This procedure could be followed with the examples *bat, sat,* and *pat.* Next, the teacher and students could try to generate as many words as possible from the *-ad* phonogram. A list of common phonograms is provided in Figure 6.6.

5. *When.* Explain when students should use what they have learned as they are reading on their own. If they are trying to decode a word that contains this vowel (*a*), they should remember that one good sound to try, particularly when the word has a particular pattern (CVC), would be the sound they have just worked on ("short *a*"). Illustrate this by decoding several "short *a*" words in actual text (language experience story, basal story, paragraph containing "short *a*" words).

FIGURE 6.6   List of Common Phonograms

ack	ay	id	ite
ad	eat	ide	ock
ade	ed	ight	old
ake	eed	ike	ook
all	eel	ill	op
ame	eep	im	ot
an	eet	in	uck
and	ell	ine	ud
ang	en	ing	un
ar	eat	ink	ung
at	et	ip	up
ate	ick	it	ut

6. *Provide independent practice in the vowel or vowel pair under study.* Suggestions are listed later in this section.

Once two sounds for one vowel or vowel pair have been introduced ("short *a*," "long *a*"), it is important to compare words containing the same vowel or vowel pair but different vowel sounds. For example, after receiving instruction in the short sound of *a* (as is usually found in words following the CVC pattern), and the long sound of *a* (as is often found in words following the CVCe pattern), a student needs practice in distinguishing between these two sounds for the symbol *a*. To do this the teacher and students might start with a list of ten words containing the letter *a*. The students would decode the words, with the teacher's help if necessary, and write them under the appropriate category, "short *a*" or "long *a*." Then, to reinforce this comparison in the context of

FIGURE 6.7   Example of Short Modified Cloze Passages to Be Used as a Practice Phonics Activity for the Symbol-Sound Correspondence for *ea*

First _____ is ground into flour. Then it is sold to a bakery. The flour is mixed with other things until it is _____ for baking. The _____ is baked and then sold to a food store.

Every winter Indians trapped _____ . They sold the thick, brown furs to men from France. In the 1600s and 1700s people in France wanted _____ coats to keep them warm and _____ hats for their _____ . This was a sign of _____ _____ .

bread	*heads*	*wheat*	*beaver*	*ready*	*wealth*	*real*
meat	*beavers*	*seal*	*seals*			

sentences, students might use these words to fill in blanks in oral sentences or written sentences. An example is provided in Figure 6.7.

It is also useful for the teacher to direct students' attention to minimal pair contrasts; in this case, words that differ only in terms of the presence or absence of the final silent *e* (*man, mane; cap, cape*). The teacher might work with the students on fill-in-the-blank activities such as "The _____ (man, mane) put his _____ (cap, cape) on his head." In this situation students have to attend to the presence or absence of the feature *e*, which distinguishes *man* from *mane*, in order to fill in the blank correctly.

When comparing words with the same vowel symbol but different vowel sounds, it is important for the teacher to stress to the students the notion of flexibility. That is, when trying to decode an unfamiliar word containing the letter *a*, the students should remember that the word might have the "short *a*" sound or the "long *a*" sound. If the word follows the CVC pattern, a good sound to try first would be the "short *a*" sound. If the word follows the CVCe pattern, a good sound to try first would be the "long *a*" sound. In multisyllabic words, students might try a second sound for *a* if the first sound does not work. What is important for students to remember is that if first attempts at decoding produces a word that does not make sense, they should be flexible and try to decode the word again using another *a* sound.

To help students apply this notion of flexibility, the teacher should be consistent when helping students with decoding during oral or silent reading. For example, after a student has finished reading aloud a page, in which he or she read *luke* for *look*, the teacher could point out the sensibility of this error, and ask the student if she could think of another sound to use for *oo* when decoding *look*. If that does not help, the teacher should offer the student a meaning clue such as, "It means to see." Or, if a student has asked for help with the word *bread*, the teacher should ask the student if he or she could think of two common sounds for *ea* or, if necessary, provide words already known to the student such as *head* and *meat*. The teacher should remind the student to try each sound, "short *e*" and "long *e*," when attempting to decode *bread*.

One common type of phonics lesson or practice activity involving vowels or vowel pairs is the comparison of words with the same vowel sound but different vowel symbols. This type of comparison is useful for spelling but not for reading. When trying to spell *plate*, it is useful for students to know that the "long *a*" sound might be spelled with the CVCe pattern (*plate*), or with *ay* (*playt*), or with *ai* (*plait*). They can try these different symbols in their attempt to come up with the correct spelling. However, it is not useful for students to know that the "long *a*" sound is represented by *ay* and *ai* as well as the CVCe pattern when they are trying to decode *display*. Therefore, it is more useful for students to engage in reading instruction or practice activities in which they compare words with the same vowel symbol but different vowel sounds. The reverse would be true when providing students with instruction or practice in spelling. Teachers sometimes mix instruction in a way that confuses students on this important concept.

This section is about strategies for helping students learn symbol-sound correspondences. In a later section entitled, "Using a General Word Recognition Strategy," techniques for helping students apply this phonic knowledge to the reading of actual text will be examined more clearly.

Using Key Words and Pictures to Learn Symbol-Sound Correspondences   In several studies, teaching students mnemonics to help them learn symbol-sound correspondences has been found to be effective.[22] Ehri, Deffner, and Wilce (1984) found that picture mnemonics, in which the letter to be learned is highlighted in a picture of a word (for example, a *g* is highlighted in a picture of a pair of glasses), is particularly effective in terms of helping young children learn symbol-sound correspondences. For students having difficulty learning the symbol-sound correspondences for consonants or "short" vowel sounds, the following procedure, similar to that developed by Ehri, Deffner and Wilce, might be used.

The teacher gives students a work sheet containing the letter to be learned and a corresponding picture. Examples of pictures for the different letters of the alphabet are presented in Figure 6.8. The teacher says the name of the picture, explains that is begins with the letter _____, and points out the letter in the picture. The word is segmented into its component sounds and, consequently, the sound of the letter under study is isolated and pronounced. The teacher explains to the students that when they are trying to decode a difficult word containing this letter and they cannot remember its sound, they should think of the picture and the sound it starts with to help them remember the sound the letter makes. Students trace the picture on the work sheet, draw the picture freehand next to the picture, and then try to draw the picture from memory. In all instances of drawing, the shape of the letter should be emphasized.

Vowel sounds often seem to be particularly difficult for poor readers or beginning readers to learn.[23] It is not surprising that symbol-sound correspondences for vowels or vowel pairs are more difficult to learn than for consonants; single vowels and many vowel pairs have more than one sound, which generally is not the case for consonants. The key-word-picture approach described above may not be as effective with vowels or vowel pairs as with consonants for the reason that vowels and many vowel pairs have more than one sound. Therefore, it may be useful to provide students who are having considerable difficulty remembering vowel sounds with an alternative set of pictures and key words for the vowel sounds causing them difficulty. For example, the "short *a*" sound might be represented by the word *bat* and a picture of a bat. The difference between this and the above approach is that the letter(s) is not incorporated into the picture. These vowels, key words, and pictures can be listed on individual charts to which students can refer when attempting to decode difficult words while reading. Examples of key words and pictures for the

FIGURE 6.8   Picture Mnemonics for the Letters of the Alphabet

a	apple	
b	ball and bat	
c	caterpillar	
d	duck	
e	elephant	
f	flower	
g	glasses	
h	house	
i	igloo	
j	jam	
k	kite	
l	lamp	
m	monkey	
n	nest	
o	octopus	
p	puppy	
q	queen	
r	rose	
s	snake	
t	tree	
u	umbrella	

(Cont.)

FIGURE 6.8   Picture Mnemonics for the Letters of the Alphabet (*Cont.*)

v	vase	
w	wings	
x	"exit" sign	
y	yellow (colored in yellow)	
z	zzz (a person snoring)	

"long" and "short" vowel sounds and the most common vowel pair sounds are presented in Figure 6.9.

Activities to Provide Practice in Symbol-Sound Correspondences

Independent activities that might be used to provide students with necessary practice in using symbol-sound correspondences just learned include the following:

1. Direct the students to teach the newly learned symbol-sound correspondence to someone else. Even if these "students" already know the correct sound for the symbol under consideration, it will be useful for them to go through the steps of teaching the symbol-sound correspondence.

2. Have the students complete a modified cloze passage in which several words containing one or more recently learned symbol-sound correspondences are provided after each blank. Or, a list of words containing the symbol-sound correspondences could be provided at the bottom of the page. An example of the type of activity described was presented in Figure 6.7. In any fill-in-the-blank type activity it is important that students be given some incorrect and potentially confusing distractions in which they will have to come up with the correct sound for the symbol in order to fill in the blank correctly, such as "I _____ (hat, hate) to wash dishes, most of all the frying _____ (pan, pain)."

3. Let the students play a game such as bingo, concentration, rummy, or a track game. The words to be read aloud in order to advance in the game should be words containing the symbol-sound correspondence to be practiced. The cautions about games which were made in the section about basic sight words also apply to symbol-sound correspondence activities.

FIGURE 6.9   Key Words and Pictures for Vowels and Vowel Pairs

a	ă	(bat	)	or	ā	(cake	)
e	ĕ	(bell	)	or	ē	(me	)
i	ĭ	(six	)	or	ī	(five	)
o	ŏ	(sock	)	or	ō	(Coke	)
u	ŭ	(sun	)	or	ū	(cube	)
ea	ea	(head	)	or	ea	(meat	)
oa	oa	(boat	)				
oo	oo	(school	)	or	oo	(foot	)
ow	ow	(cow	)	or	ow	(snow	)
oi	oi	(oil	)				
oy	oy	(boy	)				
ee	ee	(feet	)				
ai	ai	(rain	)				
ou	ou	(house	)				

4. Let students look through old magazines to find pictures of words containing the symbol-sound correspondence under consideration. Students can make a collage of these pictures. The teacher can help the students label their pictures with letters and/or words in order to emphasize the symbol-sound correspondence.

5. Direct the students to find examples of the symbol-sound correspondence in old language experience stories or in stories they have recently read. Students may want to make a chart to keep a record of the number of examples they found on a particular day.

Good examples of phonics games and other activities for practicing with symbol-sound correspondences are provided in Johnson and Pearson (1984).

Learning to Segment, Sound, and Blend Phonemes   The ability to break a word into individual phonemes, or sounds, and blend the sounds together into a word are important reading skills. In a number of studies, high correlations between phonemic analysis and synthesis skills and beginning reading achievement have been found.[24] Furthermore, Williams (1980) has demonstrated that training in phonemic analysis and syntheses contributes to success in beginning reading.

Williams (1980) has developed a supplemental decoding program, called the ABD's of reading (for analysis, blending, and decoding) which has been used successfully to improve the decoding skills of beginning level, learning disabled readers, ranging in age from seven to twelve. A description of this technique follows:

How. First, the students are taught how to aurally analyze words at the syllable level. The students are shown how to tell what syllable occurs in the initial, middle, and final positions in a three-syllable word. Syllables are represented by individual wooden (or cardboard) squares, something that becomes important later in the program as individual sounds of specific letters are represented by squares. Then, students are shown how to aurally analyze two- and three-letter units at the phoneme level. At this point, individual phonemes are represented by individual squares. Students are shown how to break CV and CVC units into individual phonemes. Next, students are shown how to blend two- and three-phoneme CVC units together. CV-C units are blended first, followed by C-VC units, and finally C-V-C units.

After the above auditory analysis and synthesis work, symbol-sound correspondences for a small number of consonants (seven) and vowels (two) are taught. Then, students are shown how to combine the analysis and syntheses skills with this symbol-sound correspondence knowledge to decode CVC units. Letters are now written on the individual squares and students manipulate and decode all the possible CVC combinations from the seven consonants and two vowels.

After the initial analysis, blending, and decoding instruction, five new consonants and one new vowel are introduced. By manipulating the squares, students practice decoding as many CVC units as possible from the fifteen letters. They then practice decoding CCVC, CVCC, and CCVCC units. Finally, they practice decoding two-syllable patterns (for example, CVCCVC).

The content of the ABD program is taught in twelve units. For each unit the teacher demonstrates the task to be learned, then has students perform the task with other examples. To help students focus on context, words are used in sentences or are identified as nonsense words by the teacher and students. The real words are also used in simple comprehension activities and games. A more detailed description of this extensive program can be found in Williams (1979).

What, Why and *When.* It is important for the teacher to explain to students the purpose of such a decoding program. Repeatedly, the teacher should explain *what* students are doing this for: They are learning how to sound and blend simple words and nonsense words by manipulating squares. The teacher should explain *why* this is important: It will teach them how to sound and blend real words they come across when reading. In real reading, meaningfulness will help them decide whether or not the words they sound out are correct. The teacher should explain *when* they would use this as they are reading on their own: When they come to a difficult word, they should break it into individual sounds and blend the sounds back together, just as they have learned to do with the letters on the squares.

Because this program deals to a great extent with words in isolation, it should be used as a supplemental decoding program (as intended) for students reading on a primer, first-, or second-grade level. The program is useful because it teaches students more than symbol-sound correspondences; it teaches them how to apply this knowledge, through phonemic analysis and blending, to the decoding of words.

Learning to Segment, Sound, and Blend Word Parts in Multisyllabic Words

In a recent study of third-, fourth-, and sixth-grade students' decoding ability, Durkin (1984c) found that the students lacked any organized strategy for attacking difficult words and that their syllabication and blending skills were inadequate. She concluded that intermediate grade readers need more instruction in syllabication and blending to provide them with a set of organized skills for attacking difficult multisyllabic words.

Providing students with instruction and practice in formal syllabication is not recommended. Intensive drill in segmenting large quantities of words in isolation (as the dictionary would segment them), following formal syllabication rules, does not seem very useful. However, students do need to develop strategies for breaking longer words into smaller parts, or approximate syllables, so they can sound out these units and blend them together. Doing this will not be very useful, however, if applied to words that are not in a reader's listening vocabulary. In the case of low-achieving readers whose listening vocabularies often exceed decoding ability, students may be able to decode multisyllabic words if they are able to segment them into approximate syllables, sound out the syllables, and blend the syllables together. Therefore, the teacher should follow the strategy discussed below to teach students how to decode multisyllabic words.

How. The teacher should explain to students that a longer word is made up of syllables, usually with one vowel or vowel pair in each syllable. To segment a word into approximate syllables, students should break the word between the vowel and following consonant or between two consonants if there are two consonants together. If the syllable ends in a consonant, a good sound to try first when sounding out the syllable is the short vowel sound. If the syllable ends in a vowel, a good sound to try first when sounding out the syllable is the long vowel sound, but there is a good chance that the vowel might have a short sound. Following these guidelines, students should try to segment and sound out the syllables in difficult words they come across in actual reading material. After saying a word slowly at first, they should try to say it again more quickly and see if the attempted pronunciation helps them think of a word that makes sense in the context of the passage. If students cannot think of a word, they should be flexible and try to sound out each syllable again, this time giving some of the vowels different sounds.

What, *Why*, and *When*. The teacher should explain *what* the students will be learning to do and *why* this is important: They will be learning a strategy to use when they have to figure out a difficult, longer word. This is important because is will enable them to pronounce big words on their own without any help. The teacher should model the above procedure with several multisyllabic words in material that the students are currently reading. For guided practice the teacher and students should work through several other examples from the students' current reading assignment. The teacher can also instruct students to write down troublesome words and their page numbers during silent reading. The students should attempt to use the above procedure with these words. Also, at some later time the teacher can help students decode these words.

Another simple technique found to be effective is for the teacher to put dots between syllables in difficult longer words taken from actual text (for example, *con si der a tion*). This helps students decode the specific words under consideration and at the same time teaches them to break longer words into smaller parts and to look at longer words from beginning to end.

Using Contextual Analysis

Although research suggests that low-achieving readers rely on context more than good readers for help with mediated word recognition, they nevertheless use context less effectively than good readers. Low-achieving readers have been found to produce more meaning-changing substitutions in word recognition than good readers and to self-correct fewer of these erroneous substitutions.[25] They have also been found to make less use of semantic information on cloze passages than good readers.[26] These results suggest that low-achieving readers may not use context as effectively as they should to help them decode unfamiliar words and to help them self-correct substitutions that interfere with the meaning of the text.

Later in this chapter a general word recognition strategy will be discussed that encourages students to use context clues at the same time they are using their phonics knowledge to decode difficult words in actual text. In the first step of this procedure students try to think of a word that would make sense in the sentence and paragraph they are reading as they are trying to sound out a difficult word. We also present two strategies below which are designed to teach low-achieving readers to monitor themselves for meaning as they are decoding and to self-correct substitutions which do not make sense in the context of their reading.

Using Context to Self-Correct   Pflaum and Pascarella (1980) have developed a program to help students learn to use context to determine when substitutions do not make sense and to correct these substitutions to maintain meaning. The program has been effective in improving the reading level of students reading at the second-grade level or above but not at the first-grade level.

The instructional program consists of twenty-four lessons, twelve focusing on substitutions that change sentence meaning and twelve focusing on self-correction of erroneous substitution. For each lesson, students are told *what* they will be learning, *why* it is important, *how* it is related to previous lessons, and *when* they can use it in their own reading. The teacher first models the activities to be learned in a particular lesson and then helps students perform these activities. The lessons on detecting word recognition substitutions that do not make sense focus on the following activities:

1. Students underline the substitutions made by a recorded reader (on a tape) in each of ten sentences.

2. Students underline the substitutions (two in each of five paragraphs) made by a recorded reader and discuss the seriousness of each substitution (based on whether or not it interferes with meaning).

3. Students record their own reading of a short selection, listen to the tape, and underline their own substitutions.

4. Students underline twice the substitutions (one in each of five paragraphs) made by a recorded reader that interfere with the meaning of the paragraph and underline once the substitutions (one in each of five paragraphs) that do not interfere with meaning.

5. Students record their own reading and underline serious substitutions twice (ones that interfere with meaning) and less serious substitutions once (ones that do not interfere with meaning).

The twelve lessons on self-correcting substitutions that do not make sense focus on the following activities:

1. Students indicate corrections made by a recorded reader by marking them on a copy of the reading material. In some instances the recorded reader might talk aloud about substitutions that do not make sense. For example, if reading, "The horse stumbled and fell off the clith," the recorded reader could say, "Clith? That doesn't make any sense. I'd better look at that word again."

2. Students discuss the purpose of the recorded reader's corrected substitutions.

3. Students discuss words appropriate for blanks in fifteen sentences, given initial letter cues.

4. Students learn to use context first, then initial letter cues, and then final letter cues to help them come up with possible words for blanks in sentences. To do this they list a number of possible words for the blank in a sentence. Then, they eliminate those that do not fit because of initial letter and those that do not fit because of final letter.

5. Students correct the substitutions made by a recorded reader by using context and the initial and final sounds of the missing words.

6. Students record their own reading and analyze their own corrections. They can correct the substitutions they made while reading by stopping the tape when they hear a substitution and correcting it.

For many of the foregoing activities students might enjoy working with partners. Two students working together could mark substitutions of a recorded reader that did or did not make sense as well as self-corrections. Students could take turns reading into a tape recorder and then work together to mark their substitutions and self-corrections.

Oral Reading for Meaning   The oral reading for meaning technique (Taylor and Nosbush, 1983) is another procedure that can be used to teach students

These two children are listening to what they have read into the tape recorder to locate miscues. *(James Silliman)*

to self-correct substitutions that do not make sense and to use context to help them decode difficult words. In addition, the procedure can be used to provide on-the-spot instruction in needed word recognition skills based on the student's oral reading. The steps of the oral reading for meaning procedure are as follows.

How. In a one-to-one situation the student orally reads a 250- to 300-word excerpt from a book that is on his or her instructional level. The teacher may help with difficult words, but in general, lets the student read without interruptions. While the student is reading, the teacher takes notes on oral reading errors.

After the student has finished reading, the teacher first provides feedback on something the child did well in his or her oral reading. If possible, the teacher should point out instances where the student self-corrected and commend the student for doing this. The teacher should emphasize that this is what one should always do after reading a word that does not make sense.

Next, the teacher picks out two examples of senseless substitutions made by the student which are in sentences containing good context clues. The teacher shows the student his or her substitutions one at a time and asks if he or she can reread each sentence and come up with a word that makes sense. The child should use phonics cues (like beginning and ending letter sounds) to verify that the word he or she generates is correct. Again, the teacher should remind the student that when he or she decodes a word that does not make sense, he or she should stop and self-correct.

As a final step, the teacher can select a word recognition skill with which the student had difficulty during the oral reading, and can provide on-the-spot instruction in this skill. If, for example, a student had trouble with *ow* words, reading *know* for *now* and *hoe* for *how*, the teacher can point these words out to the student. The teacher can give several examples of other *ow* words that contained the same sound as *now* and give several examples of *ow* words that contain the same sound as *know*. By doing this the teacher is drawing the student's attention to the fact that the symbol *ow* has two different sounds. This on-the-spot instruction should be particularly meaningful and memorable to the student because he or she just had trouble reading two words containing *ow*.

Instead of basing on-the-spot instruction on substitutions that were just made, the teacher can review the oral reading material for examples that fit earlier instruction. If, for example, the student received instruction the previous day in different sounds for the symbol *ea*, the teacher could find *ea* words in the selection the student just read aloud and bring the words to the student's attention. The student can write the words containing *ea* under the example *head* or the example *meat*. An example of an oral reading for meaning session is presented in Figure 6.10.

What, Why, and *When.* The teacher should be sure to explain to the students *what* they are trying to accomplish through the oral reading for meaning procedure and *why* this is important: The teacher is helping the student learn to monitor himself or herself for meaning when reading and to

FIGURE 6.10 Example of an Oral Reading for Meaning Session

To Your Good Health*

Long ago there lived a king who was such a mighty ruler that whenever he *however* ˢᶜ

sneezed everyone in the whole country had to say, "To your good health!"

Everyone said it except the *sheep* shepherd with the bright blue eyes, and he would not

say it.

The king heard of this and was very angry. He sent for the shepherd to appear

before him.

The shepherd came and stood before the *thorn* throne, where the king sat looking

every very grand and powerful. But however grand or powerful he might be, the shepherd

after ˢᶜ did not feel a bit afraid of him.

"Say at once, 'To my good health!' " cried the king.

"To my good health!" replied the shepherd.

my ˢᶜ   *my* ˢᶜ *your* "To mine—to mine, you rascal!" stormed the king.

mission "To mine, to mine, Your Majesty," was the answer.

"But to mine—to my own," roared the king and beat his chest in rage.

"Well, yes; to mine, of course, to my own," cried the shepherd and gently

tapped his breast.

A fifth grade student made mistakes when reading as indicated in the preceding passage. The teacher gave the student the following feedback:

1. First, she praised the student for self-correcting after reading "however" for "whenever," "after" for "afraid," and "my" for "mine." She pointed out that the student should always self-correct when she read a word that didn't make sense.

2. Second, the teacher pointed out to the student two substitutions which didn't make sense. She showed her that she said "thorn" for "throne" and "mission" for "majesty." She helped the student decode these two words using the cues of context plus first and last letter sound. She again reminded the student that she should stop and try to correct errors like this that didn't make sense.

3. Third, the teacher helped focus the student's attention on the symbol-sound correspondence for "thr." On a sheet of paper she listed a few examples of words beginning with "thr" and then asked the student if she could think of any other words beginning with "thr." The teacher added these words to the list and then made up a few sentences, leaving a blank where one of the "thr" words on the list belonged. She had the student point to and say correct words for the blanks from the list of "thr" words. Since the student had confused "every" with "very," the teacher could have elected to provide her with some on-the-spot instruction in distinguishing between these two words instead of providing her with help in "thr" words.

* The passage in Figure 6.10 is from To Your Good Health in *A Lizard to Start With* of the READING 720 series by Theodore Clymer and others, © Copyright, 1976, by Ginn and Company. Used with permission.

self-correct substitutions that do not make sense in the context of the material being read. *When* the student recognizes a substitution that does not make sense, he or she should attempt to self-correct. To do this the student should think of a word beginning with a particular sound that would make sense in the material he or she has just read.

An important aspect of the oral reading for meaning procedure is that it be carried out on a regular basis. For the desired reading behaviors to develop, this procedure should be undertaken at least twice a week. Obviously a classroom teacher can only use this procedure on an individual basis with a few students at a time due to time constraints. But after six weeks or so, the teacher can phase the procedure out with one set of students and begin using it with a second set.

With modifications, this procedure can be used with a group of students. As students are taking turns reading aloud and a nonsemantic substitution is made, the teacher and students can stop to talk about the substitution and the fact that it does not make sense. The group can also try to correct the substitution error by using contextual and phonic analysis.

Structural Analysis

Structural analysis is the process of identifying words by breaking them into morphemes, or meaning-bearing units. Morphemes can be free or bound. Free morphemes are units that can stand by themselves, such as simple words like *book*, *judge*, and *farm*. Bound morphemes are meaning-bearing units in that they change the meanings of free morphemes. However, bound morphemes cannot stand by themselves; they must be attached to other morphemes. For example, *s*, *ment*, *ing*, *er*, and *ed* are bound morphemes, which when added to the above free morphemes would make the words *books*, *judgment*, *judging*, *farmer*, and *farmed*. Bound morphemes include inflectional endings such as plurals (*e, es*), verb tenses (*ed, ing, s*), comparisons (*er, est*), and possessives ('*s, s'*). Also included in this category are affixes (prefixes and suffixes) and contractions. Roots such as *bio* and *scribe* are also bound morphemes in that they are meaning-bearing units that cannot stand alone.

Structural analysis can be a useful word recognition skill. Readers are using structural analysis when they recognize bound or free morphemes as they are attempting to figure out a difficult word. Therefore, in addition to informal syllabication, structural analysis is a useful technique for breaking a word into parts. Prefixes and suffixes are syllables and can be analyzed as such. The reader may be able to recognize a word such as *unhappiness* after breaking off the syllables *un* and *ness*.

An additional benefit of decoding words through prefixes, base words, and suffixes is that the reader is focusing on meaning-bearing units at the same time he or she is decoding word parts, something which is not possible at the letter-sound level of decoding. This focus on meaning aids in recognizing the word being decoded as well as in comprehending what is being read.

The use of structural analysis to determine the meanings of unfamiliar words can be a valuable skill. For example, a reader may not know the meaning of the word *nonprofit* but may recognize that the word is made up of *non* and *profit*. The reader may then be able to come up with an approximate meaning for the word because he or she knows that *non* means *not* and *profit* means *to make money*. A good discussion of structural analysis in identifying words and in determining word meanings can be found in Durkin (1981b). In this chapter the discussion will be limited to structural analysis skills used in word recognition. Specifically, strategies for helping students become familiar with inflected endings and affixes will be discussed. The use of structural analysis to develop word meanings will be discussed in Chapter 10, the chapter on vocabulary instruction.

Inflectional Endings   In general, students do not need much instruction in inflectional endings. Their skill with oral language helps them read words with the proper inflections. For example, in "The two boys played ball," *two* signals *boys*. In "The boy was running," *was* signals *running*. However, if a student frequently has difficulty decoding familiar words because they have inflections added to them (for example, a student does not recognize *run* in *running*) or frequently does not self-correct substitutions involving inflections that interfere with meaning (for example, a student does not correct "the girl were walking"), instruction in inflectional endings may be useful. It is important to keep in mind that instances in which a student omits endings due to dialect should not be regarded as word recognition errors. An example of explicit instruction on inflectional endings follows.

What, Why, and *When.* As a first step, the teacher should explain to students *what* they will be working on: They will be looking at word endings. The teacher should explain *why* this is important and *when* to focus attention on word endings: It is important to recognize word endings when consciously decoding words because this may make words containing the ending easier to decode. That is, the student may not instantly recognize *helped* but if he or she notices the *ed* on the end of the word and then looks at the rest of the word, he or she may recognize that it is *help* + *ed* or *helped*. It is also important for students to notice and correct substitution errors that involve endings that do not make sense. For example, a student who reads "The girl were walking" should notice that this does not make sense and go back to correct the error because it is interfering with meaning.

How. The teacher should find examples of words with the inflectional ending to be learned from the students' language experience stories or from familiar reading material. For example, the teacher might find verbs ending in *ed*, write these words for the students, ask them what the words have in common, and ask them what the ending has done to the verbs' meaning. The teacher would ask the students to read the words in the list with and without the *ed* ending. Then, the teacher would ask the students to think of a few more verbs ending in *ed* and add them to the list. To apply this instruction to words in the context of sentences, the teacher could present students with oral or written sentences in which words are missing. The students' task would be to read the correct words from the list that fit in the blanks.

For a practice activity the students might complete a modified cloze passage in which blanks in the passage were followed by a word without the inflectional ending as well as the same word with the inflectional ending. Students would have to use context and be able to read both words to select the appropriate word for the blank (for example, "Tom *want, wanted* to go to the park." "We *want, wanted* to go to the zoo next week."). Also, for practice, students might make a collage of words with the inflectional ending that have been cut out of newspapers or magazines.

To help students apply instruction in a particular inflectional ending to reading, the teacher and students can locate words containing the ending in old language experience stories or in recently read stories. The teacher and students can break each word into the base plus the ending. This latter activity gives the students practice in decoding words by separating endings from the rest of the word, a tactic that may make a word easier to decode. For independent practice, students can be directed to search their reading materials for additional words containing the ending under study.

Affixes   Familiarizing students with common prefixes and suffixes enables them to recognize these word parts when attempting to decode unfamiliar words. For example, when confronted with the long word *unbelievable*, students might have a better chance of identifying the word if they first recognize *un* as a prefix and *able* as a suffix, thus leaving the more easily recognized base word *believe*. Therefore, when coming across multisyllabic words, students should check to see if the words contain any prefixes or suffixes. If so, the reader should first look for and read the root word and then reread it, adding the prefixes and suffixes. A list of common prefixes and suffixes is presented in Figure 6.11. Explicit instruction in recognizing affixes might look like this.

FIGURE 6.11   Common Prefixes and Suffixes

Prefixes

anti	mons
bi	non
circum	over
co (con, com, col, car)	pre
counter	re
de	semi
dis	sub
fore	super
in (im, il, ir)	trans
inter	un
intra	under
mal	
mid	

Suffixes

able	less
ance (ancy, ence, ency)	like
ation	ly
ative	ment
dom	most
er (or)	ness
fold	ous
ful	ship
hood	tion (sion, ion)
ible	ty
ic	ward
ish	y
ism	

What, Why, and *When.* The teacher should focus on a particular affix that has appeared a number of times in the students' reading material and explain that they will be learning to recognize words containing that particular affix. This will help them recognize the affix in other words not known instantly which, in turn, will help them decode the words.

How. After looking at a particular root word and affix, the teacher and students should discuss how the word changed in meaning when the affix was added. Then the teacher and students should try to generate a list of other words containing the affix under consideration. The students should read this list and then fill in the blanks of oral or written sentences with appropriate words from the list. This type of practice activity is commonly found in basal reader programs.

For an additional practice activity, students can play a concentration game that involves pairing root words and affixes after receiving instruction in a number of affixes. Or, students can see how many words they could generate from a word wheel containing affixes and root words.

To help students apply knowledge of affixes to reading, the teacher and students should locate words containing prefixes and suffixes when reading and practice decoding these words by breaking off the prefixes and suffixes from the remainder of the word. For independent practice, students can locate and keep a list of additional words containing affixes when reading independently.

Using a General Word Recognition Strategy

What, Why, and *When.* Students may know the most common symbol-sound correspondences but may not know how to use this knowledge in decoding unfamiliar words when actually reading. Consequently, it is important that students be taught a general word recognition strategy to use when reading on their own. Also, it is important to devote enough time to guided practice in using this general strategy. To provide students with a strategy for decoding a difficult word, we recommend the following steps:

I. *Use context clues.* Read to the end of the sentence and remember to be thinking of a word that would make sense in the sentence as you engage in step IIa or IIb.

IIa. *Sound out a one-syllable word.*
1. *C + V _____.* If the word is one syllable, see if the word has a common phonogram you recognize. If so, blend the beginning sound with the phonogram to come up with the word (for example, *s-ight, sight*).
2. *CVC or CVCC.* If you still do not recognize the word and if the word has a CVC or CVCC pattern, try the short vowel sound first as you sound out each letter in the word. Blend the sounds together. Try the long vowel sound if necessary. Use your vowel key word chart (p. 149) if you have forgotten the sound of a particular vowel.
3. *CVCe.* If the word has a CVCe pattern, try the long vowel sound first as you sound out each letter. Blend the sounds together. If necessary, try the short vowel sound. Use your vowel key word chart if necessary.
4. *CVVC.* If the word has a CVVC pattern, try one common sound that comes to mind for the vowel pair as you sound out each letter in the word. Blend the sounds together. If necessary, try another common sound for the vowel pair. Use your vowel key word chart if you cannot remember sounds to try for the vowel pair.

IIb. *Sound out a 2+ syllable word.* If the word is a multisyllabic word, break the word into parts with one vowel or vowel pair per part.

Sound out each part, trying a short vowel sound first in a CVC segment and trying a long vowel sound first in a CV segment. Blend the sounds of the word parts together. Remember that you should be trying to think of a word you know that would make sense in the sentence. Remember to be flexible and try different vowel sounds for different word parts.

III. *Ask for help or skip the word.* If you still do not recognize the word, ask for help or skip the word and read on.

How. To initially teach this general word recognition strategy, the teacher should write the steps on a chart, using as few words as possible to keep it simple, and go over the steps with the students. A chart for students reading on a first- or second-grade level might contain the following:

I. Use context

II. Sound it out (C + V _____, CVC or CVCC, CVCe, CVVC)

III. Ask for help or skip it.

Then, the teacher should model the strategy for the students. The teacher reads from a text and lets the students follow along. The teacher pretends to find a word that he or she does not know and then talks aloud as he or she goes through the steps in figuring out the word. This discussion should include various examples, such as coming up with a word after recognizing a common phonogram and blending it with the initial sound. Alternately, the teacher should provide examples of looking at the spelling pattern in a one-syllable word (CVC, CVCe, or CVVC), sounding out the word, blending the sounds together, and checking to make sure that the word makes sense. Also, the teacher should provide examples of skipping the word and going on with the reading. An example of a lesson in which the teacher models the general word recognition strategy is provided in Figure 6.12.

After modeling the strategy for the students, the teacher asks them to restate the steps they should follow when coming to an unfamiliar word. The teacher rereads the chart with the students and then lets them take turns orally reading actual text. The group should stop at difficult words to go through the steps of the general word recognition strategy.

The procedure described above will have to be repeated with the students, at least in some modified form, a number of different times. Also, it is important to be consistent when students read aloud or ask for help with an unfamiliar word. Instead of simply telling students words or telling them to sound the word out, the teacher should remind them of the general word recognition strategy and help them go through its steps in an attempt to decode the word.

To provide students with practice in learning this general word recognition strategy, the teacher can let students listen to a tape in which the reader is

FIGURE 6.12   Lesson on the General Word Recognition Strategy

TEACHER: Today we are going to work some more on the steps to follow when you come to a word you don't know as you are reading. The steps of the general word recognition strategy are: (1) use context clues, (2) sound the word out, (3) ask for help or skip the word. I'm going to show you how to follow these steps. It is important to know how to do this, because there will be times you won't know a word and you will need to try to figure the word out to better understand what you are reading.

Let's imagine I am reading along and come to a word I don't know, *r-a-k-e* in the sentence, "In the fall we *r-a-k-e* . . . ." First, I use context clues. To do this, I read to the end of the sentence, "In the fall we _____ leaves." The word has something to do with leaves in the fall. Second, I see if I can sound out the word, remembering the context. To do this, I see if I can figure the word out by looking at the first letter plus the rest of the word. *R* plus "ake." Well, I recognize *ake*. *R* plus *ake* is *rake*. That makes sense. "In the fall we rake leaves."

Now, let's imagine I come to another word I don't know. "One tree was a beautiful *s-h-a-d-e* . . . ." I read to the end of the sentence, "One tree was a beautiful _____ of red." It has something to do with a red tree. Let's see, *sh* plus *a-d-e*, I don't really recognize *a-d-e*. Let's see, the word ends in an *e* so the *a* must be long. /sh/ + /ā/ + /d/. Oh, *shade*. That makes sense. "One tree was a beautiful shade of red."

Now let's turn to the story "The Messy Room" on page 12 in our reading book. We'll take turns reading aloud. When one person comes to a word he/she doesn't know, the rest should not shout out the word. Together we'll go through the steps of the general word recognition strategy to figure out the word. Okay, Sara, why don't you start reading.

SARA: "One day Kate's mother said Kate had to clean her room. It was very messy. Her clothes were in a . . . ." I don't know that word.

TEACHER: Okay. What should Sara do first? Roger?

ROGER: Read to the end of the sentence.

TEACHER: Good. Sara, can you read to the end of the sentence?

SARA: Her clothes were in a _____ by her bed."

TEACHER: Okay, the word has something to do with clothes by the bed. What should Sara do next to try to figure out this word *h-e-a-p*, Mike?

MIKE: See if she can sound it out by looking at the first letter plus the rest of the word.

TEACHER: Great! Sara, can you do this?

SARA: No. I don't know *e-a-p*.

TEACHER: That's okay. Can you think of what to do next?

SARA: No.

(Cont.)

FIGURE 6.12   Lesson on the General Word Recognition Strategy (*Cont.*)

TEACHER: Who knows? Mike?

MIKE: She should try to sound it out letter by letter.

TEACHER: How should she do this?

MIKE: Well, one sound to try for *ea* would be /ē/; /h/ + /ē/ + /p/, /hēp/. That makes sense. "Her clothes were in a heap by her bed."

TEACHER: Very good. Good try Sara. Roger, will you please read next.

modeling the strategy. The reader should demonstrate or model how to use the general word recognition strategy by coming to unknown words and talking through the use of the different steps in the procedure. Students can follow along by reading from the same book. They can write down the words not known by the reader and indicate whether or not the reader used the general word recognition strategy effectively. For example, if the reader came up with the word *heap* after she read to the end of the sentence, looked for a common phonogram but did not recognize *eap*, and then sounded out the word, trying two different sounds for *ea*, students would write *yes* by the word *heap* on a sheet of paper. If the reader did not read to the end of the sentence, sounded out the word as *hep* and continued, students would write *no* by the word *heap*. At the end of the reading, the reader on the tape could discuss with the students what they wrote down on their papers.

To practice applying the general word recognition strategy to actual reading, students can read aloud into a tape recorder. Then, working in pairs, they can play the tape back, list the unfamiliar words they had to decode, and indicate if they used the general word recognition strategy effectively. Or, working in pairs, students can simply take turns reading aloud and monitor one another in terms of whether or not they were following the general word recognition strategy they had learned.

WORD RECOGNITION FLUENCY

Developing Word Recognition Automaticity

To this point discussion has focused on techniques for helping low-achieving readers learn to decode words accurately as they read. In addition to identifying words correctly, emerging readers must learn how to identify words automatically and rapidly as skilled readers do. The benefit of rapid, context-free, automatic word identification is that it frees attentional capacity and short-term memory space for use in comprehension.

Generally, automaticity in word recognition develops through repeated exposure to words through reading. Therefore, wide reading experience is recommended to help develop students' word recognition automaticity (as well as beginning readers' word recognition accuracy and all readers' comprehension abilities). In addition, several specific strategies to develop students' automaticity will be discussed below.

Repeated Reading   Samuels (1979) has developed the following procedure to develop students' automaticity and reading rate. It consists of rereading short passages a number of times until certain levels of word recognition and reading rate are reached. Explicit instruction in this procedure might look something like this.

What and *Why*. The teacher explains to students that they will be rereading short interesting passages several times until they can read them accurately and at a faster rate than when they started. This will help them learn to read faster and with better comprehension.

How. The teacher helps students select short, interesting passages (50-200 words) that are relatively easy for them to read. They read one passage aloud into a tape recorder, to an aide, or to a partner and record their reading rate and number of word recognition errors. Students practice rereading the passage (silently or orally) several times and then they read it aloud again and, using a stopwatch, record their word recognition errors and rate. They do this until they are able to read the passage with less than two errors and at a criterion rate which is 50 words per minute better than their first attempt. After each timed reading, a comprehension question can be asked to focus students' attention on comprehension as well as on word recognition accuracy and rate. Students then go on to a new passage which they continue to reread until they again reach their criterion reading rate (as determined from the first passage) and their same low error rate.

Samuels has found that on subsequent passages, students' initial reading rate increases. Also, it requires fewer repeated readings for students to reach their criterion reading rate. In addition to increasing reading rate, students are increasing word recognition automaticity and comprehension for individual passages as they read them repeatedly.

Group Repeated Reading   Lauritzen (1982) has modified the repeated reading technique for use with groups of students. Reading selections consist of poems, song lyrics, folktales, and other stories that have one or more of the following qualities: (1) strong rhyme, (2) definite rhythm, (3) obvious sequence, (4) strong oral literature patterns. Students are motivated to reread these selections because of their appealing nature.

The teacher first reads the story or poem aloud. The students follow along either with a copy of the book or from a copy on a chart or on the chalkboard. Next, the students echo-read a line, sentence, or paragraph of the selection. Finally, the teacher and students chorally read the selection. For independent practice the students continue to reread the story or poem individually or in pairs.

Book Memorization   Chomsky (1978) has developed a listening-while-reading technique that involves repeated reading of a single selection until it is memorized. In the process of learning to "read" a particular selection, students become automatic in terms of word recognition for the particular selection and are able to read the selection fluently.

Students select a story or selection from an appealing book. The selection should be on a second- to fifth-grade reading level and should take about fifteen minutes of listening time. It does not matter if the students are not

The teacher is using the group repeated reading technique with this picture book to develop students' fluency. *(James Silliman)*

reading at the book's level. The teacher has the individual selections put on tape and the students then listen to their reading selections over and over (perhaps ten to twenty times for first- or second-grade level readers) until they can read them without the use of the tape. Every two to three days, as students are in the process of learning their selections, the teacher listens to them read the pages they know without the tape. After one story or selection is learned, the process is repeated with a second selection.

In addition to developing automaticity, this technique offers older students who are reading on a first- or second-grade level a choice of more interesting "non-babyish" material to read. Chomsky found that low-achieving third-grade students reading on a first- or second-grade level were very motivated to learn to read their selected books and extremely pleased with themselves when they were finally able to read them to others.

Chunking   A number of studies[27] have found that students' comprehension of specific texts is enhanced when the material is segmented into meaningful phrases. The procedure may be beneficial because it enables readers to focus less attention on individual words and helps them process text in phrase or idea units, as skilled readers do. In contrast to word-by-word reading, chunking is a form of automaticity. Not only do fluent readers decode individual words automatically, they read automatically in phrase units. Consequently, attention to chunking can be useful for improving low-achieving readers' ability to read in meaningful phrases instead of word by word.

What and *Why*. Explicit instruction in chunking might look something like this. The teacher should explain to students that they will be learning how to segment text into meaningful phrase units because this will improve their reading fluency and consequently their reading comprehension.

How. First, the teacher presents text using an overhead projector and shows students how to segment it into meaningful phrase, or thought, units. The teacher points out that there are no definite places the text must be segmented except at the end of sentences. However, within sentences, fluent readers generally pause slightly before and after prepositional phrases, before or after dependent clauses, and between independent clauses, and may pause slightly between subjects and predicates or between verbs in compound predicates. It will be easiest for the teacher to instruct students in where to segment sentences through modeling. An example of a sentence segmented into meaningful phrase units would be as follows: "In the morning/John got up/and got dressed/before he went downstairs/for breakfast."

Next, the teacher and students chorally read the chunked text. An unsegmented section of text and another that has been segmented in inappropriate places are also read and compared to the meaningfully segmented text. Students then reread the meaningfully segmented text one or two times and attempt to segment a second passage with teacher guidance. This second passage is read several times.

For individual practice students read a new teacher-segmented passage several times then segment a passage on their own and practice reading it in meaningful phrase units.

When. The teacher should explain to students that instead of reading in a word-by-word manner, they should attempt to mentally segment text into meaningful phrases whenever they read.

Developing Reading Rate

Fluent adult readers read at a rate of about 250 to 300 words per minute. Average readers have reached the lower end of this range (250 words per minute) by ninth grade. As with word recognition automaticity, wide reading is the best means of developing an adequate reading rate. Generally, as students gain experience with reading, they begin to read automatically at an adequate reading rate. However, low-achieving readers who have learned to read automatically on at least a fourth-grade level but do so at a slow rate may benefit from specific instruction and practice in increasing their reading rate. Slow reading rates for various reading levels are presented in Table 6.2.

One technique that is designed to develop reading rate as well as automaticity, the method of repeated reading, has been described. Learning how to read in phrases should also lead to gains in reading rate. Below the use of timed readings to develop reading rate will be discussed.

TABLE 6.2   Average and Slow Reading Rates

Grade Level	Range of Rates (wpm)	Slow Rate (wmp)
2	70–100	
3	95–130	
4	120–170	120
5	160–210	160
6	180–230	180
7	180–240	180
8	195–240	195
9	215–260	215
12	225–260	225

SOURCE: Adapted by Richek, List, and Learner (1983), Reading problems: Diagnosis and remediation, from Harris and Sipay, *How to increase reading ability,* 7th ed., Longman Inc., 1980.

Timed Reading—What and Why   The teacher explains to students that they will be timing their reading and keeping a chart of their reading rate in an attempt to increase it. If they learn how to read a little bit faster, their reading fluency will improve and there is a good chance that their reading comprehension will improve as well. Also, because they have a considerable amount of reading to do in school, it will be beneficial to learn how to read a little bit more quickly.

To do timed readings, students simply read short (100–300 word), interesting passages and answer several comprehension questions on the material. They record their reading rate in words per minute and their percent of comprehension accuracy on a graph. It is important that students select passages that are not above their instructional level so they will not have to struggle with decoding.

We do not recommend the use of reading machines to increase reading rate if students have to read in an unnatural manner, such as line by line. However, intact short passages that are shown on the computer for a certain amount of time would be another tool for students to use to increase their reading rate.

SUMMARY

This chapter examined strategies for developing low-achieving readers' word recognition accuracy and fluency. It stressed the importance of explicit instruction in word recognition, in which the teacher explains *what* a particular skill is and models *how* to perform it, discusses with students *why* the skill is important, and explains *when* they can use it as they are reading on their own.

Word recognition instruction was presented as an important component of the reading comprehension process. Without word recognition, comprehension of text cannot take place. However, word recognition should not be regarded as an end in itself. For this reason, instruction and practice in word recognition should focus as much as possible on the reading of connected text; work with words in isolation should be kept to a minimum. Throughout this chapter, examples were provided of instructional strategies that will help students learn how to apply word recognition skill to actual reading.

SUGGESTED ACTIVITIES

1. Use the individual language experience approach on at least three occasions with one child who is reading on a first-grade level or lower. Make a booklet of stories for the child and be certain that the student repeatedly rereads the stories in his or her booklet.

2. Teach the symbol-sound correspondence for a vowel or vowel pair to a child or small group of children who do not know the correspondence, following the steps outlined in the chapter. Be sure to help the student(s) attack words in actual text containing the symbol-sound correspondence being taught. If children are not available, "teach" the symbol-sound correspondence to a group of peers in your class.

3. Use the oral reading for meaning procedure, preferably once or twice a week, with a student who frequently makes nonsemantic substitutions and does not tend to correct these miscues.

4. Teach a student to use the general word recognition strategy outlined in the chapter. After modeling the strategy, be sure to use the strategy with the student while reading actual text. If a child is not available, "teach" the general word recognition strategy to a peer in your class.

5. Use the repeated reading procedure with a student who is not a very fluent reader.

NOTES

1. See Ehri and Wilce (1983), Juel (1983), and Stanovich, Cunningham, and Feeman (1984a).
2. See DiBennedetto, Richardson, and Kochnower (1983), Ehri and Wilce (1983), Juel and Roper-Schneider (1985), Manis (1985), Mason (1976), Perfetti (1985), Rosso and Emans (1981), and Venezky and Johnson (1973).
3. See Durkin (1984c), Lewkowicz (1980), Stanovich, Cunningham, and Feeman (1984a), and Williams (1980).
4. See Durkin (1984c).
5. See Juel (1980, 1983), Stanovich (1980), and Stanovich, Cunningham, and Feeman (1984a).
6. See Juel (1980, 1983), and Stanovich (1980).
7. See Beebe (1980), D'Angelo (1982), Leslie (1980), Pflaum and Pascarella (1980), and Willows and Ryan (1981).
8. See Ehri and Wilce (1981), LaBerge and Samuels (1974), Manis (1985), Stanovich (1980), and Stanovich, Cunningham and Feeman (1984a and 1984b).
9. See Ehri and Wilce (1983), Manis (1985), Stanovich (1980), and Stanovich, Cunningham, and Feeman (1984a).
10. See Mason (1983).
11. See Durkin (1978–1979, 1984b), and Mason (1983).
12. See Williams (1985).
13. The reader is referred to Johnson and Pearson (1984) for a more detailed discussion on developing a basic sight vocabulary.
14. See Dolch (1942), Moe (1973), and Otto and Chester (1972).
15. See Arlin, Scott, and Webster (1978–1979), Ehri and Roberts (1979), Ehri and Wilce (1980), Nemko (1984), Rash, Johnson, and Gleadow (1984), and Singer, Samuels, and Spiroff (1974).

16. The reader is referred to Hall (1981) for an in depth discussion of the language experience approach.
17. See Johnson (1976). See also Figure 6.1.
18. See Anderson, Hiebert, Scott, and Wilkinson (1985), Bond and Dykstra (1967), Chall (1983), and Pflaum, Walberg, Karegianes, and Rasher (1980).
19. See Anderson, Hiebert, Scott, and Wilkinson (1985).
20. See Anderson, Hiebert, Scott, and Wilkinson (1985) and Chall (1983).
21. See Haddock (1976).
22. See Ehri, Deffner, and Wilce (1984) and Marsh and Desberg (1978).
23. See DiBennedetto, Richardson, and Kochnower (1983) and Mason (1976).
24. See Calfee, Lindamood, and Lindamood (1973), Chall, Roswell, and Blumenthal (1963), Fox and Routh (1975), Helfgott (1976), and Liberman (1970).
25. See Leslie (1980), Pflaum and Bryan (1980), and Willows and Ryan (1981).
26. See Willows and Ryan (1981).
27. See Brozo, Schmelze, and Spires (1983), Mason and Kendall (1979), O'Shea and Sindelar (1983), and Stevens (1981).

SUGGESTED READINGS

BRIDGE, C. A., WINOGRAD, P. N., AND HALEY, D. (1983). Using predictable materials vs. preprimers to teach beginning sight words. *The Reading Teacher* 36: 884–891.
The authors discuss how to use predictable books to teach basic sight words.

HALL, M. (1981). *Teaching reading as a language experience* (3rd ed.). Columbus, OH: C. E. Merrill.
Hall describes the language experience approach in detail and discusses how it can be implemented in the classroom.

JOHNSON, D. D., AND PEARSON, P. D. (1984). *Teaching reading vocabulary* (2nd ed.). New York: Holt, Rinehart and Winston.
This book provides many good suggestions for developing a basic sight vocabulary and for teaching phonics.

PFLAUM, S. W., AND PASCARELLA, E. T. (1980). Interactive effects of prior reading achievement and training in context on the reading of learning-disabled children. *Reading Research Quarterly* 16: 138–158.
The authors describe the program they use to improve learning disabled students' contextual analysis skills.

SAMUELS, S. J. (1979). The method of repeated readings. *The Reading Teacher* 32: 403–408.
The importance of automaticity and a technique to develop automaticity in low-achieving readers are discussed.

TAYLOR, B. M., AND NOSBUSH, L. (1983). Oral reading for meaning: A technique for improving word identification. *The Reading Teacher* 37: 234–237.
Taylor and Nosbush describe the oral reading for meaning procedure they developed to improve low-achieving readers' self-correction ability.

WILLIAMS, J. P. (1979). The ABD's of reading: A program for the learning-disabled. In L. B. Resnick and P. A. Weaver (Eds.), *Theory and practice in beginning reading, vol. 3.* Hillsdale, NJ: Erlbaum.
An effective program for developing beginning readers' ability to sound and blend words is presented.

Chapter 7

Word Recognition Assessment

OVERVIEW

As you read this chapter use the following list of main ideas to guide your understanding and reflection.

Oral reading analysis is an effective technique for assessing a student's word recognition abilities when actually reading.

Oral reading analysis should be conducted once or twice a week with low-achieving readers experiencing difficulty in word recognition.

It is essential that written records be kept of students' oral reading performance so that patterns of errors or difficulties can be determined over time.

Based on a student's relative strengths and weaknesses in word recognition, as assessed through oral reading analysis, a teacher can determine the most appropriate types of remedial instruction.

This chapter first discusses oral reading analysis, an assessment technique used to gather information pertaining to different aspects of word recognition. Strategies for specific areas of word recognition, such as phonics knowledge or contextual analysis are then assessed. This latter discussion will parallel the discussion of word recognition instruction presented in Chapter 6.

ORAL READING ANALYSIS

In oral reading analysis the teacher listens to an individual student read aloud, records the miscues, and notes on an oral reading analysis sheet unfamiliar words succssfully decoded by the student. By unfamiliar we mean words not readily known by a student, words the student had to consciously, or deliberately decode. The teacher then aggregates the data from a number of oral reading samples to determine the reader's general strengths and weaknesses in word recognition as revealed by patterns of behaviors. Also, if the teacher has provided instruction in a skill, he or she can use these data to evaluate the student's progress in applying that skill. Oral reading analysis can reveal valuable information about a reader's habitual approach to decoding as well as the reader's basic sight word and symbol-sound correspondence knowledge. The reader's ability to use word-level fix-up strategies, to apply phonics knowledge to reading, and to use context clues to attack difficult words can also be detected. Ideally, oral reading analysis should be conducted once or twice a week with low-achieving readers who are reading below grade level or who reach frustration level, at least in part, because of difficulties in word recognition.

It should be pointed out that oral reading analysis has the advantage of being an assessment procedure that focuses on students' word recognition skills in actual reading situations.[1] Furthermore, if carried out regularly, oral reading analysis has the added advantage of being an assessment procedure occurring in a nonthreatening, nontestlike environment.

Many teachers shy away from oral reading analysis for one or more of the following reasons: (1) It is threatening to the children; they get uptight when they know they are on the spot. (2) It is difficult and time-consuming to collect and, especially, to analyze the data. (3) Teachers believe that data gathered from "real" published tests are needed to assess low-achieving readers. (4) Diagnosis is unnecessary once students are placed in the basal reader at their instructional level.

With regard to students feeling threatened, it is found that oral reading analysis is not threatening to students if it occurs regularly. Children come to view the teacher's notetaking during oral reading as a "business as usual" activity.

With regard to time involved, it is relatively easy to take notes during oral reading if an appropriate form is available (such as the one presented in Figure 7.1 and explained later in the chapter). What is important is that the teacher get into the *habit* of taking notes when students read aloud. Since it is time-consuming to analyze data collected from oral reading analysis, dated analysis should only be conducted with low-achieving readers who have word recognition difficulties. Teachers should also collect data on an oral reading analysis sheet to facilitate data interpretation and that they do one or more of the following to analyze the data: (1) Take time to fill in as much of the oral reading analysis sheet as possible immediately after a student has read (while completing the sheet have students reread the material to partners. (2) Build time into their schedule, such as an hour once or twice a month, to analyze data from four or more oral reading sessions per low-achieving reader. (3) Get assistance with data analysis from the reading resource teacher.

With regard to the necessity of using formal diagnostic tests, remember that formal published tests are of questionable content validity and generally are based on unnatural reading tasks (see the discussion of informal assessment in Chapters 5 and 13). On the other hand, data collected by the teacher during oral reading analysis are based on actual reading of text and become reliable over time because they are based on repeated measurements. What is important is that a teacher know how to recognize significant recurring word recognition problems. The remainder of this chapter will be devoted to those aspects of word recognition performance that are most important for the teacher to consider when analyzing oral reading notes in search of significant word recognition problems.

With regard to the necessity of using oral reading analysis, once students are placed at the appropriate level in the basal, we again emphasize that diagnosis is essential for students experiencing difficulty in word recognition and that oral reading analysis is an excellent method that is based on actual text.

Conducting Oral Reading Analysis

To conduct oral reading analysis, a teacher begins by listening to a student orally read a 50–200 word segment from his or her regular reading material (basal, textbook, or trade book). The amount to be read depends on the reading level of the student (younger children read shorter passages). The teacher records on an oral reading analysis sheet the student's oral reading errors and the correct words, along with any unfamiliar words that were deliberately and successfully decoded. The book and page numbers are also recorded. An example of the type of sheet that might be used is presented in Figure 7.1.

It is important that the material read aloud be on the student's instructional level. Research has found that students make different kinds of errors when reading material at instructional and frustration levels.[2] In general, readers make more nonresponse and graphophonic errors (errors that are phonetically similar) and rely less on meaning and context clues when at their frustration level than at their instructional level.[3] Presumably, this is because readers are directing so much attention to decoding when reading at their frustration level that they pay less attention to context and meaning. Instructional plans should be built around error patterns revealed during instructional level reading.

While listening to a student read aloud, the teacher should record notes on the elements listed below on an oral reading analysis sheet. A suggested recording system is also listed.

This teacher is conducting oral reading for meaning with an individual student.
(Laimute E. Druskis/Taurus)

Type of Element	Recording System
Substitution	Write the word substituted above the actual word. If an ending or part of a word has been omitted, circle what was omitted.
Repetition	Draw a wavy line under the repeated words.
Insertion	Insert the word or words with a caret.
Omission	Circle the omitted word or words.
Teacher Pronunciation	Put "TP" above the unknown word to indicate that the teacher pronounced the word for the student after waiting at least five seconds.
Self-Correction	Put "SC" after a substitution to indicate that the word was corrected spontaneously by the student. The original substitution should also be recorded.
Successfully Decoded Word	A word that obviously was not known instantly but was successfully decoded by a student should be listed.

An example of a teacher's notes based on a student's oral reading is provided in Figure 7.2. (Ignore columns 2 through 6 of this chart for now. They will be explained later in the chapter.)

FIGURE 7.1   Oral Reading Analysis Sheet

Column 1   Substitution is written above the actual word from the text.

Column 2   Indicates whether or not the general word recognition strategy was used: + = used successfully; − = not used successfully; 0 = student didn't try (word consciously omitted or pronounced by the teacher); blank = not applicable (student decoded word automatically even though he or she did not read the correct word).

Column 3   Indicates whether or not a nonsemantic substitution was self-corrected: + = nonsemantic substitution self-corrected; − = nonsemantic substitution not self-corrected; 0 = semantic substitution.

Column 4   Indicates whether or not substitution involved incorrect analysis of a 1 syllable word.

Column 5   Indicates whether or not substitution involved incorrect analysis of a 2+ syllable word.

Column 6   Indicates apparent difficulty in terms of symbol-sound correspondence knowledge. Other notes can be made here as well, such as difficulty with basic sight words, inflectional endings, affixes.

Column 7   Indicates unfamiliar words that were deliberately and successfully decoded.

1	2 General Word Recognition Strategy	3 Nonsemantic Substitution	4 1 Syllable Word	5 2+ Syllable Word	6 Apparent Difficulty	7 Successfully Decoded
Error						

Number of words _____   Word recognition accuracy _____

Number of times nonsemantic substitutions self-corrected/total number of nonsemantic substitutions _____

Oral reading analysis can be conducted with students on an individual basis or in a reading group. The advantage of working with a student individually is that, in addition to collecting diagnostic information, the teacher can take more time to provide individualized instruction as the student is reading. If students read orally in a group, the teacher should be sure to take notes on individual students' performance and insist that other students *not* call out a word that is not instantly known; otherwise the reader will have no time to figure out the unknown word.

So far we have discussed how to conduct oral reading analysis but have

FIGURE 7.2   Teacher's Notes Based on Student's Oral Reading

A Swim

Toad and Frog went down to the *river* river.

"What a day for a swim," said Frog.

"Yes," said Toad, "I will go behind these *this* rock(s) and put on my bathing *TP* suit *TP*."

"I don't wear a bathing suit," said Frog.

"Well, I do," said Toad. "After I put on my bathing suit, you must not look at me

until I get in the water."

"Why(not)?" asked Frog.

"Because I *like* sc look funny in my ^*new* bathing suit. That is why," said Toad.

Frog closed his eyes when Toad came out from behind the rocks. Toad was
weering
wearing his new bathing suit.

Do not
"Don't peek," he said.

	1 Error	2 General Word Recognition Strategy	3 Nonsemantic Substitution	4 1 Syllable Word	5 2+ Syllable Word	6 Apparent Difficulty	7 Successfully Decoded
P. 40	river river	—	—			ĭ	
	this these		0				
	rock(s)		0			(s)	
	bathing TP	0					
	suit TP	0					
P. 42	(not)						water
	like SC look	+	+				funny
	new ^bathing suit						
	weering wearing	—	—			ea	
	Do not Don't		0			n't	

FIGURE 7.2   Teacher's Notes Based on Student's Oral Reading (*Cont.*)

9 errors in 100 words = 91% accuracy in word recognition
Number of times nonsemantic substitutions self-corrected out of total number of
    nonsemantic substitutions 1/3
Column 1   Substitution is written above actual word from text.
Column 2   Indicates whether or not general word recognition strategy was used:
            + = used successfully; − = not used successfully; 0 = student
            didn't try (word consciously omitted or pronounced by the teacher);
            blank = not applicable (student decoded word automatically even
            though he or she did not read the correct word)
Column 3   Indicates whether or not a nonsemantic substitution self-corrected; +
            = nonsemantic substitution corrected; − = nonsemantic substitution
            not corrected; 0 = semantic substitution.
Column 6   Notes about apparent difficulty with a particular word.
Column 7   Indicates unfamiliar words that were successfully decoded.

NOTE: An expanded version of the oral reading analysis sheet below is presented in Figure 7.4.

SOURCE: The passage in Figure 7.2 is from *Frog and Toad Are Friends,* pp. 40–42, by Arnold
Lobel. Copyright © 1970 by Arnold Lobel. Reprinted by permission of Harper & Row, Publishers,
Inc.

said very little about how to actually use the collected information for diagnostic
and evaluative purposes. The interpretation of data collected from oral reading
will be discussed as specific aspects of word recognition are examined.

BASIC SIGHT VOCABULARY

As discussed in Chapter 6, basic sight words are high-frequency words that
students should be able to recognize instantly. It it important to assess the
basic sight word knowledge of low-achieving readers reading at or below a
third-grade level. Students reading above this level probably know most of
the words on a basic sight word list, such as Johnson's list presented in Chapter
6. Any frequently missed basic sight words for students reading above grade
level will become apparent through oral reading analysis and other daily
reading activities.

The conventional way to evaluate a student's ability to identify basic sight
words is to use word cards in an individual assessment. To do this, the teacher
prints all of the words from a basic sight word list on one side of a card. The
teacher also writes the word in a simple sentence on the back of the card,
using surrounding words that he or she thinks early readers might know.
Then, the teacher simply shows, or flashes, the words to the student, beginning
with the first-grade words. If a word is not known, the teacher flips the card

over to see if the student can read the word in the context of a sentence. Those not known by a student either in isolation or in the context of a sentence comprise the body of words with which to begin that student's instruction. Later, some attention may also be directed to basic sight words known in a sentence but not known in isolation.

After students have received instruction and practice in learning specific basic sight words, this approach can be used several times a week to assess their knowledge of the words they have been working on. The number of words known can be recorded on a progress chart, or specific words known can be checked off on a progress chart.

Another useful method for screening students on their knowledge of sight words has been described by Johnson and Pearson (1978). This procedure is a paper and pencil task that involves the teacher's reading a basic sight word and the student's circling the correct word from among four choices that are visually similar. A portion of the test might look like this:

Words Read by Teacher	Student's Paper
1. where	1. were, where, when, went
2. then	2. then, they, there, the
3. our	3. are, out, our, oar

Johnson (1976) found correlations ranging between .86 and .91 for scores derived from such a test and also from the flashcard approach described earlier. An advantage of the circle-the-word test is that it can be administered to a group of students. A disadvantage is that it assesses students' ability to *recognize* basic sight words but not their ability to *read* them. There is no guarantee that because students circle a word correctly on the test they will be able to identify the word when coming across it in text. Nevertheless, the paper and pencil assessment of basic sight word knowledge may be useful as an initial screening device. If a student does poorly on the circle-the-word test (missing even a few words from a word list that is below his or her instructional reading level), further assessment is probably needed.

However, the most useful assessment of a student's basic sight word knowledge comes from observation of the student's performance during actual reading. From records of a student's oral reading, the teacher can determine if any basic vocabulary words have been repeatedly missed. These words then become a point of focus during instruction. These same records reveal which basic sight words have been read correctly by the student during actual reading. If a student missed *the* once when reading aloud but read the word correctly in context on ten other occasions, this would indicate that there was no need for the student to drill on the word *the*.

GENERAL WORD RECOGNITION STRATEGY

A general word recognition strategy involves following a set of steps to decode a word not recognized instantly. Students' knowledge and use of a general word recognition strategy should be assessed if word recognition difficulties contribute to their reading below grade level. One way to assess a student's knowledge of what to do with an unknown word is to ask the student directly. The teacher asks the student to list the steps to follow when coming to an unknown word and also to explain what he or she actually does in such situations. In both cases it would be useful to record the student's responses to see if his or her knowledge of correct decoding procedures matched his or her actual decoding behavior during real reading.

This leads directly to the second suggestion for assessing a student's use of a general word recognition strategy. When taking notes on a student's oral reading the teacher should record information on what the student does when the student comes to unfamiliar words. For example, the student (1) might try to decode a word not known instantly and then successfully pronounce the correct word; (2) try to decode the word but produce a miscue; (3) not even try to decode the word but look at the teacher to give him or her the word; or (4) omit the word and continue reading. Words deliberately but incorrectly decoded are listed under the substitution column of the oral reading analysis sheet. (These substitutions are marked with a minus [−], for unsuccessfully decoded, in column 2 of Figures 7.2 and 7.4.) Words not attempted and either pronounced by the teacher or omitted are also recorded in the substitution column. (These substitutions are marked with a "0," for not attempted, in column 2 in Figures 7.2 and 7.4.) Words incorrectly decoded and subsequently self-corrected are recorded in the substitution column. (These substitutions are marked with a plus [+], for correctly decoded, in column 2 in Figures 7.2 and 7.4.) Words not known instantly that are decoded correctly are also listed on the oral reading analysis sheet (see Figure 7.2, column 7 and Figure 7.4, column 7) because they provide data on the frequency with which a student is successfully decoding difficult words.

Frequently a student may identify a word automatically but incorrectly (for example, *this* for *the*). The miscue may or may not be self-corrected by the student. In either case the student has not deliberately attempted to decode an unknown word, and, consequently, there would be no notes about the student's use of a general word recognition strategy. (This type of miscue is indicated by a blank in column 2 of Figures 7.2 and 7.4.)

Teachers should study several samples of a student's word analysis attempts gathered over time in an effort to understand how the student generally deals with difficult words. It may become apparent, for example, that the student habitually waits for the teacher to pronounce the words or omits the words altogether and continues reading. Or, the student may try to attack most unknown words but with little success. After instruction in the general word recognition strategy presented in Chapter 6, the incidence of unknown words deliberately and successfully decoded, as recorded on oral reading analysis sheets, should increase if instruction has been effective.

PHONIC ANALYSIS

The phonic analysis skills of students having difficulty with word recognition also should be assessed. This section discusses two aspects of phonic analysis, symbol-sound correspondence knowledge and the ability to analyze, or segment, one-syllable and multisyllabic words correctly. Assessing students' symbol-sound correspondence knowledge should be done in a manner that moves from symbol to sound as opposed to sound to symbol and should be based on actual reading. We also recommend assessing students' ability to analyze words correctly through examination of their word attack performance during actual reading.

Before discussing specific strategies for assessing phonics knowledge, several problems seen with many phonics tests should be addressed. One common problem is that students are often given sounds and asked to provide symbols instead of being given symbols and asked to provide sounds. Furthermore, some paper and pencil tests provide three or four words that have the same beginning sound or vowel sound as a picture that is shown or a stimulus word pronounced by the teacher and then ask students to circle the correct word. The choices are not read to the students, so they have to know the letter that represents the sound in the picture or stimulus word and be able to find the correct word. For example, the teacher asks the students to circle the word that begins with the same sound as *sun* from among the following choices: *ship, sat, chin, zoo*. Or, the teacher asks them to write the letter that they hear at the beginning of the word *sun*. When assessing vowels, the teacher may read a word and ask the students to circle the correct word from among three or four choices. For example, the teacher reads the word *pin* and has students circle the correct word from among the choices *pine, pan, pin, pain*.

The problem with sound to symbol assessment is that it does not tell us about the phonics skills a reader must use when decoding words not known instantly. The fact that a reader can provide the correct symbol for a sound is no guarantee that he or she can give the correct sound for the same symbol. In other words, a student may be able to tell you that *sat* begins with the same sound as *sun*, given the choices *ship, sat, chin*, and *zoo*, but you still do not know if the student will "give" the word *sunny* the *s* sound when trying to decode it. Phonics knowledge is often tested in such a "recognition" mode (for example, what word from among the four choices begins with the same sound as a stimulus word or picture?) because it can be assessed through a group paper and pencil test. However, such assessments do not necessarily tell you what a student does when he or she "sees" a symbol and has to produce a sound, which is, of course, precisely what must be done in decoding an unfamiliar word.

Phonics tests that attempt to assess from symbol to sound by asking students to read lists of words overlook the fact that students may be reading some of the words as sight words. If so, there is no guarantee that the student really knows the symbol-sound correspondence for the phonics element being tested.[4] For example, if a student reads *seat* as a sight word, the teacher really does not know whether the student knows that the "long a" sound is one of the sounds that the symbol *ea* may have.

Another common approach to phonics testing is to ask a student to pronounce letters in isolation. The problem with this approach is that it is difficult to isolate some sounds. For example, the sound for the letter *b* often comes out as /buh/; a vowel sound has been attached. Similarly, even though some students may be able to sound out unknown words, they may not be able to sound out the individual letters in words. Conversely, some students may be able to give a sound in isolation for a consonant, blend, vowel, or vowel combination, but be unable to apply this phonics knowledge when attempting to decode a word.

Informal Phonics Inventory

One useful way to assess symbol-sound correspondence knowledge that avoids the problems listed above is to use an informal phonics inventory similar to that presented by Ekwall and Shanker (1983). Such an inventory begins with five or six simple words such as *am, on, in, it, all, up*, which a student must know to be able to take the test. If a student does not know the words, the teacher should review them with the student before beginning the inventory. Then the student reads a list of nonsense words constructed from the five or six simple words. In the area of initial consonant sounds, sample items on the inventory might include the following: *bin, con, dat, fon, gat, hin, jall, kat, lin, mon, nall, pon, quin, rin, all, tat, von, wat, yit, zall.* An item is counted as wrong only if the phonic element being tested is pronounced incorrectly. For example, if a student reads *din* for *bin*, this would suggest that the student may have difficulty with the symbol-sound correspondence for *b*. However, if the student reads *bine* for *bin*, this would not be counted as an error in the category of initial consonant sounds.

In addition to initial consonants, other categories to be assessed would include initial consonant blends, consonant digraphs, final consonant sounds, long and short vowel sounds, and vowel combinations. An example of an informal phonics inventory is presented in Figure 7.3.

Informal phonics inventories are useful screening devices for determining a student's general strengths and weaknesses in symbol-sound correspondence knowledge. For example, assume a student misses only one item under initial consonants, two items under initial consonant blends, three items under long and short vowels, but ten items under vowel combinations. This suggests that

FIGURE 7.3   Informal Phonics Inventory

DIRECTIONS   The student must know the following words: *in, on, am, all, it, up.*
Then, have the student read the nonsense words in column 1 of each category
followed by the nonsense words in column 2. Stop in a particular category if
the student misses five consecutive words or seems unduly frustrated. If the
student does not give the desired vowel sound, ask him or her to try the word
again, this time giving it a different vowel sound.

Initial Consonant Sounds

1	2
bin	bon
con	cit
din	dall
fon	fun
gam	git
hin	hon
jall	jit
kam	kon
lin	lall
mon	min
nall	nit
pon	pall
quin	quam
rin	rit
sup	sall
tam	tip
von	vall
wup	wam
yit	yon
zall	zin

Initial Consonant Blends

1	2
blin	blam
brit	bron
clup	clit
crin	crup
drall	dron
dwam	dwin
flup	flam
fram	frall
glon	glit
grup	gron
plin	plon
prit	prin
scup	scam
skall	skup
slin	slon
smit	smup
snam	snall
spon	spam
stin	ston
swup	swin
trall	trup
twam	twall
wrup	writ

Triple Blends

1	2
schall	schin
scrin	scrup
shrup	shrall

1	2
splon	splam
sprin	sprit
squit	squin
strall	stron
thrup	thrall

Final Consonant Sounds

	1	2
x	bax	rox
ld	pild	buld
mp	tamp	fomp

	1	2
nd	jand	lund
ng	ding	pong
nk	tink	dank
nt	fent	bint
rk	sark	hirk

FIGURE 7.3   Informal Phonics Inventory (*Cont.*)

Digraphs

Vowel Combinations

		1	2
ch	(church)	chall	cham
sh		shup	shon
th	(think)	tham	thit
th	(then)	tham	thit
wh	(which)	whup	whan
wh	(who)	whup	wham
ph		phon	pham

		1	2
ai	(rain)	bain	mait
ay	(day)	nay	tay
au	(author)	taud	raul
aw	(law)	faw	baw
ea	(meat)	teap	tead
ea	(head)	teap	tead
ee	(seed)	jeed	neep
ei	(weight)	peight	feight
ei	(receive)	ceip	ceif
ew	(few)	rew	tew
oa	(boat)	soat	koad
oi	(boil)	doil	doin
oo	(book)	fook	nood
oo	(moon)	foon	nood
ou	(cloud)	poud	pouse
ow	(slow)	fow	jow
ow	(now)	fow	jow

Long and Short Vowels

	1	2
ă	sab	hap
ā	dade	lafe
ĕ	ret	fem
ē	bege	lete
ĭ	mip	sim
ī	dite	hipe
ŏ	jod	mot
ō	kope	noke
ŭ	fut	pum
ū	sume	bule

the student knows the symbol-sound correspondence for the first three categories fairly well but needs to work on vowel combinations.

Several words of caution, however. The fact that a student misses one or two items involving the consonant cluster *sl,* for example, does not "prove" that the student needs instruction in the symbol-sound correspondence of *sl.* It only suggests such a possibility. It also suggests that the teacher should begin paying particular attention to *sl* words the student decodes during oral reading.

One additional limitation of an informal phonics inventory is worth mentioning. Most informal phonics inventories assess words (or nonsense words) in isolation. However, missing no items on such a test does not guarantee that a student is applying this phonics knowledge appropriately when decoding unfamiliar words during actual reading. Again, oral reading analysis provides a more valid assessment of a student's ability to use phonic analysis in word recognition during actual reading.

In sum, an informal phonics inventory gives a teacher some idea of how well a student can decode symbols into sounds when no other cuing systems are in operation (the syntactic, semantic, and knowledge systems that are present when the student reads real text). As long as teachers keep this basic limitation in mind and remember that the best assessment lies in an analysis of how a student reads real text, such isolated tests can be marginally useful.

Group Paper and Pencil Phonics Test

A second approach used to assess a student's knowledge of phonics is described by Johnson and Pearson (1978). As with the informal phonics inventory, nonsense words are used in this approach. A student is directed to read a nonsense word that contains an underlined letter and then to circle the real word (from among three choices), which has the same sound as the underlined letter in the nonsense word. Examples of several test items are presented below.

*c*ibe	kite	say	cat
*c*ate	king	sad	cent
*g*ipe	game	gym	got
*g*ade	got	gem	gym
fa*y*	made	hat	car
p*af*	car	at	late

An advantage of this paper and pencil phonics test, compared to the informal phonics inventory described earlier, is that it can be administered to a group instead of on an individual basis. It is particularly useful for testing students' knowledge of single letters or letter pairs that have more than one sound. If students do not know the real words, these can be read to them. However, the nonsense words should be left for the students to decode on their own.

This test, like others, has limitations. Often what it really tests is students' ability to recognize variant spellings for the same sound (for example, *cate-king, fay-made*).

Phonics Assessment Through Oral Reading Analysis

To assess a student's weaknesses in symbol-sound correspondence knowledge based on his or her ability to analyze words correctly when reading, it is important to keep careful records and analyses of a number of oral reading samples. A record could be kept of the following:

1. Substitutions involving a single, distinct, readily apparent symbol-sound correspondence mismatch. In this case an incorrect sound is given for a particular symbol (*began* for *begin* would be recorded as a distinct symbol-sound mismatch whereas *cran* for *canyon* would be recorded as a more complex substitution involving a multisyllabic syllable word).

2. Substitutions involving a one-syllable word being incorrectly segmented into phonemes. The substitution may not contain the same number of

phonemes as the actual word (*family* for *flame*) or the phonemes may not be in the proper order (*quiet* for *quite*). In many instances, this type of substitution would also involve one or more symbol-sound correspondence mismatches which were readily apparent ("short i" for "short u" in the case of *striked* for *struck*).

3. Substitutions involving multisyllabic words being incorrectly segmented into syllables (*eliss* ["short e"] for *easily*; *expeller* for *explore*) or syllables being incorrectly analyzed into phonemes (*growling* for *glowing*). In many instances this type of substitution would also involve one or more symbol-sound correspondence mismatches that were readily apparent ("short e" for *ea* in the case of *eliss* or *easily*).

An example of the type of record keeping that is recommended is presented in Figure 7.4 in the form of oral reading analysis sheets. (Column 3 of the chart will be explained later in the chapter in the section on contextual analysis.) In addition to indicating whether or not word recognition substitutions involved incorrect analysis of 1 syllable or 2+ syllable words (see columns 4 and 5 in Figure 7.4), the teacher should list apparent symbol-sound correspondence mismatches ("short e" for *ea* in *easily*, see column 6 in Figure 7.4).

Based on such data, the teacher should look for recurring problems such as frequent substitutions involving a particular symbol-sound correspondence (for example, *ea*) or a high incidence of substitutions involving incorrect analysis of one-syllable or multisyllabic words.

Consider, for example, a teacher's notebook entries based on one student's oral reading in Figure 7.4. Billy Stone, a fifth-grade student, is reading on a third-grade level. Over four samples Billy made fifteen word recognition substitutions involving symbol-sound correspondence knowledge; three of these involved the CVCe pattern, three involved *i*, and three involved *ea*. Billy made seven substitutions involving the analysis of 1 syllable words and nine substitutions involving 2+ syllable words. This would suggest that Billy may benefit from instruction in the CVCe pattern, in sounds for *i*, and in sounds for *ea* as well as instruction in applying this knowledge to actual reading. Billy may also benefit from instruction in how to segment, sound, and blend 1 syllable and 2+ syllable words. After instruction, the number of substitutions Billy makes during oral reading involving words with the CVCe pattern, *i*, *ea*, and 1 syllable and 2+ syllable words should decrease.

Actually, if a teacher were listening to a student read on a regular basis, such as twice a week, he or she would have more than four samples on which to base decisions about areas in need of instruction. In other words, four oral reading samples are not sufficient for assessment but are here included only for the purpose of illustration.

Another technique used to investigate a student's weaknesses in the area of phonics involves a self-report procedure. The student is asked to write down all words encountered during independent reading that he or she has difficulty decoding. The teacher discusses with the student why he or she had difficulty

FIGURE 7.4 Oral Reading Analysis Sheets Based on Four Sessions

Column 1   Substitution is written above the actual word from the text.

Column 2   Indicates whether or not the general word recognition strategy was used: + = used successfully; − = not used successfully; 0 = student didn't try (word consciously omitted or pronounced by the teacher); blank = not applicable (student decoded word automatically even though he or she did not read the correct word).

Column 3   Indicates whether or not a nonsemantic substitution was self-corrected: + = nonsemantic substitution self-corrected; − = nonsemantic substitution not self-corrected; 0 = semantic substitution.

Column 4   Indicates whether or not substitution involved incorrect analysis of a 1 syllable word.

Column 5   Indicates whether or not substitution involved incorrect analysis of a 2+ syllable word.

Column 6   Indicates apparent difficulty in terms of symbol-sound correspondence knowledge. Other notes can be made here as well, such as difficulty with basic sight words, inflectional endings, affixes.

Column 7   Indicates unfamiliar words that were deliberately and successfully decoded.

10/2

	1 Error	2 General Word Recognition Strategy	3 Nonsemantic Substitution	4 1 Syllable Word	5 2+ Syllable Word	6 Apparent Difficulty	7 Successfully Decoded
p. 78	striked struck		0	X		ŭ ed	whiz
	began begin		0			ĭ	swish
	scared screamed	−	−	X		scr ea	
	cheeks SC knees	+	+				
p. 79	game came	−				ca	crack
	plat plate no SC	−	−			ā (CVCe)	
	now	+	+				
Totals	5	2− 2+	2/5	2	0		3+

Number of words <u>118</u>   Word recognition accuracy <u>96%</u>

Number of times nonsemantic substitutions self-corrected/total number of nonsemantic substitution <u>2/5</u> = <u>40%</u>

FIGURE 7.4 Oral Reading Analysis Sheets Based on Four Sessions (*Cont.*)

10/5 Error	General Word Recognition Strategy	Nonsemantic Substitution	1 Syllable Word	2 + Syllable Word	Apparent Difficulty	Successfully Decoded
p. 85 ĕliss easily	−	−		X	ea	mouth
father farther		−			ar	fearful
expeller explore	−	∕ −		X		candle
suched touched	−	−				
p. 86 take SC look		+				
family flame	−	−	X		ā (CVCe)	relight
frice fierce	−	−	X		ier/ri	finally
growling glowing	−			X		
shout SC shouted		0				
recozicle recognize	−	−		X		
Totals 8	7 −	1/9	2	4		5 +

Number of words 143   Word recognition accuracy 94%

Number of times nonsemantic substitutions self-corrected/total number of nonsemantic substitutions 1/9 = 11%

10/12 Error	General Word Recognition Strategy	Nonsemantic Substitution	1 Syllable Word	2 + Syllable Word	Apparent Difficulty	Successfully Decoded
p. 99 cran canyon	−	−		X		decided
nature national	−	0		X	tion	
grōg gorge	−	−	X		gor/gro	

(*Cont.*)

FIGURE 7.4 Oral Reading Analysis Sheets Based on Four Sessions (*Cont.*)

10/12 Error	General Word Recognition Strategy	Nonsemantic Substitution	1 Syllable Word	2+ Syllable Word	Apparent Difficulty	Successfully Decoded
p.100 where were	−	−			were	squirrel
wĭnding winding	−	−			ī	lizards
cross chose	−	−	X		ō (CVCe)	weather
Totals 6	6−	0/5	2	2		4+

Number of words 118   Word recognition accuracy 96%

Number of times nonsemantic substitutions self-corrected/total number of nonsemantic substitutions 0/5 = 0%

10/16 Error	General Word Recognition Strategy	Nonsemantic Substitution	1 Syllable Word	2+ Syllable Word	Apparent Difficulty	Successfully Decoded
p.103 neighborhood neighbor's	−	−			's	clever
neighborhood SC						
neighbor		+				
was is		0			is	
p.104 bouncing TP	0			X		lemonade
basket breakfast	−	−		X	ea	honey
silling					ī	
sliding	−	−		X	sli/sli	
around^my car						
quiet quite	−	−	X		ite/iet	
Totals 6	4−	1/5	1	3		3+

Number of words 113   Word recognition accuracy 94%

Number of times nonsemantic substitution self-corrected/total number of nonsemantic substitutions 1/5 = 20%

with a particular word. For example, a student might say that he or she had trouble with *screamed* because he or she did not know the sound for *scr*. From discussions with the student and from an analysis of the words identified by the student as troublesome, the teacher may be able to discern several patterns of errors. Armed with this information and the information gathered during oral reading, an appropriate instructional program can be planned.

STRUCTURAL ANALYSIS

As with phonic analysis, teachers should assess the structural analysis skills of students having difficulty with word recognition. This section discusses assessment of students' decoding of inflectional endings and affixes.

Inflectional Endings

Substitutions involving inflectional endings (see Chapter 6) can be a problem for readers if the errors interfere with meaning. When a student appears to be having difficulty with inflectional endings, there are several assessment strategies that may be used to determine the student's initial performance level and to evaluate progress following instruction.

However, pronunciations of words due to dialect, such as a variation of Black English, should not be regarded as errors. Students who speak Black English should not receive instruction and practice in inflectional endings simply because their dialect typically omits many inflectional endings. For example, one of the common features of Black English is a principle called final consonant cluster reduction. The rule for final consonant cluster reduction says that whenever a word ends in a consonant cluster of two or more sounds, reduce the cluster to the first of the consonants. So, a student who speaks Black English would likely say /han/ for *hand* and /pas/ for *past* of *passed*. A teacher who infers that /pas/ for *passed* indicates a lack of attention to inflections makes a grievous instructional error were he or she to drill the child in inflections.

One technique for assessing a student's skill in reading inflections correctly involves a paper and pencil task similar to many work book activities. A sentence containing a blank is presented along with several words. For example:

1. Tina _____ to go to the game. (wanted, wanting)

2. Last night my dad _____ me with my homework. (helps, helped)

The student is asked to select the correct word for the blank. Choices comprise the same word with different endings. If the student does not know all of the words in a particular sentence, the teacher should read the sentence to the student. Even the base word of the answer can be read aloud if necessary, but the two choices should be read by the student.

If a student is having difficulty with inflectional endings, his or her performance on this type of activity should improve following instruction. A progress chart can be kept indicating percentage of blanks filled in correctly on a series of assessments taken over time. One advantage of this type of task is that it can be administered to a group. A disadvantage is that it does not really tell the teacher what a reader is doing during actual reading.

A second procedure for assessing a student's skill in reading inflectional endings is to keep a record of the word recognition substitutions involving inflectional endings made during oral reading. A high incidence of substitutions involving inflectional endings that interfered with meaning indicates that instruction in inflectional endings is needed.

Affixes

Recognizing affixes (see Chapter 6) aids students in the syllabication and decoding of unknown words. A group-administered paper and pencil task could be used to assess students' skill in recognizing affixes in text. Such an assessment might involve asking students to circle all of the prefixes and suffixes they could find in a given text segment. A short story or article, work book page, or skill sheet on which the students can write might serve as the reading material for this task. Alternatively, a piece of acetate can be placed over a page in the student's basal reader so that, using actual reading material, the student can locate affixes with a grease pencil or overhead transparency pen. The teacher should keep a record of the number of affixes missed, and after instruction, this number should decrease, indicating greater student awareness of affixes.

An advantage of this approach is that it can be administered to a group. A serious limitation is that it assesses a student's ability to recognize affixes during teacher directed activities but not during natural reading activity.

Another technique that assesses skill in decoding affixes involves recording word recognition substitutions during oral reading. A high incidence of substitutions involving affixes indicates that the student was not attending to affixes and that instruction in using affixes as an aide in decoding might be needed. A progress chart can be kept and should demonstrate improvements in this area after instruction.

CONTEXTUAL ANALYSIS

As with phonic and structural analysis, the contextual analysis skills of students having difficulty with word recognition should be assessed. One method for doing this is through oral reading analysis. Of particular interest is the incidence of nonsemantic substitutions that are self-corrected by a student during oral reading (see substitutions marked with a plus [+] in column 3 of Figures 7.2 and 7.4). A nonsemantic substitution is a miscue that does not make sense in the context of its passage (see substitutions marked with a minus [−] in column 3 of Figures 7.2 and 7.4). A semantic substitution, by contrast, is a miscue that does make sense in the context of its passage (see substitutions marked with a 0 in column 3 of Figures 7.2 and 7.4). As pointed out in Chapter 6, low-achieving readers tend to make more and correct fewer nonsemantic substitutions than good readers. A relatively low incidence of self-corrections on nonsemantic substitutions would indicate that a student was not monitoring for meaning as he or she was decoding and not using context to help her decode difficult words.

A record can be kept of the ratio of nonsemantic substitutions that were self-corrected during a number of oral reading activities. Looking once again at Figure 7.4, we see that two of Billy's five nonsemantic substitutions on Day 1 were self-corrected, one out of nine on Day 2, zero out of five on Day 3, and one out of five on Day 4. These data indicate that Billy did not self-correct most word recognition substitutions that interfered with meaning. Following instruction, the incidence of a student's nonsemantic substitutions should decrease and the incidence of nonsemantic substitutions self-corrected should increase.

FLUENCY

To assess a student's ability to read automatically and with good phrasing, teachers should pay particular attention to fluency during oral reading. A student who has to consciously or deliberately decode many words is not reading automatically. A student who is reading in a word-by-word manner is not reading in phrase units. Comments on a student's automaticity or lack thereof should be recorded on the reading difficulties record sheet (see Figure 7.5). After instruction in automaticity and phrasing, progress in these areas should be seen during oral reading. Audio tapes could be kept over time to demonstrate to students their progress in automaticity and phrasing.

Working on a student's reading rate should not be tackled until the student has mastered the basics of decoding and is doing so automatically. However, once a student is decoding fairly automatically, the teacher should assess the silent reading rate of instructional level materials and compare it to the rate listed as slow in Table 6.2. Several samples should be used initially to determine a student's reading rate. Also, several comprehension questions and a retelling of the story should be used to determine if the student has comprehended the material. A progress chart, indicating the reading rate in words per minute and the comprehension score for each passage read, can be kept. Also, data on a student's reading rate should be recorded.

USING THE READING DIFFICULTIES RECORD SHEET TO PLAN INSTRUCTION

This chapter has discussed a number of ways to collect and analyze oral reading data in order to locate sources of word recognition difficulty. To this point the discussion has centered on teachers' interpretation of these data. The remainder of this section will discuss ways to assist the teacher with interpretation of these data.

Students who are not recognizing grade level words with approximately 90 to 95 percent accuracy can be considered to have difficulty with word recognition. Given a student with difficulty in word recognition, the teacher's task is to determine the most appropriate types of corrective instruction. One way to approach this task is to look for *relative strengths and weaknesses* in a student's word recognition performance. The first few pages of the reading difficulties record sheet, presented in Figure 7.5, can be used to summarize data collected from a student's oral reading sessions. The data in Figure 7.5 summarizes the information in Figure 7.4.

Billy Stone is in the fifth grade but has been placed in a 3^1 (first half of third grade) reader for instruction. Ongoing assessment of Billy's instructional level reveals that the 3^1 level appears to be a good instructional level for Billy (see IB of Figure 7.5). Because Billy is not decoding with 90 to 95 percent accuracy at his grade level, the teacher should suspect that he has difficulty with word recognition.

From Figure 7.5 it can be seen that the teacher believes the data from the oral reading analysis suggests that Billy would benefit from instruction in the general word recognition strategy. Four samples of oral reading reveal that Billy was unable to decode most of the unfamiliar words he encountered.

Billy has made repeated symbol-sound correspondence mismatches that involve the CVCe pattern (three substitutions), words with *i* (three substitutions), and words with *ea* (three substitutions). It can also be seen that 7/25 (or 28 percent) of Billy's substitutions involved inappropriate analysis of one-syllable words, and 9/25 (or 36 percent) of his errors involved inappropriate analysis of multisyllabic words. These data suggest the need for instruction in vowel sounds for words with the CVCe pattern, sounds for the symbols *i* and *ea* and analysis, or segmentation, sounding, and blending, of one-syllable, and multisyllabic words.

The data also suggest that Billy is not monitoring for meaning. He self-corrected nonsemantic substitutions only 17 percent of the time (only four nonsemantic substitutions out of twenty-four). This would suggest focusing instruction on the use of context as an aid in decoding.

On the other hand, Billy does not appear to need special instruction at this time in basic sight words or in structural analysis. Very few of his substitutions involved basic sight words and no basic sight words were missed frequently. Also, very few errors involved inflectional endings and affixes.

Again, we want to point out that a student's reading difficulties record

FIGURE 7.5   Reading Difficulties Record Sheet
Instructional Level and Word Recognition

Student's Name <u>Billy Stone</u>

Age _____   Grade __5__

I.   Instructional Level

A.	IRI	Level	Word Recognition Accuracy	Average Comprehension	Oral Comprehension	Silent Comprehension
Date	9/16	2^2	96	85	90	80
Instr. level	3'	3^1	95	75	75	75
		3^2	89	70	75	65
		4	85	60	70	50

Comments:

B.   Ongoing assessment of instructional level (from oral reading analysis sheets and comprehension questions)

Date	Pages/Book	Word Recognition Accuracy	Comprehension
10/2	78–84; lvl 3'	96 (p. 79)	85
10/5	85–90, 3'	94 (p. 86)	75
10/12	99–102, 3'	96 (p. 100)	70
10/16	103–108, 3'	94 (p. 104)	65

Comments:

10/19   WR Acc. and Comp. okay at level 3'.

II. Word Recognition

A.   Basic sight words not known frequently missed (from informal test and/or oral reading analysis)

Comments:
10/19   None from 10/2–10/16

B.   General word recognition strategy

1. Student's comments:
10/5   He says he tries to sound out a word he doesn't know.

(Cont.)

**FIGURE 7.5   Reading Difficulties Record Sheet
Instructional Level and Word Recognition (*Cont.*)**

2. Degree to which unfamiliar words deliberately and successfully decoded (from oral reading analysis sheets)

Comments:
10/19   On 10/2, 5 SD*/2 NSD; on 10/5 5 SD/7 NSD; on 10/12, 4 SD/6 NSD; on 10/16, 3 SD/4 NSD. Could use help with general word recognition strategy.
*SD = successfully decoded; NSD = not successfully decoded

C. Phonic analysis

1. Informal phonics inventory Date _____

Results:

2. Consistent errors in symbol-sound correspondence knowledge and/or ability to analyze 1 and 2+ syllable words (from oral reading analysis sheets)

Comments:
10/19   From 10/2–10/16, 3 errors with CVCe, 3 errors with *i*, 3 errors with ea. Review of each of these needed. From 10/2–10/16, 7 errors with 1 syllable words, 9 errors with 2+ syllable words. Needs help analyzing 1 and 2+ syllable words.

D. Structural analysis—infectional endings and/or knowledge of affixes

1. Informal testing
   Date   % Correct/Comments

2. Consistent errors (from oral reading analysis sheets)
   10/19   From 10/2–10/16, none.

E. Contextual analysis

Self-correction of nonsemantic substitutions (from oral reading analysis sheets)

Comments
10/19   From 10/2–10/16:2/5, 1/9, 0/9, 1/5 nonsemantic substitutions corrected. Seems to need help with this. Try oral reading for meaning.

F. Fluency

1. Rate
   Date   Pages/Book   Words per Min.   Comp.

Comments:

2. Automaticity/phrasing

Comments:

This teacher is keeping oral reading analysis notes as students are engaged in oral reading. *(Peter Vadnai)*

sheet should be based on more than four reading samples. Four samples have been included here for the purpose of illustration. In the classroom or clinic, low-achieving readers with difficulties in word recognition should be reading aloud to the teacher at least once or twice a week. This will provide numerous samples that can be analyzed for initial and ongoing assessment and evaluation of pupil progress.

Classroom teachers may be wondering how they would have time to collect the type of data presented in Figures 7.4 and 7.5. It is important to remember that this would be done only for those students who are low-achieving readers with word recognition difficulties.

When listening to a student read, the teacher needs to record only word recognition substitutions (column 1) and words successfully decoded (column 7) on a chart as shown in Figure 7.4, along with notations indicating whether or not the general word recognition strategy was used successfully in decoding efforts. The rest of the information in Figure 7.4 (columns 3, 4, 5, and 6) can be filled in at a later date. The teacher should devote twenty minutes to oral reading analysis several times a week. The teacher can work with an entire reading group for a ten-minute period, focusing on students with word recognition difficulties and making notes as individuals read aloud. The students can then reread this material in pairs as the teacher spends the next ten minutes completing columns 3 through 6. Additional suggestions for scheduling time to help low-achieving readers during the reading period will be discussed in Chapter 15.

To enter data on the reading difficulties record sheet, the teacher should periodically (such as every four to six weeks) analyze the data from four or more oral reading sessions. An aide can take the class for an hour twice a month, or the teacher can ask the principal to provide time during the day when this task could be completed. Once the data from a number of oral reading sessions have been collected, a person with expertise in remedial reading, such as the classroom teacher or the reading resource teacher, can enter the data on the reading difficulties record sheet (Figure 7.5), analyze it, and decide on recommendations for remediation.

In Chapter 15 all of the remedial instruction recommendations made for Billy Stone in the areas of word recognition, comprehension, and vocabulary will be reviewed and a specific remedial program recommended.

SUMMARY   This chapter recommended oral reading analysis as the primary assessment tool used by a classroom teacher or special reading teacher to determine a low-achieving reader's strengths and weaknesses in word recognition. The chapter demonstrated how oral reading analysis can be used to gain information about a student's basic sight vocabulary, use of a general word recognition strategy, skill in phonic, contextual, and structural analysis, and fluency. The use of a reading difficulties record sheet to collect data based on a student's oral reading was discussed, along with ways to plan instruction.

SUGGESTED   1. Conduct oral reading analysis on at least three occasions with a student
ACTIVITIES   who is not proficient in word recognition. Record necessary information (columns 1, 2, and 7 for Figure 7.4) on an oral reading analysis sheet as the student is reading, and complete the chart after the student has finished reading (columns 3 to 6 of Figure 7.4).

2. Based on the data from three or more oral reading analysis sheets, fill out the word recognition section of a reading difficulties record sheet for a student. If you have not been able to complete oral reading analysis sheets because a child was not available, you may be able to complete a reading difficulties sheet on a student based on oral reading analysis sheets provided by your instructor.

NOTES   1. See Wixson (1979).
2. See Pikulski and Shannon (1982b).

3. See Biemiller (1979), Kibby (1979), Leslie and Osol (1978), and Williamson and Young (1974).

EKWALL, E. E., AND SHANKER, J. L. (1983). *Diagnosis and remediation of the disabled reader* (2nd ed.). Boston: Allyn and Bacon.
The authors provide a good discussion of some of the problems inherent in phonics testing. They also describe an informal phonics inventory they have developed.

JOHNSON, D. D., AND PEARSON, P. D. (1978). *Teaching reading vocabulary*. New York: Holt, Rinehart and Winston.
Johnson and Pearson discuss a number of paper and pencil word recognition tests which the classroom teacher may find useful.

SUGGESTED READINGS

Chapter 8

Comprehension Instruction

OVERVIEW

As you read this chapter use the following list of main ideas to guide your understanding and reflection.

Metacognition, in which readers are aware of and have control over their comprehension, is an important part of the reading comprehension process.

Low-achieving readers may need instruction in specific strategies they can use when reading on their own to foster good comprehension.

Low-achieving readers may need instruction in comprehension monitoring and the use of fix-up strategies to improve poor comprehension.

Explicit instruction in a comprehension strategy will explain to students *what* a strategy is, *why* it is important, *how* to perform the strategy, and *when* to use the strategy when reading actual text.

Effective reading comprehension involves more than understanding the message on a printed page. Reading comprehension is also a metacognitive process in which readers are aware of and have control over their comprehension. Successful comprehenders of text generally understand that the purpose of reading is to read for meaning. They know how to use specific strategies to facilitate comprehension, and they monitor their own comprehension as they read, implementing fix-up strategies when comprehension has failed.[1]

Low-achieving readers may have trouble with reading comprehension for a number of reasons. They may not actively read for meaning, focusing more on reading as a decoding process than as a meaning-getting process.[2] Also, they may not know how to use comprehension-fostering strategies and may not be as effective as good readers at monitoring their own comprehension.[3]

Reading instruction designed to improve low-achieving readers' comprehension of text should stress that meaning getting is the purpose of reading. Students should be taught specific comprehension strategies they can use when reading on their own, and they should be taught why these strategies are important. Low-achieving readers should also be taught to monitor their reading comprehension and to stop and apply appropriate fix-up strategies when they do not understand what they are reading.

PROBLEMS WITH CONVENTIONAL READING COMPREHENSION INSTRUCTION

Unfortunately, conventional reading comprehension instruction, developmental or corrective, is often inadequate for a number of reasons. First, many teachers do not provide students with explicit instruction in how to perform comprehension strategies. Too often they merely mention skills (for example, "The main idea is the most important idea in a paragraph") and then help students complete work sheets on these skills. In a study of thirty-nine intermediate grade classrooms, Durkin (1978–1979) found that comprehension instruction in which teachers did or said something to improve students' ability to comprehend actual text occurred less than 1 percent of the time during the reading period. In a survey of basal reader manuals, Durkin (1981a) found that comprehension skills were mentioned but explicit suggestions for how to model them were not provided.

In addition to the lack of explicit instruction, reading comprehension instruction often fails to provide for adequate transfer to actual reading of connected text. Far too often reading comprehension skills are practiced in isolation on skill sheets, and students are not taught how to transfer these skills to real reading situations.[4] There is no guarantee that skills covered on skills sheets will be used by students when they read actual text on their own.

For example, Taylor, Olson, Prenn, Rybczynski, and Zakaluk (1985) found that sixth-grade students who appeared to be quite skilled at "reading for main ideas" on the basis of their performance on multiple choice skill sheets (88 percent correct), did significantly less well when asked to answer multiple choice questions on main ideas in their social studies book (73 percent correct), and did very poorly when asked to generate main ideas for paragraphs in their social studies book (40 percent correct). Similar results were found in a second study.[5]

Low-achieving readers need to be shown explicitly how and when comprehension strategies should be used when engaged in independent reading. Although they cannot possibly use all of the comprehension strategies that have been taught, there are times when the conscious use of a particular strategy will be useful or even essential.

The third concern deals with the overwhelming number of skills that are "taught" or practiced, many of which will not be useful to students when they are reading connected text on their own. For example, it would be difficult to explain to students how numbering sentences in the sequence in which they appear would enhance their comprehension. Instead, teachers need to focus their comprehension instruction on strategies that students can actually use when reading independently.

The final concern is that students are not taught to be metacognitively aware of their own understanding as they read. That is, they have not learned to be aware of when they do or do not understand what they are reading. They are also not taught how to use specific fix-up strategies when their reading comprehension has failed. Many good readers may have learned to do this on their own, but many poor readers appear to be in need of instruction in comprehension monitoring.

MODEL FOR READING COMPREHENSION INSTRUCTION

The remainder of this chapter provides suggestions for sound reading comprehension instruction. Strategies are discussed that will help students become better comprehenders when reading on their own. The strategies fall under one or more of the following aspects of comprehension, all of which are essential:

1. Monitoring comprehension

2. Fostering general comprehension

3. Drawing inferences

4. Reading for important ideas

5. Studying

6. Using prior knowledge

In most cases the strategy is presented using the following steps:

1. An explanation of *what* the strategy consists of

2. An explanation about *why* the strategy is important

3. An explanation of *how* teachers can model the strategy

4. An explanation of *when* the strategy should be used in independent reading

5. Provisions for guided practice with actual text

6. Provisions for independent practice with actual text

Obviously teachers should do certain things routinely to enhance students' comprehension of specific texts. For example, sound developmental reading instruction includes introducing difficult vocabulary, activating students' prior knowledge, and asking thought-provoking questions for basal reader stories.[6] The focus in this chapter, however, will be on student-directed, as opposed to teacher-directed, comprehension strategies which poor comprehenders can learn to use independently. Not all strategies should be taught to all low-achieving readers. Chapter 9 provides guidance on which strategies to teach to particular students based on diagnosed needs.

COMPREHENSION STRATEGIES

Unlike good readers, many low-achieving readers do not check their comprehension as they read.[7] That is, they are not aware of whether they do or do not understand what they are reading. Furthermore, they have inadequate fix-up strategies for improving their comprehension.[8] This section discusses a specific strategy for teaching poor comprehenders to monitor and improve their comprehension of text.

Comprehension Rating

A four-step instructional procedure developed by Davey and Porter (1982) has been found to be effective in improving low-achieving readers' comprehension monitoring skills. The procedure is designed to help students (1) understand the purpose of print, (2) focus their attention on meaning while reading, (3) evaluate their comprehension while reading, and (4) develop fix-up strategies to improve their comprehension.

How. Step 1 of the procedure, helping students to understand the purpose of print, involves teacher demonstration and modeling. Through the use of cloze passages the teacher can show students that even if they do not read every word in a paragraph, they can still understand what they are reading. After discussing the importance of comprehension, some personal fix-up strategies, like rereading or looking up a difficult word in the dictionary, can be introduced. The teacher can also model comprehension monitoring while reading aloud to the students. ("I understand this paragraph, so I'll go on," "This paragraph doesn't make sense; I'd better reread it").

Step 2, focusing attention on meaning during silent reading, involves a comprehension-rating task. Students are given single sentences to read and rate for comprehension. Some sentences make sense ("Susie was crying because she fell down"). Some sentences do not make sense because they contain nonsense words ("The flug was happy"). Some sentences do not make sense even though they are made up of real words because of faulty logic ("Jimmy went to bed and then he brushed his teeth"). Working first in groups and then independently, students rate their comprehension of the sentences, using a plus (+) for sentences they do understand and a minus (−) for sentences they do not understand.

After demonstrating accurate comprehension ratings for sentences, students are given paragraphs to read and rate for comprehension. Some paragraphs make sense; some do not make sense because of faulty logic, inserted sentences that are out of context, or ideas that are nonsensical ("The window has one son"). Students first work in groups and then individually, rating paragraphs as either making sense (+) or not making sense (−).

Step 3, establishing criteria for understanding, involves a three-point comprehension-rating task. First working in groups and then working individually, students rate sentences, paragraphs, and longer texts as (1) "I understand well" (I have a clear, complete picture in my head and could explain it to someone else), (2) "I sort of understand" (I have an incomplete picture in my head and I couldn't explain it to someone else), or (3) "I don't understand." The teacher and students share their ratings for different sentences, paragraphs, and texts and discuss their reasons for particular ratings.

Students are also shown how to locate sources of comprehension difficulty in naturally occurring text, working first with nonsense words and out-of-context sentences and then moving to paragraphs and longer texts containing faulty logic and either nonsensical or confusing ideas. Examples of texts that might be used are presented in Figure 8.1.

Step 4, developing fix-up strategies, is implemented once students show competence with the first three steps. Attention is directed to both word level and idea level fix-up strategies.

Word level fix-up strategies include:

1. Read around the word (maybe you can skip the word without much loss of comprehension or can figure the word out from context clues).

2. Use context clues for help in decoding or predicting what a word means.

3. Look for structural clues within words.

4. Sound out words.

5. Use a dictionary.

6. Ask for help.

FIGURE 8.1   Examples of Passages to Use with the Comprehension-Rating Task

The sources of comprehension difficulty that students should identify are in italics.

Nonsense word   Kristie was so happy. She found a *dug* and put it in a jar.

Out-of-context sentence   Dan got up. He brushed his teeth. *The driver slammed on his brakes.* Then Dan got dressed.

Faulty logic   After Mrs. Jones put the roast in the oven, she got it out of the refrigerator. It smelled so good as it was cooking.

Nonsensical idea   It was a sunny summer afternoon. Nick wanted to go out to play. He put on his *raincoat* and ran out the door.

Confusing idea in actual text   London is a beautiful city. There are many famous old buildings like the Houses of Parliament and Westminster Abbey. *Many are buried there.*

The firefighters worked hard all morning. Sam was really hungry. *She* went to lunch at 11:00 A.M.

Dust storms swept across the Great Plains in the 1930s. Farmland was destroyed. *Many people moved away.*

Idea level fix-up strategies include:

1. Read on to make it clearer.

2. Reread carefully to make it clearer.

3. Look again at the title, pictures, headings.

4. Ask yourself questions.

5. Put ideas into your own words as you go along.

6. Picture the ideas in your head while you read.

7. Relate ideas to your personal experience.

8. Ask someone to clarify things.

Students are given a list of these fix-up strategies. Each strategy is modeled by the teacher (the teacher talks aloud as he or she performs the strategy) and then practiced by the students. Finally, students practice choosing and using fix-up strategies when they experience comprehension difficulties during actual reading. They are asked to make notes or mark places in the text where they use fix-up strategies, and later to explain to the teacher what strategies they used. If they are unable to do this independently, they can read individually with the teacher, receiving guidance about what fix-up strategies to use when they know they are experiencing comprehension difficulties.

This teacher is modeling the technique of comprehension monitoring for a group of intermediate grade students. *(Peter Vadnai)*

What, Why, When. The preceding discussion focused on *how* to model various aspects of the Davey and Porter comprehension-rating procedure and how Steps 3 and 4 can be used with actual text during guided and independent practice. In addition, it is important for the teacher to do the following:

1. *What*—Explain to students that they will be learning to monitor their reading comprehension.

2. *Why*—Explain to students that this is important because the purpose of reading is to understand the written message.

3. *When*—Explain to students that they should use comprehension monitoring as they are reading on their own. They should stop at the end of every paragraph or page (or any time they notice they are not understanding their text), and ask themselves whether or not they understand what they just read. If their answer is *no*, they should decide on the reason they are having difficulty and select an appropriate word level or idea level fix-up strategy.

The comprehension-rating procedure described above was used with fifth- and sixth-grade students who were poor comprehenders. Compared to a control group, students trained in the procedure had better scores on a reading comprehension test, generated better summaries of what they read, and were more successful in identifying idea level comprehension difficulties.[9]

GENERAL COMPREHENSION STRATEGIES

This section discusses a number of strategies that have been found to improve students' general ability to comprehend text when reading on their own.

Student-Generated Questioning

Student-generated questions during or after reading helps students to interact with the text, improves their comprehension, and makes them more independent as learners.[10] It has also been found to (1) increase involvement in the process of comprehension; (2) help focus attention on important information; (3) improve text processing time, and (4) help readers monitor their own comprehension.[11] Generally, however, students must be taught a specific self-questioning strategy for improved comprehension to occur. Simply telling students to ask themselves questions while reading will be ineffective.

Self-Questioning While Reading Narrative Text   A self-questioning technique that has proved successful with both elementary[12] and secondary students was developed by Singer and Donlan (1982). It involves students asking themselves story-specific questions about elements such as character, goal, obstacles, outcome, and theme. Only one story element is covered in a particular lesson. Examples of general and specific questions for the story "The Three Little Pigs" are presented in Figure 8.2.

Specific instructional steps to follow in this self-questioning procedure are presented below.

What. Students are told they will be learning how to ask and answer questions about stories they read.

Why. Students are told this is important because it will improve their ability to understand the stories they are reading.

How. Students are shown how to ask themselves certain kinds of questions as they read stories. The teacher begins with a story element, such as character, and explains that a story can either be about one character or a group of characters working together toward a common goal. The teacher then asks a general question about the main character, shows how to convert it into a story-specific question, and finally answers the question. Several other examples of story-specific questions that could have been asked are then presented. (Is this story about all three pigs or is it mostly about the third pig? Is this story about the wolf or the third pig?) Several questions are also discussed that are inappropriate because they do not pertain to the main character(s). (Where does this story take place? What other characters are in this story besides the three pigs and the wolf?) On subsequent days the same modeling procedure is repeated with the other story elements.

When. Students are told to ask and answer questions about the major story elements whenever they are reading a story that seems difficult to understand.

For guided practice, the teacher and students work together generating

FIGURE 8.2   General and Specific Questions for "The Three Little Pigs"

Story Element	General and Specific Questions
Character	GQ Who is the leading character?
	SQ Is this story more about the wolf or the third pig?
Goal	GQ What is the leading character trying to accomplish?
	SQ What does the third pig hope to accomplish in this story?
Obstacles	GQ What obstacles does the leading character encounter?
	SQ How does the wolf create problems for the third pig?
Outcome	GQ Does the leading character reach his or her goal?
	SQ How does the third pig overcome the wolf?
Theme	GQ Why did the author write this story?
	What does the author want to show us about life?
	SQ What did I learn from the story "The Three Little Pigs?"

story-specific questions on the main character for other stories in their basal reader. Good and bad story-specific questions are discussed. For independent practice, students work through several more stories on their own, generating and answering story-specific questions about the main character.

After teaching students how to generate and answer a story-specific question about the main character, the teacher can extend the discussion to the element of goal. For guided and independent practice, students should generate and answer questions about both the leading character and that character's goal. By the time that all story elements have been covered, students should be able to generate and answer story-specific questions about the main character, goal, obstacles, outcomes, and the theme of stories they read.

Reciprocal Questioning   Helfeldt and Lalik (1976) found that their reciprocal student-teacher questioning strategy, based on the ReQuest procedure,[13] had a positive effect on fifth-grade students' reading comprehension. This is a very simple procedure whereby students learn how to ask thought-provoking questions that help them interpret or better understand the material they have read. Steps include the following:

What. Students are told they will be learning how to generate questions that ask readers to interpret material they have read. Often these are "why" and "how" questions instead of "what," "where," or "when" questions. They require students to make inferences, or to interpret what is happening in a story.

Why. Students are told that if they ask each other interpretive questions about material they have read in small groups, their understanding of the material improves.

How. The teacher introduces vocabulary and asks several questions to motivate reading. The students read the assigned text and answer the motivating question in a small group discussion. Then, the teacher begins to ask thought-provoking, interpretive questions about the material. Every time a student correctly answers a question, the student then gets to ask the teacher a question. The student question then is followed by another teacher question. By observing and imitating teacher questions, students learn to ask good interpretive questions. Helfeldt and Lalik found that after fourteen 45-minute lessons with the teacher, students' inferential reading comprehension improved. An example of teacher-student questioning for a story is presented in Figure 8.3.

When. Students are told that after completing a reading assignment, they may want to work in groups of three or four and ask each other interpretive questions about the material they have read. Whoever answers a question correctly gets to ask the next question.

Guided practice occurs whenever the teacher and students engage in the reciprocal questioning model. For independent practice, students can work in small groups of three or four and ask each other questions about a story or informative selection they have read.

Reciprocal Teaching

A reciprocal teaching model that develops low-achieving readers' skill in monitoring and improving their comprehension has been developed by Palincsar and Brown (1984). The model involves students taking turns assuming the role of teacher and engaging a small group of readers in the study activities of questioning, summarizing, clarifying, and predicting. Palincsar and Brown found that students who learn to use the reciprocal teaching model make substantial improvements in their ability to answer comprehension questions based on textbook material, gains that are maintained over time. For example, Palincsar and Brown found that seventh-grade students who initially answered comprehension questions with only 40 percent accuracy after independent reading were able to read with 70 to 80 percent accuracy after engaging in the reciprocal teaching model for fifteen days. Students have also made significant gains on other reading comprehension measures after learning how to use the model. Recently, Palincsar and Brown have applied the strategy to whole class instructional settings with similar success.

How. The teacher works with a group of five or six poor comprehenders, modeling how to lead a dialogue about a paragraph of textbook material. After the group reads one paragraph, the teacher calls on one student to answer an important question regarding the paragraph. Then, the teacher summarizes the paragraph in a sentence or two. Confusing aspects of the paragraph, if any, are discussed and clarified, and a prediction about future content is made if one comes to mind. The procedure is then repeated with the next paragraph.

At first, students tend to be relatively passive observers but become more

FIGURE 8.3   Example of Reciprocal Teacher-Student Questioning Based on the Story "Tico and the Golden Wings" by Leo Lionni

Story Summary of "Tico and the Golden Wings"

Tico was a bird who had no wings. Luckily, the other birds were his friends and brought him food. Tico wished that he could fly like the other birds. One night he dreamt that he had golden wings. When he woke up, his dream had come true. Tico was happy and flew around all day with his new golden wings. The other birds left Tico alone. They thought Tico felt he was better than the rest of them because he had golden wings. Tico was sad and lonely. One day Tico gave a golden wing to a man who needed money to buy medicine for his sick child. Tico now had a black feather where the golden feather had been. One by one Tico gave away the rest of his golden feathers to people who needed help. His wings turned completely black. Tico flew back to his friends, the other birds. They were glad to see him because now he was just like them. Tico was happy and excited. But even though he looked the same as the others, he felt he was different because of his memories and dreams.

Reciprocal Questioning

TEACHER: How did Tico feel when he had no wings?

STUDENT A: He felt sad.

TEACHER: Good. Now you ask me a question that will really make me think about the story.

STUDENT A: What did Tico dream?

TEACHER: He dreamt he had golden wings. That question is okay, but the answer is right in the story. Try to ask another question that doesn't have an answer right in the story but will help me understand the story better. Maybe you can think of a question that starts with "how" or "why."

STUDENT A: How did Tico's friends feel about him when he had golden wings?

TEACHER: Good question. They were jealous. They thought he felt better than everybody else, but he didn't really feel this way. Here's another question. Why was Tico happy and excited at the end of the story?

STUDENT B: He was happy to be back with his friends.

TEACHER: Good. Any other reasons he may have been happy?

STUDENT B: Maybe he was happy about things he had done.

TEACHER: Great. Now you ask me a question about the story that will make me think.

STUDENT B: Do you think Tico should have gone back to the other birds at the end of the story?

TEACHER: Great question. Yes, because I think he was happy they accepted him again. But even though they thought he was just like them, he still felt a little special because of his memories of the good things he had done.

The teacher provides feedback as a group of four students practices the reciprocal teaching technique. *(Peter Vadnai)*

actively involved in the model as they attempt to assume the role of "teacher." As one student attempts to lead the group through the four activities of questioning, summarizing, clarifying, and predicting, the teacher offers a considerable amount of guidance and feedback. The teacher helps students generate important questions and reword unclear questions, and initially may even construct questions for students to mimic. ("What would be a good question about monarch butterflies that starts with 'why?' " *No response.* "How about 'Why do monarch butterflies fly south for the winter?' ") The teacher also provides many clues at first about what would be good summary statements for paragraphs. ("What's this paragraph about? How about, 'Monarch butterflies fly south for the winter because _____.' ") In addition the teacher offers much praise and positive feedback. ("That was a clear, important question. You came up with a good summary statement. I like your prediction.")

Palincsar and Brown have found that after fifteen lessons students learn through practice, guidance, and feedback how to ask important questions and generate good summary statements for paragraphs. An example of a reciprocal dialogue on the fifteenth day of instruction is presented in Figure 8.4

What, Why, and *When.* During each lesson, it is important to explain to students that they are learning how to ask important questions that help summarize, clarify, and make predictions about paragraphs of informative text.

FIGURE 8.4   Example of a Reciprocal Dialogue After Fifteen Lessons

TEXT:	A dolphin is a mammal, not a fish. A baby dolphin gets milk from its mother until it is about a year and a half old. At six months it also begins to eat small squid. Adult dolphins live on fish and squid.
STUDENT A (TEACHER):	What does a baby dolphin eat?
STUDENT B:	Milk and squid.
STUDENT A:	Correct, very good. My summary for this paragraph is that it is about what dolphins eat.
TEACHER:	Very good. Would you please select the next teacher?
TEXT:	The dolphin breathes through a hole on the top of its head. The hole closes every time the dolphin goes under water. The dolphin can stay under water for about six minutes before it has to rise for more air.
STUDENT C (TEACHER):	How does a dolphin breathe?
STUDENT D:	Through its mouth.
STUDENT C:	No.
STUDENT A:	Through a hole on the top of its head.
STUDENT C:	Correct. This paragraph is about how dolphins breathe.
TEACHER:	Great job!
STUDENT B:	I have a prediction to make.
TEACHER:	Good.
STUDENT B:	I think it might tell about how dolphins swim.
TEACHER:	Okay. Can we have another teacher?
TEXT:	A dolphin lives for about thirty years. During that time, it doesn't sleep very much. A dolphin sleeps for just a few minutes at a time and then wakes up. Most of the time a dolphin is awake and ready to go.
STUDENT D (TEACHER):	Does a dolphin sleep very much?
STUDENT B:	No.
STUDENT D:	That's correct. To summarize: A dolphin doesn't sleep very much.
TEACHER:	That is a good start, Billy, but I think there might be something else to say in the summary. There is more important information to include. In addition to learning that a dolphin doesn't sleep very much, what else do we learn that is important and related to this idea?
STUDENT D:	That a dolphin lives for thirty years?
TEACHER:	Okay. But what else do we learn about sleeping?
STUDENT C:	That a dolphin sleeps for just a few minutes at a time.

FIGURE 8.4 Example of a Reciprocal Dialogue After Fifteen Lessons (*Cont.*)

TEACHER:	Great. This paragraph is mostly about how dolphins sleep. Okay. Next teacher.
TEXT:	Dolphins swim very fast. They can move through the water at 30 miles an hour. Their bodies bend easily so they can move well as they swim through the waves.
STUDENT B (TEACHER):	My question is, How do dolphins swim? I got my prediction right!
TEACHER:	Great. Okay, someone; how do dolphins swim?
STUDENT A:	Fast.
STUDENT B:	Why?
STUDENT A:	Because their bodies bend with the waves.
STUDENT C:	I don't understand exactly what that means.
TEACHER:	Does anyone think he or she can explain it?
STUDENT B:	I think it means they bend to go with the waves instead of through them.
TEACHER:	Good.

They should be told that this is important because these strategies will help them better understand what they are reading. They should also be encouraged to use this technique whenever they are reading on their own.

Text Lookbacks

Students are often asked to answer questions about what they have read. A seemingly obvious strategy to use when they are uncertain about an answer involves looking back in the text for the answer. However, poor comprehenders are not as skilled in using text lookbacks to answer questions.[14]

A simple strategy developed by Garner and colleagues (1984) has been found to improve middle grade students' use of text lookbacks. The teacher uses (or prepares) short 200-word passages that are printed on two pages. Two text-based questions (the answers can be found in the text) and one reader-based question (the answer comes from students' prior knowledge) are written on a third page. An example is presented in Figure 8.5.

The steps of the procedure include the following:

What. Students are told they will be learning to look back in the text to help them answer questions.

Why. Students are told this is important because looking back can help them find the answers to questions. As simple as this sounds, many students do not use text lookbacks when they need to.

How. The teacher models the text lookback strategy by looking back to the first or second page of the prepared passage to answer the two text-based

FIGURE 8.5 Example of a Passage and Questions to Use with the Text Lookback Strategy

PAGE 1 Every fall monarch butterflies fly south. Some fly almost 2,000 miles from Canada to Mexico. They fly about 11 miles an hour and may cover about 80 miles in one day. They fly during the day and stop at night. They find a tree like a pine tree to roost in because they can easily cling to pine needles.

PAGE 2 People used to think that the monarch butterfly slept through the winter. But monarchs cannot live in a place where it stays below freezing for several days. That is why they have to fly south before winter comes.

No one knows exactly how monarchs find their way south. They cannot see very well, so they cannot find their way by landmarks. It remains a puzzle to scientists.

PAGE 3 *Text-based question:* How many miles does a monarch butterfly travel in one day?

Text-based question: Why do monarchs fly south for the winter?

Reader-based question: How do you think the monarch finds its way south?

questions. The teacher then explains that it will not help to look back for the reader-based question.

When. Students are told to use this strategy whenever they cannot answer questions about what they read.

For guided practice, the teacher and students first work through several of the short three-page passage and question sets. Then, they use the procedure with questions written for a two- or three-page segment in either their basal reader or a content textbook. For independent practice, students first work with several more three-page passage and question sets and then work with questions written for two- or three-page segments in one of their textbooks. They should keep a progress chart indicating how many questions they answered correctly and how many times they used the text lookback strategy to help them answer questions.

STRATEGIES TO IMPROVE INFERENCING

Inferencing is an inevitable part of the reading process. Readers must make inferences across sentences, such as in connecting anaphoric terms (for example, pronouns) with their antecedents. Readers must make slot-filling inferences, in which they insert unstated information, such as causal relationships, to make text comprehensible (for example, Mary was crying. [because] She fell down). Readers also make many elaborative inferences as they read, connecting text with prior knowledge.[15]

In addition to inferences that readers make automatically as they read, students are frequently asked to answer inference questions after reading in order to expand their comprehension of what they have read. Inference questions also serve as a window into what is going on in the reader's mind while processing text. Consequently, inference questions are important from both an instructional and an assessment perspective. Low-achieving readers, as compared to good readers, appear to have difficulty making inferences as they read[16] and also in answering inferential questions after reading.[17]

The remainder of this section will present several instructional techniques designed to improve students' general ability to draw inferences as they read or answer questions. Inferencing and inference questions cover many of the traditional comprehension skills commonly found in basal reader programs such as cause-effect, sequence, anaphoric relationships, drawing conclusions, and predicting outcomes. Inferencing will not be segmented into specific subskills, however, because readers do not do this on a conscious level as they read. That is, readers do not consciously say, "Oh, here is a cause-effect relationship," or "I must connect this anaphoric term to its antecedent," as they are reading. Inferencing is a process that occurs holistically as readers are making sense of text.

Question-Answer Relationships

Raphael[18] has developed a successful instructional program to improve students' ability to answer inferential questions. Students are taught to identify how they come up with an answer to a question which may be literal (the question and answer come from one sentence), textually inferential (the question and answer come from more than one sentence and require a connecting inference), or scriptally inferential (the answer is not in the text and therefore must come from the reader's general knowledge base). Raphael has found that instruction and practice in identifying question-answer relationships (QARs) are particularly effective in terms of improving poor readers' question answering ability.

How. Instruction begins with an explanation of the three different types of QARs. An example of each of the QARs is presented below with an accompanying passage. It is important to keep in mind that both the question and the answer must be considered in order to come up with the appropriate label.

> Billy went to the zoo. He saw a snake in a cage. Billy's mom knew he was scared.
> *Literal QAR:* Where did Billy see a snake?
>   In a cage.
> *Textually Inferential QAR:* Why was Billy scared?
>   He saw a snake.
> *Scriptally Inferential QAR:* How did Billy's mom know Billy was scared?
>   He probably started to cry when he saw the snake.

Literal QARs are labeled "Right There"; textually inferential QARs, "Think and Search"; and scriptally inferential QARs, "On My Own." The teacher presents several brief passages and one question from each of the QAR categories for each passage and then explains why the QAR label for each question is appropriate. Next, students are asked to explain QAR labels for questions and answers related to particular passages. After this, students are given text, questions, and answers and asked to provide labels and justifications. Finally, students are given texts and questions and asked to answer the question and provide QAR labels.

What, Why, and *When.* In addition to these steps, it is important that the teacher explain to students that they will be learning how to figure out where answers to questions come from and that this is important because answers come from different places. This understanding will improve their ability to answer questions after reading. The teacher should also explain that students should use this skill as they are working on their own and seem to be having a hard time answering questions. Students should then think about the type of questions they are answering and label them as either "Right There," "Think and Search," or "On My Own" questions.

Using a Self-Monitoring Checklist

Carr, Dewitz, and Patberg (1983) found that teaching sixth-grade students to ask themselves questions about their answers to inferential questions improved their inferential comprehension. Questions that students asked themselves focused on forward and backward clues (explained below) that could be used to answer inferential questions. They found that the instruction was particularly beneficial for low-achieving readers.

How. Instruction in this strategy begins with the completion of cloze passages. First, the teacher presents several single sentences with one cloze blank per sentence to demonstrate the cloze procedure. For a sentence such as, "Most of the houses on the block are painted _____," students are asked to generate a number of possible answers, such as "white," "yellow," and "purple," which are listed on the board. The teacher and students discuss why some answers seem to be more appropriate than others. Also, the teacher points out that students have to rely primarily on background knowledge to fill in the blank in this type of situation.

Second, the teacher presents several short passages in which students use a "forward" clue; they must read past the cloze blank to fill in the blank with an appropriate answer. For a passage like, "Most of the houses on the street are painted _____. When it snows there is almost no color on the street at all," students provide a variety of answers. The teacher and students discuss how "snow" is a forward clue that helps students come up with the answer "white" for the cloze blank.

Third, the teacher presents several short passages in which students use a "backward" clue; they must refer to information previous to the cloze blank to fill in the blank with an appropriate answer. For a passage like, "After the rain Rover was rolling on the ground. Susie ran to catch her dog and slipped in the _____," students provide a variety of answers. The teacher and students discuss how "ground," "rain," and "slipped" are backward clues that help students come up with the answer "mud" for the cloze blank.

Fourth, students are given an excerpted three-to-five-page passage from a content textbook in which cloze blanks have been inserted. After filling in the cloze blanks, the teacher and students discuss appropriate answers and whether forward or backward clues were helpful in coming up with these answers.

Fifth, students are asked inferential questions about the completed passage. The questions are similar to the cloze exercises in that they require students to use forward and backward clues to find one-word answers. The teacher and students discuss appropriate answers as well as the forward and backward clues that helped them come up with these answers.

Sixth, students are shown how to use a self-monitoring checklist to help themselves fill in cloze blanks and answer inferential questions. The self-monitoring checklist from Carr, Dewitz, and Patberg (1983) is as follows:

1. Does the answer make sense?

2. Does the answer make sense in the sentence?

3. Is the answer based on a combination of knowledge you had before you read the passage and clues in the passage?

4. Is there a forward clue in the same sentence, paragraph, or passage?

5. Is there a backward clue in the same sentence, paragraph, or passage?

6. Did the clue make you change your answer or is your answer the same?

The teacher models for the students how to use the checklist. Students are given individual copies of the checklist and instructed to ask themselves the questions on the checklist when completing cloze blanks or answering questions on content textbook material.

What, Why, and *When.* Lessons, including Steps 4 through 6 in the preceding list, should be carried out for about fifteen days over a six- to eight-week period. In addition to the procedure explained above, it is important that the teacher explain to the students that they are learning how to ask themselves questions about their answers to questions on content textbook material and how to use forward and backward clues to help them answer the content textbook questions. Students should be told that using forward and backward clues and the self-monitoring checklist will help them do a better job answering inferential questions about material they read in their content textbooks. They should also be told to use the self-monitoring checklist whenever they are asked to answer questions about content textbook material.

Inference Awareness

Gordon (1985) has found an inference awareness strategy that improves students' ability to successfully answer inference questions. It involves the teacher showing students how to use both textual information and personal knowledge to answer inference questions and to provide the reasoning that led to each answer.

What, *Why*, and *How*. First, the teacher explains that inference awareness is the skill of using clues from the text and the reader's own background knowledge to guess what the author has implied but not directly stated. The teacher explains that if students do this, they will have better comprehension and will do a better job of answering inference questions. The teacher then models the inference process by reading a paragraph, asking and answering a question, and providing the reasoning involved. A think-aloud procedure is then used to make the reasoning process explicit. An example is presented below:

1. Teacher reads text: "Billy's ball was headed for the window. There was the shattering of glass. Mr. Jones came out of the house. He was yelling in an angry voice."

2. Teacher asks: "Why was Mr. Jones angry?"

3. Teacher answers: "Mr. Jones was probably angry because the ball broke his window."

4. Teacher provides reasoning: "Well. I know from my own experience that if a ball is heading for a window and there is a shattering of glass, the ball probably broke the window. The text says the ball was heading for the window, there was a shattering of glass, and Mr. Jones was angry. I combine my own experience with information from the text to determine that the window broke. I can use that information to answer the question: Mr. Jones was angry because Billy's ball broke his window. That's my reasoning. I put together my own ideas and experiences with what the author has written to get a new idea of my own."

After modeling the process several times, the teacher and students engage in guided practice. The teacher reads a paragraph or two from a basal reader or content textbook, asks a question, and gives an answer. Students write down evidence from the text and their experience that led to the answer. The teacher and students discuss the reasoning and the information that led to the answer.

Next, the teacher reads a paragraph or two of text and asks a question which students answer. The teacher then cites evidence from the text and from background knowledge that led to the answer. This is followed by a teacher-student discussion about the reasoning process that produced the answer. An example is presented below:

1. Teacher reads: "After school, Carl and Tom stopped at the drug store. Then Carl went to Tom's house for a while. When Carl got home, his mom said dinner was ready. Carl told his mom he wasn't hungry yet."

2. Teacher asks: "Why did Carl tell his mom he wasn't hungry yet?"

3. Students answer: "Maybe he had something to eat before he got home."

4. Teacher cites evidence: "From the text—drug store, Tom's house; from my head—get candy at drug store, snack at friend's house, full before dinner."

5. Teacher-student discussion: "On the way home from school Carl and his friend stopped at the drug store and probably bought some candy. Then Carl went to Tom's house and probably had a snack. So, by the time Carl got home, he was not hungry for dinner."

Finally, the teacher asks an inference question for a paragraph or two of text. Students answer the question, support the answer with evidence, and explain the reasoning involved in coming up with the answer to the question.

When. The teacher explains to the students that if they are having difficulty answering a question, they should look for evidence in the text and their own experience and think about how these clues could lead to a reasonable answer. In addition, the teacher can explain to students how to use this skill when reading on their own. If they finish a paragraph that does not make very much sense, they should look for a confusing sentence in the paragraph. Then, they should ask themselves a question, most likely a "why" question, about the confusing sentence. For example, if readers felt confused at the end of the paragraph about Carl, they might ask themselves, "Why wasn't Carl hungry yet?" The only difference, in this case, from the example provided earlier, is that readers are responding to their own question instead of responding to a teacher-generated question.

STRATEGIES TO HELP STUDENTS READ FOR IMPORTANT IDEAS

Reading for important ideas is an essential comprehension skill when dealing with informative text. Although readers cannot possibly remember all the ideas in their textbooks, it is essential that they be able to pick out the most important ones when reading for information. Whereas skilled adult readers mentally summarize important ideas after reading and studying text,[19] students, particularly low-achieving readers, often have difficulty doing so.[20]

Understanding Main Ideas and Supporting Details in Paragraphs and Short Passages

Baumann (1984) has developed a direct instruction program that improves sixth-grade students' understanding of the main ideas in individual paragraphs and in short passages of two to three paragraphs. Individual lessons focus on the following:

1. Identifying an explicit main idea (topic sentence) and its supporting details.

2. Identifying an implicit main idea and its supporting details.

3. Identifying the explicit main idea (theme statement) of a short passage and associating explicit paragraph main ideas with the theme statement.

4. Identifying an implicit main idea (theme statement) of a short passage and associating explicit and implicit paragraph main ideas with the overall theme statement

5. Constructing a main idea outline for a short passage consisting of an explicit theme statement and explicit paragraph main ideas; constructing a main idea outline for a short passage consisting of an implicit theme statement and explicit and implicit paragraph main ideas.

What and *Why*. For each type of lesson the teacher describes the targeted skill, provides an example, and explains that figuring out main ideas and themes will help students better understand and remember the most important information in the materials they read.

When. For the lessons involving individual paragraphs (1 and 2), the teacher models how to identify the main idea after reading a paragraph. This involves identifying one or two words that explain the topic of the paragraph, then listing on the board all the ideas in the paragraph related to the topic. These ideas are identified as supporting details. Then, after reading over the supporting details, the teacher decides what important idea goes with all the supporting details. There may be an explicit main idea sentence in the paragraph or the main idea may have to be implied. An example is provided in Figure 8.6.

For guided practice, the teacher and students work through several examples of explicit and implicit main idea statements following the steps that were modeled by the teacher. For independent practice, the students identify the main ideas for several paragraphs they have read, first through a multiple-choice format and then by writing down the main idea.

The lessons for short passages (3 and 4) are similar to the lessons involving individual paragraphs. The teacher first models how to identify (1) the topic for a short passage and (2) the explicit or implicit main ideas for the paragraphs in the passage. The teacher then uses these paragraph main ideas to identify

FIGURE 8.6   Determining an Implicit Paragraph Main Idea

Some birds build nests on tree branches. Some build them in holes in the ground. Other birds build nests in bird houses.

Step 1	*Determining topic:*	building nests
Step 2	*Determining details*	tree branches holes in ground bird houses
Step 3	*Determining main idea*	Birds build nests in different places.

an explicit or implicit theme statement, that is, the main idea for the entire passage. Thus teacher modeling is followed by guided and individual practice.

The lessons in which students learn how to construct main idea outlines (5) are similar to the above (3 and 4) lessons, except that they require a written response from the students. The teacher first models how to identify and write down explicit paragraph main ideas and an explicit overall theme statement for a passage. Finally, students are shown how to identify and write down either explicit or implicit paragraph main ideas and theme statements for a passage. Again, all teacher modeling is followed by guided and independent practice. An example of a main ideas outline is presented in Figure 8.7.

When. Although not spelled out by Baumann, there are several different ways in which the teacher can explain when the above skills can be useful during independent reading. Whereas several studies have found that having students generate a main idea sentence in their own words after every

FIGURE 8.7   Creating a Main Idea Outline

Elephants live in herds. They help each other in time of trouble.

A strong female travels first. She is followed by other females and their young. Last come the bulls. If there is danger, the bulls form a circle around the females and young elephants.

If one elephant gets sick, the other elephants in the herd stop traveling until the sick elephant is better. If an elephant is hurt, it travels between two other elephants.

When a female elephant is about to have a baby, she leaves the herd for a while. Another female goes with her to help.

Step 2 *Determining theme statement*   Elephants help each other in time of trouble. (*explicit*)

Step 1 *Determining paragraph main ideas*
   1. Elephants travel in a certain pattern for safety. (*implicit*)
   2. Elephants help a member of the herd who is in trouble. (*implicit*)
   3. A female elephant helps another female who is having a baby. (*implicit*)

paragraph of informative text enhances their comprehension of the material,[21] this is too time-consuming and probably unnecessary. However, students might be advised to reread and generate a main idea outline whenever they encounter a section of text they do not fully understand. Or, if students immediately notice that the material they are reading is very difficult for them, they may want to take the time initially to generate a main idea outline, either mentally or in writing.

Summarizing Textbook Selections

Taylor (1982)[22] has developed a summarizing study procedure which has been found to improve middle grade students' comprehension and memory of the important ideas contained in their content textbooks. The procedure focuses on teaching students how to summarize several important ideas after reading sections of text and how to study the summaries they generate.

What and *Why.* First, the teacher explains to the students that summarizing means being able to list or explain the most important ideas contained in a section of text. Students are told that they cannot possibly remember all the ideas contained in their content textbooks so it is important to learn how to identify and remember the most important ideas.

How. The teacher models how to read one section of textbook material at a time (a section goes from one heading to another and is usually two to four paragraphs long) and how to select two or three words from the section heading that reflects its topic. Talking aloud, the teacher then shows how to turn the topic into a complete sentence that reflects the most important idea from the section, and writes this main idea on the board. Next, one to three other important ideas from the section are written down. It is important that the teacher state these ideas in his or her own words. It is important that students learn how to limit the number of important ideas from a section; they have a tendency to write down too many ideas. Teacher modeling involves explaining why certain ideas would not be good main idea statements because they are either too general or too specific and why others are not important enough to write down after the main idea.

The above procedure is repeated for a few more sections until a typical three- to five-page reading assignment from a content textbook has been covered. Finally, the teacher models how to study from the written summary by reading it over and reciting the important ideas it contains. An example of a summary is presented in Figure 8.8.

For guided practice the teacher and students work together through several sections of a reading assignment, summarizing in the manner specified above. The teacher can provide instructional support to the extent necessary. For example, as illustrated in Chapter 5, the teacher may give students extra clues as to what topics might be included in a summary, he or she may direct students to specific parts of the text, or he or she may provide students with several possible summaries and have them pick the one that is best. Also, a

FIGURE 8.8   Example of a Summary for a Textbook Selection

Egypt Is a Developing Nation.

A. *Egypt depends on the Nile.* Most of the people in Egypt live along the Nile because so much of the country is a desert. The Egyptians use the Nile for irrigation and for generating electricity.

B. *Cairo is a mixture of the old and the new.* Cairo, the capital of Egypt, has many modern buildings and people in Western dress. There are also old buildings and people in clothes of the type worn long ago.

C. *Farming in Egypt is old-fashioned but becoming modernized.* Many farmers are poor and use animals instead of machines. Some farmers are starting to use machines and modern methods.

D. *Egypt's leaders are working hard to solve the nation's problems.* Egypt doesn't have enough food for all its people. It also needs to become more industrialized.

discussion contrasting good and poor main idea statements for sections as well as good and poor "other" ideas seems to be useful in helping students choose a few important ideas to remember from a section. For independent practice, the students working alone or with a partner summarize the remaining section or two from a reading assignment and then practice studying their summary.

When. It is important that the teacher explain to students that if they cannot summarize a page or section of text, they need to reread it and use a fix-up strategy, such as identifying main ideas for individual paragraphs, to improve their comprehension. If students are reading particularly difficult material and realize they are going to have difficulty comprehending it, they should consider writing a summary for each section as they go along and then review what they have written down.

Self-Questioning on Main Ideas

A self-questioning study technique developed by Andre and Anderson (1978–1979) has been found to improve comprehension among low verbal ability secondary students. Students are taught to identify the main idea of each paragraph as they are reading and are then shown how to generate and answer a question about that main idea. They repeat this procedure with the next paragraph.

For example, given a passage on monarch butterflies, students might identify main ideas and generate questions such as those in Figure 8.9.

Specific steps to follow in this self-questioning study procedure are:

What. Students are told that they will be learning how to ask and answer questions about the main ideas of paragraphs as they read informative text.

Why. Students are told that this is important because they will have better comprehension of the material they are studying.

FIGURE 8.9   Example of the Main Idea Self-Questioning Procedure

Every fall monarch butterflies fly south. Some fly almost 2,000 miles from Canada to Mexico. They fly about 11 miles an hour and may cover about 80 miles in one day. They fly during the day and stop at night. They find a tree like a pine tree to roost in because they can easily cling to pine needles.

People used to think that the monarch butterfly slept through the winter. But monarchs cannot live in a place where it stays below freezing for several days. That is why they have to fly south before winter comes.

No one knows exactly how monarchs find their way south. They cannot see very well, so they cannot find their way by landmarks. It remains a puzzle to scientists.

Topic of paragraph 1 Monarchs fly south

Main idea of paragraph 1 Monarch butterflies fly south every winter just like birds.

Possible question What do monarch butterflies do every winter?

Topic of paragraph 2 Why monarchs fly south

Main idea of paragraph 2 Monarchs have to fly south for the winter or they will freeze.

Possible question Why do monarchs fly south for the winter?

Topic of paragraph 3 How monarchs fly south

Main idea of paragraph 3 No one knows exactly how monarchs migrate.

Possible question How do monarchs find their way as they are flying south?

How. First, the teacher models how to identify main ideas for paragraphs, then decides on one or two words that state the topic of the paragraph. Next, a main idea sentence about the topic of the paragraph is generated. The teacher provides several examples of possible main idea sentences for a particular paragraph as well as several inappropriate main idea sentences. Then the students are shown how to generate and answer a question about the main idea and are provided with several examples of possible questions that could have been generated for a particular paragraph. Several inappropriate questions are also discussed.

When. Students are told to use the self-questioning procedure whenever they are reading textbook material that seems particularly difficult to understand. They should then start over, identifying main ideas for paragraphs and generating and answering questions on these main ideas.

For guided practice, the teacher and students work through several paragraphs together. Good and bad main idea statements for paragraphs and good and bad questions on the main ideas are discussed. For independent practice, students work through several more paragraphs on their own and discuss their main idea statements and questions with a partner or larger group.

STRATEGY TO HELP STUDENTS STUDY

Many middle grade students have not learned how to study textbook material effectively, a skill which they will need as they continue into junior and senior high school and beyond. Adams, Carnine, and Gersten (1982) have developed a study strategy, adapted from the SQ3R procedure[23] which has been found to improve fifth-grade students' comprehension and memory of social studies material. Students who could effectively decode material in their social studies textbook but did not effectively study the text when instructed to do so received individual instruction in this study strategy.

How. The teacher models each step of the study strategy shown below. The student then repeats the teacher's modeling and uses each step independently with new material. After several lessons, the teacher modeling ceases and the student studies silently except for reciting aloud to the teacher (Steps 5 and 6, below). The teacher gives the student feedback on whether he or she is accurately following the study strategy and is selecting important information to study. The steps of the study strategy are listed below. An example is presented in Figure 8.10.

1. Preview the passage (600 to 800 words) by reading the headings and subheadings.

2. Recite one subheading at a time.

3. Ask yourself a question about what would be important to learn from the section, based on the subheading.

4. Read the section (from one subheading to the next) to find important information. Try to find the answer to your question and also identify other important information to remember.

5. Reread the subheadings and recite the important information. State the answer to your question as well as other important information you learned about in the section. Repeat Steps 2 through 5 with the next section.

6. Rehearse. After completing Steps 2 through 5 for each section, reread each subheading, look up from the passage, and try to recall the important information from each section. Repeat Steps 2 through 5 for a section if you cannot recall any information from the section.

What, Why, and *When.* In addition to teaching students how to use the study strategy, the teacher should explain that they will be learning a procedure that will help them learn textbook material. The teacher should explain that this is important because throughout school (junior high, senior high, and so

FIGURE 8.10   Example of the Modified SQ3R Study Procedure Used with a Passage on Egypt (outlined in Figure 8.8)

1. Read the heading and subheadings (title and subheadings for sections A through D)

2a. Recite the first subheading (Egypt and the Nile River)

3a. Ask a question about this section (Why is the Nile River something important to Egypt?)

4a. Read the section to come up with an answer to the question and to remember other important information.

5a. Reread the subheading and recite the important information (Egypt and the Nile River—The Nile River is important to Egypt because Egypt uses the Nile for electricity and irrigation. Most of the people in Egypt live along the Nile.)

2b. Recite the second subheading (A Mixture of the Old and the New)

3b. Ask a question about this section (In what ways is Cairo a mixture of the old and the new?)

4b. Read the section to come up with an answer to the question and to remember other important information.

5b. Reread the subheading and recite the important information (A Mixture of the Old and the New—Cairo is a mixture of the old and the new. Cairo has many modern buildings and people in Western dress. There are also old buildings and people in clothes of the type worn long ago.

Steps 2 through 5 are repeated for the third and fourth sections. At the end students reread the subheadings and try to recall the important information from each section.

on) students will be expected to read and study textbook material independently in order to pass examinations and to prepare themselves for further schooling.

STRATEGIES TO HELP STUDENTS USE BACKGROUND KNOWLEDGE

A reader's background knowledge plays a crucial part in the reading comprehension process. People comprehend reading material by relating the new information in the text to their background knowledge.[24] Readers use their background knowledge as they read in order to make inferences regarding unstated information and also to make elaborations that enhance their comprehension.[25]

Research has shown that the more background knowledge readers have about the content of a reading selection, the greater their comprehension of the material.[26] Consequently, taking the time to build students' background for unfamiliar reading material is important and beneficial.[27]

Although students are rarely given reading material about which they have little or no background knowledge, it is important that this knowledge be activated and used in the reading process. Research has shown that helping students activate and use their relevant background knowledge before reading enhances their comprehension of the material.[28]

In the remainder of this chapter, three effective strategies that help students activate and use their background knowledge will be described.[29] Unlike the other strategies described in this chapter, these are teacher-directed; that is, they are not designed to be used by students independently. However, because the use of background knowledge in the reading process is so important, the following teacher-directed strategies should be included.

Using the Experience-Text-Relationship Method to Discuss Stories

Au (1979, 1981) has developed a questioning strategy that has been successfully used as the basic approach to comprehension instruction in the Kamehameha Early Education Program (KEEP) for Polynesian-Hawaiian children who have a potentially high risk for educational failure.[30] In this approach, students at the same reading levels meet in small groups of about five to read and discuss a basal story with the teacher.

How. The lesson begins with an *experience* phase. The teacher activates students' background knowledge and builds their interest by asking a question related to their personal experience. For example, given a story entitled "The Noisy House," the teacher might ask students what the phrase *noisy house* means to them. The teacher then encourages the students to talk about their own experiences related to this topic. Alternatively, the teacher might have them look at a picture from the story and guess what the story will be about or ask about a problem they may have had that is similar to the problem in the story. For example, the teacher might ask, "Did your mother or father ever complain that your neighbors were too noisy?"

One or more *text* phases follow the experience phase. Here the teacher has the students silently read several passages of a basal story after first setting a purpose for their reading, such as, "Read to find out which house was the noisy one." When the students have finished reading, the teacher asks a question related to the purpose-setting statement as well as other questions about the text they have just read. An attempt is made to ask questions from a variety of levels. Through the text-based questions the students get the opportunity to practice conventional comprehension skills like cause-effect, sequence, and main idea.

A *relationship* phase follows the *text* phase. This may occur several times during a story or only at the end of a story. Here the teacher asks questions to help the students make connections between the story and their own experiences. The teacher may ask students to compare their own experiences in dealing with a particular problem with those of the main character. For example, the teacher might ask, "What have you done or would you do if you had noisy neighbors like those in the story?" The teacher may ask the students if their predictions made at the beginning of the story were correct. Often, the teacher tries to develop an important idea in the story by relating it to the students' lives.

Au (1981) reports that students who have been involved with the ETR method on a regular basis often begin to internalize certain aspects of the process and to use it when reading on their own. These students have been found to have better reading comprehension than others who have not received the lessons.

Using Background Knowledge to Draw Inferences

Hansen and Pearson (1983) have developed an approach to story discussion that draws heavily on students' background knowledge. The approach was found to be effective in improving elementary grade readers' inferential comprehension.

What and *Why*. The first step in the procedure is to engage students in a metacognitive discussion prior to reading a basal story. This discussion encourages them to prepare for the story by thinking about similar experiences they have had. After reading the basal story the students are asked about the purpose of the preparatory discussion. The students respond that they have been comparing their own real-life experiences to what will happen in the story. The teacher then asks why they have done this and they respond that this will help them understand and remember the story better. The teacher might then ask them to repeat this process with another story, such as one about a circus. After thinking about how this topic may also be related to their own experiences, they may come up with answers such as, "I might think about a circus I've been to" or "We could see if the circus in the story is like one we've been to." The purpose of this metacognitive discussion is to remind students that as they are reading it is important to think about their own related experiences.

How. After engaging in a brief metacognitive discussion, the teacher leads the students in a strategy discussion. The teacher asks students to compare something from their own lives to something that might happen in the upcoming story. To do this the teacher selects three important concepts from the story and generates a pair of questions for each concept. For example, for a story about a boy who dislikes coyotes the teacher might ask the following:

1a. This story is about a boy who doesn't like a certain kind of wild animal. Tell us about a wild animal you don't like.

1b. In the story, Antonio doesn't like coyotes. Why do you think he doesn't like coyotes?

2a. Try to recall a time when an adult tried to give you some advice. Tell us how you reacted.

2b. In the story, Antonio's grandfather tries to give him some advice. How do you suppose he will respond to this advice?

3a. Tell about a time when you changed your mind about a person or animal you didn't like.

3b. In the story, Antonio changes his mind about the coyote. Why do you think he does this?

The point of this discussion is to lead the students through the inferencing process they should use as they read; that is, the relating of new information to old information. It is by relating the new (information in the text) to the known (background knowledge) that comprehension of the text occurs.

After the metacognitive and strategy discussions, which usually take about twenty minutes, the students read the basal story and engage in a postreading discussion. The teacher then asks about ten inference questions in which the students have to combine information in the text with their own background experience. For example, the teacher might ask, "How do you think Antonio felt at the end of the story?" "Why do you suppose the coyote tried to take care of the lost puppy?" "Why do you think people often change first impressions?" Such questions help students realize the need to use their background knowledge in order to help them interpret what they are reading.

Using the PReP Procedure

Langer (1984) has developed a Pre-Reading Plan (PReP) to assess and activate students' background knowledge for key concepts in a content reading assignment. The procedure is used with a group of about ten students prior to reading the assigned textbook material. PReP is a quick, effective way for the teacher to assess students' level of background knowledge for a particular reading assignment. The procedure has also been found to improve students' comprehension of content textbook material.

Before using the procedure, the teacher selects about three major concepts from a 700- to 800-word content textbook reading selection. For example, from a passage about farming on the Great Plains the teacher might select dry farming, dust storms, and conservation.

What and *Why*. The teacher explains to students that they will be drawing upon what they already know about important concepts that will appear in the material they are going to read. The students are told that the prereading discussion will enable the teacher to determine if any background building discussion is necessary before reading the story. They are also told that the discussion will activate their existing background experience which, in turn, will improve their comprehension of the material because people comprehend new information by relating it to what they already know.

How. The first step is to have students make associations with the first important concept. "Tell anything that comes to mind when you hear the term

FIGURE 8.11   PReP Procedure: An Example of Students' Responses to Key Concepts

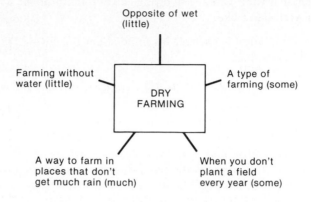

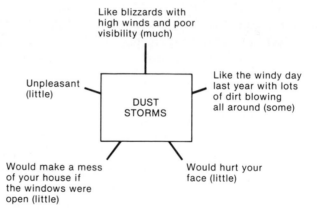

dry farming." The teacher jots down students' responses on the board. An example is presented in Figure 8.11.

The second step is for the teacher to ask students to reflect on their initial associations. "What made you think about _____?" This helps students to further develop their associations with the concept under discussion and to listen to the ideas of others.

The third step is to ask students to reformulate their knowledge about the concepts being discussed: "Based on our discussion, do you have any new ideas about _____?" This step allows students to talk about any new or modified associations, based on the discussion. The procedure is then repeated for the next major concept.

Based on the students' responses during Steps 1 and 3 of the procedure the teacher will be able to determine whether students have much, some, or little background knowledge about the concept being discussed. If students have much background knowledge about the concept being discussed, responses will take the form of superordinate concepts ("Dry farming is one way to farm in a place that gets very little rainfall"); precise definitions; analogies, or the linking of one concept to another ("Dust storms and blizzards both have high winds and make it difficult to see"). If students have some background knowledge about the concept being discussed, responses will take the form of examples ("Dust storms are like what happened last year when it was very dry and the wind blew lots of dirt into the air"); attributes, or defining characteristics ("Dry farming is when you don't plant a field every year"). If students have little background knowledge about the concept being discussed, responses will focus on low-level associations, such as tangential links ("Dry farming is the opposite of wet farming"); morphemes, such as prefixes, suffixes, and root words ("conserve"); words that sound like the stimulus word ("conservation-reservation"); and first-hand experiences that focus on tangential information ("Dust storms must hurt your face").

Langer (1981) has found that students with "much" or "some" background for the major concepts in the reading material will be able to read the text with adequate comprehension assuming, of course, they have relatively little difficulty in terms of decoding. Students with "little" background knowledge of the major concepts in the reading material usually will benefit from a more extensive background discussion designed to build their background knowledge prior to reading.

In addition to being a useful assessment tool, PReP enhances students' comprehension of a particular text. The procedure helps students activate relevant background knowledge and make links between important text concepts and their past experiences.

SUMMARY

Readers of this chapter may have wondered why particular strategies were organized as they were. In fact, it may be helpful to summarize what is covered in this chapter by organizing the strategies somewhat differently, according to comprehension monitoring and comprehension fostering activities. Basically, all of the strategies discussed in this chapter are useful comprehension monitoring and/or comprehension fostering activities designed to improve students' reading comprehension.

Several of the strategies discussed are useful as *comprehension-monitoring strategies* and many are useful as fix-up strategies. For example, in addition to the general comprehension-monitoring strategies involved in the comprehension-rating procedure, the summarizing procedure and the self-monitoring checklist procedure are useful comprehension-monitoring activities. Students can use these activities either to check their understanding as they are reading or as they are answering questions.

In addition to general fix-up strategies discussed as part of the comprehension-rating task, the text lookback strategy, the QAR procedure, and the inference awareness procedure are useful fix-up strategies for students to use when answering questions proves difficult. The reading for main idea activities are useful fix-up strategies for students to consider using when comprehension has failed.

Many of the strategies discussed are useful in enhancing comprehension in a general sense, in improving students' inferential comprehension, or in improving students' ability to read for main ideas. In particular, two self-questioning procedures and the reciprocal teaching procedure are considered general *comprehension-fostering strategies*. The procedures dealing with background knowledge are regarded as general comprehension-fostering activities.

The strategies dealing with inferences—the text lookback procedure, the reciprocal questioning procedure, the QAR procedure, the self-monitoring checklist procedure, the inference awareness procedure, and the background knowledge procedure—are regarded as useful in instructing students to do a better job drawing inferences as they read. Many of these strategies are also designed to help students do a better job answering inferential questions after reading.

The strategies dealing with important information—the main idea self-questioning procedure, the reciprocal teaching procedure, the reading for main idea activities, the summarizing procedure, and the study procedure—are seen as useful in instructing students how to do a better job reading for and studying main ideas when they deal with informative text. Although most of the strategies discussed seem to be useful with narrative or informative text, strategies focusing on reading for main ideas, summarizing, and studying are seen as useful primarily for informative text, or text in which one is reading to learn new information.

All of the strategies covered in this chapter can be taught through small-group, as opposed to individual, instruction. In fact, some strategies, such as the reciprocal questioning procedure and the reciprocal teaching procedure actually require group instruction. Chapter 9 discusses informal assessment strategies that can be used to determine which students in a classroom or clinic may benefit from small-group instruction in comprehension-monitoring activities, fix-up strategies, general comprehension-fostering activities, and/or comprehension instruction in drawing inferences or reading for main ideas.

SUGGESTED ACTIVITIES

1. Prepare appropriate materials and teach the comprehension rating procedure to a student or small group of students. If a child is not available, "teach" the procedure to a group of peers in your class.

2. Locate appropriate reading material and teach the reciprocal teaching procedure to a group of two or three students. If children are not available, work with peers in your class. With children, the procedure should be carried out on more than one occasion (children will not learn the technique in one lesson). Keep a chart of the student's performance on comprehension questions answered after reading the material. As you are teaching this procedure, be sure to stress *what, why, how,* and *when* as discussed in the chapter.

3. Prepare appropriate examples and teach the QAR procedure to a student or small group of students. If children are not available, "teach" the procedure to a group of peers in your class. Be sure to stress the *what, why, how,* and *when* of the procedure, as discussed in the chapter.

4. Locate appropriate reading material and try out the PReP procedure with several students or a group of peers in your class.

NOTES

1. See Baker and Brown (1984) and Paris and Jacobs (1984).
2. See Baker and Brown (1984) and Ryan (1981).
3. See Baker and Brown (1984), Paris and Myers (1981), and Wagoner (1983).
4. See Durkin (1984a, 1984b).
5. See Taylor (1985b).
6. See Tierney and Cunningham (1984).
7. See Garner (1980) and Owings, Peterson, Bransford, Morris, and Stein (1980).
8. See Davey and Porter (1982), Garner and Reis (1981), and Golinkoff (1975–1976).
9. See Davey and Porter (1982).
10. See Anderson and Biddle (1975).
11. See Andre and Anderson (1978–1979), Baker and Brown (1984), and Singer (1978a).
12. See Nolte and Singer (1985) and Singer and Donlan (1982).
13. See Manzo (1969).
14. See Garner and Reis (1981), and Garner, Wagoner, and Smith (1983).
15. See Anderson and Pearson (1984) and Reder (1980).
16. See Bridge and Tierney (1981), Bransford et al., (1982), and Reder (1980.
17. See Holmes (1983), Raphael, Winograd, and Pearson (1980), and Wilson (1979).
18. See Raphael and Pearson (1985) and Raphael and Wonnacutt (1985).
19. See van Dijk and Kintsch (1983).
20. See Brown and Day (1983), Taylor (1985c), and Winograd (1984).
21. See Doctorow, Wittrock, and Marks (1978) and Taylor and Berkowitz (1980).
22. Taylor and Beach (1984), and Taylor (1985a, 1986).
23. See Robinson (1941).
24. See Anderson and Pearson (1984).
25. See Reder (1980).
26. See Johnston (1984a), Langer (1984), and Pearson, Hansen, and Gordon (1979).
27. See Hayes and Tierney (1982) and Stevens (1982).
28. See Hansen (1981) and Langer (1984).
29. See Au (1979), Hansen (1981), and Langer (1984).
30. See Tharp (1982).

SUGGESTED READINGS   BAUMANN, J. F. (1984). The effectiveness of a direct instructional paradigm for teaching main idea comprehension. *Reading Research Quarterly* 20: 93–115.
The author provides a good description of the components of direct instruction and presents a direct instruction program for teaching students to read for main ideas.

DAVEY, B., AND PORTER, S. M. (1982). Comprehension-rating; A procedure to assist poor comprehenders. *Journal of Reading* 26: 197–202.
A program to develop students' comprehension-monitoring ability and their use of fix-up strategies is presented.

LANGER, J. A. (1981). From theory to practice: A prereading plan. *Journal of Reading* 25: 152–156.
A technique for assessing and activating students' background knowledge prior to reading is presented.

PALINCSAR, A., AND BROWN, A. L. (1984). Reciprocal teaching of comprehension-fostering and comprehension-monitoring activities. *Cognition and Instruction* 1: 117–175.
Palincsar and Brown describe a successful procedure called reciprocal teaching which they developed to improve low-achieving readers' comprehension of expository text.

PARIS, S. G. (1986). Teaching children to guide their reading and learning. In T. Raphael (Ed.), *The contexts of school-based literacy*. New York: Random House.
Paris discusses the importance of strategic reading which includes the use of comprehension-fostering, comprehension-monitoring, and fix-up strategies. He also discusses the importance of direct instruction and discusses a direct instruction program he developed to teach students to become more strategic readers.

TAYLOR, B. M. (1986). Teaching middle grade students to summarize content textbook material. In J. Baumann (Ed.), *Teaching main idea comprehension*. Newark, DE: International Reading Association.
Taylor discusses the importance of teaching students to summarize main ideas and presents several techniques for doing so.

Chapter 9

Comprehension Assessment

OVERVIEW

As you read this chapter use the following list of main ideas to guide your understanding and reflection.

Initial assessment and ongoing evaluation of students' reading comprehension should be based primarily on regular classroom materials and reading assignments.

In the area of comprehension monitoring, it is important to determine the extent to which students do and do not understand what they are reading, their ability to locate sources of comprehension difficulty, and their success in using appropriate fix-up strategies to remediate comprehension failures.

In addition to having students answer questions to assess general comprehension, a teacher might ask them to generate questions or to select the best summary for a text.

To better understand students' inferencing ability, a teacher can ask students to explain how they have come up with their answers to questions.

It is essential that written records be kept of low-achieving readers' performance on comprehension tasks so that strengths and weaknesses can be determined and the most appropriate remedial instruction can be implemented.

After completing their assignment, the students will record their progress on the chart behind them. *(Peter Vadnai)*

As with word recognition, regular classroom materials should be used as much as possible for initial assessment and ongoing evaluation of comprehension. In general, this assessment should be based on frequent samples of students' ability to answer different kinds of questions and to use various comprehension strategies while reading instructional level material. The teacher should then use these data to plan appropriate instructional activities.

The discussion of specific comprehension assessment strategies will parallel the discussion of comprehension instruction presented in Chapter 8. First, assessment of students' comprehension monitoring skills is discussed. Next, assessment of students' general reading comprehension ability is presented. Students' inferencing ability and their ability to read for important ideas is then discussed. The chapter concludes with a discussion of how to use the reading difficulties record sheet in the area of comprehension.

It should be stressed that comprehension assessment must be based on students' reading of instructional level material. If students are struggling with decoding (for example, reading with less than 90 percent accuracy in word recognition), comprehension performance will be distorted and therefore not useful as assessment data on which to make instructional decisions.

COMPREHENSION MONITORING

There are three questions to answer about comprehension monitoring: (1) Do students know when they do and do not understand what they are reading? (2) Can students locate sources of comprehension difficulty when they know comprehension is faltering? (3) Can students select and use appropriate fix-up strategies to remediate their comprehension failures? Because comprehension monitoring is essential for reading, comprehension-monitoring skills of all low-achieving readers should be assessed, even when it appears that word recognition, and not comprehension, is the primary area of difficulty.

Do Students Know When Comprehension Is or Is Not Occurring?

To assess students' comprehension monitoring skill, they can be asked to rate individual paragraphs and sections of text (such as three- to four-page sections in a content textbook). A three-point rating system, such as the one developed by Davey and Porter (1982) discussed in Chapter 8, could be used. It allows students to rate paragraphs and longer sections of text as something they understand very well, moderately well, or not very well. Reading material could be copied so that blanks for ratings could be built into the material. An example is provided in Figure 9.1.

These ratings should be compared to the students' scores on the comprehension questions at the end of the material (see Figure 9.1). A positive relationship should be apparent. That is, students' comprehension scores on specific paragraphs and passages should roughly match their comprehension ratings on these same paragraphs and passages. It is apparent that in Figure 9.1 the student was not very skilled in rating his comprehension because in almost all cases he rated his comprehension as high despite missing quite a few questions. Students who are repeatedly unable to tell with any degree of accuracy when they do and do not understand what they are reading need instruction in self-monitoring (see the comprehension rating procedure discussed in Chapter 8).

Can Students Locate Sources of Comprehension Difficulty?

To assess students' skill in locating sources of comprehension difficulty, the teacher could question students on an individual basis. The teacher should ask students to look over a comprehension rating assessment activity, such as the one presented in Figure 9.1, and point out or explain what caused them comprehension difficulties in places where they rated their comprehension as poor. Alternatively, the teacher could ask students to reread material on which they had low comprehension scores and to try to explain the cause of their difficulty. Using notes taken on students' comprehension monitoring ability, the teacher should decide whether individual students needed specific instruc-

FIGURE 9.1   Example of a Comprehension Rating Task

DIRECTIONS: In each blank at the end of the paragraph put a 1 if you understood the paragraph well, a 2 if you understood the paragraph some-what, and a 3 if you did not understand the paragraph. In the box at the end of the page also put a 1, 2, or 3 to indicate your understanding of the entire passage. Then answer the comprehension questions.

Please Pass the Potato Chips!

1. Americans buy more than 600 million bags of potato chips each year. If people had to make potato chips in their own kitchens, they might not eat so many.   _1_

2. From field to factory, potato chips are made by machines. A machine digs the potatoes in the field. A second machine puts them in sacks. A truck takes them to the factory. There, they are fed into a peeling machine. They are tumbled over rough machinery that scrapes away the skins.   _2_

3. The next machine cuts the potatoes into slices, which are washed in cold water. The slices are cooked in hot oil in a frying machine.   _1_

4. The potatoes turn a golden color. They are now thin chips that ride along on a moving steel belt. Salt is sprinkled on them from above. Any chips that are broken or too brown are removed. The finished chips go into a machine that makes bags and puts in the chips. This machine also weighs and seals the bags.   _2_

5. When you put your hand into the bag, you are the first to touch the chips. Machines have done all the work.   _1_

_1_

X 1. The machine that is used in potato fields
   (a.) takes the potatoes to the factory.
   b. cuts the potatoes into pieces.
   c. digs the potatoes.
   d. peels the potatoes.

X 2. The word in paragraph 2 that means *not smooth* is _scrapes_ .

X 3. The words "weighs and seals the bags" in paragraph 4 tell about the word _machine_ .

4. The story does not say so, but it makes you think that
   a. potato chips are washed just before they go into bags.
   b. potato chips are made by hand.
   (c.) potato chips are a favorite American snack.

X 5. The golden potato chips ride along on a belt made of
   (a.) rubber.
   b. paper.
   c. wood.
   d. steel.

FIGURE 9.1   Example of a Comprehension Rating Task (Cont.)

6. Potatoes are sliced in the field.
   Yes   (No)   Does not say
7. On the whole, this story is about
   (a.) making potato chips.
   b. digging potatoes.
   c. how potato chips are sorted.

X 8. Why are potato chips made by machines? (Check the story again.)
   a. It is a faster way to make millions of chips.
   (b.) Workers would break too many of the potato chips.
   c. Workers would eat too many of the chips.

X 9. Which of these sentences do you think is right?
   (a.) Potato chips are made from the skins of potatoes.
   b. Potato chips are cooked in hot water.
   c. Several machines are used in making potato chips.

Number correct _3/9_

The passage and questions in Figure 9.1 are from *Reading for Concepts*, level D, 2/e, by William Liddle, © Copyright, 1970, by Webster Division, McGraw-Hill Book Company. Used with permission.

tion in locating sources of comprehension difficulty. Again, the comprehension rating procedure by Davey and Porter (1982) could be used for instruction.

Can Students Select and Use Appropriate Fix-Up Strategies?

To assess students' skill in using appropriate fix-up strategies, the teacher can use a self-report procedure. The teacher can ask students to list what they usually do when they are having trouble understanding what they read either because: (1) a specific word is unknown or (2) an idea, sentence, or paragraph is not clear. The teacher could also have students tell or write down what they do to fix up comprehension difficulties in specific instances, such as on the comprehension rating assessment task in Figure 9.1, where they indicated poor comprehension. In addition, the teacher could ask students to keep notes whenever they encounter comprehension difficulties in independent reading and also on their attempts to remedy the problem. An example of a record sheet students could use for this activity is presented in Figure 9.2.

The teacher might have students complete a questionnaire on fix-up strategies. Items for both word-level and idea-level fix-up strategies could be included. An example is provided in Figure 9.3.

Finally, the teacher could work with students individually or in a small group and have them read until they noticed a comprehension difficulty. The teacher could then ask the student to explain what was causing the problem and what should be done in terms of a fix-up strategy. The teacher should

FIGURE 9.2 Example of a Comprehension Rating Record Sheet (based on passage in Figure 9.1)

DIRECTIONS: In the spaces below write down the page and paragraph number when you notice you are having trouble understanding what you are reading. Write down what you think is causing the problem (a particular word or a sentence) and write down what you did to fix up your comprehension failure.

Page and Paragraph	Cause of Difficulty	Fix-Up Strategy
106, no. 2	tumbled	reread, sounded out
106, no. 4	1st sentence	read on

keep notes on students' ability to select and successfully use appropriate fix-up strategies to remediate comprehension failure. Assessment activities such as these can serve as the basis for teacher decision making about a student's need for special instruction in the use of word-level and idea-level fix-up strategies.

Metacognitive Skills When Answering Questions

In addition to assessing students' use of metacognitive skills when reading, the teacher should also assess their use of metacognitive skills when answering questions. For example, low-achieving readers may not realize when their answer to a question does not make sense. To assess their ability, the teacher could ask students to put an X by questions and answers they were uncertain about. Students who seldom put X's by questions they answered incorrectly would appear to need metacognitive instruction.

Similarly, low-achieving readers also may not know what to do when confronted with a question they cannot answer. Working with students individually or in small groups, they teacher could ask students what they might do to produce reasonable answers to difficult questions. Students who have little to say would appear to be either unaware or unable to use fix-up strategies to answer difficult questions. The section on drawing inferences will discuss assessment of students' knowledge of how to go about answering a difficult inference question.

Students unaware of either their own difficulty in answering questions or of what to do about it might benefit from the text-lookback procedure, the QAR procedure, the inference checklist procedure, and/or the inference awareness procedure, all of which were discussed in Chapter 8 as strategies to help students answer questions.

FIGURE 9.3 Example of a Questionnaire on Use of Fix-Up Strategies

1. When you do not understand a word you are reading how often do you do these things?
   a. Skip over the word
   b. Sound out the word
   c. Use context clues to decode the word
   d. Use context clues to predict what the word means
   e. Use a dictionary
   f. Ask for help
2. When you do not understand a sentence, paragraph, or page you have read, how often do you do these things?
   a. Keep reading
   b. Reread carefully
   c. Look at the title, pictures, headings
   d. Ask yourself important questions
   e. Put important ideas in your own words
   f. Picture the ideas in your head as you read
   g. Relate ideas to your personal experience
   h. Ask someone to clarify things

ASSESSING GENERAL COMPREHENSION

This section will discuss the use of questions and other strategies that can be used to measure general comprehension. It will discuss students' ability to comprehend narrative and expository text as well as their literal and inferential comprehension ability.

Consistent with the general preference for frequent and informal assessment, "acceptable" performance on a comprehension task should be based on teacher judgment, not arbitrary levels of acceptable performance. Teachers should collect frequent data on actual reading tasks to decide (1) whether or not a student has difficulty with a comprehension task after reading and, if so, why, and (2) if a student's performance on similar comprehension tasks improves following instruction.

Comprehension depends on a number of factors such as background knowledge, motivation, and task understanding. Students with little background knowledge about a topic, students who are not motivated, and students who do not understand what they are supposed to do will perform poorly on almost any comprehension task. Consequently, teachers should record anecdotal evidence about these variables in order to explain comprehension difficulties.

Using Questions to Assess Comprehension

Of all the techniques used to determine comprehension of text, the oldest and still the most popular is to ask students a few questions about what they have

Students' performance on daily comprehension tasks provides valuable assessment data. *(Peter Vadnai)*

read. Questions are the staple of comprehension tests, workbook pages, classroom discussions of stories, and normal everyday conversation. There is nothing inherently wrong with using questions to assess students' comprehension. But . . . there are questions and there are questions! Some kinds of questions provide more appropriate and useful assessments of comprehension than do others.

The ultimate criterion a teacher should use to judge the quality of comprehension questions is simple: Do the questions focus upon what is important to understand about the text? In other words, good questions should focus on important ideas, not trivial details.

A few other words of caution about questions are in order. Students who have difficulty understanding what they are reading may have learned to answer questions by writing down "any old answer" as quickly as possible in order to get the task completed. For assessment purposes, teachers should supervise students closely when answering questions to be sure that they are working carefully. A teacher may find that some students actually do quite well on questions when they slow down and work carefully.

It is also important for teachers to bear in mind that some students do poorly when answering comprehension questions because they have difficulty *writing*. Consequently, it is a good idea for teachers to keep records of both written and oral question answering activities so that they can determine if a student's difficulty with writing clouds their judgment about the student's comprehension.

Narrative and Expository Text

One way to assess students' general ability to comprehend narrative and expository text is to keep records of their success in answering questions based on instructional level text. Alternatively, a teacher might have students generate questions about such text. Students often find this task enjoyable because it is something different. The teacher should stress that questions should be about important information, not unimportant details. Based on teacher judgment, inability to ask important questions about narrative or expository text would be an indication of poor general comprehension of the material. Following appropriate instruction, students' ability to answer or ask important questions after reading should improve.

Students might also be asked to select the best questions among a set of choices. Inability to select the best questions for recently read narrative or expository material would be another indication of poor general comprehension.

Students' ability to select the best summary of a narrative or expository selection from among two or three choices could be used as yet another indication of their general comprehension. Such summaries should be concise statements of the important ideas, or major points, the author was trying to make in expository text or should highlight the important story elements in narrative text. Students generally find it easier to select appropriate summaries for texts than to generate them.

Students in need of instruction in understanding either expository or narrative text would benefit from such comprehension-fostering procedures (discussed in Chapter 8), as self-questioning, reciprocal questioning, and reciprocal teaching.

Literal and Inferential Comprehension

In addition to assessing students' general comprehension of narrative and expository text, the teacher should consider students' literal and inferential comprehension ability. One way to do this is to keep records of students' performance on literal and inferential questions. Literal questions have both the question and answer in one sentence (see "Right There" QARs in Chapter 8). Inference questions, however, require the reader to combine information from two or more sentences to generate an appropriate answer ("Think and Search" QARs, or text-based inference questions), or to combine information in the text with personal knowledge to generate an appropriate answer ("On My Own" QARs, or prior knowledge-based inference questions). Material on which assessment questions are based should be at students' instructional level and should consist of both narrative and expository text.

Students doing poorly on written and oral literal questions probably have a need for instruction in literal comprehension such as the text lookback procedure and the QAR procedure discussed in Chapter 8. Students doing poorly on written and oral inference questions probably have a need for instruction in inferential comprehension. To better understand why a student is having difficulty with inferential comprehension, the procedures in the next section on drawing inferences should be followed. Students in need of instruction in inferential comprehension would benefit from instruction in the QAR procedure, the self-monitoring checklist procedure, and the inference awareness procedure discussed in Chapter 8.

DRAWING INFERENCES

As mentioned in Chapter 8, students' answers to inference questions serve as a convenient window to their inference processing ability when reading. However, a teacher should go beyond students' initial answers to inference questions and ask additional probing questions. A teacher can inquire about and take notes on how students came up with particular answers or about what might be done to answer questions left unanswered. A teacher can help students answer difficult questions and take notes on what kind and how much support has to be provided. A teacher can also provide several answers for an inference question and ask a student to explain why one answer appears to be better than another.

A group discussion is presented in Figure 9.4 to illustrate the approach to inference assessment that is recommended. In this discussion the teacher asks students to explain how they come up with their answers and whether they have used the book or their background knowledge to help them. The teacher also gives student clues when they cannot answer questions.

It is important that periodically a teacher take notes on such a questioning session for the purpose of collecting assessment data. Notes from the discussion presented in Figure 9.4 might look like the following:

> Lisa—Good job explaining text-based inference question (TBIQ, or "Think and Search" QAR). Unable to answer or explain how to answer prior knowledge-based inference question (PKBIQ, or "On My Own" QAR).

> Pat—At first, answered TBIQ incorrectly. Couldn't explain how he came up with answer. Could find 1 of 2 clues and could then answer question correctly.

> Jimmy—Found clue to a TBIQ. Used picture and prior knowledge to answer second TBIQ. Couldn't locate clue in text.

> Susan—Answered and explained 2 PKBIQs.

FIGURE 9.4   Example of Probing Questions to Assess Students' Inferencing Ability

A reading group consisting of four low-achieving readers in the third grade has just finished reading a story about a little girl who puts on a magic show. The teacher asks the students inference questions on the story and also asks them how they came up with their answers.

TEACHER: Why was Madge special? (*text-based inference*)

LISA: She was a magician.

TEACHER: Good. Tell me how you came up with your answer?

LISA: Well, it said so.

TEACHER: Show me where.

LISA: It says, "Madge was very special. She was a great magician."

TEACHER: Good. How did Jimmy Smith feel about Madge's magic tricks at first? (*text-based inference*)

PAT: He liked them. (*incorrect answer*)

TEACHER: How did you come up with this answer?

PAT: I don't know.

TEACHER: Do you see a clue at the bottom of page 127?

PAT: It says, "Everyone clapped. Jimmy Smith didn't."

TEACHER: Good. Do you see another clue at the top of page 128?

PAT: No.

JIMMY: It says he said her first trick was not so hard.

TEACHER: Good. Now, Pat, based on these two clues how do you think Jimmy Smith felt about Madge's magic tricks?

PAT: He didn't think they were very good.

TEACHER: Great! Could Madge have pulled a chicken, fox, and goat out of her hat? (*prior knowledge-based inference*)

SUSAN: No.

TEACHER: How do you know?

SUSAN: Well, a fox and a goat are too big.

TEACHER: That's right. How did you come up with your answer? Did you use the book or your head?

SUSAN: I guess I used my head.

TEACHER: Great. How did Jimmy Smith feel about Madge's last trick of pulling a rabbit out of the hat? (*text-based inference*)

JIMMY: He liked it.

TEACHER: Good. How did you come up with your answer?

JIMMY: I don't know. He looks happy in the picture.

TEACHER: Okay, but look for a clue at the bottom of page 131.   (*Cont.*)

FIGURE 9.4 Example of Probing Questions to Assess Students' Inferencing Ability (*Cont.*)

JIMMY: I don't see anything. I think pulling a rabbit out of a hat was a good trick.

LISA: It says, "Gee," said Jimmy Smith. "A real rabbit. How did you do it?" That shows he liked it.

TEACHER: Good. How do you think Madge learned to be a magician? (*prior knowledge-based inference*)

LISA: I don't know.

TEACHER: Why do you think you can't answer the question?

LISA: It doesn't say anything about that.

TEACHER: How could we answer the question?

LISA: I don't know.

SUSAN: You can learn magic tricks from books. Maybe Madge did that.

TEACHER: Good. Where did you get your answer, from the book or from your head?

SUSAN: From my head.

Such notes collected over time enable a teacher to understand and evaluate a student's inferencing ability. The teacher can look for patterns in his or her notes that may reflect one or more of the following problems: difficulty answer text-based inference questions; difficulty answering prior knowledge-based inference questions; difficulty locating clues in text to answer text-based inference questions; difficulty determining whether answers to questions come from the text or prior knowledge.

Once students have learned the question-answer relationship technique presented in Chapter 8, assessment data on students' inferencing ability can be collected in the form of a paper and pencil task. Students can be directed to answer text-based and prior knowledge-based inference questions and to indicate whether answers to questions are literal, text-based inferences ("Think and Search"), or prior knowledge-based inferences ("On My Own"). Records can be kept of students' ability to answer successfully these two different types of inference questions and to determine successfully where their answers have come from.

READING FOR IMPORTANT IDEAS

As discussed in Chapter 8, reading for important ideas is an essential skill when reading expository, or informative text, yet is a skill with which many students have difficulty. At about the third-grade level it becomes important to begin assessing students' skill in reading for main ideas in the expository paragraphs that will increasingly confront them. At about the fourth-grade level teachers should begin assessing students' ability to summarize the important ideas contained in the longer passages of their content textbooks.

To assess students' skill in reading for main ideas of instructional level paragraphs, records can be kept of students' success in generating main idea statements. The teacher can instruct students to number their papers according to the number of paragraphs in a two- to three-page section of regular textbook material. The students' task is to list a topic and write a main idea sentence for each paragraph without copying from the text. It is important for the teacher to demonstrate this task and have students practice it a few times before keeping records on their performance because it is probably a new task for them.

To determine if low-achieving readers needed special instruction in this skill, the teacher may want to compare their performance, based on a number of instructional level passages, to that of peers reading at grade level. Because most students have difficulty reading for main ideas of paragraphs,[1] instruction in this skill may benefit the entire class. After instruction, records of students' performance in generating main ideas for paragraphs should show improvement.

As discussed in Chapter 8, summarizing important ideas involves stating a few important ideas to remember from a section of text as opposed to stating a main idea for every paragraph in the section. To assess students' skill in summarizing the important ideas of two to three pages of informative text, records can be kept of students' success in writing summaries of instructional level material. Students' summaries can be scored for number of important ideas included in X number of sections, a section being designated by a heading. Ideally, a summary should contain approximately one to three important ideas per section of text.[2] The teacher would put a check by the sentences in students' summaries that express important ideas as opposed to those relating relatively unimportant details. An example of this type of scoring is provided in Figure 9.5.

As with reading for main ideas of paragraphs, the teacher may want to compare low-achieving readers' summarizing skills with those of peers' reading grade level material.

Chapter 8 discussed teacher support in the form of providing summarizing clues and alternative summaries. When providing such instructional support with an individual or a small group, a teacher can collect assessment data by noting how much instructional support has to be provided in order for a student to succeed at the task. For example, the teacher might jot down that Fred, Sara, and Chris were unable to summarize a section of their social studies text when clues were provided as to what topics to include in the summary (for example, "I think the summary should say something about the Nile River, Cairo, farming in Egypt, and Egypt's problems."). However, the teacher might also note that they were able to select the best summary for the section given two choices. Over time such notes should reflect the need to provide less instructional support.

FIGURE 9.5   Example of a Summary Scored for Important Ideas

Section	Type of Idea	
1	*+*	*(+)* Israel is an ancient nation fighting to become a modern one. *(0)* In one city there are enough teachers and schools that all the children can get an education.
1	*0*	
2,2	*+,+*	*(+)* Israel's biggest problem is its land. *(+)* Most of it is unusable for farmland. *(0)* Some of it can be used for grazing. *(+)* But new steps are being taken to make more farmland like draining swamps and irrigating fields.
2	*0*	
2	*+*	
3	*+*	*(+)* May 14, 1948, is an important date for Israel because that is the day it became a nation. *(X)* Israel is still fighting today.
3	*X*	

SCORING: + = important idea; 0 = unimportant idea; X = idea that does not come from the text

5 important ideas in 3 sections = 1.7 important ideas per section.

ASSESSING BACKGROUND KNOWLEDGE

When making judgments about a reader's comprehension of specific material, the teacher should consider the extent of the student's background knowledge of the material to be read. Any reader's comprehension will suffer when very little is known about the topic. In some instances a student's poor performance on comprehension questions may be due primarily to this fact.

There are a number of ways a teacher can assess students' background knowledge of material they will read. In Chapter 8 the PReP technique was discussed in which the teacher asks students to relate what they know about several of the major concepts developed in the reading material. Based on the students' knowledge, the teacher judges whether students' background knowledge is high, moderate, or low.

A similar procedure has been described by Zakaluk, Samuels, and Taylor (1986). The teacher has individuals free-associate orally or in writing with several key concepts from material they are about to read. For example, a series of free associations for Egypt might look like the following: Egypt–Nile, Egypt–desert, Egypt–Cairo, Egypt–Sadat, Egypt–pyramids, Egypt–Africa. A series of free associations for Cairo might look like the following: Cairo–Egypt, Cairo–big city, Cairo–nice. Based on this information the teacher might conclude that an individual knew a moderate amount about Egypt but very little about Cairo.

A teacher might also make a list of terms, some of which were related to material to be read and some of which were unrelated. Students could be asked to put check marks next to all the words on the list related to the topic about which they were going to read. For example, a list for a section in their social studies book on Alaska might look like the following: oil, resorts, tundra, permafrost, cattle, mountains, desert, farmland, big cities, hydroplanes, pipeline. Based on an individual's performance on this task, the teacher could determine whether the student had high, moderate, or low background knowledge of the material to be read.

Records of students' comprehension should reflect the extent of their background knowledge for material they have read. For example, in Figure 9.6 under the section on general comprehension a column on background knowledge has been included and completed.

COMPLETING AND USING THE READING DIFFICULTIES RECORD SHEET

This chapter has discussed a number of ways to assess students' comprehension abilities. As with word recognition, assessment has depended heavily on teacher interpretation. In this section the teacher is provided with suggestions for interpreting these data.

Chapter 7 considered Billy Stone's performance on the Reading Difficulties Record Sheet in the area of word recognition. It was determined that Billy, a fifth-grade student reading at a beginning third-grade level, had difficulty with particular aspects of word recognition. We will now investigate Billy's performance in the area of comprehension to determine his need for special remedial instruction and, if so, what types of comprehension instruction would be most beneficial for him.

The comprehension-monitoring section of Figure 9.6 shows that Billy is not particularly skilled at monitoring his comprehension of text. In four instances, Billy rated his comprehension of what he was reading as good or 1 = I understand (see the comprehension rating task in Chapter 7), even though his performance on comprehension questions ranged from 65 to 85 percent. Also, on two occasions, Billy was unable to locate sources of comprehension difficulty and had little to say in terms of word-level and idea-level fix-up strategies. Based on this information, the teacher believes that Billy may benefit from instruction in the comprehension-rating procedure, described in Chapter 8.

Section B of Figure 9.6 shows that Billy appears to have more difficulty answering questions after reading expository text, less difficulty with narrative text. The teacher believes that Billy would benefit from the reciprocal teaching procedure, a general comprehension-fostering technique designed for use with expository text.

Section B also reveals that Billy appears to have difficulty with inference questions. Section C reveals that Billy has difficulty explaining where answers to inference questions come from. The teacher believes that the QAR procedure designed to help students answer inference questions would benefit Billy.

FIGURE 9.6 Reading Difficulties Record Sheet: Comprehension

III. Comprehension
A. Comprehension monitoring
    1. Knowing when do/don't understand

Date	Pages/Book	Overall Rating	Comprehension (%)
10/2	78–84, level 3'	1	85
10/5	85–90, 3'	1	75
10/12	99–102, 3'	1	70
10/16	103–108, 3'	1	65

       Comments:
       10/19   Always thinks he understands well.

    2. Locating sources of comprehension difficulty
       Comments:
       10/5   Unable to do this, pp. 85–86, 3' book
       10/6   Unable to do this, pp. 103–104, 3' book

    3. Using fix-up strategies
       a. Student's comments:
       10/5   For a word—"Ask the teacher," idea/paragraph—"I don't know."
       10/16 For a word—"Ask someone," idea/paragraph—"I don't know."
       b. Comments:
       10/19 Doesn't really understand notion of fix-up strategies.

    4. General comments
       10/14 Would benefit from comprehension rating procedure.

B. General comprehension

Date	Pages	Book	% Accuracy Narrative	% Accuracy Expository	% Accuracy Literal	% Accuracy Inferential	Background Knowledge	Other Notes
10/2	78–84	3'	85 (17/20)		90 (9/10)	80 (8/10)	H	
10/5	85–90	3'	75 (15/20)		90 (7/10)	60 (6/10)	M	
10/12	99–102	3'		70 (14/20)	80 (8/10)	60 (6/10)	M	
10/16	103–108	3'		65 (13/20)	80 (8/10)	50 (5/10)	L	poor attention

    Comments:
    10/19   More trouble with expository than narrative text. Okay with literal questions. Some trouble with inference questions. Would benefit from reciprocal teaching procedure.

FIGURE 9.6   Reading Difficulties Record Sheet: Comprehension (*Cont.*)

C. Drawing Inferences

Date	Pages	Book	Notes
10/6	85–90	3'	Missed 2 TBIQ$_s^*$ and 2 PKBIQ$_s^*$. Couldn't tell whether answers came from text or head.
10/14	99–102	3'	Missed 2 TBIQ$_s$ and 2 PKBIQ$_s$. Still unable to tell where answers to questions came from.

*TBIQ = text-based inference question; PKBIQ = prior knowledge-based inference question

Comments
    10/19   Seems to need help with text-based and prior knowledge-based inference questions. Try QAR procedure.

D. Reading for important ideas

Date	Pages	Book	% Correct/ Paragraph M.I.	No. Important Ideas/ No. Sections
10/12	99–100	3'	30 (3/10)	
10/16	103–104	3'	20 (2/10)	
10/18	2 pgs.	library book	30 (3/10)	

Comments:
    10/19   Can give topic sometimes but not main idea. Needs instruction.

Section D of Figure 9.6 reveals that Billy has considerable difficulty generating main ideas for paragraphs. The teacher believes this is an area in which Billy would benefit from special instruction.

Chapter 7 pointed out that instructional decisions should be based on more than four reading samples. Only three or four samples of comprehension performance have been included for illustration purposes. However, even after four or five samples a teacher may want to summarize findings and begin with instruction in areas of clear need, adding instruction in other areas as weaknesses become apparent and as time allows.

You may be wondering at this point how a teacher would have time to provide Billy and six to eight other low-achieving readers with special remedial instruction in both word recognition and comprehension. As noted in Chapter 7, all of the special instruction recommendations for Billy (word identification, comprehension and vocabulary) will be considered in Chapter 15. Chapter 15 will also discuss how a teacher would plan for and implement special remedial instruction for six to eight low-achieving readers in the classroom.

SUMMARY   This chapter discussed ways to assess students' comprehension-monitoring abilities. The use of questions as well as less traditional tasks, such as question generation and summary selection, to assess students' general reading comprehension were discussed. The chapter described the use of probe questions to assess students' referencing ability. After discussing the assessment of students' inability to read for important ideas and presenting techniques for assessing students' background knowledge, the chapter concluded with a discussion of how to complete the Reading Difficulties Record Sheet and plan for remedial instruction in comprehension.

SUGGESTED ACTIVITIES

1. Prepare appropriate materials and have a student rate his or her understanding of paragraphs within longer passages and answer questions on the passages. Based on the student's ratings and answers to questions, determine whether or not the student has been accurately rating his or her comprehension. If a student is not available, your instructor may be able to provide you with three or more passages on which a student has rated comprehension and answered comprehension questions.

2. For one or two students, look at their answers to questions for three expository texts and three narrative texts (provided by your instructor). You will also need to look at the texts. Based on the student's performance, complete section III.B. of Figure 9.6. To do this you will need to decide which questions were literal and which were inferential.

3. Direct a student to summarize the main ideas (important ideas only) of two or three informative passages. Score the summaries, based on the procedures discussed in the chapter. If a student is not available, you can score several summaries written by a peer in class or your instructor may be able to provide you with several summaries written by a student, along with the corresponding texts.

NOTES   1. See Taylor, Olsen, Prenn, Rybczynski, and Zakuluk (1985).
2. See Taylor (1984).

SUGGESTED READINGS   TAYLOR, B. M. (1984). The search for a meaningful approach to assessing comprehension of expository text. In J. Niles and L. Harris (Eds.), *Changing perspectives on research in reading/language processing and instruction* (pp. 257–263). Albany, NY: National Reading Conference.

Taylor presents an approach to assessing students' comprehension of expository text based on their recall of important information.

VAUGHAN, J. L., AND ESTES, T. H. (1986). *Reading and reasoning beyond the primary grades.* Boston: Allyn and Bacon.
The authors present a number of useful suggestions for assessing students' reading comprehension through the use of retellings and questions.

Chapter **10**

Vocabulary Instruction

OVERVIEW

As you read this chapter use the following list of main ideas to guide your understanding and reflection.

Vocabulary knowledge is highly related to reading comprehension.

Contextual analysis, the use of context to determine approximate meanings for words, is a valuable vocabulary strategy which students can use when they are reading independently.

Vocabulary strategies in which students relate new words to personal experience, such as semantic mapping, have been found to be particularly effective.

Vocabulary knowledge has been found to be highly related to reading comprehension.[1] Davis (1944, 1968) investigated the reading process by factor analyzing reading comprehension subskills and concluded that reading comprehension was comprised of two primary skills, knowledge of word meanings, or vocabulary, and reasoning ability. In addition, Thorndike (1973) found correlations between vocabulary knowledge and reading comprehension to range from .66 to .75 for ten-, fourteen-, and seventeen-year olds in fifteen countries.

Vocabulary knowledge is important in the reading comprehension process for a number of reasons.[2] One view is that people with larger vocabularies normally have greater verbal ability which, in turn, facilitates their reading comprehension. A second view is that readers with larger vocabularies come across fewer unfamiliar words that interrupt the fluency of their reading, thereby enhancing comprehension. A third view is that readers with larger vocabularies have broader background knowledge and richer conceptual networks that facilitate comprehension.

VOCABULARY DEVELOPMENT: INCIDENTAL LEARNING VERSUS EXPLICIT INSTRUCTION

The three notions just described about the relationship between vocabulary knowledge and reading comprehension lead to different approaches to vocabulary development. The first view suggests that direct instruction makes little difference in terms of vocabulary development whereas the second view suggests that direct instruction in specific words is extremely beneficial. The third view suggests that vocabulary development will be enhanced if students learn to relate new concepts to their existing concepts and background knowledge.

There is considerable debate about the best way to develop students' vocabulary because there is little agreement as to which of the above three views is most accurate. The debate is further fueled by a related question concerning the degree to which readers develop vocabulary through incidental learning as they are exposed to unfamiliar words in context.

Nagy, Herman, and Anderson (1985)[3] have argued that direct instruction in specific words is a slow and inefficient method of vocabulary development. They have shown that readers do use context to learn the meanings of unfamiliar words. In fact, Nagy, Herman, and Anderson (1985) have argued that this is *the primary means* of vocabulary development and that wide reading experience is probably the best means of developing students' reading vocabulary.

In contrast, others have argued that direct instruction in vocabulary is essential for good vocabulary growth.[4] They believe the process of learning new words incidentally through repeated exposures in context is a slow and difficult means of vocabulary development. In their view, many repeated exposures to unfamiliar words in text are required before meanings are learned. Furthermore, adults have been found to frequently skip over unfamiliar words as they read.[5] It has also been demonstrated in several studies that intermediate grade students are not very skilled at using context to determine meanings of unfamiliar words.[6]

Advocates of direct instruction in vocabulary also point out that comprehension of specific reading passages is enhanced through passage-specific vocabulary instruction.[7] Additionally, it has been found that certain unfamiliar words are learned better through direct instruction than through incidental exposures in reading material.[8]

Although there is some validity to all three views of vocabulary development presented at the beginning of this chapter, the view of Nagy, Herman, and Anderson (1985) that wide reading is probably the best means of vocabulary development has the most validity. However, there are some general vocabulary strategies that students can be taught to use when reading on their own. Furthermore, direct instruction in passage-specific vocabulary benefits comprehension, and certainly is not detrimental to general vocabulary growth. Finally, recent research suggests that future recall of new words will be increased if direct instruction focuses on relating words to students' background knowledge.[9]

PROBLEMS WITH CONVENTIONAL VOCABULARY INSTRUCTION

One problem with vocabulary instruction as it often occurs in the classroom is that very little direct instruction is provided.[10] At best, target words are presented by the teacher in isolation or in sentences before a selection is read, the words decoded by the students, and their meanings determined either from the context of the sentences or by looking them up in a glossary or dictionary. Sometimes students are asked to use the target words in sentences of their own, and after reading the selection in which the words occur, students may be asked to complete a practice sheet that uses the words. At worst, target words are either not introduced at all or they are simply listed on the board, pronounced, and their meanings briefly discussed.

A second problem with conventional vocabulary instruction is that it tends to focus on rote drill and memorization as opposed to activities that help students actively relate new words to their existing knowledge and conceptual network.[11] Recent research on effective vocabulary instruction has shown that for optimal learning, students need to be actively involved in learning new words and need repeated exposures to the words.[12] These exposures should be related to students' background knowledge and experiences to facilitate retention and recall.[13]

A third problem with conventional vocabulary instruction is the lack of focus on strategies that students can use to determine meanings, or approximate meanings, of unfamiliar words when reading on their own. Students need to become independent learners to maximize vocabulary growth.

GENERAL MODEL OF VOCABULARY INSTRUCTION

This chapter looks at vocabulary development in two different ways. First, it discusses strategies that students can learn to use when reading on their own, such as the use of contextual analysis, structural analysis, and the dictionary. As with word recognition and comprehension strategies, it is important that, in addition to explaining these strategies, the teacher be explicit about why they are important and when students can use them when reading on their own.

Second, this chapter discusses strategies for providing direct instruction in specific target words either before or after reading occurs. The focus will be on strategies that provide students with active experiences, repeated exposures, and opportunities to relate the target words to other known concepts and background experiences.

Although the activities suggested in this chapter are valuable for both good and poor readers alike, teachers may need to spend more time directing them at low-achieving readers. Certainly vocabulary development should not be neglected simply because a great deal of time is devoted to word recognition and comprehension instruction.

VOCABULARY STRATEGIES THAT TRANSFER TO INDEPENDENT READING

Contextual Analysis

As discussed above, elementary school children do make use of contextual analysis when reading, thus developing their reading vocabulary. However, they are not particularly skilled in the use of this strategy. Sometimes, of course, distinct context clues for unfamiliar words are not provided in naturally occurring text. However, even when context clues do occur, elementary students have been found to have difficulty. For example, Carnine, Kameenui, and Coyle (1984) found that sixth-grade students were able to determine the meanings of unfamiliar words through the use of context clues only about 40 percent of the time. Students appeared to have the greatest difficulty when contextual information was separated from unfamiliar words (for example, "Farmers usually plow around hills instead of up and down. This method is called *contour* plowing"), and when they had to make an inference to determine a word's meaning ("The class was having an end-of-year party. It was a very *raucous* affair"), as opposed to when they encounter a synonym.

Fortunately, elementary students can be taught to improve their skill in using context clues to determine approximate word meanings. A modification of an instructional technique developed by Carnine, Kameenui, and Coyle (1984), is presented below.

What, Why, and *When.* First, the teacher explains to students *what* they will be working on and *why* this is important. They will be learning how to look for meaning clues for unfamiliar words that will help them better understand what they are reading. Contextual analysis is a convenient skill to use when reading because if students are able to generate an approximate meaning for an unfamiliar word, they will not be forced to stop and use the dictionary. Although using the dictionary is often a good idea, it does interfere with students' train of thought as they are reading.

How. Next, the teacher models contextual analysis using whatever reading material the students are currently studying. The teacher reads aloud a paragraph containing an unfamiliar word (for example, "I don't know what *raucous* means") and talks about other words in the same sentence or in nearby sentences that provide clues to the word's meaning ("*End-of-the-year* and *party* seem like clue words for *raucous*). The teacher then puts this information together to come up with an approximate meaning for the word ("Well, a party at the end of the year would probably be pretty noisy. Kids would be excited about school ending and summer vacation starting. I think *raucous* must mean noisy"). After modeling the process several times, the teacher and students together locate clues words and derive approximate meanings for unfamiliar words in the students' reading material.

For independent practice, students can continue to read on their own. They can stop to write down clue words and approximate meanings for unfamiliar words which have been targeted by the teacher or which they have noticed on their own. The teacher should explain that this skill should be used whenever they are having difficulty comprehending a paragraph because of an unfamiliar word.

Although it is not important for students to label context clues, it is useful for teachers to differentiate the following types of context clues (target words and clue words are in italics):

1. Direct definition: We have more *pollution* today than in the past. Pollution is *waste that has been added to natural resources.*

2. Restatement: The farmers planted *shelterbelts*, or *rows of trees*, by their fields to break the wind.

3. Synonym: The students had a *raucous* end-of-year party. The party was so *noisy* that the principal stopped in to see what was happening.

4. Comparison: A *dust storm* is like a *blizzard.*

5. Contrast: Dan is a *diligent* student whereas Paul is *lazy.*

6. Inference based on text information and/or prior knowledge or experience: Jason was *furious.* As soon as he finished putting the puzzle together, his *baby brother pushed it from the table onto the floor.*

7. Example: Everyone in the family was *slight.* Michelle, for instance, *weighed only seventy pounds but was twelve years old.*

Discussions about what the author did to provide a context clue for a particular word (for example, gave a direct definition, made a comparison) may teach students to look for these types of context clues when they are reading independently.

Another approach to using context clues is the vocabulary overview guide[14] which will be discussed following the next section on using the dictionary.

Using the Dictionary

Helping students learn to use the dictionary to locate the meaning of an unfamiliar word is obviously an important activity. After learning how to locate a word in the dictionary (or glossary), the next step is learning how to select the most appropriate definition for the word. Words seldom have only one meaning, yet students have the tendency to write down the first dictionary definition provided.

It is inadvisable to ask students to look up the meanings of unfamiliar words presented in isolation prior to reading. Instead, target words should be presented in the context of sentences and, if necessary, they should be looked up in the dictionary during or after reading. In this way, students will have a context for each word they locate in the dictionary. They should be encouraged to read through all of the definitions provided for a word before selecting the one that seems to be most appropriate to the text usage. Group discussion in which students are asked to explain their reasons for selecting one particular definition over others should follow dictionary work.

Another activity, which may be particularly beneficial for low-achieving readers, involves students keeping a list of unfamiliar words they come across during reading. These words might come from either assigned or independent reading material. Group meetings with the teacher can focus on unfamiliar words from common reading assignments, and students can meet individually with the teacher to discuss unfamiliar words from independent reading material. After relocating the words in the reading material in which they occurred, the teacher and students use contextual analysis plus the dictionary to determine meanings for the unfamiliar words.

The Vocabulary Overview Guide

Carr (1985) has developed a useful metacognitive vocabulary strategy that teaches students to locate unfamiliar words as they are reading on their own, to define these words, and to relate them to their personal experience.

What, *Why*, and *How*. First the teacher explains to students that they will be learning how to locate and define unfamiliar words as they are reading and to relate these words to their own experience. This will help them better understand a particular selection they are reading and develop their general vocabulary. The teacher then models the procedure as he or she reads a particular selection and writes unfamiliar words and their page numbers on the board or a piece of paper. The teacher uses context clues first and then the dictionary to determine and write down the meanings of the unfamiliar words.

Next, the teacher shows students how to complete the vocabulary overview guide. The title of the reading selection is listed at the top of a sheet of paper. Category titles, reflecting the topics of unfamiliar words, are listed under the

FIGURE 10.1   **Example of a Vocabulary Overview Guide**

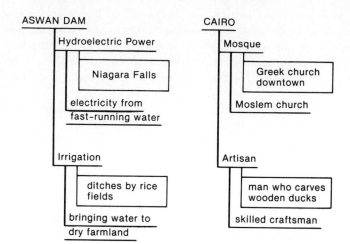

title of the reading selection. The unfamiliar words may describe or be associated with these category titles. For example, a section from students' social studies book entitled "Egypt—A Developing Nation" might contain unfamiliar terms such as *hydroelectric power* and *irrigation* that are associated with the category title, "the Aswan Dam." Similarly, *mosque* and *artisan* would be associated with the category title "Cairo." The unfamiliar words are listed under the appropriate category titles. Next, definitions or synonyms, as determined from context or the dictionary, are written under the unfamiliar words. Finally, personal clues that connect the unfamiliar words to personal experiences are written in boxes below the unfamiliar words. For example, for the unfamiliar word *mosque* a student might write the personal clue, "like Greek Orthodox church downtown." An example of a vocabulary overview guide is presented in Figure 10.1.

When. In addition to teaching the above procedure to students, the teacher should explain to them when to use the vocabulary overview guide as they are reading on their own. The teacher should explain that whenever they are reading on their own and they encounter an unknown word, they should use context clues to generate an approximate word meaning and should look the word up in the dictionary if they feel a more precise definition is needed. After completing a reading assignment, they should prepare a vocabulary overview guide that includes the unfamiliar words they encountered.

Using Structural Analysis

Knowing the meanings of common prefixes, suffixes, and roots can be useful when trying to determine the meanings of unfamiliar words containing these elements. For example, if students know that *trans* means *across*, then they will probably understand that a trip was made across the Atlantic Ocean when they read the sentence, "The pilgrims made a transatlantic voyage." Common prefixes, suffixes, and roots are listed in Figure 10.2.

In general, isolated discussions and drills on lists of prefixes, suffixes, and roots will not be very effective with low-achieving readers. The most appropriate time to discuss their meaning is when students come across an example in their reading. The teacher should write the word containing the element on the board, along with several other examples. If possible, these examples should consist of words already known by the students. The teacher can ask the students for their ideas about the possible meaning of the element being studied. Since most affixes and roots have more than one meaning, all examples introduced at one time should demonstrate the same meaning. However, the teacher should make a point of stressing that the meaning for the affix or root, as used in the examples, is just one of several meanings that the element may have.

For reinforcement, the students may be provided with sentences containing examples of the affix or root just studied. The students' task is to use a combination of context clues and structural analysis knowledge to generate meanings for the various unfamiliar words. To check their meanings, students can locate the words in the dictionary. Variations of this type of practice activity are common in basal reader materials. An example is provided in Figure 10.3.

Interpreting Ambiguous Words: Secondary Meanings and Homographs

Many words in the English language have multiple meanings, a primary meaning and one or more secondary meanings. Children are less likely to know the secondary meanings of familiar words they encounter in reading materials.[15] This, in turn, may cause confusion and impair comprehension. Therefore, it is important for the teacher to help students attend to and determine the secondary meanings of familiar words they come across in their reading. Also, by focusing on secondary meanings, teachers will help students learn to deal with them. That is, students will become less confused when confronted by familiar words whose primary meanings do not make sense.

As a follow-up to discussing secondary meanings of words encountered in assigned reading, the teacher can ask students to keep a list of unfamiliar secondary meanings they encounter in their independent reading. These lists can be shared at later meetings. As an additional follow-up activity, the teacher can provide a practice activity consisting of a pair of sentences containing underlined words that have both a primary and a secondary meaning. The students' task is to use the sentence context to generate the appropriate meaning for each underlined word. Responses can be checked by locating the

FIGURE 10.2 Common Prefixes, Suffixes, and Roots

Prefixes	Examples
anti (against, opposing)	antifreeze, antisocial
bi (two, twice)	bicycle, biweekly
circum (around)	circumnavigate, circumvent
co, con, com, col (with, together; to the same degree)	cooperate, conversation, coauthor
counter (contrary, opposing; complementary)	counterproductive, counterpart
de (do the opposite of, remove, reduce, get off)	deemphasis, dethrone, devalue, detrain
dis (deprive of, opposite, not)	disable, disunion, disagreeable
in, im, il, ir (not, in)	illogical, imperil
inter (between, reciprocal)	international, interrelation
intra (within)	intramural, intravenous
mis (bad, badly; lack of)	misjudge, mistrust
non (not)	nonconformity, noncommercial
post (after, behind)	postwar, postlude
pre (before, in front of)	prehistoric, premolar
pro (before, in front of; favoring)	proclaim, pro-America
re (again, back)	retell, recall
retro (backward)	retroactive, retrospective
semi (half, to some extent)	semiannual, semiconscious
sub (under, secondary, less than completely)	subsoil, subtropic, substandard
super (more than, over, above)	superhuman, superior
trans (across, change)	transatlantic, transfer
un (not, do the opposite of, remove from)	unskilled, unfold, unhand

Suffixes	Examples
able, ible (able to)	capable, forcible
al (pertaining to)	fictional
ance (action or process, quality or state)	performance, despondence
ation (action or process)	discoloration
ative (of, tending to)	authoritative, talkative
dom (realm, state of being)	kingdom, freedom
er, or, ist (performer of)	farmer, pianist
ful (full of, having qualities of, quantity)	eventful, peaceful, roomful
hood (state of being, instance of a quality)	boyhood, falsehood
ic (of, containing, characterized by)	panoramic, alcoholic, allergic
ish (being, characteristic of, somewhat)	Spanish, boyish, purplish
ism (act of, condition of)	criticism, barbarianism

FIGURE 10.2 Common Prefixes, Suffixes, and Roots (*Cont.*)

less (not having, unable to act)	childless, helpless
ly (like, every, in a specified manner)	fatherly, hourly, slowly
ment (action or process, condition)	development, amazement
ness (state of, quality of)	goodness
ous (having)	poisonous
ship (quality, profession)	friendship, authorship
tion, sion, ion (the act of)	decision, motion
ty, ry, ity (condition of)	safety, purity
ward (in the direction of, in spatial or temporal direction)	leftward, upward

Roots	Examples
audio (hear)	audiometer, audiovisual
auto (self)	automobile, automatic
bene (good)	beneficial, benefit
bio (life)	biology, biography
chrono (time)	chronological, chronic
cosmo (world)	cosmopolitan, cosmos
fac, fact, fic (make, do)	facilitate, factory
geo (earth)	geology, geography
gram, graph (written, or drawn)	telegram, telegraph
logo (speech)	logic, catalog
logy (science of)	biology, geology
mal (bad, inadequate)	malpractice, malformed
micro (small)	microcomputer, microcosm
mis, mit (send)	submit, admit
mov, mot (move)	move, motion
phobia (fear)	claustrophobia, hydrophobia
poly (many)	polygamous, polyunsaturated
port (carry)	portage, transportation
scope (instrument for seeing)	telescope, microscope
scrib, scrip (write)	prescription, scribble
spect, spic (look, see)	spectacles, inspect
ven, vent (come)	convention, event
vid, vis (see)	visible, video

words in the dictionary and should also be shared in a group discussion. An example of a practice activity focusing on primary and secondary meanings is presented in Figure 10.4.

Homographs are words that are spelled alike but do not sound the same and have different meanings, such as de*sert* (leave) and *de*sert (dry land). As with secondary meanings, homographs may cause students problems if they do not expect them. Again, it is important that the teacher discuss homographs when they occur in assigned reading. Students should be encouraged to use

FIGURE 10.3 Prefix Practice Activity

DIRECTIONS: Write meanings for the following underlined words. To do this use context clues plus your knowledge of the meaning of *circum*. If necessary, also use the dictionary.

1. The small sailing vessel set out to <u>circumnavigate</u> the globe.

   _____

2. A barbed wire fence <u>circumscribed</u> the farm. _____

3. John <u>circumvented</u> the problem of taking Mary out to eat after the movie by going with her to his parents' house for dinner before the movie.

   _____

4. Mr. Jones instructed his class to calculate the <u>circumference</u> of the circle. _____

5. The <u>circumspect</u> mother fox stood on guard as her babies played in the sun. _____

FIGURE 10.4   Practice Activity Focusing on Primary and Secondary Meanings

DIRECTIONS: Write meanings for the following underlined words

1. a. The old shed in the backyard <u>lists</u> to one side. _____
   _____

   b. Did you make a <u>list</u> of the things we need to buy at the grocery? _____

2. a. Tom didn't know how to get out of the <u>scrape</u> he was in; he had a date with Mary and with Sue for Saturday night. _____
   b. Timmy <u>scraped</u> his knee when he fell off his bike. _____
   _____

3. a. Eating all of Aunt Matilda's cookies before I got home was a <u>base</u> thing to do. _____
   _____

   b. Peggy hit the ball and ran to first <u>base</u>. _____
   _____

4. a. At the <u>face</u> of the building are four beautiful marble columns. _____
   b. Billy has a lot of freckles on his <u>face</u>. _____

5. a. You can get the answer <u>key</u> from me when you have completed all of the math problems. _____
   b. Grandma used an old skeleton <u>key</u> to open the door to the attic. _____
   _____

context to determine the appropriate meaning and pronunciation for a particular homograph. As a follow-up to a discussion of homographs, students should be encouraged to keep and share a list of homographs which they find in their independent reading. For practice, students can be asked to generate the appropriate meaning for each member of a homograph pair in a set of sentences. An example is provided below.

1. I hope he did not *contract* the disease. _____

2. Ms. Smith pointed out that making the morning coffee was not in her *contract*. _____

Another practice activity would be for students to generate sentences using both members of a homograph pair. These sentences could be shared in the students' reading group. Two examples are provided below.

He made a bow to the girl with a bow in her hair.

She had a tear in her eye because of the tear in her dress.

A list of common homographs is provided in Figure 10.5.

DIRECT INSTRUCTION IN SPECIFIC WORDS

As mentioned earlier, direct instruction in unfamiliar words enhances students' comprehension of specific reading material and contributes to their vocabulary growth. This section discusses a number of effective strategies for teaching vocabulary.

Using Context, Learning Definitions, and Relating Unfamiliar Words to Personal Experience

Gipe (1978–1979) has developed an effective approach to vocabulary instruction that primarily uses contextual analysis and definitions but also incorporates two important aspects of vocabulary learning: (1) receiving repeated exposures to unfamiliar words and (2) relating these words to personal experiences. A modification of this procedure is presented in the following section.

Prior to reading a particular assignment, unfamiliar words are presented one at a time on the board. The teacher reads aloud two sentences containing each word that provide good context clues to the word's meaning. The teacher asks students to write down the word and what they think it means. Approximate meanings generated by the students are discussed. In a third sentence the

FIGURE 10.5   Common Homographs

aged	converse	lead	relay
arch	convert	live	sewer
brass	desert	minute	shower
bow	digest	object	sow
bowed	do	perfect	subject
close	does	permit	tear
collect	dove	present	transfer
compact	entrance	primer	use
conduct	excuse	project	wind
console	incense	read	wound
content	intimate	record	
contract	invalid	refuse	

word is presented along with a definition. Then, students are asked to answer a question in which they relate the word to their own experience.

For example, for the word *clumsy*, the teacher writes the word on the board and reads, "The clumsy child stumbled and knocked the glass off the table. Someone who is clumsy may trip frequently and bump into things." The teacher directs students to write the word *clumsy* on a sheet of paper and to also write what they think it means. Possible meanings are discussed. Then, the teacher reads a sentence containing a definition for the word *clumsy*, "*Clumsy* means moving in an awkward manner." The students are then directed to answer the following question, "What might a clumsy shopper do at the grocery store?" Students share answers to this question.

Sentences and a question for the word *surplus* might include the following: "We had a surplus of food after the party was over. Our surplus showed us that we had bought too much food for the party. *Surplus* means having more of something than is needed. Do you or your family have a surplus of anything?" By participating in this sequence of activities, students receive several meaningful exposures to each unfamiliar word prior to reading. This will aid their retention of each word as well as its meaning.

Using the Key-Word Method

Another effective technique for learning meanings of unfamiliar words is the key-word method.[16] This method involves using mnemonics and imagery to learn the meanings of unfamiliar words.

Mnemonic techniques, strategies for transforming to-be-learned material into a form that makes the material easier to learn and remember, are known to facilitate memory. In addition, images or pictures seem to be particularly effective devices for coding information mnemonically.[17]

The key-word method involves presenting a vocabulary word along with a key word, that is, a familiar word that is phonetically similar to part or all of

FIGURE 10.6   Example of a Key-Word Illustration

SURPLUS (SYRUP) having some left over,
having more than was needed

SOURCE: From J. R. Levin et al. (1982), Mnemonic versus nonmnemonic vocabulary-learning strategies for children, *American Educational Research Journal, 19,* 127. Copyright 1982, *American Educational Research Journal,* Washington, DC.

the vocabulary word. For example, *syrup* could be presented as a key word for *surplus, purse* for *persuade,* and *angel* for *angler.*

A picture is then presented that relates the key word to the meaning of the vocabulary word. For example, a cupboard full of syrup could be presented to illustrate a surplus, a woman being persuaded by her friend to buy a purse could illustrate the meaning of persuade, and an angel fishing could illustrate the meaning of angler. To clarify each picture, two characters in the picture are speaking. One character's comments contain the key word and the other's the vocabulary word. At the bottom of the picture, the vocabulary word is presented, followed by the key word in parentheses and a definition of the vocabulary word. An example of a key word illustration is presented in Figure 10.6.

The teacher reads the characters' comments and the vocabulary word, key word and definition at the bottom of the page. After discussing what is happening in the picture, the teacher explains or has the students explain how they will remember the meaning of the vocabulary word by thinking of the key word and picture.

In research using the key-word technique with children, actual pictures have been provided. Although pictures may be less practical for the classroom, it is important that the teacher help students develop an appropriate key-word illustration in the form of a mental image. The key-word procedure is not as effective when the students are expected to generate key-word images on their own.[18] For example, even if no picture such as the one in Figure 10.6 were available to help students learn the meaning of surplus, the teacher should help students come up with this or a similar image in their heads. The teacher could tell students to imagine a boy pouring a great amount of syrup on his pancakes because there are five more bottles of syrup in the cupboard. Next, the teacher could tell students that the boy was not worried about using too much syrup because he knows there is a "surplus of syrup" in the cupboard. Then the teacher could write the words *syrup* and *surplus* on the board and provide students with a definition for the word *surplus*.

Because it is a somewhat lengthy procedure, the key-word method is not an appropriate technique for introducing a large number of words before students read assigned material. Instead, the key-word method might be reserved for particularly important, difficult words.

Semantic Mapping

People learn by relating the new to the known; that is, by relating new concepts to existing concepts and knowledge. In several recent studies it has been found that vocabulary instruction that helps students relate unfamiliar words and their meanings to known concepts has been more effective than conventional approaches that focus on learning definitions or using context to determine meanings of unfamiliar words.[19]

Semantic mapping[20] is one such technique that has been found to be effective.[21] It involves linking a vocabulary word to as many related words as possible. It is a useful way to focus on a particularly important word that students have come across in a reading assignment.

Assume, for example, that students have just read a section in their social studies book about dry farming on the Great Plains. The teacher might develop a semantic map for the concept *dry farming* on the board while students make copies on individual sheets of paper.

First, the teacher puts *dry farming* in the middle of the board. As the students free-associate with this word, the teacher lists their ideas on the board. Then, different categories of information pertaining to the word and the free associations are developed by the class. One category might be "definition," and the students would provide a definition for *dry farming*. A second category might be "reasons for dry farming," and students would list the reasons. A third category might be "types of crops grown through dry farming," and students would list crops such as wheat and oats. A fourth category might be "places where dry farming is used," and students would list states such as Montana, Colorado, and Wyoming. An example of a semantic map for the concept *dry farming* is presented in Figure 10.7.

Another approach to semantic mapping involves taking a familiar concept

FIGURE 10.7 Semantic Map

<u>definition</u>

1/2 land planted
1/2 land fallow

<u>reasons for using</u>

not much rainfall
soil dry

Dry Farming

<u>where used</u>

Montana
Wyoming
Colorado

<u>types of crops</u>

wheat
oats

pertaining to a pending reading selection and having students generate ideas related to the concept. After reading, new concepts gleaned from the material can be added to the map.[22]

For example, if students are going to read a story in their basal reader about the circus, the teacher and students can generate a semantic map for the word *circus* before reading. After reading, new words can be added to the map. An example of such a pre-post semantic map is presented in Figure 10.8. Words included in the map before reading, based on students' background knowledge, are those in regular type. New words added after reading are

FIGURE 10.8 Pre-Post Semantic Map

<u>performers</u>

acrobats
trapeze artists
lion *trainer*
tightrope walker

<u>animals</u>

lions
tigers
elephants
monkeys

Circus

<u>clowns</u>

WHITEFACE
AUGUST
ACROBAT
MIDGET
TALL (ON *STILTS*)

<u>clown tricks</u>

TINY CAR TRICK
SAW-A-CLOWN-IN-*HALF*

NOTE: Words included in the map before reading, based on students' background knowledge, are in regular type. New words added after reading are in capitals. Vocabulary words that were selected by the basal authors of this story about the circus as words in need of attention are indicated by asterisks.

those in capital letters. Vocabulary words selected by the basal authors for this particular story are indicated by asterisks.

Semantic Feature Analysis

Semantic feature analysis[23] is another technique that helps students learn the meanings of unfamiliar words by relating them to known words. The technique involves looking at the similarities and differences of related concepts. Like semantic mapping, semantic feature analysis has been found to be an effective technique for developing students' vocabulary.[24]

Semantic feature analysis involves the teacher's taking a category such as *fruit* and listing in the left-hand column a few members of the category, such as *apple, peach*, and *plum*. Features germane to the category, such as *smooth skin, seeds*, and *pit*, are listed in a row across the top of the grid. The teacher and students use a system of pluses and minuses to determine which members of the category under investigation have which features. If one of the category members is a newly introduced vocabulary word, students will be able to see how this new word is similar to, yet different from, other words already known.

For example, if the new vocabulary word is *canoe*, the teacher introduces the category *boats*. The teacher lists *canoe* at the top of the column of category members and asks students to add other types of boats to the grid. Next, students are asked to add boat features to the grid. They complete the grid by using pluses and minuses to match boats and features. An example of a semantic feature analysis grid is provided in Figure 10.9. A plus means *yes* (this category member has this feature), a minus means *no*, and a question mark means *maybe*.

After completing the grid, the teacher and students discuss the category members and features. Questions such as, "What two category members are most alike?" and "What two category members are most different?" can be asked to stimulate discussion. Students may also think of other category members or features to add to the grid.

DEVELOPING STUDENTS' INTEREST IN WORDS

This chapter concludes with a number of suggestions for developing students' interest in words. It is important that teachers be enthusiastic about new words and their meanings and to instill this enthusiasm in their students. One of the best ways to build students' enthusiasm for words is to engage them in vocabulary games and other entertaining vocabulary-related activities. It is hoped that through such activities students will develop their vocabulary knowledge and become more attentive to new words they encounter.

Sharing New Words Heard Outside of School

Students often enjoy what is actually a sophisticated version of "show and tell" in which they share with the class new words they have learned outside of

FIGURE 10.9   Example of a Semantic Feature Analysis Grid

Category—Types of Boats

Category Members	Manpower	Tips Easily	Fast	Expensive	Use on Rivers	Use on Lakes
Canoe	+	+	−	−	+	+
Sailboat	−	?	−	?	−	+
Rowboat	+	−	−	−	−	+
Powerboat	−	−	+	+	?	+

school. The teacher can simply set aside ten minutes once or twice a week for students to present and define new words they have encountered. Students should be prepared to tell how they came across a particular word and to explain the context in which the word was used. For example, students might pick up new words at the dinner table, on TV, from the newspaper or a book they are reading, or from a list of unfamiliar words they have been keeping as part of their reading in school. Students' attention to unfamiliar words usually increases if they know they have the opportunity to share them in school. As an additional motivator, students can keep personal lists of new words on

This student is sharing his new vocabulary word with the rest of the class.
(Peter Vadnai)

charts displayed in their classroom. Every time someone brings in a new word to share, it can be added to his or her list.

Illustrating New Words

Students often enjoy using pictures to illustrate new words they have learned. One possible activity involves cartoons. Students can make cartoons to go with new words, or they can simply add new captions to existing cartoons. For example, in a "Peanuts" cartoon in which Charlie Brown asks Snoopy if he wants to go downtown with him, the vocabulary word *accompany* might replace *go*. Similarly, students can write captions for magazine pictures that illustrate vocabulary words. The captions should contain the new vocabulary words. For example, to illustrate the word *adorned* a student might find a picture of a person wearing a bizarre object and write a caption beneath the picture using the word *adorned*.

Completing Crossword Puzzles

Many students enjoy crossword puzzles, which may or may not be made up of new vocabulary words. Often, basal reader materials have crossword puzzles featuring new words. However, even if crossword puzzles are not made up of new vocabulary words, they are useful for general vocabulary development and for developing students' interest in words.

Students often enjoy making simple crossword puzzles for others to complete. An example of a simple crossword puzzle is provided in Figure 10.10. In this example, in only one instance do the letters in a column spell an actual word. If students were making their own crossword puzzles, they may want to create words for rows but not columns to keep their task simple.

Playing Vocabulary Games

A number of commercial games are available, such as "Scrabble" and "Spill-and-Spell," that are valuable for promoting general vocabulary growth as well as for developing students' interest in words. A rule for such games might be that students give a definition for any word they have constructed, or at least an example of its use to demonstrate they know what the word means.

"Concentration" is another vocabulary game that is easy to prepare. For example, the teacher or students can make pairs from vocabulary words and synonyms or antonyms for these words. Or, new vocabulary words can be matched with definitions.

SUMMARY   This chapter discussed the fact that vocabulary development is an important but often neglected aspect of both developmental and remedial reading

FIGURE 10.10 Simple Crossword Puzzle

DIRECTIONS: Use the words below to answer the questions and to fill in the crossword puzzle.

learned	electric	pilot
immortal	trade	quarrel

1. What do you do if you give a friend a baseball card and get one from them?
2. What would you be if you never died?
3. What type of clock has to be plugged in?
4. What does the teacher hope you have done after you've read your science book?
5. What is someone who flies a plane called?
6. What is a fight with words called?

*

1. _t_ _r_ _a_ _d_ _e_
2. _i_ _m_ _m_ _o_ _r_ _t_ _a_ _l_
3. _e_ _l_ _e_ _c_ _t_ _r_ _i_ _c_
4. _l_ _e_ _a_ _r_ _n_ _e_ _d_
5. _p_ _i_ _l_ _o_ _t_
6. _q_ _u_ _a_ _r_ _r_ _e_ _l_

Read the word spelled downward under the star. It spells the name of a famous person you will read about. Write the name on the line.

Amelia

programs. Suggestions for initial vocabulary instruction focusing on strategies students can use when reading on their own were provided. The primary purpose of these strategies is to help students obtain meanings for unfamiliar words while reading so their comprehension is not impaired. In addition, general vocabulary growth occurs as students attend to unfamiliar words.

Suggestions for vocabulary instruction in specific words were also provided.

Vocabulary games are a good way to develop students' interest in words.
(James Silliman)

Three of the strategies presented involve relating new vocabulary words to already known words, and/or to students' own experiences. A fourth strategy given involves using mnemonics and imagery to help students remember the meanings of new words.

Finally, activities for developing students' interest in words and word meanings were discussed. Collecting words outside of school, illustrating vocabulary words, and playing vocabulary games were offered as ways to heighten students' awareness of and interest in words.

SUGGESTED ACTIVITIES

1. Locate appropriate material and teach two or three students how to use context clues to determine word meanings. If students are not available, "teach" the technique to peers in your class.

2. Locate two or three important words in a student textbook and prepare key-word illustrations, dialogue, and definitions for these words.

3. Locate two or three important words in a student textbook and develop a semantic map for each of these words with a group of two or three students or with peers in your class.

1. See Anderson and Freebody (1981) and Sternberg and Powell (1983).
2. See Anderson and Freebody (1981).
3. See Nagy and Anderson (1984) and Nagy and Herman (1984).
4. See Beck, McKeown, and McCaslin (1983), Graves (1987), and Omanson, Beck, McKeown, and Perfetti (1984).
5. See Freebody and Anderson (1983).
6. See Carnine, Kameenui, and Coyle (1984) and Rankin and Overholser (1969).
7. See Beck, Perfetti, and McKeown (1982), Jenkins, Stein, and Wysocki (1984), Kameenui, Carnine, and Freschi (1982), and Stahl (1983).
8. See Beck, McKeown, and McCaslin (1983), Jenkins, Pany, and Schreck (1978), and Omanson et al. (1984).
9. See McNeil (1984).
10. See Beck, McKeown, McCaslin, and Burkes (1979), Durkin (1978–1979), Graves (1987), and Jenkins and Dixon (1983).
11. See Blachowicz (1985) and Eeds and Cockrum (1985).
12. See Beck, Perfetti, and McKeown (1982), Jenkins, Stein, and Wysocki (1984), McKeown, Beck, Omanson, and Perfetti (1983), and Mezynski (1983).
13. See Eeds and Cockrum (1985), Jenkins, Pany, and Schreck (1978), Johnson, Toms-Bronowski and Pittelman (1982), and Margosein, Pascarella, and Pflaum (1928).
14. See Carr (1985).
15. See Mason, Knisely, and Kendall (1979).
16. See Levin et al. (1984), Levin, et al. (1982), and Pressley, Levin, and Miller (1981).
17. See Levin (1981).
18. See Levin (1981).
19. See Eeds and Cockrum (1985), Johnson, Toms-Bronowski, and Pittelman (1982), and Margosein, Pascarella, and Pflaum (1982).
20. See Johnson and Pearson (1984).
21. See Johnson, Toms-Bronowski, and Pittelman (1982) and Margosein, Pascarella, and Pflaum (1982).
22. See Johnson, Toms-Bronowski, and Pittelman (1982).
23. See Johnson and Pearson (1984).
24. See Johnson, Toms-Bronowski, and Pittelman (1982).

BLACHOWITZ, C. (1985). Vocabulary development and reading: From research to instruction. *The Reading Teacher* 38: 876–881.
Techniques for relating new words to students' background knowledge are discussed.

CARNINE, D. W., KAMEENUI, E. J., AND COYLE, G. (1984). Utilization of contextual information in determining the meanings of unfamiliar words. *Reading Research Quarterly* 19: 184–204.
The authors present a technique for teaching students to use context clues to determine word meanings.

CARR, E. (1985). The vocabulary overview guide: A metacognitive strategy to improve vocabulary comprehension and retention. *Journal of Reading* 28: 684–687.

Carr presents a technique that helps students learn new words by relating them to their background knowledge.

EEDS, M., AND COCKRUM, W. A. (1985). Teaching word meanings by expanding schemata vs. dictionary work vs. reading in context. *Journal of Reading* 28: 492–497.

The importance of relating to background in vocabulary instruction is stressed.

JOHNSON. D., TOMS-BRONOWSKI, S., AND PITTELMAN, S. (1982). *An investigation of the effectiveness of semantic mapping and semantic feature analysis with intermediate grade level children* (Progress Report No. 83–3). Madison, WI: Wisconsin Center for Educational Research.

The authors describe how to conduct semantic mapping and semantic feature analysis to promote vocabulary learning.

LEVIN, J. R. (1981). The mnemonic 80s: Keywords in the classroom. *Educational Psychologist* 16: 65–82.

Discusses the key-word technique.

Chapter **11**

Vocabulary Assessment

OVERVIEW

As you read this chapter use the following list of main ideas to guide your understanding and reflection.

General vocabulary knowledge is difficult to assess and can probably best be achieved through the use of commercial standardized tests.

A constructed answer format is preferable to a multiple choice format for vocabulary assessment because it more closely approximates what a reader must do when he or she encounters an unfamiliar word in text.

For vocabulary assessment an unfamiliar word should be presented within the context of sentences because a word's meaning depends on its context.

This chapter on vocabulary assessment first discusses assessment of students' general vocabulary knowledge, then provides suggestions for assessing specific vocabulary skills that students can use when they encounter unknown words in their reading. Such skills include using context and the dictionary, structural analysis, and interpreting ambiguous words. The discussion then turns to strategies for assessing students' learning of specific words. These may be words discussed before and/or after students have read basal reader stories, content textbooks, or other instructional level material. These suggestions for assessment will closely parallel the suggestions for instruction provided in

Chapter 10. The chapter concludes with a discussion about using the reading difficulties record sheet in the area of vocabulary.

The suggestions for vocabulary assessment presented in this chapter assume that vocabulary words are presented within the context of sentences because words' meanings depend on their context. Although examples are provided using both the constructed answer (for example, students are asked to provide definitions or give meanings for words) and multiple-choice formats, the constructed answer format is stressed because this approach more closely approximates real reading. In independent reading, a student is not provided with several choices for a word's meaning when confronted with an unfamiliar word. Instead, the student will most likely generate an approximate meaning for a word and continue reading. The student may occasionally stop to look up an unknown word in the dictionary, but this is not something that readers do on a regular basis.

ASSESSMENT OF GENERAL VOCABULARY KNOWLEDGE

Assessment of general vocabulary knowledge is difficult because of the problems associated with developing an appropriate sample of words.[1] Random sampling of words from the dictionary does not take into account word frequency. Selecting words from a frequency list is more appropriate, yet determining the numbers of words to select from different frequency levels remains a problem. Using a commercial standardized test is recommended, as opposed to a teacher-made test, to obtain an indication of a student's reading vocabulary because general vocabulary knowledge is so difficult to assess.

Most achievement tests include some measure of reading vocabulary knowledge. General achievement tests that contain vocabulary subtests include the following: Comprehensive Tests of Basic Skills (1981), Iowa Test of Basic Skills (1982), Metropolitan Achievement Tests (1978), Sequential Tests of Educational Progress (1979), and SRA Achievement Series (1978). Other reading tests that contain vocabulary subtests include the following: Gates-MacGinitie Reading Tests (1978) and Nelson Denny Reading Test (1981). The Diagnostic Reading Scale (1981), the Durrell Analysis of Reading Difficulties (1980), the Gates-McKillop-Horowitz Reading Diagnostic Tests (1981), and the Stanford Diagnostic Reading Test (1984) are diagnostic reading tests that include measures of auditory vocabulary. Finally, the Peabody Picture Vocabulary Test (1981) is an individually administered test of verbal knowledge.

The above tests employ different approaches and have limitations that need to be acknowledged if used. For example, many of these tests present words in isolation. This represents an unnatural situation since words are almost always encountered in some context. The tests mentioned above by no means provide a comprehensive list of all vocabulary tests that are currently available to assess general vocabulary knowledge. For more complete information on available tests as well as specific descriptions of other information concerning individual tests, teachers should consult *Buros Mental Measurements Yearbook* and the actual tests themselves.

Using Context

Contextual analysis to determine word meanings is a skill that becomes important at about the third-grade reading level. Generally, below this level there are not many words students encounter in their reading whose meanings are unfamiliar to them. Consequently, teachers should begin assessing students' ability to use context to determine word meanings at this level and above.

To assess a student's ability to use context clues to determine word meanings, the teacher should use words that the student does not already know. These words can be determined by presenting students with a list of eight or ten less frequently encountered vocabulary words from their basal reader or other instructional level material. The students are asked to write down meanings for any words they know (Task 1). Initially, the words should be presented in sentences with minimal context clues to determine if students know particular words even without the benefit of good context clues. Next, the teacher should present the same eight or ten words in sentences containing good context clues and ask the students to generate meanings for the words (Task 2). When students complete these tasks independently, the sentences should not contain words that would cause decoding problems. Alternately, the teacher or an aide could be on hand to assist students with decoding problems. For each student the teacher should come up with a score indicating the number of words defined correctly from context (Task 2) out of the total number of words not originally known (Task 1). An example of a student's performance on such an informal context test is presented in Figure 11.1.

It is important to score responses on this type of test leniently, since different meanings, based on context, may be possible. The goal of this test is to assess a student's ability to use context to determine word meanings and, consequently, reasonable responses should be accepted. Consider, for example, the following sentence: "Mrs. Jones forbids Tommy to go near the river because it is dangerous." For the word *forbids*, response such as *does not want* would be reasonable, even if it is not as accurate as a response such as *will not allow*.

One informal context test containing eight or ten items does not provide a teacher with sufficient information concerning a student's ability to use context clues to determine word meanings. As mentioned in Chapter 5, a more reliable technique is to take a number of samples over time of a student's performance on a skill. After initial assessment, a teacher must judge whether or not a student's use of context analysis to determine word meanings indicates that special remedial instruction in this skill is needed. One way to help form this judgment is to compare a low-achieving reader's performance with that of average reading peers. However, it is important for the teacher to bear in

FIGURE 11.1 Student's Performance on an Informal Context

NOTE: Parts 1 and 2 should be on separate sheets of paper.

    ✓ = word meaning known in Part 1.
    ✓ ✓ = correct word meaning given in Part 2 for word not known in Part 1.

PART 1 DIRECTIONS: Write as many definitions or synonyms as you know for the following underlined words:

✓ a. She complained of an ache. _____ *pain* _____

✓ b. The building was ancient. _____ *old* _____

    c. The crystal was on the shelf. _____

    d. I will dye the shirt. _____ *to not be alive* _____

    e. The man wanted to express his gratitude. _____

    f. There was a musket in the closet. *animal like a weasel*

    g. John will navigate. _____

    h. The man seized a child in the crowd. _____

PART 2 DIRECTIONS: Give a meaning for each underlined word:

✓ a. Susie has a stomach ache after eating so much candy.
_____ *pain* _____

✓ b. Tom said the church was ancient because it was built in 1683. _____ *old* _____

✓ ✓ c. Mrs. Jones's good crystal bowl shattered when it fell off the shelf. _____ *glass* _____

✓ ✓ d. The children had a pleasant time dyeing Easter eggs.
_____ *coloring* _____

    e. When you get a present from someone, you should show your gratitude by sending them a thank-you note.
_____ *happy* _____

✓ ✓ f. The pioneer shot the wolf with his musket. _____ *gun* _____

✓ ✓ g. The man navigated his boat across the Atlantic Ocean.
_____ *sailed* _____

    h. The bank robber seized someone in the bank to be his hostage. _____ *shot* _____

Total number not known in Part 1 __6__

Number correct in Part 2 out of number not known in Part 1 __4/6__ mind that different words and different context sentences or texts were used with the low-achieving readers, thus making direct comparisons with better readers impossible.

A variation of this assessment procedure involves having students locate vocabulary words used in sentences with good context clues in their basal reader or other instruction level material. The teacher should first determine which words students already know. This can be done by asking students to provide meanings for words in sentences with minimal context clues. Then, the teacher directs students to locate the same words on particular pages in their basal reader and to use context to come up with approximate meanings for the words. Students should be encouraged to read the entire paragraph containing a target vocabulary word because context clues often are provided in neighboring sentences as well as in the sentence where the word occurs. An example of this type of test is presented in Figure 11.2.

This second (basal reader) approach to assessing students' use of context is particularly appealing because it involves students in an activity that is similar to real reading. In both approaches the targeted vocabulary words should come from the students' basal reader or other instructional level material so that students will be assessed on the type of material that they will be expected to read.

A third approach to assessing students' use of context clues involves a multiple-choice format. First, students are asked to provide meanings for eight or ten vocabulary words presented in sentences with minimal context clues. Then, students are presented with a set of eight or ten sentences, each one containing an underlined vocabulary word followed by three or four synonyms or brief definitions. The students' task is to use the context of the sentence to select that definition or heading that best fits the underlined word. Again, it is important to use vocabulary words from a students' basal reader or from material on the student's instructional level. An example of this type of test format is:

Mrs. Jones's good *crystal* bowl shattered when it fell off the shelf.
(plastic, glass, wood)

The multiple-choice approach to assessing the use of context has several advantages. First, the test is easier for students to complete because they do not have to generate responses in the second part of the test. Also, the responses can be scored objectively. The biggest disadvantage of this approach is its inability to approximate a natural reading situation in which students must generate their own meanings for unfamiliar words.

Using the Dictionary

Like contextual analysis, using the dictionary to locate appropriate definitions for unfamiliar words is a skill that becomes important once students are reading

FIGURE 11.2   Informal Context Test Using the Students' Basal Reader

NOTE: Parts 1 and 2 should be on separate sheets of paper.

PART 1 DIRECTIONS: Write as many definitions or synonyms as you know for the following underlined words:

a. She complained of an ache. _____

b. The building was ancient. _____

c. The crystal was on the shelf. _____

d. I will dye the shirt. _____

e. The man wanted to express his gratitude. _____

f. There was a musket in the closet. _____

g. John will navigate. _____

h. The man seized a child in the crowd. _____

PART 2 DIRECTIONS: Locate each word on the page in your basal reader that is listed. Read the paragraph that the word is in. Then give a meaning for each of the following words:

a. ache: page 92 _____

b. ancient: page 95 _____

c. crystal: page 97 _____

d. dye: page 97 _____

d. gratitude: page 101 _____

f. musket: page 102 _____

g. navigate: page 105 _____

h. seize: page 107 _____

at about the third-grade level. Therefore, assessing students' ability to use the dictionary is recommended when they are reading on a third-grade level or above, or whenever they have received instruction in this skill.

To assess students' ability to locate appropriate dictionary definitions for specific vocabulary words, it is essential that the words be presented in sentences and that students be confronted with vocabulary words that have not been formally studied.

One approach simply involves presenting five to ten underlined words in the same number of sentences. Students should locate the underlined words in the dictionary and select the definitions that best fit the words as they were used in the sentences. Examples are provided in Figure 11.3.

These students are using the dictionary to select the best meaning for an unfamiliar word. *(Peter Vadnai)*

Another approach involves students locating five to ten words in a textbook, finding each of the words in the dictionary, and using the context of the textbook passage to select the most appropriate dictionary definition. An advantage of this approach is that it approximates a normal reading situation. In either case it is important to use sentences or passages which do not present serious decoding difficulties. Passages should be from books written on a student's instructional level and either the teacher or an aide should be present to assist with reading definitions in the dictionary.

As with skill in using context clues, the teacher initially will have to use his or her judgment about the instructional needs of low-achieving readers. Their performance on this skill can be compared to that of average reading peers reading from grade level material. However, as was pointed out previously, it is important for the teacher to remember that different materials have been used in the two situations and different words assessed. After instruction and practice in locating words in the dictionary and selecting appropriate definitions, improvements should be seen in students' performance on the type of informal test shown in Figure 11.3.

Using Structural Analysis

Students' use of structural analysis as an aid in determining word meanings should be assessed once it appears in the basal, which is generally at about the third- or fourth-grade level, or once students have received instruction in it. Generally, students' knowledge of prefixes, suffixes, and roots is best

FIGURE 11.3   Informal Test on Using the Dictionary to Determine Words' Meanings

DIRECTIONS: Look up each underlined word in the dictionary. Read all of the definitions and then write on your paper the definition that best fits the underlined word as it is used in these sentences.

1. John held the school record for the 100-yard dash.

   definition: _____

2. Sally was not able to figure out the answer to the math problem.

   definition: _____

3. Tom likes to read the sports column in the newspaper.

   definition: _____

4. Jane did not have a solution to her problem.

   definition: _____

5. Tina bought a beautiful violet dress.

   definition: _____

assessed in conjunction with their skill in using context clues since affixes and roots seldom have just one meaning. One needs to know the context in which an affix or root occurs to determine the appropriate meaning of the element. Therefore, students' knowledge of affix or root meanings is best assessed by presenting sentences with underlined words containing the affixed or roots that have been studied.

The students' task would be to provide meanings for the underlined words and for each prefix, suffix, or root as it was used in a particular sentence. Three or four examples of a particular affix or root should be included in a single test. Therefore, only a few affixes or roots should be tested at one time. An example of an informal structural analysis test is presented in Figure 11.4. This type of activity is often found in basal reader skill sheet materials.

The examples in Figure 11.4 use sentences that provide good context clues. When interpreting students' performance on this type of test, the teacher has to keep in mind that the test provides a measure of students' knowledge of specific affix or root meanings along with their ability to use context clues to generate word meanings.

Because it is relatively unimportant for students to memorize meanings for various prefixes, suffixes, or roots, minimal amounts of additional drill and practice on structural elements that a student has not learned is recommended. It is more important that a student perform well (that is, approximately as well as better reading peers) on informal structural analysis tests, or show improve-

FIGURE 11.4   Informal Test of Students' Knowledge of Prefixes, Suffixes, or Roots

DIRECTIONS: Read each sentence below and write down what you think is the meaning of each word (which has one line under it) and each prefix (which has two lines under it).

1. Mr. Wilson took the subway to work instead of the bus because it was a lot quicker.

   subway _____

   sub _____

2. Temperatures in the sixties in August are subnormal for Texas.

   subnormal _____

   sub _____

3. The wizard transformed the frog into a beautiful princess.

   transformed _____

   trans _____

4. Ms. Smith was a supervisor who had twenty people working under her.

   supervisor _____

   super _____

5. Mr. and Mrs. Peters took a transatlantic voyage from New York to London.

   transatlantic _____

   trans _____

6. They ship oil to the United States from the Middle East in supertankers.

   supertanker _____

   super _____

ment following instruction. This suggests that instruction in the meanings of prefixes, suffixes, and roots has been effective.

Interpreting Ambiguous Words

Teachers may want to assess students' ability to interpret secondary meanings and homographs once students have received instruction in them, or if they appear to be a frequent source of confusion. Informal tests of students' ability to interpret ambiguous words should include both words previously studied and words never seen before. In the first case, a teacher would be assessing students' knowledge of secondary meanings or meanings for homographs they had already studied. In the second case, a teacher would be assessing students' ability to use their general knowledge of secondary meanings and homographs to help them interpret new words with secondary meanings and new homographs.

To illustrate the latter point, if students have received instruction in some secondary meanings, they should have learned to anticipate word usage beyond the most common meanings. They should be ready to use context to help them generate approximate secondary meanings.

As with prefixes, suffixes, and roots, words demonstrating secondary meanings and homographs should not be presented in isolation. Instead, examples should be presented in sentences even though this approach will confound the assessment of students' ability to interpret ambiguous words with their ability to use context clues. However, this is not a serious problem since ambiguous words seldom occur in isolation. Furthermore, it is only through context that ambiguous words become unambiguous.

One approach to assessing students' knowledge of secondary meanings and homographs involves a constructed answer format. The students are presented with a set of eight or ten sentences containing underlined words that are either homographs or words with secondary meanings. The students' task is to generate meanings for the underlined words. Examples are provided below. In the blanks students should write what they think each underlined word means.

1. Several old houses by the river *list* to one side and look like they're going to fall over._____

2. The cowboys chased the wild horses across the *plain*._____

Another approach to assessing students' ability to interpret ambiguous words involves a multiple-choice format. Instead of generating responses, as in the above examples, students are asked to select from among three or four choices the most appropriate definitions or meanings for the underlined terms. Examples of this format are also provided below.

1. Several old houses by the river *list* to one side and look like they're going to fall over. (a series, leans)

2. The cowboys chased the wild horses across the *plain*. (flat stretch of land, not fancy)

ASSESSING STUDENTS' LEARNING
OF SPECIFIC WORDS

To assess students' ability to provide synonyms or definitions for specific vocabulary words that have been studied, it is best to use a multiple-choice format. This is because using a constructed response format, in which students are asked to generate meanings for isolated words, is a difficult and unnatural task. Students will seldom need to provide synonyms or definitions for words in isolation, except on vocabulary tests.

Because words do not normally appear in isolation, even multiple-choice tests should present vocabulary words in sentences. To separate word knowledge from the ability to use context clues, the test sentences should provide minimal context clues. An example is provided below.

Kristie was *furious* when she knew what had happened.
a. happy   c. sad
b. angry   d. disappointed

In this example, all of the responses would make sense in the context of the sentence. The student has to know the meaning of *furious* to come up with the correct synonym for the word. However, selecting the appropriate synonym in the above example is easier than defining the word in isolation because the sentence implies that *furious* is an emotional response.

An alternative approach to assessing students' knowledge of specific words involves a fill-in-the-blank format. Students could be given approximately ten sentences in which a vocabulary word is missing from each one as indicated by a blank. The ten missing vocabulary words could be listed at the bottom of the page. The students' task would be to write the vocabulary words in the appropriate blanks. To do this, the students would have to know the meanings of the missing words. An example of this type of test is presented in Figure 11.5. As Figure 11.5 shows, it is important for the sentences to provide adequate context clues in order to enable students to fill in the blanks correctly.

Progress can be determined by keeping individual records of the percent of correct meanings selected or blanks filled in correctly over time. Teachers will have to use their judgment as to whether or not students' performance is satisfactory. Low-achieving readers' performance could be compared to that of average reading peers on similar vocabulary tests. Unsatisfactory progress would indicate that more instructional time or new approaches are needed.

ASSESSING INTEREST IN UNFAMILIAR WORDS

In addition to assessing students' abilities in specific vocabulary skills, such as using context clues or finding appropriate definitions in the dictionary, it is

FIGURE 11.5   Informal Word Meanings Test

DIRECTIONS: Use the words at the bottom of the page to fill in the blanks in the sentences below.

1. Mr. Wilson was _____ when he found out that rabbits had eaten all of the lettuce in his garden.

2. A yellow flashing light means to go through the intersection with

   _____ .

3. The dog was _____ when it quit running.

4. He _____ a dime from his mother's purse.

5. I did not _____ that you were trying to tell me it was time to go home.

6. Jerry _____ his old car that quit running by the side of the road and started to walk into town.

7. A diamond is a _____ gem.

8. The cat was _____ the mouse.

abandoned	panting	furious	realize
filched	caution	precious	stalking

important to keep records that document changes in students' interest in words. One way to do this is through individual progress charts indicating the number of unfamiliar words collected by students every week or two from their independent reading. These charts should show increases if students have been paying more attention to unfamiliar words during independent reading. This same technique can be used to track the number of unfamiliar words brought in by students from sources outside of school. Again, one- or two-week recording intervals could be used. Charts such as this should be shared with parents in addition to information from formal and informal tests of vocabulary.

COMPLETING THE READING DIFFICULTIES SUMMARY SHEET

This chapter has discussed a number of ways to assess students' ability to determine meanings for unfamiliar words they encounter in their reading as well as their knowledge of specific vocabulary words that have been studied. Again, evaluation of the data depends heavily upon the teacher for interpretation. The remainder of this chapter helps the teacher with the task of data interpretation by considering Billy Stone's performance in vocabulary.

Figure 11.6 shows that Billy is performing with 59 percent accuracy on

FIGURE 11.6   Reading Difficulties Record Sheet: Vocabulary

IV. Vocabulary

A. General knowledge (from formal test)

B. Using context

10/6	4/6 (Number of words defined correctly out of number not known)
10/13	3/5
10/20	4/6
10/27	2/5

Comments:
11/2   13/22 correct. Performing with 59% accuracy. Could use instruction in using context clues (when time allows).

C. Using the dictionary

10/6	7/10 (number correct)
10/13	8/10
10/20	7/10
10/27	6/10

Comments:
11/2   28/49 correct. Performing with 70% accuracy. Not as high a priority for instruction as using context to determine word meanings.

D. Structural analysis

Comments:
11/2   Not assessed at this time.

E. Secondary meanings/homographs

Comments:
11/2   Not assessed at this time.

F. Learning of specific words

10/6	5/10 (fill-in-the-blank format)
10/13	7/10
10/20	6/10
10/27	6/10

Comments:
11/2   24/40 correct. Performing with 60% accuracy. Would benefit from more time spent on unfamiliar vocabulary words. Try to do more with semantic mapping.

G. Interest in unfamiliar words

Comments:
11/2   Has added only 5 new words to his progress chart since 10/1. Let him illustrate new words he locates since he likes to draw.

tests assessing his ability to use context clues. The teacher believes that instruction in this area is needed.

Billy is performing with 70 percent accuracy on tests assessing his ability to use the dictionary to determine word meanings. Because he is performing reasonably well and doing better at this skill than at using context clues, the teacher believes dictionary instruction is not a high priority at this time.

The teacher has not assessed Billy's skill in structural analysis (knowledge of affixes and/or roots) and secondary meanings or homographs. The teacher does not feel these are important to assess at this time because Billy is only reading on a beginning third-grade level and has not been encountering many words with affixes and secondary meanings, or homographs.

In terms of learning specific words, Billy is performing with about 60 percent accuracy on vocabulary tests. The teacher believes that Billy needs to spend more time on new words and that the semantic mapping technique may be a beneficial way to do this.

As was pointed out in earlier chapters, all of the recommendations made for Billy Stone will be considered in Chapter 15.

SUMMARY This chapter discussed assessment of vocabulary skills that students can use to determine word meanings when reading independently. It also discussed assessment of students' learning of specific words. The chapter concluded with a discussion of the use of the Reading Difficulties Record Sheet to plan for remedial vocabulary instruction.

SUGGESTED ACTIVITIES 1. Prepare an appropriate informal context test (as described in the chapter and illustrated in Figure 11.1). Have a student complete the test if possible and then score the test. As an alternative, your instructor may be able to provide you with several informal context tests completed by one student. Your task would be to score these tests and complete section IV.B of Figure 11.6.

2. Locate appropriate material and have a student select the best dictionary definition for relatively unfamiliar words you located in the material. As an alternative, your instructor may be able to provide you with several informal dictionary tests (like the one described above) which were completed by one student. Your task would be to score those tests and complete section IV.C of Figure 11.6

NOTE 1. See Anderson and Freebody (1981).

ANDERSON, R. C., AND FREEBODY, P. (1981). Vocabulary knowledge. In J. Guthrie (Ed.), *Comprehension and teaching: Research reviews* (pp. 77–117). Newark, DE: International Reading Association.

Issues pertaining to vocabulary assessment are discussed.

SUGGESTED READING

Part 3

Traditional Approaches to Reading Difficulties

In the previous parts of this book an approach to remedial reading instruction was taken that emphasizes the close relationship that should exist between instruction and assessment. The classroom teacher is in an excellent position to determine how a child is responding to a lesson through observation and other informal means of assessment. This close connection between instruction and assessment is not characteristic of many traditional remedial programs, which begin with testing as the primary form of assessment and then follow with instruction that is aimed at overcoming the difficulties identified by the test(s). Progress in such a program is often evaluated by the use of another test. This test-teach-test pattern relies much more heavily on formal measures of reading than seems appropriate. Of course, traditional approaches to remediation are not all bad, nor are they likely to disappear anytime soon. The third part of this book, in order to provide some balance and a basis for making comparisons, will look closely at the tests and methods that are so prominent in traditional remedial reading programs.

Chapter 12

Assessment Principles Applied to Remedial Reading

OVERVIEW

As you read this chapter use the following list of main ideas to guide your understanding and reflection.

Tests and testing can easily assume an importance in remedial reading that is undeserved and even harmful.

Test scores gain meaning when they are placed in context by virtue of specification of test content or comparisons with other scores.

Teachers have a responsibility to provide parents with information that helps them understand the nature and content of a test their child has taken, the purpose for giving the test, and how to interpret a particular score.

Norms indicate how pupils have done on a test, not how they should do.

The primary purpose for all assessment in reading is decision making.

To be useful in educational decision making, tests must be reliable and valid.

A test that is valid for one purpose may not be valid for another purpose.

A reading test must match a teacher's notions of what is important in the reading process to be valid for his or her purposes.

Low-achieving readers may perform below their potential on reading tests because of poor test-taking abilities and because norm-referenced tests are geared to the average pupil.

Reading tests may fail to reveal what children have gained from instruction because program objectives do not match well with what the tests measure.

Gloria Sanchez and Audrea Berg walked to the corner bus stop in front of Thomas Jefferson Elementary School in brooding silence. Not until they had boarded a crowded bus and worked their way to standing positions near the rear exit doors did either woman speak. Finally Audrea asked her companion with some hesitation, "Did Renaldo's teacher have good things to say in your conference, Gloria?"

"It was better than I expected, Audrea. How did your conference with Joey's teacher go?" Gloria responded.

And with this tentative beginning the conversation rapidly gained momentum. Both mothers had been dreading the first parent-teacher conference of the year and appreciated the chance to share their thoughts, questions, and concerns with each other. As the bus turned at the final intersection before entering the block where their row houses stood side-by-side, Gloria volunteered the information they had both been avoiding.

"Renaldo got a 63 on his reading test," she said.

Mrs. Berg turned to face her friend with a warm smile saying, "Why, that's not so bad, Gloria. Joey got a 70. I think they must both be doing well in reading."

"I'm not so sure," Mrs. Sanchez moaned. "Sixty-three sounds like a low score to me. It sure isn't as good as a 70."

Mrs. Berg suggested they continue their discussion over a cup of coffee. Between sips the two concerned mothers began to wonder out loud just what the scores they had been told really meant.

This conversation is probably not at all uncommon. Many parents, and indeed many teachers and administrators, are not sure about some basic measurement principles. What does a test score of 63 mean? What other information is needed in order to judge it as a "good" or a "bad" score? How should Renaldo's score affect his teacher's plan for helping him progress in reading? This chapter identifies and explores some fundamental issues that bear on these and related issues. For those readers who have had a course in educational measurement, this chapter will serve as a review. For others, this chapter will only introduce topics that require further study.

The fact that reading in general and remedial reading in particular are closely linked in the minds of many people with tests and test interpretation present a genuine dilemma. Although the heavy use of formal tests is not recommended, remedial programs are often driven by them. Tests are used to identify low-achieving readers, their needs and weaknesses, and the progress that results from their remedial instruction. Tests are even used to evaluate the overall effectiveness of remedial programs.

In view of all this, it seems prudent to deal with testing in this and the following chapter if only to put the topic in perspective. Consequently, this chapter lays the groundwork by (1) dealing with the nature of test interpretation, (2) reviewing some fundamental principles of educational measurement, and (3) giving an overview of the various types of reading tests. The following chapter will then provide an introduction to specific tests that are illustrative of those likely to be used in schools.

WHAT'S IN A SCORE?

For some reason Mrs. Sanchez believed that Renaldo's score of 63 was not very good. But why? In isolation the number 63 has virtually no meaning. It represents a quantity, but without some context, some frame of reference, it cannot be interpreted. Mrs. Sanchez was apparently making some assumption that caused her to feel 63 was a poor score. She may have assumed the number represented a percent, for example. In this case, her previous experience with

Parents can easily see how well their children perform certain physical skills but need help from teachers in knowing how to interpret test scores. *(Peter Vadnai)*

schools and teachers may have led her to assume that 95 to 100 percent earns an A or excellent, 85 to 94 percent earns a B or good, and so forth. Against this system a "score" of 63 would probably receive an F or fail.

There are some obvious difficulties with an absolute system of this sort, the most serious being that no allowance is made for the fallibility of the test or the test maker. Let us suppose that 63 did represent a percent. Was Mrs. Sanchez right to think the score was poor? Not unless or until she has several other pieces of information. She needs to know, for example, how much progress a score of 63 percent represents for Renaldo. It may be that over the past three weeks he has doubled or tripled his performance on whatever the test measures. A single score can take on a different flavor if viewed in this context.

She might also consider what the test includes. Suppose Renaldo got 63 percent of the items right on the vocabulary test. This score takes on one complexion if the words were simple, high-frequency words from a basal reader and quite another complexion if they were technical terms taken from a science book. Also the fact that Renaldo is in second grade rather than seventh grade makes a percentage score of 63 on a basal reader test less alarming.

Let us now alter our assumption about the 63 being a percentage score and consider it as a raw score. Typically this would mean Renaldo got 63 items correct (though it might mean he got even more items than that right but had his score reduced by some factor intended to "correct for guessing," such as the number of items answered incorrectly). Is a raw score of 63 poor, as Mrs. Sanchez seemed to think? Suppose the test only included 64 items? In that case, Renaldo got all but one item correct. One could not do much better. But even here the issues raised earlier apply. The content of the test might be such that a perfect score is expected (for example, circling the letters of the alphabet when they are called by the teacher is a task a second grader should perform with close to 100 percent accuracy). It would also be helpful to know how much progress a raw score of 63 represents for Renaldo on the content of this particular test.

Whether 63 is a percentage or a raw score, another kind of information is still required in order to more completely interpret Renaldo's performance. We typically want to know how other pupils did on the same test. Even though the meaning of a score can be established through self-comparisons and progress toward a criterion, comparisons with other pupils can also provide useful information. Criterion-referenced testing will be examined in a moment, but first consider comparisons among pupils.

COMPARISONS TO OTHER PUPILS

Let us return to the Sanchez-Berg conversation. Suppose Mrs. Sanchez also reported that other scores on the test ranged from a high of 78 to a low of 40. With this information, Mrs. Berg would realize that Renaldo is much closer to the top than to the bottom of the group. This would seem to be "good" performance, yet her response might still be sympathetic if she thought Renaldo should be at the top. In any case, knowledge of the range of scores gives useful information insofar as interpreting a score is concerned.

Another piece of information parents often need is knowledge concerning the "average" score. There are several measures of central tendency including the mode (score achieved most frequently by the students), the median (score that has half the group above and half below), and the mean (the arithmetic average). If Mrs. Sanchez said the average score was 55, Mrs. Berg would realize that Renaldo's score is some distance above the average. This information also helps in interpreting an individual student's performance on a test.

Most parents are probably sufficiently informed to judge the merit of their child's score, given the top and bottom score in the class, and the mean (average) score. Some will realize that to interpret more completely the meaning of a score, it is also critical to know the "spread" or variability of the test scores. To illustrate, if the scores of Renaldo's classmates are tightly grouped around the mean of 55, his score of 63 is more extraordinary than if they are spread evenly from top to bottom. The statistic needed to know how much spread exists in the scores is the *standard deviation*. Without going into unnecessary detail, suffice it to say that the standard deviation is an index of how much scores vary on the average from the mean. A standard deviation of ± 5 would indicate greater spread around the mean than ± 2, for example. If Renaldo's score of 63 were achieved on a test where the mean score was 55 and the standard deviation ± 2, he would be among the top 1 percent of pupils taking the test. A larger standard deviation would indicate that scores are scattered further from the mean and that Renaldo's score is not quite so exceptional. The normal curve diagram in Figure 12.1 shows what percentage of a population usually falls within one and two standard deviations of the mean.

If Renaldo's teacher had given Mrs. Sanchez a more complete picture of his test score, the conversation at the beginning of this chapter might have sounded something like this.

"Renaldo's teacher told me he got a score of 63 in a published survey test the children at Thomas Jefferson always take in the fall of the year," Mrs. Sanchez reported. "The test has a vocabulary section and a paragraph comprehension section. Renaldo's class had an average score of 55. The standard deviation was ± 5 and the range of scores was from 40 to 78. The teacher said the same test will be given again in the spring so we can see what progress Renaldo has made. Meanwhile she will use the test results to help her form reading groups."

With the above information, Mrs. Sanchez is in a much better position to understand and, therefore, support what the teacher is doing. The teacher has shown professional competence by providing adequate information to the parent concerning the type of test given, the purpose for giving the test, how the class did as a whole, how Renaldo did in particular, and what use will be

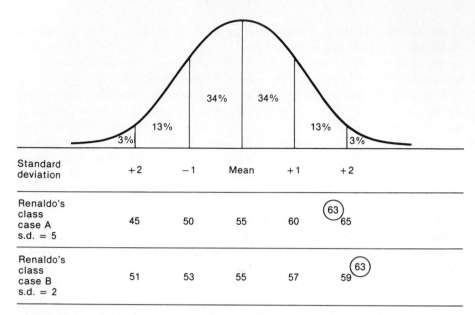

Standard deviation	+2	−1	Mean	+1	+2
Renaldo's class case A s.d. = 5	45	50	55	60	⓺⓷ 65
Renaldo's class case B s.d. = 2	51	53	55	57	59 ⓺⓷

FIGURE 12.1   Percentage of Population Falling Within One and Two Standard Deviations of the Mean

made of the results in the future. There is a great deal more the teacher might have shared, information on test reliability and validity, for example, and how the class compared to national norms, but these facts are more important for the teacher and principal than for parents.

Now, to carry the scenario one step further, suppose that Audrea Berg listened to Gloria Sanchez's report with growing interest.

"That's fascinating," Audrea states. "Joey's class took the same test and his teacher gave me entirely different figures for her group. The class average was 61, the standard deviation was ±7 and the range was 45 to 91. Joey's class did better overall than Renaldo's, but I wonder which group is the most typical? Is Joey's class really high or is Renaldo's really low?" These are appropriate questions to ask if one really wants to make comparisons.

Whether appropriate or not, the American obsession with comparisons is a fact of life, and test publishers respond by supplying various types of norms. The following section looks more closely at norms and what they mean.

NORMS FOR COMPARING TEST PERFORMANCE

Test norms are nothing more than a summary of the scores achieved by a large group of pupils with known characteristics. They are, in a real sense, averages that permit comparisons. It is common for tests that are sold to a national market to have national norms, though state and local norms are often more useful and revealing depending on one's purposes. In any case, norms should not be confused with standards to be achieved. Norms indicate how pupils have done on a test, not how they should do. Four types of norms will be examined here: percentile rank, grade equivalents, standard scores, and stanines.

Percentile Rank Norms

How percentile rank norms work can be illustrated by looking at the score Renaldo achieved on his reading test. Renaldo's raw score of 63 on the test falls at the ninetieth percentile, meaning it is better than 90 percent of the second graders who took the test when it was being normed. Joey's score of 70 falls at the ninety-eighth percentile, meaning only 2 percent of the second graders taking the test did better when it was normed. By using the norms in the test manual, Renaldo's and Joey's teachers can translate the scores of all their students into percentile ranks, thereby enabling anyone who is interested to see how a score compares to those of other pupils. To answer Mrs. Berg's question about how the second-grade classrooms at Thomas Jefferson compare to typical schools the teachers should consult the test manual for specific norms that permit school comparisons.

Percentile ranks are straightforward and relatively easy to understand, but they can still be misinterpreted. Most parents can understand that percentile ranks simply indicate what percentage of pupils in a particular group scored lower on a test than their child. Nevertheless, we should point out that national norms are sometimes inappropriate for judging a pupil's achievement because pupils included in the national pool come from a broad range of environments. Although this broad range is necessary for norms to be truly representative of all segments of the population, it may be more useful to know how pupils at Thomas Jefferson compare with other inner-city schools. In this case, special norms would be necessary.

Another limitation of percentile ranks is that units on percentile scale are not equal due to the preponderance of scores near the mean and the sparsity of scores at the extremes. (See Fig. 12.1.) As a result, percentile ranks are not very useful when it comes to assessing growth. Moving ten percentile points, from the sixtieth to the seventieth percentile, for example, represents a much smaller variation in achievement than moving from the tenth to the twentieth percentile. Another concept that some have difficulty accepting is that a child who maintains his or her rank over time is making normal growth. A similar problem, which is also a reflection of human nature, is that most people believe that they (or their children) are better than average. As a consequence, most people expect to be someplace above the fiftieth percentile. Although half the population must fall below average on any variable, this fact seems easy to forget when scores are being translated using a table of norms.

Grade Equivalents

Another type of norm that is not quite so straightforward as percentile ranks is grade norms (sometimes called grade equivalents). Suppose Mrs. Sanchez told her friend Audrea that Renaldo scored at the third-grade level on the reading test. What does that mean? Should Renaldo be promoted to third grade immediately? Does this mean he should be reading a "third-grade book" even though he is in the second grade? To answer these questions, consider how a raw score of 63 gets translated into a grade equivalent of 3.6 (read third grade, sixth months).

Just as with percentile ranks, grade norms are determined by summarizing the test results achieved by the norming population. The scores of second-grade children are analyzed and some score, say 53, is found to be the mean. This raw score is then set equal to 2.0. The performance of third graders is examined and the average score found to be 60. This score is set equal to 3.0 and on it goes. The difference between a raw score of 53 and 60 is spread evenly (interpolated) across the interval 2.0 to 3.0 so that a raw score of 56 is equated to 2.5, 58 is equated to 2.7, and so forth.

Renaldo's score of 63 is somewhat higher than the average score of the third graders, so his grade equivalent equals 3.6. What can be said is that on this particular test Renaldo did slightly better than the average third grader. That is all it means.

Grade equivalents have been roundly criticized by professional organizations such as the International Reading Association and American Educational Research Association because of their susceptibility to misinterpretation. There is no universal agreement regarding what constitutes second, third, or any other grade level achievement in reading, so to report a pupil's test score according to grade level may *falsely* suggest that he or she should be placed in that grade for reading instruction. This mistaken notion ignores the fact that a given text inevitably ignores many other aspects of reading a typical third grader can perform. Furthermore, the grade level equivalents reported for standardized tests do not match well with the difficulty levels of various reading material. Yet the temptation is strong to conclude that the reading level achieved on a given test is a good indication of which book(s) a child can or should read. It is probable that reading tests often overstate the level at which a child can read for daily instruction.

Finally, critics of reading instruction frequently build their case on the fact that a larger percentage of pupils read *below* grade level. Since the mean score is set equal to the grade in which pupils are enrolled, half the children *should* be below grade level. This is merely another example of the point made earlier that half of any group is below average. These and other misunderstandings regarding the meaning of grade norms make them potentially harmful. Their use should be avoided altogether.

Standard Scores

A third type of norm is the standard score. This calculation involves translating raw scores into a regularized scale. One scale sets the mean equal to 50 and the standard deviation equal to 10. IQ scores are commonly reported as standard scores on a scale having 100 as the mean and 15 as the standard deviation. Other scales are also commonly used. In all cases the raw score is converted by subtracting the mean of the standard scale from the raw score and dividing by the standard deviation. Any basic measurement book will describe the steps involved.

The advantage of standard scores is that the results of several tests can be compared, even added and averaged. This is not acceptable with raw scores unless they have been converted to standard scores because differences in the variability of the several score distributions can easily distort the relative importance of each test. With some help parents can learn to interpret standard scores as evidenced by the general understanding that seems to exist for IQ and SAT scores. We would recommend that the results of teacher-made tests be translated into standard scores for the sake of clarity and uniformity.

Stanines

A fourth type of norm that receives less attention than it deserves is the stanine, which is actually a variation on percentiles that breaks the full range of scores into nine groups as follows:

Stanine	Percentile Range	Group
9	96–100	Superior
8	89–96	Above average
7	77–89	Above average
6	60–77	Average
5	40–60	Average
4	23–40	Average
3	11–23	Below average
2	4–7	Below average
1	0–4	Far below average

Stanines are particularly useful in reporting a pupil's relative score because the false precision conveyed by a percentile rank is softened somewhat. Allowances for error due to measurement are made with stanines by grouping scores together that are probably not reliability different anyway. Children near the upper or lower cutoff points for any given stanine are still treated inappropriately perhaps, but this limitation justifies the risk involved when the advantages of stanines over straight percentile ranks are considered. Renaldo's test score falls into the eighth stanine, whereas Joey's is in the ninth stanine. Mrs. Sanchez's intuitive feeling that 63 is significantly lower than 70 on the test is supported by this transformation to stanines (although both scores are high).

CRITERION REFERENCED MEASURES

Earlier it was suggested that performance on a reading test can be judged in a way that is not dependent upon comparisons among pupils. Knowing the letters of the alphabet was used as an example, an important bit of knowledge that all literate people must master sooner or later. In this case, accomplishing the learning objective is the critical issue, not whether a student masters a skill at the same time it is mastered by other pupils.

To illustrate, suppose that Joey scores at the ninety-eighth percentile on knowing the letters of the alphabet. He is clearly near the top of the group. Yet it is still possible that no one in the group knows the entire alphabet. Relative to his peers Joey is superior, but against the objective he is still inadequate. If the average reader only knows thirteen of the twenty-six letters, this becomes the fiftieth percentile. Joey may know twenty-one of twenty-six letters, making him well above average, but he still falls short of mastery (often called competence).

Over the past ten to fifteen years there has been a concern for accountability in education. The public mood has demanded that clear-cut objectives for instruction be established and pupil mastery of those objectives be monitored. In this atmosphere, criterion-referenced testing (CRT) flourished. Some publishers and consulting firms even got into the business of performance contracting with school districts, an arrangement whereby they received payment for instruction they contracted to deliver only if a certain percentage of pupils mastered a set of targeted learning objectives as measured by criterion-referenced tests.[1] Although performance contracting seems to have gone the way of most educational panaceas, criterion-referenced tests and mastery of discrete skills are still very much in evidence today. Various skills management programs are available either as part of a basal reading program or as a separate system that is compatible with nearly any set of instructional materials. The next chapter will look closely at such a system. Here it is important to say that the actual items on a norm-referenced test are virtually indistinguishable from those on a criterion-referenced test (CRTs). How the items are packaged to form a test is somewhat different (that is, norm-referenced tests include items on a wide range of skills, whereas CRTs have many items on one specific skill), and how they are interpreted is markedly different.

Like most parents, Mrs. Sanchez and Mrs. Berg probably do not know the difference between norm-referenced and criterion-referenced tests. Consequently it becomes the teacher's job to clarify for parents what type of test was used and how to correctly interpret the score according to either norms or performance criteria. Any test that claims to be both norm-referenced and criterion-referenced is likely to have serious flaws since the underlying purpose of the two tests is markedly different. Norm-referenced tests must spread pupils over a wide range of scores and do so by including items that are intentionally difficult (no one should get a perfect score). Criterion-referenced tests have no such purpose and therefore include only items that pupils should be able to answer correctly if they have mastered the concept or skill being tested.

More will be said about CRTs later when different types of tests are described. Here the point should be made that interpretation of test results is an important and necessary task for the teacher. Interpretation is normally accomplished by referring to how others in a class, school, or norming group did on the same test, or by comparing performance to a performance criterion. A frame of reference makes interpretation possible. Without interpretation, without some use of the results, the act of measuring reading performance is without justification. Next turn to a consideration of why reading performance is measured.

WHY GIVE TESTS ANYWAY?

As Mrs. Sanchez and Mrs. Berg sat drinking coffee, it seems reasonable to assume that their conversation might eventually have touched on why their sons took a reading test at all. Renaldo's teacher gave an answer of sorts when she indicated that fall and spring performance on the same test would be used as a measure of reading progress. But why is a measure of progress necessary? Although there could be a number of answers to that question, a central thread running throughout all of them relates to instructional decision making. On the basis of measured progress the instructional program might be revised, Renaldo might be placed in a particular group, or the teacher might be encouraged to participate in an inservice program. Decisions will (must) be made about these and dozens of other matters that affect the instruction of Renaldo and Joey. To the extent that such decisions can be based on reliable, valid information, the decisions are likely to be defensible. To the extent that decisions are made on the basis of whim, folklore, or bias, they are likely to be indefensible.

Of course, reading performance can be measured in a number of ways. The most convenient and obvious way is to give a paper and pencil test. Another way is to have a pupil read orally from a graded textbook. Or, the teacher can simply observe how the child responds to questions about the reading material. Even flash cards can be used as a way of assessing reading ability. Although these examples only scratch the surface, they serve to illustrate the vast number of ways in which teachers can assess a pupil's reading ability.

It might be useful at this point to distinguish between two terms used in the preceding paragraph. Thus far the terms *measure* and *assess* have been

Test results are most valuable to a classroom teacher when they help in making decisions about the instructional program. *(James Silliman)*

used to describe the act of gathering information about a pupil's performance. The two terms have similar though not identical meanings. Measurement involves "a comparison of something with a known standard . . . and often involves . . . assigning numbers to objects to represent some property or characteristic."[2] For example, measurement is often done with a ruler or a scale (for example, a thermometer), the result being a number of some sort. In reading, performance is usually measured with a test. Assessment, like measurement, involves gathering data, but seems to be a broader term not so closely associated with quantification and the use of a known standard. Assessment includes testing as well as observation and interviewing conducted for the purpose of identifying strengths and weaknesses.[3]

This leads us to a crucial point about "measuring" reading performance. *Even the slickest, most sophisticated-looking test is nothing more than a way of sampling reading behaviors.* It may seem to be precise in the same way that measuring distance with a ruler is precise, but in reality the paper and pencil test is subject to the same limitations as are such informal measures as teacher observation. The danger is that test results are often used in a way that overestimates their accuracy. Much as young children tend to believe anything they read in a book, adults seem prone to believe anything they get from a test. If tests can be "demythed," the results will be used more wisely and more effectively.

SOME BASIC MEASUREMENT PRINCIPLES

The more confidence people have in the accuracy of the samples of reading behavior that are gathered, the more faith they can have in generalizations based on those samples. Earlier the concepts of reliability and validity were invoked, but were not discussed in any detail. It is now time for that discussion.

Test Reliability

The reliability of a test has to do with the consistency of its results. In other words, a reliable test is one that is not subject to variation because of factors that are uncontrolled or unaccounted for. Whenever a test is given one hopes to get a true picture of how much a person knows or how well he or she can perform in some domain. Ideally the test will be 100 percent accurate, which means the results will not be subject to any error. In other words, the only test items Renaldo will get right are those he has the knowledge or skill to answer and the only ones he will get wrong are those he does not have the knowledge or skill to answer. The name given by measurement experts to this unsullied score is the true score (X_t). Yet there is no direct way available to determine how a person's observed score (X_o) compares to his or her true score. If the test is subject to errors (X_e) that are unrelated to what the test is supposed to be measuring, the observed score could be quite different from the true score. The true score is found by subtracting measurement error from the observed score $(X_t = X_o - X_e)$. To have some idea of how much confidence one can have in the observed score, the notion of reliability is introduced. Using a procedure that will be described shortly, an estimate of measurement error is made. If reliability is high, measurement errors are minimal and the observed score is thought to be a close (good) estimate of the true score. If reliability is low, measurement errors are frequent and the observed score could be far from the true score. This seems simple enough if one knows how reliable the test is. But how is reliability determined?

Reliability is expressed as a correlation coefficient. A correlation coefficient shows what relationship exists between two sets of scores. A perfect relationship (that is, the same person had the highest rank score on each test, and so on down the line) is represented by a coefficient of ± 1.0. (A perfect negative relationship is shown by a coefficient of -1.0. In this case the highest score on one test is paired with the lowest score on the other test, and so forth.) No relationship between scores yields a correlation coefficient of 0. Most reliability coefficients for standardized tests are in the range of $+.6$ to $+.9$ suggesting a positive, but imperfect relationship between two sets of test scores.

Estimates of reliability are obtained by computing correlation coefficients based on the manipulation of test scores. Three approaches are often taken by the publisher or author. The test can be taken twice (with little or no time lapse between administrations to avoid the effects of additional learning). This is usually depicted as A_1 and A_2 (administration one and administration two) and is called *test-retest reliability*. The reason the test is taken twice is to see what agreement there is between the two set of scores. If agreement is high (that is, results are consistent) the observed scores are thought to be a close estimate of the true score. This means error due to measurement is minimal and greater confidence can be placed in scores obtained from the test.

A second approach involves using alternate forms of a test (assuming they exist) and is depicted as A and B (two forms.) This is called *alternate forms reliability*.

The third approach to determining test reliability is to give the test only once but to treat half the items as test one and half the items as test two (often performance on odd-numbered items is compared to performance on even-numbered items). This approach is depicted as $\frac{1}{2}$ A and $\frac{1}{2}$ A and is called *split-half reliability*. Thus reliability can be calculated in three ways:

1. A_1–A_2 (test-retest)

2. A–B (alternate forms)

3. $\frac{1}{2}$ A–$\frac{1}{2}$ A (split half)

It should be clear that each approach has certain limitations insofar as estimating the amount of error is concerned. From a theoretical standpoint the test maker's goal is to eliminate measurement error. Any difference between the scores of two individuals on a test should reflect differences in the knowledge or skill being measured. If the test itself introduces variation in scores because of uncontrolled factors, this reduces the reliability of the results. In other words, such errors make it more difficult to determine how well the pupil knows what is being tested.

What can make a test unreliable? If guessing is not eliminated or at least minimized, this can introduce a variable that affects reliability. If only a few behaviors are sampled, performance can be affected because the domain being tested is not covered systematically. If a test is so long it causes fatigue, this can reduce reliability. The discussion could go on since literally dozens of factors can come into play, but the point is made.

It must be obvious from what has been said thus far that unless a test is fairly reliable it makes little sense to use it. If the results are subject to considerable measurement error, one cannot have much faith in their accuracy. If scores are not accurate, why use them? Any decision made using the results of an unreliable test could be made just as well by flipping a coin or drawing straws.

What level of reliability can be demanded of published standardized tests? Any test having reliability estimates below $+.70$ accounts for less of the variance (49 percent)[4] in scores than uncontrolled factors such as student motivation and guessing. It would seem a good rule of thumb to expect published tests to at least exceed this level. It should also be remembered that reliability coefficients are calculated in various ways. Split-half reliability coefficients are typically higher, as they should be, considering the way they estimate errors (that is, one administration of the test only).

Having said all of the above, it should be pointed out that some reading tests do not report any kind of reliability coefficient. When this occurs one's suspicions should rise. These questions should be asked: Why has this fundamental step not been taken? Is another test available for which reliability estimates have been determined? Will it serve the user's needs just as well? Most reputable publishers and test authors take pains to develop a reliable test and readily share the appropriate information with the test user. In most cases reliability coefficients in the +.80 to +.95 range for the overall test will be found. Subtests typically have lower reliabilities than the total test because they have fewer items. This simply tells the users not to place much faith in the separate parts of the test but to use the total score for their decision making.

Test Validity

The fact that a test is reliable is a necessary condition for its use. However, test reliability alone is not sufficient. A test must also be valid, which means the test is capable of achieving certain aims to a high degree. At a basic level, validity is concerned with whether a test measures what it claims to measure. This means, for example, that a test of intelligence should not measure some other ability, such as reading. Many tests fail to meet this fundamental criterion—they measure something other than what they claim to measure. For example, a readiness test may measure the child's ability to follow directions more than it measures ability to discriminate among letters of the alphabet, or a spelling test may measure ability to recognize incorrect spellings more than it measures ability to *write* words correctly. These tests are not valid for the intended purpose.

Beyond this basic issue, the determination of a test's validity becomes increasingly complex. This is because a test that is perfectly suited to one aim—valid for one purpose—may be quite unsuited to another aim. No test publisher can be expected to anticipate the many uses to which a test may be put; consequently, the user must determine this aspect of validity. Too often the user incorrectly concludes that a published test must be valid or it would not be popular. It should be remembered, though, that the way some people use a test may be perfectly valid, and the way others use it quite invalid. To illustrate, suppose Mrs. James uses overall scores on the *Metropolitan Readiness Test* (1976) to group children for readiness instruction. This would seem to be a legitimate use of that test. Suppose another teacher, Mrs. Moberg, uses scores on the *Metropolitan* to give semester grades in reading. The test seems inappropriate for that purpose unless the content of the instructional program is closely tied to what is measured on the *Metropolitan*. A more dramatic example would involve using a typing test as a way of hiring teachers. Using this approach, better typists would get hired as teachers, although typing clearly is not a valid measure of teaching ability. Yet a typing test would be quite appropriate for hiring secretaries (provided that is an important duty for secretaries to perform). Again, a test that is valid for one purpose is not necessarily valid for other purposes.

Validity coefficients are sometimes reported for published tests. When they are reported they often represent the extent to which the scores they yield agree with scores from some other measure of the same thing (this is criterion validity). Group intelligence test scores are often correlated with the scores from an individually administered IQ test such as the Stanford-Binet, for example, with the intent of showing that a high degree of agreement exists between scores on both tests. To the extent that the Stanford-Binet is a true measure of intelligence, it can be a legitimate standard for establishing the validity of the group test.

The scores on reading tests are seldom compared with each other to demonstrate criterion validity. Those who develop reading tests often think their product is better than any other test available and, consequently, they are unlikely to recognize any other test as a standard of comparison. Instead, other ways of claiming validity are used. Content validity is claimed, for example, by describing how the content of the test matches up with a definition or conceptualization of reading. This is a highly subjective process, of course, and particularly limited if the test user's definition of reading is different in part or in whole from that of the developers of the test. Even when the developers are quite explicit in stating their definition of reading, the user must still examine the test to see how the tasks the pupil performs relate to that definition. It is an easy matter to say in a definition that comprehension is fundamental, for example, then to include relatively few tasks on a test that probe anything other than general knowledge (answering questions, for example).

An Example of Test Reliability and Validity

To illustrate how reliability and validity work, let us leave the field of reading for an area most adults have experienced first-hand, the behind-the-wheel driver's test. Certainly the citizens of a state are anxious to know that unsafe drivers are kept off the roads. Consequently, the behind-the-wheel test must be structured in such a way as to provide reliable and valid results. Under normal circumstances, the more behavior samples gathered, the greater the reliability. In the case of the driver's test, it is hoped that incompetent drivers would fail every time they took the behind-the-wheel test because the tasks performed measure most of the important behaviors involved in safe driving. Obviously, the less time the examiner spends with the driver, the fewer the behaviors that can be sampled. Thus a five-minute ride around the block offers fewer opportunities to observe faulty performance than a thirty-minute drive that includes highway driving, driving in heavy traffic, left- as well as right-hand turns, parallel parking, emergency stops, and so forth. Likewise a behind-the-wheel test that lasted several days could sample, for example, driving at night and driving in rain. Even then, driving in snow could be observed only if the test took place in the winter. One could question the reliability of a driver's test that did not sample enough of these diverse behaviors to be sure the domain of safe driving had been adequately covered. In short, the reliability of any test is dependent on sampling sufficient behaviors to be confident of the results.

The reliability of a test can also be affected by factors related to its administration and scoring. In a driver's test it would be extremely important for the examiner to know what behaviors constitute a proper left turn. Something as simple as when and how to signal the turn must be specified so that points can be awarded in a reliable fashion. If the examiner is not guided by explicit standards and deducts points in a haphazard manner depending on his or her mood or personal feelings toward the driver, this introduces an uncontrolled factor that lowers the reliability (and ultimately the safety of everyone on the road). If a signal must be given at least 200 feet from an intersection, for example, but some drivers get by with a signal at only 150 feet, inconsistent scoring affects the results. Likewise, if one examiner scores left-hand turns one way and another examiner scores them another way, the reliability of the test is reduced.

In the case of a reading test that is reliable, the results should not be affected by who gives or scores the test. An error should be an error regardless of who makes it or who records it. Most standardized tests are fairly consistent because of the format used to elicit responses. Scoring masks are used to check a child's answers, and so forth. Of course, reliability may be gained at some cost since a standardized test eliminates some of the interaction between examinee and examineer that may provide unexpected insights into how a child approaches a reading task.

The person who knows the most about a driver's ability is his or her teacher—the person who sits alongside the learner watching progress and providing instruction when problems occur. Unless the examiner spends as much time with the driver under the same variety of conditions as the teacher, the "snapshot" taken during the test is not as reliable (or as valid) as the assessment the instructor has made over weeks and months. The teacher of remedial reading has much the same opportunity to observe over time. The day-to-day interaction of teaching-learning has built-in reliability that a brief test cannot achieve. Yet often the results of a reading test are believed even when they conflict with a teacher's knowledge of a child's ability.

Using the behind-the-wheel driver's test, it can also be seen how validity works by noting that actual driving performance is required. This is evidence of face validity. A paper and pencil test might be useful in determining a driver's knowledge of the laws that affect driving, but knowing the law is not the same as driving in a manner that conforms to the law. Only by observing a driver perform the act of driving can face validity be guaranteed. Is the behind-the-wheel test a valid test of driving ability in *all* respects? Not necessarily. Validity could be lowered if the driving sample is observed on the deserted streets of the local fair grounds during the off season rather than in normal city traffic, for example. Additionally, suppose the test were conducted in an automobile having an automatic transmission but the driver will use a car with a standard shift transmission once he or she passes the exam. Is this test a valid measure? Does it assure citizens that the driver is competent? Certainly not, because validity is lacking. The test of driving ability must sample behaviors that are critical to the domain supposedly being tested.

Our driving test example allows us to demonstrate several types of validity but does not address another type of validity that is extremely important to the assessment of reading ability: content validity. Driving ability is concrete in the sense that it can be observed in action, but reading is a mental operation not open to direct observation. What is happening in the reader's head must be inferred from what can be observed—oral reading, for example, or question answering. Yet oral reading is not an infallible way of measuring reading ability. Neither is question answering. Therefore, content validity is always problematic on a reading test. To obtain it the test author must make a clear statement about what conceptualization of reading undergirds the test. Then the tasks given in the test must be shown to relate directly to that conceptualization.

If content validity is approached in this way, users can decide whether they accept the test author's underlying conceptualization and whether the tasks performed by the examinee are appropriate. For example, a test that ignores comprehension and focuses all attention on vocabulary and word identification would not merit the label "reading test." Such a test would have to be described more accurately so that users would recognize its scope and limitations. Unfortunately, this basic requisite is met by very few published reading tests. In most cases the user must decide what a test really measures and whether that information is of any value. The fact that some publisher prints and promotes the test does not make it a valid measure of reading.

When selecting a reading test, the teacher must first make a conscious effort to clarify what purpose is to be served by the test. Once this is done, various tests can be examined against that purpose. *Tests must never dictate what the teacher will measure. The teacher must decide what is important to measure.* Just because something is included in a test does not make it important or worthwhile. This approach places a great deal of responsibility on the teacher, and while that may seem awesome, that is how it should be if teachers are to function as professional decision makers.

But the teacher is not alone in finding and appraising tests. Help is available in a number of places and forms. Those sources of information on reading tests are discussed next.

SOURCES OF INFORMATION ON TESTS

Suppose you have decided to go to a movie this weekend and there are several choices available at nearby theaters. How would you normally decide which movie to see? Your approach is probably not much different from others. The first step is to ask friends if they have seen any of the films playing at the nearby theaters. If a friend whose tastes you respect endorses a particular film, chances are good that you might choose it. A similar sequence of events is often followed when selecting a book for recreational reading.

Another source of information on movies and books are the published reviews that appear in magazines, newspapers, and on television. The reviewer is normally an expert who has seen the movie or read the book recently and whose review tells enough about the film or book to give you a sense of its content and quality. Although you must still decide whether to invest your own money in a ticket, without reviews you would have precious little information on how to make a decision.

A movie and book review schema have been invoked so that test reviews may be discussed in this context. Although you are capable of evaluating a test by yourself, test reviews are readily available to assist your decision-making process. Test reviews appear in a number of sources, the most common being professional journals and the *Mental Measurements Yearbook*.

The Mental Measurements Yearbook

In 1938 O. K. Buros produced the first *Mental Measurements Yearbook (MMY)*. Eight additional editions have appeared since then, the latest in 1985. The *MMY* is most noteworthy for its collection of high-quality reviews of tests. Because of his own high standards and the caliber of people he asked to review for the *MMY*, Buros assembled penetrating, well-documented opinions about hundreds of tests. Reviewers were instructed by Buros to prepare their reviews with these objectives in mind:

1. To provide test users with carefully prepared appraisals of tests for their guidance in selecting and using tests.

2. To stimulate progress toward higher professional standards of test construction by censuring poor work, and by suggesting improvements.

3. To impel test authors and publishers to present more detailed information on the construction, validity, reliability, norms, uses, and possible misuses of their test.

O. K. Buros actually hoped to make it unprofitable financially and professionally for poor tests to be published. It is a judgment call as to how successful he has been in meeting that goal. Plenty of poor tests are published, purchased, and used even today but the situation might be even worse if the *MMY* had not been available. Since his death in 1978, the work of Buros' Institute of Mental Measurements has shifted to the University of Nebraska at Lincoln.

The *MMY* makes it possible for any test user to see what several experts have to say about a test. Reviews are relatively brief (600 to 1200 words in length), but are typically hard-hitting and frank in their appraisal. Just as you can disregard the advice of a friend or the reviewer for a local newspaper regarding a movie, you can ignore the advice of experts, but you do so having been alerted to their concerns.

The *MMY* includes reviews written especially for the *Yearbook* as well as reviews first published elsewhere. It is a reference any reading teacher should know first-hand and any school district should have available.

Reading Tests and Reviews

Because a test that was reviewed in a previous edition of the *MMY* was seldom reviewed in a subsequent edition (unless revision of the test had occurred), Buros saw a need to gather all reading test reviews from across all editions together into a single volume. This resulted in the publication of *Reading Tests and Reviews* in 1968.[6] An update of the 1968 publication was published in 1975.

Reviews in Professional Journals

Many professional journals publish test reviews on a regular basis. Others review tests periodically. You should consult the following journals for reviews of reading tests: *The Reading Teacher*, *Journal of Reading*, *Reading Research and Instruction*, *Journal of Learning Disabilities*, and the *Journal of School Psychology*.

Reviews in Professional Books

Some remedial reading textbooks include reviews of reading tests. Among those with fairly extensive reviews are Spache (1981), Harris and Sipay (1985), and Bond, Tinker, and Wasson (1984). Of course, Chapter 13 of this textbook also consists of test reviews.

Publications of the IRA

Two collections of test reviews are published by the International Reading Association (IRA). They are *Reading Tests for Secondary Grades* (Blanton, Farr, and Tuinman, 1972) and *Diagnostic and Criterion-Referenced Reading Tests: Reviews and Evaluation* (Schell, 1981).

In addition, several IRA publications include useful essays on important issues related to tests, measurement, and evaluation in reading. These include

Reading: What Can Be Measured? by Farr and Carey (1986); *Reading Tests and Teachers: A Practical Guide* by Schreiner (1979); *Assessment Problems in Reading* by MacGinitie (1973); *Informal Reading Inventories* by Johnson, Kress and Pikulski (1987); *Measuring Reading Performance* by Blanton, Farr, and Tuinman (1974); *Approaches to the Informal Evaluation of Reading* by Pikulski and Shanahan (1982a); and *Reading Comprehension Assessment* by Johnston (1983).

Standards for Evaluating Tests

The first step in learning to evaluate reading tests is to take a course in educational tests and measurement. Any such course should help a user develop a set of personal standards for evaluating tests. In all likelihood the user will also be introduced to a publication of the American Psychological Association (APA) titled *Standards for Educational and Psychological Tests and Manuals* (1974). This joint publication of APA, the American Educational Research Association (AERA), and the National Council on Measurement in Education (NCME) serves to assist the test user by establishing criteria that an acceptable

In addition to consulting published reviews on a test, a teacher should also make a personal evaluation of a test with her own instructional goals and program in mind.
(James Silliman)

test must meet. The coordinator of research and evaluation in any school system should have a copy of this publication.

The following standards provide a basic set of guidelines for evaluating reading tests that can be adapted to your own purposes.

I. General Features
   A. Title
   B. Date of publication
   C. Author
   D. Level and forms
   E. Purpose as described by author
   F. Time for administration
   G. Scoring
   H. Cost

II. Technical Features
   A. Are the directions for administration clear?
   B. If norm-referenced, are the norms adequate to my purpose(s)?
   C. What evidence of overall test reliability is provided? subtest reliability?
   D. What evidence of test validity is provided?
      1. Is an explicit statement made concerning the definition of reading undergirding the test?
      2. Does the test appear to measure what I regard to be important for success in learning to read?
   E. Does the test provide information that will be useful in planning reading instruction?

III. General Considerations
   A. Does the test provide needed information beyond what I have available from other sources?
   B. Does the test match my program objectives?
   C. Is the test appropriate for my students in terms of difficulty and length?
   D. Have I taken the test myself in order to understand its content as an examinee?

IV. Recommendations
   A. On balance, is use of this test justified?
   B. Which students should take this test?

TYPES OF PUBLISHED READING TESTS

It makes a good deal of sense to group published reading tests according to their similarities. For example, tests that are appropriate for a particular grade level or ones that have a common format should be grouped together. What has emerged over time is the practice of grouping tests according to the reading functions they attempt to measure.[7] Thus tests of general silent reading ability are grouped together under the heading, "Survey Tests"; tests that measure the application of reading skills to meet a need for information are called "Study Skills Tests"; tests that identify specific strengths and weaknesses in learning to read are called "Diagnostic Tests"; and so forth.

Universal agreement on how to group tests is by no means evident in the literature. Reasonable people can disagree on how tests should be categorized and into which category a particular test fits. This should not come as any surprise since one's beliefs about the reading process have a direct bearing on how tests will be viewed. The following seven-category organizational scheme offered by Lapp and Flood (1978) appears to be functional: (1) readiness, (2) survey, (3) diagnostic, (4) oral reading, (5) study skills, (6) special and content area, and (7) miscellaneous reading tests. (The *MMY* employs the same categories with two exceptions: speed is a separate category and survey tests are simply called reading tests.) This text is concerned primarily with categories 2, 3, and 4 (survey, diagnostic, and oral reading tests). Skills management systems as an example of criterion-referenced tests will also be examined. Many basal reader programs now include tests that are based on the skills management scheme. The following section will describe each type of test and give examples. In Chapter 13 detailed reviews are given for a sample of tests in each category described here in order to illustrate each type.

Survey Reading Tests

A survey reading test is one designed to measure a student's general reading performance. Survey tests are administered on a group basis, are norm referenced, and have as a primary purpose the ranking of students from high to low in reading achievement. Consequently, items are included in the test that are expected to be easy for everyone as well as items that are expected to be hard for everyone. This provides both a "floor" and a "ceiling" for the test, enabling even poor readers to demonstrate some ability and superior ones to experience some difficulty. According to testing theory this contributes to the validity of the test by sampling the entire domain under scrutiny. In practical terms this means the test will include a large number of items the average student will get wrong. This does not reflect poorly on the child, since to rank students along a continuum, it is necessary to ask everyone to perform tasks that some will not be able to do.

It is necessary to highlight the difficulty level of survey tests in order to demonstrate their limitations to the user to help guide day-to-day instruction. (As you will see later, a diagnostic test does not artificially spread children from high to low. Diagnostic tests are akin to criterion-referenced tests in that they help identify where a student could profit from further instruction, such as knowledge of prefixes.) Survey tests do not represent in any systematic way the various subskills thought by the test author to constitute the reading process and in this sense do not guide daily instruction. Rather they determine how well the child can perform in a general reading situation.

Typically only two scores are obtained with a reading survey test: comprehension and vocabulary. As with any test, the teacher will want to note exactly how a particular survey test goes about determining the child's score (or level of achievement) in these two broad areas. For example, many times the comprehension score is based on only one means of assessment (typically through multiple-choice questions) using very brief passages. The topic of one of these passages may not be familiar or interesting to a particular student and, consequently, may distort the accurate determination of comprehension. Likewise, vocabulary measurement is fraught with many difficulties.

In short, teachers must be cautious in concluding that any test, particularly a survey test that is designed to rank children from high to low for the sake of comparison, is a totally satisfactory indicator of reading ability. With these cautions in mind, consider now how survey reading tests *can* help teachers. Survey tests are (1) useful in identifying the child's reading level, and consequently (2) are of some value in matching the child with appropriate instructional materials. They can also help teachers decide how children might be grouped for daily instruction. In other words, the distribution of scores from a test such as the *Gates-MacGinitie* (1978) can be used with other information to form tentative reading groups and to help select reading materials that are at an appropriate level of difficulty for each group. (Remember that a grade equivalent from the test does not translate neatly or directly to a comparable basal reader grade level or textbook readability score. The matching of child and book is far more complex than this and has been addressed elsewhere in this book (pp. 116–119). In other words, the children who are reading in the range 3.0–3.5 according to the Gates-MacGinitie cannot automatically be assigned to the third-grade book in the Houghton-Mifflin reading program.) Survey tests can also help teachers gain some sense of growth in general reading ability for a group of children over the course of an entire school year.

The *Gates-MacGinitie* Reading Test is reviewed in the next chapter. Other survey tests include: *California Achievement Test: Reading* (1978), *New Developmental Reading Test* (1968), *Davis Reading Tests* (1962), *Nelson-Denny Reading Tests* (1981), and the *Iowa Silent Reading Test* (1973).

Diagnostic Reading Tests

A diagnostic reading test is designed to provide a teacher with a profile of a student's relative strengths and weaknesses (see Figure 12.2). Rather than having one or two general scores that represent the child's overall reading performance (as from a survey test), diagnostic tests break reading into various subskills such as knowledge of phonics, structural analysis, literal comprehension, inferential comprehension, and reading rate, and they obtain scores for each of these areas. The rationale underlying a diagnostic test is that instruction

FIGURE 12.2   Graphic Profile

Name *John Kohler* _____ School _____

Grade *3 rd* ___ Teacher _____ Date_____

$(1.40 \times 3.1) + 1 = 5.3$

Grade equivalent

BASIC DATA	Pupil score	1.5	2.0	2.5	3.0	3.5	4.0	4.5	5.0	5.5	6.0	6.5	7.0	7.5	8.0
Grade in school	3.1														
Chronological grade	2.5														
Reading expectancy															

READING ABILITIES

Vocabulary

Literal comprehension

Creative comprehension

Average reading

WORD-RECOGNITION SKILL (Tests 1 and 2)

Total right (1 + 2)	59	11	21	29	38	49	60	65	70	75	77	80	82	84	
Words in isolation (1)	43	12	17	23	29	37	42	45	47	49	51	52	53	54	
Words in context (2)	16	1	5	7	10	15	18	21	23	25	26	28	30		

ERROR PATTERN (1 + 2)

Total omitted (1 + 2)	4	37	29	17	7		1							
Total errors (1 + 2)	21	31	29	28	27	22	17	15	13	10	7	4	2	1
Error type (1 + 2) Initial	8	9	8	7	6	5	4	3	3	2	2	1	1	0
Middle	4	10	9		6	5	4	3	2	1	1	0		
Ending	7	8	7	7	6	6	5	5	4	3	2	2	1	0
Orientation	2	8	7	7	6	6	5	4	3	2	2	1	0	

RECOGNITION TECHNIQUES (Tests 3, 4, and 5)

Total right (3 + 4 + 5)	57	19	23	27	32	38	44	50	55	58	60	69	78	83	85
Visual-structural analysis (3)	10	3	6	7	8	9	10	12	13	14	16	20	26	28	30
Syllabication (4)	20	8	11	13	15	17	19	20	21	22	23	25	26	28	30
Word synthesis (5)	19	4	6	7	9	12	14	17	19	20	22	25	28	30	

PHONIC KNOWLEDGE (Tests 6, 7, and 8)

Total right (6 + 7 + 8)	82	39	45	51	58	63	66	68	71	73	75	78	83	85	88
Beginning sounds (6)	28	9	14	17	20	22	23	23	24	25	26	27	28	29	30
Ending sounds (7)	25	8	10	12	15	17	19	20	21	22	23	25	27	28	30
Vowel and consonant sounds (8)	29	16	20	22	23	24	24	25	25	26	26	27	28	29	30

| | 1.5 | 2.0 | 2.5 | 3.0 | 3.5 | 4.0 | 4.5 | 5.0 | 5.5 | 6.0 | 6.5 | 7.0 | 7.5 | 8.0 |

Grade equivalent

can be planned to help students improve in areas where performance is low. Often referred to as diagnostic-prescriptive instruction, this approach springs from the belief that progress in reading is usually blocked by specific "weaknesses" that can be remediated once they have been identified (diagnosed).[8] For example, a teacher who sees that Terry scores at or near the expected level of achievement on all but one of the various subtests (auditory blending, for example) of the *Gates-McKillop-Horowitz* test (1981), would focus instruction on the "low" area. Thus diagnostic tests are important for identifying specific areas needing attention.

To have confidence in a diagnostic reading test, a teacher must satisfy several concerns. First, there is the question of whether the test actually measures the ability it claims to measure. A diagnostic reading test may purport to assess sight vocabulary, for example, but unless there is a way for the examiner to control how long a word is exposed, word analysis can occur. This is simply an illustration of test validity, of course. Beyond this obvious concern is a second more subtle question the teacher must resolve which also relates to test validity: Are the skills tested those that the teacher feels constitute the act of reading? Do the subtests reflect in some direct way the skills, abilities, knowledge, and attitudes that are crucial to reading?

Often subtests are included in diagnostic tests simply because tradition dictates it; at other times they are included because they seem to differentiate between good and poor readers. In either case, it is entirely possible that the subtest measures nothing of consequence or that it measures something that does not lend itself to instruction.

As various diagnostic reading tests are described in the next chapter the teacher should consider (1) whether the subtests match his or her notions about what is important in learning to read, and (2) how the "skills" are measured. Unless a test fits well with a teacher's conception of reading, it is unlikely to help him or her identify a student's strengths and weaknesses, or plan appropriate remedial instruction.

Group Diagnostic Reading Tests   Some diagnostic reading tests are designed to be given in a group setting. The obvious advantage of this type of test is that much less of the teacher's time is needed to gather and score responses. If the test is well constructed, a group diagnostic test can provide the detailed information needed to plan appropriate remedial work. The strengths and weaknesses of each child are easily identified when a profile of results is developed. The only real disadvantage of a group test is that nonverbal clues easily monitored in an individual setting are difficult to observe in a group setting.

Two of the most widely used group diagnostic reading tests are the *Stanford Diagnostic Reading Test* and the *Silent Reading Diagnostic Test*. These are reviewed in the next chapter. Other examples of group diagnostic tests include the *Doren Diagnostic Reading Test of Word Recognition* (1973) and the *McCullough Word Analysis Test* (1963).

Individual Diagnostic Reading Test   Because an individual diagnostic reading test is administered to pupils one at a time, and most tests of this type take a minimum of thirty minutes to administer (and some take as long as ninety minutes), it is difficult for a busy teacher to give such tests. Of course, the close face-to-face interaction involved in individual diagnostic testing permits the teacher to gather vital nonverbal clues and thereby develop a more complete picture of how a student reacts in a reading situation.

Individual diagnostic reading tests are of two basic types: the full battery and oral reading tests (IRI). The major distinction between these two types, which will become more apparent as descriptions of specific instruments are presented in Chapter 13, is that the full battery includes numerous subtests of specific skills in isolation whereas the IRI is a set of graded paragraphs to be read aloud. The following individually administered diagnostic test batteries are reviewed in Chapter 13.

Durrell Analysis of Reading Difficulty (1981)

Gates-McKillop-Horowitz Reading Diagnostic Tests (1981)

The Woodcock Reading Mastery Tests (1972)

Botel Reading Inventory (1978)

Diagnostic Reading Scales (1981)

Oral Reading Tests: Informal Reading Inventories

Oral reading tests, often called informal reading inventory (IRI), consist of a collection of brief passages written at various difficulty levels. Pupils typically begin the IRI at a level expected to be easy for them and read aloud while the teacher notes breaks in fluency that fit into common error categories, such as omissions, mispronunciations, substitutions, and so forth. Silent reading as well as listening can also be tested with an IRI. Comprehension is usually checked by asking the pupils questions on the content of the passages read.

An IRI is commonly used for the purpose of determining (1) what level of material pupils can read successfully on a daily basis for instruction (often called the instructional level), (2) what level of material is too difficult (frustration level), and (3) what level is easy (independent or recreational level). Judgments concerning what level of material fits each of these categories for a particular child are normally based on percentages of word recognition and comprehension accuracy. Criteria described by Betts (1946) continue to be used by many teachers, though Powell (1971), Pikulski (1974), Spache (1981), and others have questioned their validity. Betts suggests that 95 percent word recognition accuracy and 75 percent comprehension accuracy represent the child's instructional level.

In the broadest sense of the term, this determination of reading levels is a type of diagnosis. That is, information that might be useful in planning appropriate daily instruction is gathered. In a more narrow use of the term *diagnostic* (that is to determine a pupil's strengths and weaknesses in specific skill areas), the IRI enables the skilled teacher to gather information of a highly detailed nature that must be interpreted in order to be useful. Goodman and Burke (1972) describe a system for analyzing each oral reading miscue according to its graphophonic, syntactic, and semantic acceptability, for example. Other systems for examining oral reading miscues also exist.[9] In every case, the intent is the same: the examiner seeks to understand the strategies employed by children while they read as reflected in their oral reading behavior.

Several of the tests listed previously include a subtest that has many of the characteristics of an IRI. The *Durrell* and the *Spache*, for example, include several sets of graded paragraphs along with a system for recording oral reading errors and a means for checking comprehension. In a full diagnostic battery the graded passages approach is just one of many subtests.

In Chapter 13 the *Analytical Reading Inventory,* Second Edition by Woods and Moe (1981) is reviewed. Other commercial IRIs include:

Burns, Paul C., and Roe, Betty D. (1985) *Informal Reading Inventory* (2nd ed.). Boston: Houghton Mifflin.

Ekwall, Eldon E. (1979) *Ekwall Reading Inventory.* Boston: Allyn and Bacon.

Fry, Edward. (1981) *Reading Diagnosis: Informal Reading Inventories.* Providence, RI: Jamestown Publishers.

Gilmore, John V., and Gilmore, Eunice, C. (1968) *Gilmore Oral Reading Test.* Orlando, FL: Harcourt Brace Jovanovich.

Gray, William S. (1967) *Gray Oral Reading Test.* New York: Bobbs-Merrill.

Johns, Jerry. (1981) *Basic Reading Inventory.* Dubuque, IA: Kendall/Hunt.

McCracken, Robert. (1966) *Standard Reading Inventory.* Klamath Falls, OR: Klamath Printing Co.

Rinksy, Lee Ann, and DeFossard, Esta. (1980) *The Contemporary Classroom Reading Inventory.* Scottsdale, AZ: Gorsuch Scarisbrick.

Silvaroli, Nicholas. (1982) *Classroom Reading Inventory* (4th ed.). Dubuque, IA: Wm. C Brown.

Spache, George. (1981) *Diagnostic Reading Scales.* New York: CTB/McGraw-Hill.

Sucher, Floyd, and Allred, Ruel A. (1973) *Reading Placement Inventory.* Oklahoma City, OK: Economy.

Skills Management Systems

It is hard to explore the topic of diagnostic reading tests and ignore the existence of a relatively new group of devices commonly called skills management systems. They began to emerge in the late sixties and early seventies largely in response to growing public demands for accountability in education. To be accountable, it was necessary for schools to specify what they expected students to learn and to have a way of measuring who had learned it and who had not. Literacy, being a major concern to the public, was immediately tackled by those who advocated a systems approach. Today skills management systems are an integral part of nearly all basal reading programs. Additionally, systems that are not keyed to any particular set of instructional materials are also available.

The following is a partial list of skills management systems for reading:

Criterion Reading: Individualized Learning Management System. New York: Random House, 1970–1971.

Fountain Valley Reading Skills Tests. Richard L. Zweig Associates, Inc. Huntington Beach, CA: 1971–1975.

Analysis of Skills: Reading. Scholastic Testing Service, Inc. Bensenville, IL: 1974–1976.

Individual Pupil Monitoring System-Reading. Boston: Houghton Mifflin, 1974.

Mastery: An Evaluation Tool: Reading. Chicago: Science Research Associates, Inc., 1974–1976.

Objectives-Referenced Bank of Items and Tests: Reading and Communication Skills. New York: CTB/McGraw-Hill, 1980.

Prescriptive Reading Inventory. New York: CTB/McGraw-Hill, 1972–1977.

PRI/IS. New York: CTB/McGraw-Hill, 1980.

Reading: IOX Objectives-Based Tests. Instructional Objectives Exchange. Los Angeles: 1973–1976.

SPIRE Individual Reading Evaluation. New Dimensions in Education, Inc. Plainview, NY: 1970–1973.

Wisconsin Design for Reading Skill Development. Learning Multi-Systems, Inc. University of Wisconsin, Madison, WI: 1970–1972.

Although it would be inaccurate to contend that all skills management systems are identical, there are enough common features among them to enable one to generalize a bit. Most of them include a list of instructional objectives that relate to teaching children to read. Typically the objectives are stated in behavioral terms and relate to specific skills believed to be important to success in reading. They also include a series of tests that are designed to measure student achievement on each skill. The concept of skill mastery is often applied to student performance with some cutoff score being used to distinguish between those who have "mastered' a skill and those who have not. Finally, most skills management systems include a record-keeping system that permits the teacher to keep track of which skills a particular student has mastered (or, stated another way, which tests the child has "passed"). Chapter 13 will look at one particular system in greater detail to give a better idea of how all such systems work.

SPECIAL PROBLEMS IN TESTING REMEDIAL READERS

This chapter indicated earlier that tests often play an inordinately important role in the lives of low-achieving readers and in the conduct of remedial programs. In fact, a stated purpose for this chapter was to give teachers the information needed to develop an appreciation for the limits of tests. Before closing, this chapter must also take a look at the special problems encountered in testing low-achieving readers.

Remedial Readers Lack Test-Taking Skills

Many pupils identified as low-achieving readers are very poor test takers. One reaction to that statement might be, "Of course, that's because they usually lack the knowledge or skills being tested." However, lack of skills and knowledge does not usually account for the entire discrepancy between the test scores of good and poor readers. Often low-achieving readers perform worse than they should on tests because whatever knowledge or skill they do have is obscured by a lack of "test-wiseness." Here is a simple example to illustrate this point. Pupils who know how to take a timed test realize that it is self-defeating to spend an inordinate amount of time on an especially difficult question. They learn to make a guess at a correct answer and to go on to other, easier questions. If time permits, once all the relatively easy questions have been answered, the pupil can return to the more difficult questions, study them, and change the earlier guess if that seems appropriate. In contrast, poor test takers often dawdle over a difficult question hoping to figure it out before going on. By doing so they never reach many of the easier questions and, consequently, they end up with a lower score than they might have achieved.

Another case in point involves eliminating unlikely alternatives in a multiple-choice question. Good test takers increase their chances of getting an item right even when they are not sure of the correct answer by eliminating the choices they know are incorrect and guessing among the remaining alternatives. If two of four alternative choices can be eliminated, the pupil then has a 50-50 chance of guessing the right answer. According to testing theory the pupil is getting credit for knowing something about the topic being tested. In the same situation poor test takers realize they do not know which answer is correct and often fail to respond at all. Especially under directions "not to guess," poor test takers are inclined to adopt a conservative strategy resulting in no response even when they can positively eliminate one or several of the choices but are not sure which of the remaining choices is correct.

Low-achieving readers can be helped by learning how to take tests more effectively. Contrary to what some may think, this is not cheating; it is merely helping pupils to demonstrate what they know. Though much as been done to help adults improve their test-taking abilities.[10] there is little research suggesting ways that teachers can maximize the performance of children on tests.[11] Test training is advocated for all pupils, but particularly for low-achieving readers who are constantly being tested and then manipulated according to the results of those tests. Merely changing such pupils' attitudes toward test taking can be a big step in the right direction. Too often their past failure in testing discourages them from even trying on new tests.

Norm-Referenced Tests Arc Geared to the Average Pupil

Another problem in testing low-achieving readers is the fact that general screening tests (for example, achievement batteries and survey reading tests) are developed with the average pupil in mind. In other words, pupils at the extremes (high or low) are not measured as accurately by tests that are designed for a particular grade level. The reason for this is fairly straightforward—the bulk of the items on such tests are geared to the level being tested. Although a few easy and a few hard items are included to provide a ceiling and a floor, not enough of either is included to provide a reliable spread among pupils at the extremes. The result for low-achieving pupils is failure to measure what they do know. Since the test contained only a few items at their knowledge and skill level, they look more retarded in reading than is justified.

In what may seem to be a contradiction, it should also be said that the performance of low-achieving readers may be overestimated by norm-referenced tests that use grade equivalents. Even a score of zero typically has a grade level designation. As the difficulty level of the test goes higher, the grade equivalent of a score of zero goes higher as well. This absurdity only underscores the inappropriateness of giving pupils a test that is too difficult for them. Almost no useful information is gained by giving a reader operating at a primer level a survey test designed for fourth graders. What a teacher can do is use an easier form of the test in what is called out-of-level testing to see what knowledge and skills the pupil has. The norms are not applicable in this case, of course, but are probably unnecessary anyway since you already know the pupil is extremely low by comparison to his or her peers.

Tests Often Fail to Match Program Objectives

The effectiveness of remedial instruction is typically measured in a surprising way. Based on the mistaken belief that daily work is not adequate evidence of growth and progress, decision makers insist that general achievement tests such as the *Gates-MacGinitie* be used to document gains on a pre- and post-test basis due to remediation. The difficulty with this approach is that remedial instruction is almost always focused on a pupil's special needs. If the effectiveness of remediation is in question, measures are needed that relate directly to the remedial instruction. The issue of test validity is basic here. The *Gates-MacGinitie* or other survey test is a general measure that relates only in an indirect way to remedial instruction. Even diagnostic tests are ill-suited to a pre- and post-test design. Few are available in alternate forms and most lack the subtest reliability that would be required to use them for evaluation purposes.

The very best evidence available to document the effects of remedial instruction is the daily work the teacher keeps for each child. Work sheets, anecdotal records, written assignments, teacher-made progress tests, checklists, and the like provide a cumulative record of what the pupil has learned. No remedial reading teacher should passively accept standardized testing as a legitimate measure of the effectiveness of his/her program. If a test score is required by some authority, supply it but also supply the supplementary information you have accumulated over the time of instruction. The issues of reliability and validity apply to informal measures just as much as they do to formal measures, but the very nature of evidence gathered over time from daily instruction contributes to their reliability and validity.

Gains Realized During Remediation

It is natural to be interested in how much progress a pupil has made during remediation. Two problems associated with interpreting gains measured with tests should be identified. The first has to do with regression toward the mean and the second concerns using "normal growth" as a basis for comparison. It is important that you understand these concepts so that reports you read in the literature about the latest remedial innovation can be evaluated correctly and so that you will not make the mistake of claiming gains for your pupils not attributable to your instruction.

The phenomenon of regression toward the mean simply means that the chances of an extremely high or low performance being repeated or exceeded are small. Stated another way, chances are good that a person who did very poorly on something will not do as poorly next time. Applied to the measurement of reading this means the pupil who was lowest on a test will probably not be as low next time by virtue of chance alone. The student's score will probably be closer to the mean (average).

In selecting pupils for a remedial program those who score extremely low on some test are often chosen. *If no instruction were provided* these same pupils would probably do better on the next test because of regression toward the mean (some would do worse, but far more would do better). In a carefully controlled experiment the researcher is obliged to control for regression toward the mean by randomly assigning half the subjects in a remedial program to a placebo group (one not receiving the remedial instruction). Regression should operate in both groups thus making it possible to identify gains due to the treatment alone. A teacher will not have the luxury of creating a placebo group since all remedial readers deserve remediation, but an understanding of the regression phenomenon should help keep some perspective regarding any gains the pupils achieve.

Gain scores are typically figured by subtracting a pre-test score from a post-test score. As indicated earlier, such calculations are often done with grade equivalents because there is apparent meaning in a gain of 2.3 (two years three months). There are several cautions to observe concerning gain scores. First, it is normal for pupils to gain something during the course of a year because they have lived that long. To claim that all gains are due to instruction ignores that fact. Second, not all pupils should gain the same amount in a year's time. Brighter students will gain more than a year, slower students less than a year. Third, grade equivalents are like percentiles in that pupils are not spread evenly from top to bottom but form a bell-shaped curve. A gain from an extremely low score is not as difficult to achieve because there are fewer pupils at that level. The same gain in raw score points results in a greater grade equivalent gain at the lower or upper levels than it does near the middle. Finally, gains in reading do not usually occur in a steady fashion, but tend to occur in spurts and plateaus. Norms smooth out the uneven aspects of growth across an interval of grade equivalents thus masking the true nature of progress pupils normally make. A full year spurt in only three months can seem extraordinary when compared to "normal growth," yet little or no additional growth may occur in the next six to nine months.

Spache (1981) reviews several methods for judging the significance of gain scores and recommends the use of residual gains as suggested by Rankin and Tracy (1965). The technical aspects of teaching teachers to correct gain scores for initial status, intelligence, and so forth are not as important as sensitizing them to the dangers of using simple gain scores as an index of growth. In the final analysis the use of standardized test scores as the primary way of evaluating individual pupil growth or program effectiveness is not desirable.

SUMMARY

This chapter has focused on measurement principles as they are important to the teacher providing remedial reading instruction. Despite beliefs that published tests have serious limitations for day-to-day decision making in an instructional setting, it is important to know how to select and interpret tests.

Basic measurement principles related to reliability and validity have been discussed and sources of information on published tests described in this chapter. Special problems encountered in the use of tests with low-achieving readers were also examined.

SUGGESTED ACTIVITIES

1. Examine a norm-referenced reading test and a criterion-referenced reading test. Compare the types of tasks the examinee is asked to perform on each type of test. Determine how a score of 50 percent correct on each test would be interpreted. Explain why the scores on a criterion-referenced test are normally "higher" (in the sense that fewer items will be missed on the average).

2. Examine the administrator's manual for a variety of standardized reading tests. Determine whether reliability coefficients are reported or not and list the tests from high to low on the basis of the coefficients. Decide which of the reliability coefficients are based on split-half procedures and which are based on alternate forms or test-retest procedures. Do a similar analysis on the reported validity of these tests. Using reliability and validity as the only criteria, decide which of the tests would be best to use.

3. Plan a series of lessons that are designed to help children become better takers of standardized tests. Concentrate on one type of test (true-false, multiple-choice, or matching). You may wish to consult the references identified in this chapter or elsewhere on helping children become test-wise.

NOTES

1. See Hogan (1974).
2. See Harris and Hodges (1981).
3. See Harris and Hodges (1981).
4. Called the coefficient of determination and determined by squaring the correlation coefficient.
5. See Mitchell (1985).
6. See Buros (1969).
7. See Harris and Sipay (1985).
8. See Cheek and Cheek (1980).
9. See Harris and Sipay (1985); Cunningham (1978).
10. See Sherman and Wildman (1982).
11. See Prell and Prell (1986).

SUGGESTED READINGS

AHMANN, J. STANLEY, AND GLOCK, MARVIN D. (1981). *Evaluating student progress: Principles of tests and measurements* (6th ed.). Boston: Allyn and Bacon.

This is a college textbook for the basic course in tests and measurements. As such it addresses fundamental issues including the role of student evaluation in education, describes the characteristics of satisfactory measuring instruments (including test validity, reliability, and means for reporting students' relative test performance), and discusses teacher-built tests including methods by which tests of this sort can be evaluated. Standardized tests and the means for evaluating them are also discussed.

EBEL, ROBERT L., AND FRISBIE, DAVID A. (1986). *Essentials of educational measurement* (4th ed.). Englewood Cliffs, NJ: Prentice-Hall.

This is a comprehensive college textbook on educational measurement principles. Both theoretical and practical issues related to measuring student achievement and progress are included. The topics of grading and reporting student achievement are presented in a separate chapter.

FARR, ROGER, AND CAREY, ROBERT F. (1986). *Reading: What can be measured?* (2nd ed.). Newark, DE: International Reading Association.

This book reviews the professional literature concerned with measuring reading performance. It discusses the limitations of reading tests and provides guidelines for their evaluation.

MEHRENS, WILLIAM A., AND LEHMANN, IRVIN J. (1984). *Measurement and evaluation in education and psychology* (3rd ed.). New York: Holt, Rinehart and Winston.

This book provides an introduction to and overview of the basic principles involved in the construction, selection, evaluation, interpretation, and use of tests. It discusses the nature of norm- and criterion-referenced tests and how they can be used most effectively by a classroom teacher to plan and evaluate instruction. It contains an entire chapter devoted to interest, personality, and attitude inventories.

PIKULASKI, JOHN J., AND SHANAHAN, TIMOTHY (EDS.) (1982). *Approaches to the informal evaluation of reading*. Newark, DE: International Reading Association.

This book summarizes alternative approaches that classroom teachers can take to formal, standardized tests of reading achievement on the premise that such approaches are especially helpful in planning and adjusting daily instruction.

Chapter 13

Diagnostic Reading Tests

OVERVIEW

As you read this chapter use the following list of main ideas to guide your understanding and reflection.

Survey reading tests can be administered to groups of children, are norm referenced, and have as a main purpose the ranking of children from high to low. The *Gates-MacGinitie Reading Tests* are reviewed here as an example.

Diagnostic reading tests are either group or individual tests and have as a main purpose the identification of strengths and weaknesses. Reviewed here as examples of group tests are the *Stanford Diagnostic Reading Test,* and the *Silent Reading Diagnostic Test.* Individual tests reviewed are the *Durrell,* the *Gates-McKillop-Horowitz,* the *Woodcock,* the *Botel,* and the *Diagnostic Reading Scales.*

Informal reading inventories are commonly used to determine what level of reading material a child can read on a daily basis, but can also provide a skilled teacher with diagnostic information. The *Analytical Reading Inventory* is reviewed here as an illustrative example.

Skills management systems are criterion-referenced tests designed to measure how well children perform on (or have mastered) some specific type of task. The *Prescriptive Reading Inventory* is reviewed in this chapter as an example.

One fact that becomes immediately evident to anyone who is involved in the teaching of reading is that literally dozens of tests are available to measure reading ability. Whether one riffles through the specimen test file in a curriculum lab at the nearest university, consults the test collection in the resources center of a local school system, or leafs through the *Mental Measurements Yearbook* (1985) or *Reading Tests and Reviews* (1976), it is clear that reading is a favored area among writers and publishers of tests.

Lapp and Flood (1979) list a total of 260 reading and reading-related tests published in the United States. Piled one on top of another these tests alone would make a stack taller than a member of a college basketball team. Include the materials that accompany most tests (for example, administrator's manual, technical reports of test development, scoring masks, and the like) and the pile would dwarf all the members of a basketball team standing one on top of the other. Such statements are virtually meaningless, of course, but they serve to dramatize the fact that the testing of reading is hardly a neglected matter.

The various types of published reading tests were discussed in Chapter 12. The general purpose and nature of survey tests, diagnostic tests (group and individual), oral reading tests, and skills management systems (criterion-referenced tests) were described. It is the goal in this chapter to present selected examples of tests in each of the above categories as a way of introducing the teacher to the types and variety of instruments they will encounter in the marketplace. The tests chosen to be reviewed here are not necessarily the best nor the worst, the newest nor the most unusual. They simply serve as examples that will give a "feel" for what is available and enable the teacher to build a scaffolding or framework into which other reading tests can be fitted as they are encountered.

The following tests are reviewed in this chapter:

1. Survey reading test
   a. *Gates-MacGinitie Reading Tests*

2. Diagnostic reading tests
   a. Group administered
      (1) *Stanford Diagnostic Reading Test*
      (2) *Silent Reading Diagnostic Test*
   b. Individually administered
      (1) *Durrell Analysis of Reading Difficulty*
      (2) *Gates-McKillop-Horowitz Reading Diagnostic Tests*
      (3) *The Woodcock Reading Mastery Tests*
      (4) *Botel Reading Inventory*
      (5) *Diagnostic Reading Scales*

3. Informal Reading Inventory (IRI)
   a. *Analytical Reading Inventory*

4. Skills management system
   a. *Prescriptive Reading Inventory*

The reviews presented in this chapter are based on the application of standards for evaluating standardized tests described in Chapter 12. As a reminder those standards include the following key points:

Reliability: What evidence of overall test reliability is provided? subtest reliability?

Validity: Is an explicit statement made concerning the definition of reading undergirding the test? Does the test appear to measure what is regarded as important for success in learning to read?

Other Technical Features: Are the directions clear and complete? If norm-referenced, are the norms adequate to the teacher's purpose(s)?

Overall: On balance, is use of this test justified? Which students should take this test

Keeping these standards in mind as you read the reviews that follow will give you a better sense of the purposes and organization underlying the comments. Other standards described in Chapter 12 can only be applied in a specific situation where an instructional program and a group of children can be used as a frame of reference.

A SAMPLE SURVEY READING TEST: THE GATES-MACGINITIE

First, it will be helpful to gain an overview of the *Gates-MacGinitie Reading Tests* (1978) and then to look more carefully at one level to see how it works. Keep in mind that the primary purpose here is to establish a base of understanding that permits the users to compare and contrast diagnostic tests with survey tests, not to look in detail at survey tests.

The *Gates-MacGinitie* is available in seven different tests appropriate for various grade levels ranging from readiness to tenth through twelfth grades. Vocabulary and comprehension are assessed by every level of the test (except readiness). Two forms of the test are available at every level (except readiness), and three forms are available for some of the tests. The levels and areas measured are shown in Table 13.1. Each of the tests was developed from a large pool of items that had been tried out with a nationwide sample well in excess of 2,000 students at each level. Students' responses were used to determine item difficulty (number of students missing an item) and item

TABLE 13.1   Gates-MacGinitie Reading Tests

Test	Number of Forms	Grade Levels	Skill Areas
Readiness			
Primary A	2	2	Vocabulary, Comprehension
Primary B	2	3	Vocabulary, Comprehension
Primary C	2	3	Vocabulary, Comprehension
Survey D	3	4–6	Vocabulary and Comprehension
Survey E	3	7–9	Vocabulary and Comprehension
Survey F	2	10–12	Vocabulary and Comprehension

discrimination value (extent to which the item was missed by low-scoring students and answered correctly by high-scoring students). Only effective items were retained for inclusion in the final forms of the tests. During the development stage data were also gathered to be used in establishing appropriate time limits for the tests.

Once a final test form was ready, it was administered to samples of students representing communities throughout the nation that included a range of sizes, geographic locations, average educational level, and average family income. Test norms were then developed showing the average performance of students at a particular grade level. Reliability was determined through a test-retest method using alternate forms. Vocabulary and comprehension scores are generally in the .85 to .90 range for all levels; the reliability of speed scores is somewhat lower, falling in the .65 to .80 range. Extensive data describing intercorrelations among subtests, and between verbal IQ scores and the subtests are reported in the technical report accompanying each test. Technical information useful in judging differences between test scores (including gain scores) is provided.

In short, except for a lack of validity information, the *Gates-MacGinitie Tests* are technically sound. Care has been taken to employ effective items, norms have been carefully developed, and attention is given in the test manual to proper interpretation of the results. Furthermore, different tests are available for relatively narrow ranges of grades making it possible to match students with tasks that are appropriate for their particular level of achievement.

Because they are survey tests, the *Gates-MacGinitie Tests* are global in nature—measuring pupil performance in broad areas. Based on what the tests include, it can be inferred that reading is viewed by the test authors as a process involving comprehension and is heavily dependent upon knowledge of vocabulary. As will be seen later, some diagnostic tests omit comprehension from what is measured. Word recognition is omitted from this test. Yet it is doubtful that the test authors actually believe word recognition is unimportant. It simply is not part of this test. The purposes of a survey test do not require that it tap all aspects of the reading process. For example, most tests ignore attitudes toward reading, interests, study skills, and a variety of other factors often thought to be important to reading. When a test is intended for diagnosis, however, it can ill afford to omit key areas. It must be a thorough measure of critical areas because instruction will be geared to the test results. A survey test such as the *Gates-MacGinitie* cannot be used in the same way.

To illustrate, we will look at Survey D of the *Gates-MacGinitie* to gain a fuller appreciation for what one test in the package actually measures. Survey D is intended for fourth to sixth grades.

The first test is Vocabulary. It includes a total of forty-five items presenting words that grow progressively less common and more difficult. Each item consists of a word followed by five other words. The pupil chooses the word whose meaning is closest to the test word. Although this format is common to many vocabulary tests, the presentation of words in isolation is an unnatural and unrealistic format. In the absence of context, words can have a variety of meanings or shades of meaning. Fifteen minutes are allowed to complete this test.

The second test, Comprehension, contains sixteen passages followed by two, three, or four multiple-choice questions. The length and complexity of the passages increase gradually. Most of the passages are expository in nature. Topics range from sea snakes to Arkwright's spinning machine. The pupil is permitted thirty-five minutes to work on this test. Except for a concern over the obscure topics of several of the passages (for example, resist dying, the Karroo in South Africa), there seem to be no major problems with the comprehension portion of the *Gates-MacGinitie*.

Norms provided for the tests include grade equivalents, percentile scores, and standard scores. A separate technical manual provides detailed information on reliability, but gives no indication of standard error of measurement.

Other forms of the *Gates-MacGinitie* are similar though not identical to Form D. It is common practice in many schools throughout the United States to administer the *Gates-MacGinitie* or another survey reading test such as the *California Survey of Reading Achievement* (1959) or the *Iowa Silent Reading Tests* (1973) in the fall or spring of the year (or both) to obtain a measure of pupil progress in reading. All general achievement batteries such as the *SRA* (1978), *Metropolitan* (1978), *California* (1977), and *Iowa* (1982) also include a survey test of reading. What do the results of such tests tell a classroom teacher, particularly one who is concerned about pupils who need remediation? As was indicated in Chapter 12, survey tests are useful primarily as devices for ranking children from high to low on a global measure of reading ability. Almost no information that identifies specific needs is provided. For this a teacher will need to use diagnostic tests and informal techniques. Survey tests can reveal which children are reading at a level far below their peers and/or far below their level of expectancy (a level typically determined with the use of an ability measure such as an IQ test). Further diagnosis is required in order to plan appropriate instruction; a survey test is useful only for initial screening in this process.

GROUP DIAGNOSTIC READING TESTS

Some diagnostic reading tests are designed to be given in a group setting. The obvious advantage of group tests is that much less of the teacher's time is needed to gather and score responses. If the test is well-constructed, a group diagnostic test can provide the detailed information needed to plan appropriate remedial work. The strengths and weaknesses of each child are easily identified when a profile of results is developed. The only real disadvantage of a group test is that nonverbal clues easily monitored in an individual setting are difficult to observe in a group setting.

Two of the most widely used group diagnostic reading tests are the *Stanford Diagnostic Reading Test* and the *Silent Reading Diagnostic Test*. Each is described below.

Stanford Diagnostic Reading Test

The *Stanford Diagnostic Reading Test (SDRT,*1976), is available in two forms at four different levels. Level One (red level) is intended for use at the end of first grade, in second grade, and with low-achieving students in third grade and above. Subtests include auditory discrimination, basic phonic skills, auditory vocabulary, word recognition, and comprehension.

Level Two (green level) of the SDRT is designed for use in third and fourth grades and with low-achieving students in fifth grade and above. Five subtests are included to measure performance in auditory discrimination, phonetic analysis, structural analysis, auditory vocabulary, and comprehension.

Level Three (brown level) is intended for fifth through eighth grades and with low-achieving secondary school students. Subtests include phonetic analysis, structural analysis, auditory vocabulary, comprehension, and reading rate.

Level Four (blue level) of the *SDRT* is designed for use with students in ninth through twelfth grades and in community colleges. Seven subtests include phonetic analysis, structural analysis, word meaning, word parts, comprehension, reading rate, and scanning and skimming.

It is notable that decoding is assessed throughout the various levels of the *SDRT.* Phonetic analysis is one of the subtests even in the brown and blue levels. Likewise structural analysis with special attention to blending is a subtest in all but the first level test. That the upper level tests designed for high school and even college students measures knowledge of consonant sounds, for example, or ability to blend sounds is surprising. A student who can do even one item on the comprehension subtest at these levels must know enough about sounds and symbols to make it superfluous to diagnose knowledge of consonant sounds and blending. It is highly unlikely that a high school student who is experiencing reading difficulty will profit much from instruction on vowel sounds, for example. Though less unusual, the measurement of auditory discrimination in a test designed for children in third grade and above is somewhat unnecessary.

In general, the *SDRT* is somewhat mechanistic in its approach to reading. Too much is made of a skills hierarchy that builds sequentially on phonics based decoding. Despite this limitation, the *SDRT* is well-designed, thoroughly researched, and highly professional. As standardized tests go, this is one of the better group diagnostic tests.

The *SDRT* is a group test having answer sheets for either machine or hand scoring. A comprehensive manual for the test administrator provides a detailed description of the structure and content of the test. With the help of the manual, teachers should be able to determine in a fairly straightforward manner whether the conceptualization of reading underlying this test is consistent with their own. The test manual also includes a detailed listing of test objectives, a classification of each test item according to objective, and a cutoff score for judging student mastery of a particular skill. Of special note are the thorough and practical sections of the manual devoted to understanding, interpreting and using the test results. Those who misuse the SDRT have little justification for claiming "the manual didn't explain." This is a unique strength of the *SDRT*.

Reliability and standard error of measurement information are reported both for subtests and the total test. All coefficients are in the acceptable range. Two types of validity are discussed in the test manual: content validity and criterion-related validity. The former is properly identified as a matter left to those who use the test because it is only they who can determine whether the abilities assessed by the test reflect the instruction that has been provided. This determination is facilitated by a detailed listing in the manual of objectives and skill domains measured by the subtests as well as item clusters and item objectives.

Criterion-referenced validity is reported with reference to external instrument only, the Reading Tests of the *Stanford Achievement Tests*. Correlation coefficients are in the .70 to .95 range, thus indicating a high level of agreement between the two tests. However, a comparison between the *SDRT* and another diagnostic reading test would seem more appropriate and more meaningful as an indicator of validity, in our opinion. The test authors recommend that users of the test should determine validity by examining the test contents against the objectives of the instructional program.

The *SDRT* provides the usual norm-referenced scores including percentile ranks, stanines, grade equivalents, and scaled scores for comparing performance across the various forms of the test. Significantly, the test manual discusses the nature and limitations of the various types of derived scores in terms a user of the test can easily understand. Appropriate cautions are provided to assist those who use derived scores to understand what they mean.

The *SDRT* also provides a criterion-referenced feature called "Progress Indicators." Test items that assess a particular skill are gathered together so that pupil performance on those items can be compared to a cutoff score. The test manual suggests that these scores are useful for diagnosing strengths and weaknesses in specific areas. Scores falling above the cutoff score are taken as an indication of competence. Scores falling below the cutoff score indicate competence that has not yet been achieved. There are reservations about the small number of items used to make this determination of competence. A teacher must understand the importance of supplementing any test score with additional evidence, of course, but one who does can use the *SDRT* as a means for guiding instructional plans. The *SDRT* "Progress Indicators" are subject to the same limitations that characterize all criterion-referenced tests (discussed in the previous chapter). In particular, test users will need to compare their own instructional objectives to the objectives of the test, a caution that *SDRT* authors make themselves in the manual.

The *SDRT* is praiseworthy as a group test when used for initial screening. The authors' assumptions about the reading process, though traditional, are laid out clearly in the manual. The content of the test springs directly from the authors' conceptualization of reading which is clearly and explicitly stated in the test manual. Teachers who want to use this instrument will find it relatively easy to see how supplementary information can be gathered to give a more complete view of a child's reading abilities.

Silent Reading Diagnostic Tests

Another group diagnostic reading test is the *Silent Reading Diagnostic Tests* (1976). In contrast to the multileveled *Stanford*, the *SRDT* is available in only one form that is intended for pupils who read at second- through sixth-grade levels. Eight subtests yield scores in the areas of:

1. Recognizing words in isolation
2. Recognizing words in context
3. Identifying root words
4. Separating words into syllables
5. Synthesizing or blending words
6. Distinguishing beginning sounds
7. Distinguishing ending sounds
8. Distinguishing vowel and consonant sounds

Raw scores on each subtest are entered on a graphic profile which assists the teacher in identifying areas having "diagnostic significance" (meaning they deviate from the general pattern markedly). In addition, scores from certain subtests are combined to yield subtotals in critical skill areas. Tests 1 and 2 combine to form Word-Recognition Skill, Tests 3, 4, and 5 represent Recognition Techniques, and Tests 6, 7, and 8 combine to form Phonic Knowledge. Scores on these three general areas are also entered on the Graphic Profile. Finally, error patterns on Tests 1 and 2 are examined to determine whether a consistent pattern exists with respect to location of word errors (that is, initial, middle, and ending positions in words).

The *SRDT* are normally given in three different settings to primary grade children and two sittings for intermediate grade children. All but the last three subtests are timed, ten minutes being allowed for each. Thus about eighty minutes are required for the entire test plus ten to twenty minutes for instructions. The pupil records all answers directly on the test booklet which is then hand-scored by the teacher using a scoring mask.

Test 1, Words in Isolation, includes fifty-four items that require the pupil to select a word from among five choices that "tell about the picture." Not all distractors are real words with some being constructed to permit an analysis of errors in beginning, middle, and ending positions and other being scrambled or incorrect spellings of a word that could be considered a reasonable answer. For example, one item shows a picture of a kitchen sink with these options: *snik, knees, sink, sick, rink*. Kress is critical of the distractors employed complaining, "The artificiality of the task leads one to question the validity of the test except as a measure of pure sight vocabulary."[1] The extent to which the distractors invite errors can be taken as evidence of a particular weakness in the test.

Test 2, Words in Context, presents sentences with a word missing and five words from which to select the one that best fits the blank. Again, along with the correct answer, the child sees real and mutilated words. One item is:

He hit the ball ＿＿＿＿＿＿＿＿＿＿＿＿ at the window.
　striht　　aitster　　trait　　strade　　straight

Again Kress' evaluation is valid. In item 30, for example, *automobile* is the correct answer for the sentence, "He could drive the ＿＿＿＿＿＿＿＿＿＿," but the child who chooses *otomobile* may simply be unfamiliar with the correct spelling of the word. To conclude that this child has difficulty using context is unreasonable. This subtest loses some of its value because it lets possible error categories dictate the inclusion of highly artificial distractors. This subtest also includes thirty items. Tests 1 and 2 comprise the first sitting.

Tests 3, 4, and 5 are given at the next testing session. Test 3, Visual-Structural analysis, presents the pupil with a word (for example, *previewer*) and three choices (*view, preview, viewer*). The child's task is to find the root word. Ten minutes is given to do as many of the thirty items as possible. Bryant correctly observes that a test of this type encourages guessing and permits an inflated score based on random marking of answers.[2] What seems to be lacking in this subtest is any measure of the child's ability to use roots as a way of getting at the meaning of unfamiliar words.

Test 4, Syllabication, presents thirty words and asks the child to indicate the number of syllables in each word. One cannot be sure whether children answer by "applying the rules" or because they recognize the word. Although the importance of syllabication for fluency in reading is questionable, this subtest would be more revealing if nonsense words were used.

Test 5 is an interesting cloze-type measure having what is, in our opinion, the misleading title Word Synthesis. The test authors describe this subtest as one that "measures the ability to blend words together visually and phonetically." The task presented to the pupil is one of first reading a brief passage (two to four sentences in length) that has hyphenated words at the end of each line, then choosing from among several alternatives, those words that best fit into several sentences. To successfully complete the exercise, the pupil must comprehend the train of thought present in the passage, then select words for the blanks that are consistent with that message. This is a useful measure of comprehension that involves the reader in a constructive process. Whether the pupil actually engages in the "blending" of visual and phonetic cues, as the test authors suggest, cannot be determined. One might argue that "blending" occurs in all successful reading, but so does visual discrimination, memory search, and a host of other abilities that are not mentioned in the title of the subtest. The Word Synthesis subtest of the *SRDT* should be regarded as a measure of comprehension (something not measured directly by any of the other subtests with the possible exception of Words in Context). Test 5 includes eight passages and thirty blanks.

A third testing permits completion of Tests 6, 7, and 8. Each of these tests involves listening to the teacher and making a response on the answer sheet one item at a time. Consequently, the pupil must keep pace with the entire group.

In Test 6, Beginning Sounds, the teacher says a word aloud while the pupil looks at four combinations of letters in the test booklet. The pupil's task is to mark the letters that "have the same sound" as the beginning of the word given. Thirty items comprise Test 6 with about twenty seconds allowed for each item. All but five of the items begin with common blends and diagraphs (*sl*, *gr*, *th*, *str*, and so forth).

Test 7, Ending Sounds, is identical to Test 6 except that the pupil marks the letters that have the same sound as the end of the word given. Thirty items are given and about twenty seconds per item is recommended. Here common word endings predominate.

Test 8, Vowel and Consonant Sounds, is nearly identical to Test 6 even to the extent that beginning sounds are the point of focus. The only differences are that (mostly) nonsense words are read aloud rather than real words and the pupil has single letters to mark rather than combinations of letters. To illustrate, the teacher says the word *vang* and the child chooses from among: *u, y, v, w.*

Tests 6, 7, and 8 are all heavily dependent upon the teacher's clear and accurate pronunciation of words. Distortion in the pronunciations or variations due to dialect could easily influence the results. No cautions are offered in the test manual with respect to dialect in either giving or scoring responses.

No validity information is provided by the authors of the *SRDT* other than to claim content validity on the grounds that the tasks included in the test "are the kinds which adequately maturing readers are required to do in their everyday use of reading." No clear conceptualization of reading is offered to give perspective to how the subtests were chosen. Bryant observes that the *SRDT* "provides certain information about word recognition and analysis skills in silent reading that can be helpful to the classroom teacher," but cautions that "factors in silent reading beyond the word level are not measured by the *Silent Reading Diagnostic Tests.*"[3] Kress is less positive, believing that the "artificiality inherent in the stimuli employed" destroys any diagnostic value of the *SRDT.*

The subtests have some diagnostic value when used as indicators of general strength or weakness in the skills tested. Because of the highly artificial nature of the distractors we would neither place any faith in the error analysis described by the manual nor use Tests 3 and 4 (Visual-Structural Analysis and Syllabication). As a group diagnostic test, the *SRDT* would be helpful as an early screening device but needs more supplementation than does the *Stanford Diagnostic Reading Tests.*

INDIVIDUAL DIAGNOSTIC READING TESTS

Because an individual diagnostic reading test is administered to one child at a time, and because most tests of this type take a minimum of thirty minutes to administer (and some take as long a ninety minutes), a teacher who has many responsibilities can take only a limited amount of time to give such tests. Of course, the close face-to-face interaction involved in individual diagnostic testing permits the teacher to pay close attention to how a student responds. All manner of information can be gathered through nonverbal clues that permit the teacher to gather a more complete picture of how a student reacts in a reading situation.

Individual diagnostic reading tests are of two basic types: the full battery and the informal reading inventory (IRI). The major distinction between these two types, which will be more apparent as descriptions of specific instruments are presented here, relates primarily to the fact that the full battery includes numerous subtests of specific skills in isolation whereas the IRI is a set of graded paragraphs to be read aloud. The following full diagnostic batteries are described here:

Durrell Analysis of Reading Difficulty

Gates-McKillop-Horowitz Reading Diagnostic Tests

The Woodcock Reading Mastery Tests

Botel Reading Inventory

Diagnostic Reading Scales

The Durrell Analysis of Reading Difficulty

The *Durrell* (1980) is a recently revised diagnostic test administered individually in thirty to ninety minutes, depending on which subtests are used. The primary purposes of the tests are to (1) "estimate the general level of reading achievement and (2) discover weaknesses and faulty reading habits that may be corrected in a remedial program."[4] The tests consist of four sets of graded paragraphs to be used for assessing oral reading, silent reading, and listening comprehension; word cards and a tachistoscope for assessing word recognition and word analysis; subtests for listening vocabulary, sounds in isolation, visual memory of words, and sounds in words; a prereading phonics abilities inventory (with eight subtests); and a spelling test. The Individual Record Booklet provides a general checklist of instructional needs, a form to record general history data, a profile chart for summarizing the results of testing, and specific checklists for difficulties in oral reading, silent reading, listening comprehension, spelling, visual memory and handwriting. The battery is intended for those whose reading ability is below seventh grade.

The *Durrell* is described as an instrument that should be given only by those who have been trained by someone having experience in the analysis and correction of reading difficulties. This careful delineation of who should use the *Durrell* is particularly important. As will be shown in this review, considerable professional judgment is required in properly administering, scoring, and interpreting the *Durrell*. Certain features of the *Durrell* make it *appear* to be more precise than an analysis of it implies. Because of its *apparent* objectivity and thoroughness, unsuspecting users of the *Durrell* can be led to expect more than the test delivers.

Even though it is a diagnostic test, norms are used throughout the *Durrell* to provide a basis for interpreting a pupil's score. This is somewhat odd because the significance of a pupil's performance on a diagnostic test is normally thought to lie in his or her unique pattern of strengths and weaknesses. Comparisons to other students are not particularly important or necessary in this sort of analysis. In any case, new norms were established for this revised form by working with university faculty from graduate reading programs in six communities across the United States. It is *not* clear in the test manual whether pupils in the norming group all attend schools in university towns, but the description of procedures used leaves one with that impression. If this is the

The individual administration of a diagnostic reading test offers the examiner an excellent opportunity to observe how the child tackles each task and to gain a sense of the child's confidence and attitude toward reading. *(Peter Vadnai)*

case, this would be a serious limitation, since university communities are often atypical in many respects. A statement in the manual indicates that factors such as "language backgrounds, socioeconomic status, ethnic characteristics, and curriculum emphasis were taken into consideration" in selecting the norming group. Exactly what this means is not explained.

A minimum of forty children in each grade (1 through 6) at six different locations participated in the standardization of the *Durrell*. Thus norms for most parts of the test are based on the performance of over 1,200 individuals.

Although the parts of the *Durrell* can be given in any order, the manual suggests that the Oral Reading and Word Recognition and Word Analysis tests be given first in order to decide which other tests are appropriate. These tests, therefore, will be examined first.

The Oral Reading test is given to determine a child's instructional level. This test consists of eight paragraphs ranging from a short 21-word narrative about "My Cat" to a 129-word expository essay on "The History of Golf." The child reads each passage aloud while the teacher makes a written record of "errors" in four categories (omissions, mispronunciations, words supplied, and insertions). Errors self-corrected by the child are counted as one-half error per word. Repetitions, disregard of punctuation, awkward phrasing, improper intonation, and hesitations (up to five seconds) are all recorded, but *not* counted as errors. Instructions in the manual do not indicate why a self-correction is regarded as half an error or why other breaks in oral reading fluency are recorded but not counted as errors. A caution is provided that counting word errors must be "tempered by the examiner's judgment." The implications of this statement are not clarified, but left to the examiner for interpretation. Here, then, is the first example of the need for considerable professional judgment, referred to earlier. Why are all errors recorded, but certain errors counted and others not? What is the rationale for counting insertions as errors, for example, regardless, of their nature, and not counting disregard of punctuation as errors? Why is a self-correction half an error? An approach that does not count self-corrections as errors is preferable. Even a system that counts all errors equally would be acceptable. But in the *Durrell* errors count as errors, half-errors, and no errors without justification. This is difficult to accept.

In addition to recording oral reading errors, the examiner also notes the length of time it takes a pupil to read each passage aloud. When seven or more "errors" are made on a single passage *or* the time required for reading a passage exceeds the time norms, the oral reading test is stopped. Using the table of norms for the last passage read successfully, a grade equivalent is then determined using the elapsed time. Three levels of performances are given for each grade (that is, high second grade, medium second grade, and low second grade).

A procedure that assigns grade equivalents on the basis of elapsed reading time is questionable when hesitations of up to five seconds occur before the examiner supplies a word the pupil cannot read. The examiner is also instructed to correct mispronunciations that may affect comprehension. Time is racing by while these steps are taken, yet a difference of only two to five seconds in reading time can reduce the pupil's reading level by a full grade. The norms for rate of reading were based on a much smaller sample than the other norms (only 200 pupils) raising further doubts concerning the reliability of the procedure for turning time scores into grade equivalents.

One other observation seems appropriate. The manual suggests that "recurring errors that reflect minor differences in dialect" be ignored. The thought is admirable, but the execution is likely to be haphazard. Why focus on recurring errors? Is not any variation due to dialect one that should be ignored, whether it happens once or a dozen times? Furthermore, why are only minor differences ignored? Does this imply that major differences should not be ignored? What distinguishes a minor from a major difference? Without answers to these questions, it is difficult to apply the instructions given.

These attempts to "modernize" the *Durrell* according to recent research on miscue analysis are half-hearted and largely unsuccessful. Oral reading errors must be codified and analyzed according to a carefully designed scheme in order to be useful to the diagnostician. Here an outdated scoring system has been loosened and compromised in an attempt to pass inspection, but in the process it has thrown an enormous burden on the examiner. The norms provided for interpreting pupil performance on the oral reading passages cannot possibly be of any use since they were established on the basis of data collected under very loose conditions.

Comprehension is checked in the oral reading test with questions that probe recall of specific facts. More than three questions out of seven or eight (depending on the level) answered incorrectly indicates "poor" comprehension. So long as comprehension is above that level, it is not a factor in determining the pupil's instructional level. If comprehension falls into the "poor" range before reading speed exceeds the norms, an adjustment downward in the instructional level "may be appropriate." The manual indicates that this will seldom happen since pupils will be able to answer most of the comprehension questions. Despite the assurances, more specific instructions seem necessary.

A checklist of oral reading "difficulties" requires the examiner to decide whether phrasing is adequate, whether volume is too loud or too soft, whether the child loses his or her place easily, and so forth. No discussion in the manual is offered to help the instructor arrive at a judgment concerning what constitutes "poor enunciation of difficult words" or "poor posture," for example. Without this assistance the use of such a checklist is highly subjective and therefore meaningless. In fact, one would quarrel with several items on the list as true indicators of reading difficulty: "Guesses at unknown words from context," "Ignores word errors and reads on" and "Habitual addition of words," are three examples of behaviors on the checklist of "difficulties" that are often associated with success in reading, not difficulty.

The second test, Word Recognition and Word Analysis, involves the use of lists of words in isolation and a handheld tachistoscope made of cardboard. A shutter device enables the teacher to control to some extent the length of time a word is exposed to the pupil. Directions in the test manual indicate each word should be "flashed" for .5 of a second to "permit only one eye fixation." Words recognized at flash are taken as sight words or, more properly, words recognized without analysis. Spache (1981) correctly observes that .5 of a second is adequate for several fixations thus defeating the idea that no analysis occurs during the flash portion of this test. In any case, the identification of words in isolation is useful to the diagnostician in only a limited sense anyway since the words missed on this subtest might very well be recognized in context, a much more meaningful measure of reading ability.

The pupil progresses through the lists until seven successive errors are made. When a word is missed at flash, the shutter is reopened and the pupil asked to study and pronounce it again. The second exposure is untimed and taken as a measure of word analysis. The child's attempts at pronouncing a word are written phonetically in the individual record book by the teacher for both flash and untimed exposure tasks. Norms are provided to permit conversion of scores into grade levels for flash and analysis alike. A checklist is provided to facilitate easy identification of behaviors that are noted during completion of this subtest (for example, "Will not try difficult words").

Silent reading is assessed in the *Durrell* with a second set of graded paragraphs that are intended to be equal in difficulty to the oral reading paragraphs. No evidence to support the equivalence of the paragraphs is provided in the test manual, but similarity is apparent in the length of the passages, length of sentences, writing style employed, and topics presented. The purposes of the silent reading test are to (1) determine the pupil's independent reading level, and (2) compare performance in silent reading with performance in oral reading. Performance in silent reading is assessed with a measure of time and unaided recall.

Upon completion of a passage the child is asked to tell "everything you can remember of that story." The upper grade selections are actually essays not stories, but this technicality is unimportant. A breakdown of the text of each passage into ideas units is provided in the teacher's record booklet. As the child recalls an idea from the passage a check is made giving credit for that recollection. Recent developments in discourse analysis[5] make the *Durrell* scoring procedure seem crude and arbitrary by comparison, but the idea of assessing comprehension through free recall rather than question asking is noteworthy. Recent research on the validity of free recall suggests that it, too, has limitations as a measure of comprehension.[6] However, relatively few tests approach comprehension in any way other than through direct questioning. The *Durrell* procedure provides for follow-up questions to probe further recall once free recall has been exhausted. Scores are turned into grade equivalents using norms developed on the same group of 200 children in second through sixth grades that was used to develop norms for the oral reading test.

It is difficult to accept several assumptions made by the test authors with respect to the silent reading test. No rationale is given for using a different comprehension measure for silent reading (free recall) than for oral reading (question answering). This becomes a problem when performance on the two tests is then compared. Differences in performance on the two tests would be extremely difficult to interpret even if comprehension were assessed in the same manner on each test. When the assessment procedure changes, the problem of interpretation is exacerbated. It is also difficult to follow the logic of calling performance on the oral reading test the instructional level and performance on the silent reading tests the independent reading level. The only explanation given in the test manual is that unaided recall is a higher order task than question answering, which is not convincing.

The *Durrell* does not seem to conform to the traditional standards for determining reading levels (as exemplified by Betts) nor any other explicitly stated standards in determining instructional and independent levels. Although the value of comparing oral and silent reading performance is questionable, the *Durrell* explicitly states this as a goal of the test, but then fails to indicate how such a comparison should be undertaken, why such a comparison is desirable, or which differences and similarities between the two are worth noting. The manual includes no discussion of this matter and the *Individual Record Booklet* asks the examiner only to indicate whether silent reading was the same, better, or worse than oral reading in speed, recall, and "security." How such differences, once observed, are to be interpreted by the teacher is not clear. From one perspective, better performance in silent reading would be normal in all three categories.

The *Durrell* also ventures into assessing an aspect of comprehension that is experiencing a rebirth in recent years: imagery. Though Spache (1981) is critical of this aspect of the *Durrell*, the optional questions that invite reader description of what "you see in your mind" are potentially revealing. Research reported by Paivio (1971) suggests that poor readers are characterized by impoverished mental imagery as they read. No other diagnostic reading test attempts to examine this ability. The fact that prior to reading no instructions are given to the child about forming mental images while reading may be an important limitation in generalizing the imagery results obtained on the *Durrell*. It is also odd that after going to some lengths to measure imagery the only recording of the results is to indicate whether the "flow" is "rich" or "poor." No direction is given in the test manual concerning how to decide what is "poor flow" or how to remediate problems in this domain. This seems to be another example of major responsibility being thrown on the examiner without adequate direction or explanation.

A third set of passages is provided in the *Durrell* for assessing Listening Comprehension as an estimate of reading capacity. After hearing the examiner read a passage aloud the student responds to seven or eight factual (detail) questions. The student's listening level is the level where not more than two questions are missed. The listening score is apparently used to determine whether performance is substantially different from potential (though this language is not used in the examiner's manual). Though listening is often used as a way of establishing the child's "capacity" or "reading expectancy," the looseness with which the *Durrell* handles this topic is disappointing. No rationale is offered nor is any system given for judging how much discrepancy between silent reading and listening is significant. What seems especially strange is that the examiner is discouraged from establishing an upper level with the listening test. "There is little point in trying to establish an upper level since the purpose of this test is to learn whether or not reading difficulty rests upon lack of comprehension."[7] This explanation seems unsatisfactory since the stated purpose of the test is to estimate reading capacity. How can capacity be estimated unless the "top" is determined?

The *Durrell* provides a fourth set of supplementary passages that can be used for retesting in any of the areas previously mentioned (oral reading, silent reading, or listening), or to examine other abilities of interest to the teacher.

In their review of the *Durrell*, Schell and Jennings (1981) comment on the lack of information about the readability level of the four sets of graded passages. They complain that special importance is attached to the norms because no effort is made to show how the passages have been standardized. We have less concern about the actual grade level of each passage than about the relative difficulty of one passage in comparison to the next and equivalence from test to test (that is, oral reading, silent reading, and so on). Nevertheless, we agree with Schell and Jennings that the test authors are obligated to pay more attention than they have to the readability of the passages.

A new test added to this latest version of the *Durrell* makes further use of the same words included in the Word Recognition and Word Analysis Test (though the order of the words has been scrambled). Called Listening Vocabulary, this new test presents five lists of fifteen words each drawn from certain ideational clusters in *Roget's International Thesaurus*. The words on any one list fit into each of three categories. For example, one list includes words that relate to the categories of time, big, and color. When a word (for example, *red, large, year*) is called by the examiner, the child's task is to decide into which category it fits. The words grow gradually more difficult in each list. Testing is stopped in one list and moved to the next list when the child has missed and/or omitted three words in a row. A score is obtained by totaling the correct responses to all lists and consulting the table of grade norms.

The stated purpose of the Listening Vocabulary Test is to provide a second index of reading capacity and to permit a comparison of listening vocabulary and listening comprehension in recognizing the same words. It is difficult to accept the assumption that "knowing" the meaning of isolated words spoken aloud (at least well enough to classify them into one of three categories) is a particularly valid estimate of reading capacity. The test manual reports that performance on the Listening Vocabulary Test correlates at only a .38 level with scores on the *Metropolitan Reading Test* among primary grade children. This suggests that the Listening Vocabulary Test is not a particularly good predictor of actual reading achievement. With upper grade children a somewhat higher (.58), though not remarkable, correlation was found. These relationships are quite similar to those typically found between general intelligence and reading ability. The claim made in the test manual that Listening Vocabulary is a more direct measure of reading capacity than the usual measures of intelligence seems overdrawn. If a general measure of intelligence is already available for a pupil, it seems advisable to simply omit this test. The very low relationship found between Listening Comprehension and Listening Vocabulary (.22 at the primary level and .57 at the intermediate level) suggests that little agreement exits between the "two indexes" of reading capacity provided by the *Durrell*. Of the two, Listening Comprehension is preferred since it at least involves pupil response to connected discourse.

The remaining subtests of the *Durrell* are ones a teacher would use selectively. Some are intended for the nonreader or the child who is reading on a first-grade level. Other subtests are for second-grade level and below, third-grade level and below, and so forth. Although no set sequence is mandated for administering the various subtests, the oral and silent reading passages, the listening task, and the word recognition lists are typically given to all pupils first. Based on performance in those areas a determination is made concerning which additional tests to give. Thus the child who struggles with even the easiest passage during oral and silent reading and recognizes few words in isolation might normally be tested for hearing sounds in words, for example. On the other hand, a child who reads the third- or fourth-grade passage successfully might be tested for visual memory of words and spelling.

The various subtests have titles that are fairly descriptive of their content. In most subtests the assumption is made that a matching task is easiest, an identification task is somewhat more difficult, and a naming or producing task is more difficult. Thus the child who can name letters when they are shown can surely find a letter when it is named and match letters when they are shown. Conversely, when the child cannot match letters he or she probably cannot name letters. Consequently the *Durrell* is built on certain assumptions about what skills are important to success in reading. While the assumptions about which skill precedes another skill are made fairly explicit in the test manual, no discussion is given concerning what conceptualization of reading the test supports. One can infer that phonics knowledge is believed to be important and that use of context and structural analysis are believed to be unimportant by looking at the subtests provided. The subtests include:

Sounds in Isolation
    Letters
    Blends and Digraphs
    Phonograms
    Affixes (Initial)
    Affixes (Final)
Spelling

Phonic Spelling of Words (Nonsense Words)

Visual Memory of Words

Identifying Sounds in Words

Prereading Phonics Abilities Inventories
    Syntax Matching
    Identifying Letter Names in Spoken Words
    Identifying Phonemes in Spoken Words
    Naming Letters (Lower Case)
    Writing Letters from Dictation
    Naming Letters (Upper Case)
    Identifying Letters Named

In conclusion, the revised *Durrell* is disappointing. As a comprehensive test of reading it is insufficient. Important and basic aspects of reading are ignored. Oral reading errors are scored in a haphazard manner. Far too much emphasis is placed on the use of norms. Furthermore, the heavy dependence on time in judging a pupil's performance is inappropriate and misleading. Assumptions about skills hierarchies are made that are not acceptable. Information is gathered that the manual fails to justify or explain, and insufficient discussion is provided concerning how to interpret the results of the various tests. Some unique features of the *Durrell* are interesting and potentially revealing. The system for scoring comprehension with retellings and the attention given to imagery are examples of features that are intriguing. However, even in these areas problems exist. On balance, use of *Durrell* should be avoided.

Gates-McKillop-Horowitz Reading Diagnostic Tests

The *Gates-McKillop-Horowitz Reading Diagnostic Tests* are a 1981 version of a battery published originally in 1927 by Arthur I. Gates. The 1981 version is almost identical to the 1962 edition and consequently satisfies very few of the criticisms made by Singer (1978b), who observed that "the discrepancy between the *Gates-McKillop* and criteria for an excellent test increases . . . as theories and concepts of tests construction, standardization, and norming continue to improve."[8]

The authors of the *Gates-McKillop-Horowitz Tests* do not relate the instrument to a specific theory or conceptualization of the reading process. They state: "The main function of the tests is to assess the strengths and weaknesses in reading and related areas of a particular child." The tasks included in the tests are designed for use with children in first through sixth grades. A record booklet is provided to permit the examiner to make a written record of each pupil's responses. A summary page calls for raw scores, grade scores and/or ratings (for example, whether high, middle, or low by comparison to the performance of a norming sample), presumably to facilitate identification of strengths and weaknesses. The emphasis given to converting raw scores into grade norms is somewhat inconsistent with the stated diagnostic purpose of the tests. Why the procedures for comparing a particular child's performance on the various subtests are not given greater attention is a mystery (this approach *is* described, but without enough explanation to be helpful).

By using every subtest included in the *Gates-McKillop-Horowitz* a teacher would gain a detailed picture of how well a student does two things: read orally and identify words. Oral reading is assessed with seven paragraphs that form a continuous narrative and grow progressively more difficult. Errors are recorded in four major categories (omissions, additions, repetitions, and mispronunciations). Norms for assigning a grade level equivalent to oral reading performance are provided, but to use them the first four paragraphs must be read by the pupil. Except for a general suggestion that the examiner observe whether errors are of a "contextual nature," no acknowledgment of the extensive literature on qualitative analysis or oral reading miscues is evident in this test. The 1981 revision is different from the 1962 version in that self-corrections are not counted as errors, but no attention is paid to the semantic, or syntactic, acceptability or graphophonic similarity present in the reader's errors. Comprehension is not checked in any manner here or anywhere else in the *Gates-McKillop-Horowitz Tests*.

Oral reading is also tested in a subtest titled Reading Sentences. Here, four sentences comprised of decodable (phonetically regular) words are read aloud. Errors are recorded in exactly the same manner as in the passage situation.

Word identification represents the focus of the remainder of the subtests. Eleven subtests are provided to examine pupil performance in two areas: identification of words at sight and word analysis. Only one subtest deals with sight words (that is, Words: Flash). Here the pupil is shown forty words each for one-half second at a time by using a card having a rectangular opening (window) to control the length of exposure. A table of norms translates raw scores into grade norms. The remaining subtests, ten in all, measure the child's ability to analyze words and parts of words. Considerable overlap exists among the subtests. This fact is acknowledged in the test manual, which instructs the examiner to use only the parts needed for a complete picture of the pupil's abilities. The subtest on Reading Words could be skipped for the pupil who does well on the Syllabication subtest, for example, since the latter is merely a more difficult version of the former (both consist of nonsense words pupils must pronounce using their knowledge of sound-symbol relationships).

Despite the number of subtests on various aspects of work analysis, the *Gates-McKillop-Horowitz* does not explore a pupil's knowledge of or skill in the use of structural analysis or context clues. The subtests provided (untimed word recognition, syllabication, recognizing and blending common word parts, reading [nonsense] words, giving letter sounds, naming capital letters, naming lower-case letters, recognizing vowels, auditory blending, auditory discrimination, and spelling) all deal directly or indirectly with phonics. Grade norms are given in table form for the untimed word recognition test and the spelling test. All other word analysis tasks listed above were tried by the test authors with a sample of students, but grade norms are not provided. Instead the average performance of first graders, second graders, and so forth, on the various subtests are described in paragraph form. For example, with respect to giving letter sounds this statement is made: "First graders in our sample gave an average of 25 sounds correctly. Children beyond the end of first grade gave an average of 29 sounds correctly. Children who deviate from this level of performance should be studied further."

The looseness of these directions is troublesome for three reasons: First, the children included in the sample cited by the authors are not representative of the general population (that is, 600 children in first through sixth grade attending ten different schools. The sample was overwhelmingly urban [83percent] with a predominance of private schools [65percent]. Minority children constituted 36 percent of the sample). Second, the degree of "deviation" from the sample scores that is regarded as normal and abnormal are not specified. Finally, the nature and extent of "further study" is not described. The authors obviously expect that trained, experienced reading specialists will use their test. For such individuals the loose, sketchy directions for interpretation may be adequate. For anyone else, too much is assumed and too little is made explicit.

Published reviews of the 1962 *Gates-McKillop* were critical of the test for its failure to supply data on reliability and validity.[9] The 1981 revision is accompanied by several bits of information on reliability and validity that do little to satisfy the earlier criticism. Correlations between the *Gates-McKillop-Horowitz* oral reading scores and silent reading scores from the "*Gates-MacGinitie, Metropolitan Achievement Tests*, or others" reportedly range from .68 to .96 "at various grades." Such global reporting does little to comfort the prospective user in view of the fact that the scoring procedures for the oral reading section of the *Gates-McKillop-Horowitz* provide little more than gross error counts.

Oral reading scores were also studied for reliability using a test-retest procedure. The correlation coefficient of .94 seems respectable until one realizes that no information is given about what interval occurred between the two testing dates. Furthermore, the same set of paragraphs was evidently used both times since there is only one form of the test. Lastly, the small number of subjects participating in this reliability study (twenty-seven) severely limits the generalizability of the findings.

The *Gates-McKillop-Horowitz* also recommends gathering an informal writing sample on a "topic of interest" to the child. Despite the looseness of the procedures for gathering the sample (no audience is specified for the essay, for example), the examiner is instructed to evaluate it for both substance and form. No specific standards for evaluation are given although categories such as "clarity of expression," "use of pronouns," and "spacing" are listed for the examiner's attention. One reference to an article in the *Bulletin of the Orton Society* is provided to assist the examiner in determining whether evidence of learning problems is present in the writing sample.

Spache (1981) observed that the titles given some of the subtests in the 1962 version of the *Gates* do not accurately depict the skill or knowledge being tested. This flaw is noticeable in the 1981 revision as well. The syllabication test, for example, goes well beyond the ability to divide words to measure sound-symbol knowledge and blending. Spache also comments on the brevity of many of the subtests (fewer than twenty items in many cases and fewer than ten items in some cases). Reliability becomes problematic when relatively few samples of behavior are sampled. This is particularly troublesome in a diagnostic test that encourages teachers to develop a profile of strengths and weaknesses for the purpose of planning remedial instruction.

A minor concern is created by the fact that no "correct" pronunciation is given for nonsense words employed in several subtests of the *Gates-McKillop-Horowitz*. If it is safe to assume that teachers will agree on the way to say "tarculope" and "pharmoter," this concern is unwarranted. It would be preferable to see the test authors give a "correct" answer with specific directions on how to adjust to dialect differences.

Because of the concerns described, it is not recommended that teachers use the *Gates-McKillop-Horowitz*.

The Woodcock Reading Mastery Tests

Another individually administered diagnostic test, the *Woodcock* (1973), is published by American Guidance Service (AGS). A new version was published in 1987. Like several other AGS tests, the *Woodcock* is in the form of a sturdy, hard-covered, ring-type binder that serves as an easel when placed on a table between the student and the teacher. Stimulus materials are presented to the student by flipping a page from the teacher's side across the top of the easel to the child's side. Directions are visible on the teacher's side of the easel, thus facilitating smooth administration of the test while permitting good eye contact with the child.

The *Woodcock* includes two forms and is intended for kindergarten through twelfth grade. Five subtests each yield a separate score as well as contribute to a total score. The subtests are: Letter Identification, Word Identification, Word Attack, Word Comprehension, and Passage Comprehension. All student responses are made orally and are recorded by the teacher on a separate answer sheet.

The test is described as being appropriate for measuring individual reading growth, detecting reading problems, grouping students for instruction, evaluating curriculum and programs, and accountability. The test author estimates that an entire form of the test can be administered in twenty to thirty minutes, although Tuinman[10] indicates that thirty to fifty minutes is a more realistic time estimate. No special training in administerng the *Woodcock* is necessary according to the manual accompanying the test. In fact, even paraprofessionals (volunteers and teachers' aides, for example) are identified as appropriate examiners. This assertion is questionable since the value of any individually administered diagnostic test derives partly from the observations that only a skilled professional can make during the examination. Woodcock is probably correct in his assumption that, with experience, a competent paraprofessional can follow the directions sufficiently well to produce a reliable score, however.

The subtest on Letter Identification involves a straightforward task that requires the student to say the name of a letter as the examiner points to it. Forty-five letters are included in both capital and lower-case forms as well as in a variety of type faces (including cursive, gothic, roman, and italic). The value of spreading scores across a scale that ranges from first to fourth grade is a mystery. Letter identification is essentially a readiness factor that has no importance once the child is reading. Why an entire subtest of a diagnostic insturment attends to this relatively narrow matter is unclear.

The second subtest, Word Identification, presents the examinee with a list of 150 words in isolation to be read aloud without assistance. The words are presented in order of difficulty and, for the preprimer through third grade levels, are drawn from seven basal reading programs. Above that level they are drawn from the Throndike-Lorge list. Provision is made for starting each student at a point in the list appropriate to his or her expected level of achievement. It is odd that the test manual indicates, "There is no assumption that the subject . . . has ever seen the word before." This subtest is primarily a test of sight vocabulary. The way the words were selected suggests that high frequency words are involved. Since the next subtest purports to measure word attack, the author's assertion regarding the examinee's familiarity with the words seems incongruous.

The subtest on Word Attack consists of fifty nonsense words students must pronounce presumably by applying their knowledge of phonics and structural analysis. Again, items are arranged in order of difficulty; however, all examinees begin with item number one and proceed until five successive errors indicate a "ceiling" has been reached. The nonsense words have been created to test knowledge of "most consonant and vowel sounds, common prefixes and suffixes, and frequently appearing irregular spellings." Nonsense words are used, of course, to eliminate the possibility that words will be identified at sight. Yet the test manual states, "In several cases, including the sample item, the words are, in fact, real but most likely unknown to the subject."[11] Why the author states an important assumption then violates it is unknown and bothersome.

Word Comprehension, often called vocabulary, is a measure of the examinee's knowledge of word meaning. The *Woodcock Test* employs an analogy format (such as $snow - cold = sun - $ _____) to obtain a vocabulary score. A total of seventy analogies ranging from simple to complex is provided. Though one might argue that ability to manipulate concepts is a deeper and therefore better measure of word meaning than merely matching synonyms, for example, it seems evident that analogies require far *more* than knowledge of words. Problem solving and reasoning are needed in solving analogies and, therefore, analogies are not used in any other reading test. This subtest seems to be seriously flawed as a reading measure.

The final subtest of the *Woodcock*, Passage Comprehension, is described as a modified cloze procedure task. A total of eighty-five items, each requiring the student to supply a word that fits into a blank, comprise the subtest. Picture clues are given with the first twenty-two items. Initially only one phrase or sentence is used. In later more difficult items, up to three or four sentences are used. Dwyer comments on the ineffectiveness of this subtest in getting at higher level comprehension abilities and states: "There is no evidence of attempts to measure higher level reading skills such as inference, evaluation of logic, or analysis; instead, the use of abstruse materials seems to be relied on for difficulty."[12] Tuinman cautions that even students who decode poorly can do many of the items on this subtest correctly by responding exclusively to the picture clues.[13]

The author of the *Woodcock* test offers no explanation for the overall scheme used in creating this test. No attempt is made, for example, to specify how each subtest addresses a critical or important aspect of the reading process. No conceptualization of reading is offered as a point of reference for the subtests. Several of the subtests are traditionally a part of diagnostic reading tests (for example, word comprehension), but at least one (letter identification) is not. Several test reviewers have questioned the inclusion of the letter identification test.[14] It seems inappropriate to make a score from this subtest equal to the other subtests in arriving at an overall score on the *Woodcock*. Other aspects of the *Woodcock* that reviewers have justifiably questioned include (1) the claim that the test is both a norm-referenced and criterion-referenced (mastery of a skill at a particular grade level is, in part, a function of the instructional program used) and (2) the procedures used to establish test validity (important assumptions about the statistical procedure used are not met).

The conclusion drawn from this information is that the *Woodcock* test has very little value as a diagnostic instrument but might be used as a general screening device if the limitations cited here and in Buros (1978) are kept in mind.

Botel Reading Inventory

The *Botel Reading Inventory* (1981) has been included with other individual diagnostic reading tests even though parts of the *Botel* can be given in a group setting. This seems appropriate because *parts* of the *Botel* must be given individually, thus disqualifying it as a group test.

The *Botel Reading Inventory* (Form A and B) consists of four subtests: (1) Decoding, (2) Spelling, (3) Word Recognition, and (4) Word Opposites. The primary purpose of the *Botel* is to assist teachers in estimating the placement of pupils in textbooks. Given this purpose, the *Botel* might be regarded as a survey test. The test manual indicates that the *Botel* is also useful for "determining which common syllable/spelling patterns the student can decode and encode." With this information "it is then possible to plan appropriate instructional programs to advance the students' competence in those patterns not yet mastered."[15] Therefore, it is concluded that the test is diagnostic in nature although comprehension is addressed only from the standpoint of placement.

Interestingly enough, and quite in contrast with most diagnostic reading tests, the *Botel* contains absolutely no running text (connected discourse) to be read by pupils but confines itself instead to lists of words read or heard. This represents the most extreme example of breaking the act of reading into component parts. In effect, here is a test of reading that does not require the pupil to read in the normal sense of the word. This is a significant point that must be considered in evaluating the *Botel*.

The decoding competency section of the *Botel* includes twelve subtests of ten items each that are organized into seven levels. Each level appears to build on previous levels in a skills hierarchy that moves from simple to more complex. Thus Level One (Parts 1 through 3) is labeled "Awareness of Sounds and Letter Correspondences" and consists of subtests on Letter Naming, Beginning Consonant Sound/Letter Patterns. Subtests in Level One may be given in a group setting. The remaining tests (Parts 4 through 12) are given individually to one child at a time. Level Two (Parts 4 through 5) is labeled "Decoding Simple, Highly Regular Syllables" and includes subtests on CVC pattern words and CVCe pattern words. Subsequent levels (Parts 6 through 12) step through progressively longer and less regular words with subtests on various consonant-vowel patterns. Level Six (Part 11) focuses on different parts of speech (for example, muscle-muscular) and Level Seven (Part 12) uses nonsense words.

In Part 1 (Letter Naming) the student's task is to draw a line under one of six letters in a row when the teacher says its name. Part 2 is identical except that initial consonants are marked when a word that begins with a particular letter is given. Part 3 uses the same approach except that a word that rhymes with two stimulus words given aloud is underlined. Parts 4 through 12 require the student to read words aloud to the examiner.

The mastery level is set at 80 percent correct for all subtests in the Decoding section. This is a change from the 1970 edition, in which 100 percent success was expected. Like the 1970 edition, the 1981 version indicates that instruction should focus on the skills where test performance falls below the mastery level.

There are several problems with the Decoding subtests. First, the subtests seem too short to have satisfactory reliability. Given what is known about error in measurement, it is hazardous to draw conclusions about a student's knowledge of consonants, for example, using only ten items. Coupled with the concern for the inadequate sample of behaviors gathered by the *Botel* is dissatisfaction with the assumption made here about the hierarchial nature of reading. Certainly no empirical evidence exists to support the need to master consonant sounds before learning vowel sounds. We question the logic of such an assertion, yet a faithful follower of this test is directed to embrace such an approach.

The second subtest of the *Botel*, Spelling Placement, is a traditional spelling test. That is, the teacher says a word aloud, uses it in a sentence, then repeats the word. Subjects write the word on their paper. The *Botel* includes five graded lists of twenty words each for this subtest; one list for first and second grade, and a separate list each for third through sixth grade. The first level at which a student's score falls below 80 percent accuracy is identified as the instructional level. Systematic instruction at this level is recommended by the *Botel*. No explanation is given concerning why a spelling subtest is included in a reading test, nor is any discussion offered as to how the results of this subtest should be used diagnostically for planning specific spelling lessons by the teacher.

The subtest on word recognition is administered individually and consists of eight lists of words with twenty words per list. Each list corresponds to a "reading level"—preprimer through fourth grade. Words were chosen for the preprimer through third-grade lists from common words found in five major basal readers. The fourth-grade words were drawn from the Thorndike-Lorge list. The student's task on this subtest is to read each word aloud beginning with a level where "he is likely to have 100 percent correct." The teacher records three types of errors: (1) mispronunciation, (2) substitutions, and (3) refusals (no response). Once performance falls below 70 percent accuracy on two successive levels, the testing is stopped. The instructional reading level is determined by identifying the highest list read with 70 percent accuracy or above. The reading level of subjects who pass the hardest word list (fourth grade) is determined by performance on a different subtest, the Word Opposites Test.

It is important to note that Goodman (1969) and others have demonstrated that the identification of words in isolation is more difficult than in context. Whatever limitation this places on the *Botel* is widely shared among diagnostic tests since nearly all have a subtest identical or similar to the *Botel* (using words in isolation). More significant is the approach taken in the *Botel* to scoring errors. The examiner is encouraged to make a written record of the child's incorrect responses presumably for the purpose of making a qualitative examination of errors. Yet no assistance is given in differentiating between a mispronunciation and a substitution. Without the benefit of context the examiner would be hard pressed to know when an error qualifies as a substitution and when it is a mispronunciation. The *Botel* also suggests that variations associated with regional and dialectual differences be accepted, but no examples are given to help the teacher understand what this means or how it can be accomplished. The *Botel's* directions with respect to hesitations (no response) are vague. Hesitations (up to six seconds) are not errors, but "more than several such responses at any level are indicative of insecurity and should be considered when establishing the pupil's reading level." This raises the following questions: Exactly how many hesitations qualify as "more than several?" What constitutes "consideration" of the errors? Should the reading level be reduced a full step, two steps, or more?

The Word Opposites subtest can be given in a group setting. It presents pupils with an isolated word and three alternative choices. The task is to pick the word that "means the opposite or nearly the opposite." The example given is:

1. no   ok   *yes*   not.

Ten lists beginning at grade one and ranging up to senior high level in difficulty are included. Words for this subtest were selected in the same manner as words for the Word Recognition Test.

Performance on the Word Opposites is compared to a 80 percent accuracy standard. Once the pupil's performance falls below this standard on two successive lists (grade levels), testing is stopped and the instructional reading level determined to be the level at which better than 80 percent accuracy was achieved.

The test manual does not caution teachers to be sure that the meaning of *opposite* is known by the pupil. With only one example given prior to testing, the possibility exists that some students will fail to realize what is expected on this subtest. This same format is often used in workbooks and tests for identification of synonyms.

The presentation of words in isolation in the *Botel* is an artificial and unrealistic task insofar as normal reading is concerned; shades of meaning for many words are often unclear until they are used in context. For example, the word *colorless* is given with these alternatives: *jovial, glamorous, ignorant, drastic*. Which means the opposite of *colorless*? The keyed answer is *glamorous*. But consider these uses of the alternative responses.

The atmosphere at the carnival was *jovial*.
The brightest yellow paint was a *drastic* change in the appearance of the room.

Is *glamorous* the best opposite of colorless? None of these choices seem particularly good to us, but *jovial* and *drastic* can be as appropriate as *glamorous* in some contexts.

The Word Opposites test is normally given as a reading test, that is, students work through the items on their own reading the words silently. Used in this way, the test is intended to provide an estimate of comprehension. Unless one has a terrribly narrow view of how reading comprehension occurs, this subtest seems to raise more questions about pupil performance than it gives answers.

Used as a listening test (teachers read to pupils while they follow along marking their own answers), the Word Opposites test is described as a measure of "reading potential." Given a "wide difference" (not quantified beyond this in the manual) between the silent reading and listening scores (presumably) on two forms of the *Botel*, the vague claim is made that the test indicates "a remedial program could be started to bring performance more in line." No rationale is offered for this claim. No research supporting the use of listening comprehension as a measure of reading potential is cited, nor are any clues given as to what such a remedial program would include.

A point has been made in each test review presented in this chapter to examine what conceptualization of reading a particular test seems to reflect. Test authors have an obligaton to make an explicit statement about what they think is important in the reading process and to discuss how their test addresses those elements. (This is referred to as "content validity.") Relatively few test authors meet this fundamental expectation in an explicit manner. Most test authors come at the task in a roundabout way. The *Botel* is a good example of the latter approach.

One can infer that Dr. Botel believes two aspects of the reading act are important and measurable: word recognition and comprehension. Word recognition evidently occurs in Botel's view by learning to recognize particular spelling patterns. Furthermore, an optimal sequence exists for mastering those patterns if the nature of the test format and instructions for interpretation are any indication of the author's beliefs. Decoding evidently leads to comprehension in a linear fashion beginning with letter naming and progressing through various consonant and vowel combinations. Comprehension occurs if the meanings of words recognized are known by the reader.

This seems a gross oversimplification of the reading process. Furthermore, the subtests of the *Botel* in many cases do not measure what the labels indicate. The Word Recognition subtests based on words that follow certain spelling patterns, for example, tell only whether the pupil is familiar with particular words, not whether a student can generalize about sound-symbol relationships in certain combinations of letters. In other words, the word *hope* in part 5 of the Decoding subtest might be a sight word for a child, but the *Botel* includes it in a list of words that represent the CVCe pattern. Does the child who reads it know the "final silent e rule" or is this a word he or she recognizes at sight? It is also questionable whether ten items sufficiently sample each "skill domain" to provide a reliable measure. And, finally, Botel's argument that mastery of one decoding "skill must precede instruction on the next skill" is unconvincing.

The Word Recognition and Decoding sections of the *Botel* are narrow and insufficient, in our estimation, but the assessment of comprehension is grossly inadequate. Knowledge of word meanings is identified by the *Botel* as "the most important factor" in determining reading comprehension. From this premise the shaky conclusion is drawn that a single measure of word meanings using a word opposites task is appropriate for assessing comprehension. To compound this problem, isolated words are used to get at the pupil's knowledge of words. Although it is true that no claims are made in the test manual concerning the diagnostic value of the *Botel* in the area of comprehension, even accurate placement of a pupil in appropriate reading material requires a more sensitive measure of comprehension than this.

Validity is claimed for the *Botel* in several ways. Criterion-related validity (meaning the test correlates positively with some respected measure) is established by comparing scores on two subtests of the *Botel* (Word Recognition and Word Opposites) with actual placement in the Ginn basal readers. Although a fairly good sample of pupils was involved in this effort (over 600), several limitations seem evident. What is true for the Ginn program as it is used in one school district is not an especially accurate criterion for judging correct matching of pupils and materials.[16]

A second study based on the IRI scores of only thirty fourth-grade students produced correlation coefficients in the .77 to .94 range; however, such a small sample makes these results difficult to interpret.

High reliability is claimed for the *Botel* for both alternate forms and for internal consistency. There is no reason to doubt that results of the two forms would agree; the word lists come from common pools. However, the reported internal consistency appears to be oddly conceived. Scores for the Word Recognition and Word Opposites subtests were compared. The high correlations (.88 to .95) are cited as evidence of high reliability, but present a probability that both subtests are simply measuring the same abilities. How this demonstrates reliability is difficult to fathom. It seems to suggest that one can get at whatever the *Botel* measures regardless of which subtest one uses. This, in turn, casts considerable doubt on the accuracy of the labels assigned to the subtests and fails to address reliability altogether.

One last concern in the area of validity and reliability seems relevant. Nowhere are the Spelling and Decoding subtests compared with the results of other tests or placement results. This omission is especially troublesome given the general concern for the narrowness of the Decoding subtests. Since it is the Decoding subtests of the *Botel* that are described as having diagnostic value, this omission is a serious limitation. On balance, we cannot recommend the *Botel* for use by a classroom teacher.

Diagnostic Reading Scales

The *Diagnostic Reading Scales* were revised in 1981. The full test battery includes a graded word list (divided into three levels), two sets of graded reading passages (eleven in each set), and twelve separate word analysis and phonics tests intended for supplementary use. The *Scales* are administered individually to the student, who makes all responses orally. The entire test can be given in about sixty minutes. A prudent caution in the *Examiner's Manual* indicates that the professional judgment involved in using and interpreting this test (and the caution should include any diagnostic test) requires supervised training in a clinical setting. In response to feedback from those who have used the *Scales*, the 1981 version includes a ninety-minute tape cassette designed for inservice training in correct administration of the test. Special emphasis is given in the tape, as well as in the *Examiner's Manual*, to testing a student who speaks a "nonstandard" English dialect. This addition makes the *Scales* unique among diagnostic tests and enhances its value significantly.

The *Scales* are designed for use with students who are functioning at first through seventh grade levels. Stated purposes for the tests include the evaluation of oral and silent reading abilities and auditory comprehension. Although the manual indicates that the *Scales* are intended to help in the identification of a student's functional reading levels (that is, instructional, independent, and potential), an explicit disclaimer is made to distinguish between these levels as defined by Spache and the levels obtained from an IRI (in the manner of Betts). The criteria were established for determining the reading levels through actual tryouts with children. Thus success with the 2.2 level paragraph, for example, is judged by comparing the student's oral reading error rate with that of other students on that same material, not by applying a general word recognition accuracy level (for example 95 percent) regardless of the passage read.

The first subtest of the *Scales* requires the student to read aloud from a word list until five consecutive words are missed. The words came from the Durrell Word list and are grouped by difficulty on the basis of trials with about

100 students at each level of the *Scales*. The word lists are used, in part, as a pretest to determine which level should be used when entering the reading selection subtest. The manual also indicates that sight-word vocabulary and decoding strategies on words in isolation can be studied with the Word Recognition Lists. A word analysis checklist near the end of the *Examiner's Manual* is provided to help the teacher summarize observations about techniques the student uses on words in isolation and in context. Discussion in the *Examiner's Manual* indicates that performance on lists of isolated words is predictive of the child's instructional level. The test author, George Spache, is careful to point out that reading words in isolation requires different skills than reading words in context (except, he notes, for beginning readers). Information on how well the child reads words in context is obtained from the next subtest. Spache suggests that different instructional needs are revealed if a student is more successful with words in isolation or words in context. Errors detected under these two conditions should not be combined for analysis according to the *Manual*, a proper caution in our view.

A table is provided in the *Examiner's Manual* that enables the teacher to determine at which level to enter the reading selections for oral reading. This decision is made by using the number of isolated words read correctly in the first subtest.

The second subtest, Reading Selections, consists of eleven graded paragraphs ranging from grade levels 1.4 to 7.5 in difficulty. Two forms or sets of selections are provided to permit retesting on new material. Both narrative and expository material are included. As the pupil reads a selection aloud the teacher notes errors in the following categories: omission, addition, substitution, repetition, and reversal. Hesitations are not counted as errors and no provision is made for aiding the child. After a five-second pause, the child is encouraged to try a word, then skip it and go on if no response is given. Errors corrected spontaneously by the child are not counted. Multiple errors on the same word or phrase are counted as only one error.

The number of errors noted during oral reading of a passage is important in determining the child's instructional level. Each passage indicates the maximum number of errors permitted. Once that number has been exceeded, the previous level (where the maximum was not exceeded) is taken as the child's instructional level *if comprehension is adequate*.

Comprehension is assessed by means of questions the child answers orally when asked by the teacher. Seven questions are asked at levels 1.4–2.2, eight questions at level 2.4 and above. All questions are of a recall nature but involve language manipulations (transformations) that avoid mere rote answers. Field testing was conducted during development of the *Scales* to eliminate questions that were clearly not passage-dependent. The test author maintains that what may appear to be general knowledge to an adult may be unknown to a child, thus making a question passage-dependent for the child. Performance criteria for judging the child's comprehension are based on a 60 percent standard. Thus passages with seven questions require four correct responses and passages with eight questions require five correct responses for minimally acceptable performance. Several reviewers have questioned the use of a 60 percent criterion in earlier versions of the *Scales* for correct placement of students.[17] The 1981 *Examiner's Manual* states that more stringent standards yield underestimates of reading ability as determined by tryouts of the test with children using other oral reading tests, teacher judgment, and mental age as the external criterion.

The child's instructional level is found by determining the level at which oral reading accuracy *and* comprehension meet the minimum levels indicated. Thus a child who makes only ten errors on the 5.5 passage (below the maximum of thirteen allowed) but misses four of eight comprehension questions has failed one of the criteria. The instructional level in this case would be 4.5, the previous level where both criteria were met. The converse is also true: a child could answer seven of eight questions correctly, but not "pass" at a level because of excessive oral errors. The test manual suggests that in this case the teacher should decide if the reading errors are significant ones and if sufficient understanding is evidenced to override the oral error performance. By going on to the next passage a teacher can usually get further information to assist in judging which is the student's instructional level.

It should be noted that no attempt is made in the *Scales* to undertake qualitative analysis of oral reading miscues. Except for the practice of eliminating errors that are self-corrected and disregarding dialect differences, the *Scales* takes a quantitative approach to oral reading errors in determining instructional level. The *Examiner's Manual* is careful to explain that some types of errors are more significant than others, but that the difficulty level of the material being read is a factor in the kinds of errors made at different levels. Furthermore, to be reliable, miscue analysis must be based on a significant number of errors—probably fifty at the minimum. Because the passages in the *Scales* are short, they will not generate a sufficient number of miscues to make detailed analysis meaningful. Suggestions are given in the *Examiner's Manual* for looking at the graphic, phonic, syntactic, and semantic content of errors in an informal, though unsystematic way, for possible insights into the child's reading strategies. These insights can be recorded in the Word Analysis Checklist provided in the *Examiner's Record Book*.

After determining the child's instructional reading level via oral reading, the *Scales* direct the examiner to have the student silently read the selection one level above the orally read selection that was failed. While the pupil reads the teacher takes note of the time required to complete the selection. The teacher then asks the comprehension questions and records in the record book whether or not they are answered correctly. When the child's performance drops below 60 percent correct the silent reading test is terminated. The highest level at which the child reads with minimum accuracy is taken as the independent reading level.

Finally, the potential reading level is determined by having the teacher read to the pupil beginning one level above the last level read silently. Again the comprehension questions are asked following the completion of each selection. The 60 percent criterion is applied here in exactly the same manner as in determining the independent level.

The *Examiner's Manual* defines the instructional, independent, and potential levels and describes the use of each level in a classroom. The instructional level indicates the level of materials to be used for daily instruction. The independent level indicates the level of materials to be used for practice reading in both group oral reading and individual silent reading. It should be pointed out that because the terms are used in an unconventional way by Spache, for most children the independent level will be higher than the instructional level, a relationship that is normally reversed. Since the *Manual is* clear concerning just how the terms are being used, no problem arises with this difference as long as teachers are alert to the way the terms are defined. In any case, the independent level as determined by the *Scales* is not comparable to the independent level as it is usually designated by conventional informal reading inventories.[18] The potential level represents the level to which a child's reading performance can be raised with appropriate instruction. This notion is given considerable elaboration in the *Examiner's Manual* along with factors that must be considered in judging a child's potential.

The first two subtests in the *Scales*, the Word Recognition Lists and the Graded Reading Selections, are normally given to all students according to the sequence described above. Depending on what is learned from these tests, the teacher may decide to give some, all, or none of the remaining subtests. The Word Analysis and Phonics subtests have been sequenced according to their approximate difficulty for primary students, but can be given in any order. These subtests are not recommended by the manual for students reading above the fourth grade level for the very good reason that the skills tested are not directly related to reading comprehension.

Few tests are as direct and clear as this one in identifying assumptions made about the definition of reading being employed by the author. Additionally, Spache indicates that the supplementary subtests are not reliable enough to justify detailed interpretation of the scores. Appropriate cautions are also given about not judging pupil performance on the various subtests without allowing for the effects of the instructional program in place. Pupils in a program that deemphasizes phonics, for example, will not do as well on these subtests. The development of local standards is recommended for the Word Analysis and Phonics Tests.

The 1981 version of the *Scales* has expanded the number of supplementary word analysis tests from eight to twelve. Subtests now include:

1. Initial Consonants

2. Final Consonants

3. Consonant Digraphs

4. Consonant Blends

5. Initial Consonant Substitution

6. Initial Consonant Sounds Recognized Auditorily

7. Auditory Discrimination

8. Short and Long Vowel Sounds

9. Vowels with R

10. Vowel Diphthongs and Digraphs

11. Common Syllables or Phonograms

12. Blending

It is significant that nonsense words and real words beyond the sight word vocabulary of third graders are used in these subtests. This has been done to reduce the chances that children's performance will reflect their ability to recognize a word at sight rather than by applying their knowledge of the ability being tested. Thus, obvious care has been taken to make each subtest a valid measure of the ability indicated. For example, Test 6, Initial Consonant Sounds Recognized Auditorily, requires the child to listen to a word pronounced by the teacher and tell with which letter the word begins. Twenty-three items are included in this subtest. Three of the supplementary subtests have only nine or ten items (Initial Consonant Substitution, Vowels with r, and Blending). All others have fifteen or more items. The increased length of the supplementary tests is a positive feature of the 1981 revision of the *Scales*.

A review of the 1975 edition of the *Scales* by Schreiner is critical of the clarity of the test manual.[19] The 1981 version is markedly improved in this regard. A question and answer format is followed that is particularly clear and useful. Most questions raised were anticipated, and full yet succinct answers were provided. Proper cautions in using, interpreting, and supplementing the *Scales* are given in the *Manual*.

Reliability and validity data for the *Scales* are reported in a *Technical Report* (no date) available from the publisher. Evidence is reported to demonstrate that the 1981 revision corrects the tendency of earlier versions to overestimate students' reading ability. Some of this evidence relates to analysis of the reading passages using current readability formulas. Other evidence relates to the results of testing conducted by the publisher with students in first to eighth grades. Scores obtained with the *Scales* were compared to pupil performance on various standardized tests (for example, *Gates-MacGinitie Reading Tests*, *Iowa Test of Basic Skill*, etc.), the level of classroom reader assigned, and a teacher estimate of the child's reading level. High intercorrelations (at or above .80) were found among these variables.

Reliability was determined by retesting students after a period of two to eight weeks with the alternate set of reading selections: A correlation coefficient of .89 was found, thus suggesting a fair amount of consistency for test results obtained with the *Scales*. The Word Analysis and Phonics Tests yielded correlation coefficients on a test-retest basis in the .60 and above range for first and second grade with only one significant deviation (i.e., Initial Consonant Sounds Recognized Auditorily). These findings lend importance to the caution raised earlier about not placing confidence in the scores of individual subtests (a caution the *Examiner's Manual* is careful to make). On balance, the validity and reliability of the *Scales* seems well documented.

The *Examiner's Manual* specifies a general theory of reading diagnosis underlying the *Scales* and explains how each subtest relates to the reading process. One can make inferences about what view of reading the author holds. Both bottom-up and top-down processes are acknowledged in the discussion, but the tests themselves appear to focus more on textual factors. However, the test is not an embodiment of one reading theory. A rationale is given for the content of each subtest. The relationship between various reading abilities measured by the subtests is discussed. An extensive section of the *Manual* is devoted to interpretation of the results. The *Diagnostic Reading Scales* would be useful to a classroom teacher.

COMMERCIAL IRIs: ANALYTIC READING INVENTORY

Recent summaries by Jongsma and Jongsma (1981) and Harris and Niles (1982) compared and contrasted over a dozen commercial IRIs. While marked differences were found to exist among the inventories examined, there was also a commonality that distinguished IRIs from other instruments. The Woods and Moe (1981) *Analytical Reading Inventory* is typical of most IRIs in the following respects: (1) lists of high-frequency words in isolation are provided for testing word identification and for determining which passages should be used as a starting point; (2) graded passages from the primer level through ninth grade are provided in three separate forms; (3) comprehension questions are given to probe understanding at both a factual and inferential level; (4) forms are provided for recording and summarizing a student's performance; and (5) criteria are stated for judging the student's level of performance on each passage (independent, instructional, and frustrational levels).

The development of the *ARI* is described in fair detail in the test booklet. Topics of interest to children were selected and an attempt was made to make each form of the inventory comparable. The difficulty level of each passage was examined via readability procedures, the number of different words was controlled as were average sentence length, and the longest sentence for each level was controlled. Comprehension questions of six types were developed according to a taxonomy and care was taken to make each question passage–dependent. The inventory was field-tested with children and revised on the basis of difficulties encountered. Not all IRIs are developed with attention to the above details, nor is the process of development always described in the test booklet.

The *ARI* manual includes very little assistance for the teacher beyond

In an IRI testing situation the teacher makes notes concerning each deviation from the test as a child reads aloud. *(Peter Vadnai)*

how to administer the inventory and record the results. Roughly two pages of text are devoted to interpreting the results and providing appropriate follow-up instruction.

Seven types of oral reading miscues are noted in the *ARI*. They are: omissions, insertions, substitutions, aided words, repetitions, reversals, and hesitations. Provision is made for noting self-corrections, but it is not clear whether an error corrected by the pupil still counts toward the percentages used in calculating word recognition accuracy. A brief note in the manual cautions the teacher that, "Because not all deviations from the text are equally serious, the concern with the quality of the response is important." The teacher is then referred to the Goodman and Burke (1972) *Reading Miscue Inventory Manual*, but the full implications of this caveat are not addressed anywhere in the manual. A simplified "Qualitative Analysis Summary Sheet" focuses attention on whether a meaning change is involved in each miscue. The *ARI* does not give miscue analysis the full discussion it deserves. This may lull the unsuspecting teacher into the belief that quantitative analysis of miscues is sufficient for estimating placement and that qualitative analysis is necessary only in rare cases.

One other aspect of the *ARI* deserving special mention is the fact that the topic of each passage is briefly described for the examiner. The manual cautions that cuing prior to reading should be minimized but that some sort of introduction is appropriate if the student would otherwise be "confused" about the topic. The effect of introducing a passage when giving an IRI is unknown. According to Harris and Niles (1982), only three of twelve IRIs they examined included introductory statements. It is entirely possible that some students perform better when an advanced organizer is employed. The looseness of the *ARI* instructions on this matter are troublesome. How does the examiner decide who is "confused" and who is not? How much background should be built? One is inclined to avoid any kind of introductory remarks when giving an IRI. Interestingly, unlike some IRIs, *ARI* does not provide a title for each passage. This, too, is a variable that may affect IRI performance in an unknown way. Some IRIs (*Silvaroli*, for example) give both a title and a brief introduction to the passage (some also provide an illustration).

SKILLS MANAGEMENT SYSTEMS: PRESCRIPTIVE READING INVENTORY

A general description of skills management systems was provided on pages (323–324) of the previous chapter. An in-depth look at one such system follows.

The *Prescriptive Reading Inventory* (1977) was first published in 1972 and has been updated and refined periodically since that time. The *PRI* is described by the publisher as a "criterion-referenced testing system that measures mastery of reading objectives commonly taught in kindergarten through grade 6.5."

We have made it a point in our test reviews to discuss the implicit or explicit conceptualization of reading that the authors of a test use to develop their instrument. The *PRI*, like many other tests, is not explicit in specifying an underlying definition of reading. Unlike most other tests, the claim is made that the *PRI* is "constructed upon a set of behaviorally stated objectives most widely found in the national curriculum." On further examination it becomes clear that what this means is that five of the "most widely used basal reading programs" were taken to represent the "national curriculum." The test objectives were developed by identifying the reading behaviors implicit in the instructional programs of the five basals, pooling those objectives, grouping them according to similarities, and organizing them on a continuum from early decoding skills to critical thinking.

This procedure initially resulted in the identification of 1,248 behavioral objectives. The publisher carefully explains that these objectives merely represent common instructional methods and do not imply a definition of reading. The disagreement is, of course, that what gets tested becomes what is important. In this approach, reading becomes the sum of the parts after being broken into specific skills the pupil will be asked to master. It is true that the *PRI* suggests repeatedly that teachers should decide how well the test objectives match their instruction and adjust their use of the tests accordingly. Despite these cautions, however, the *PRI* by its very nature invites the teacher to regard reading as a set of separate behaviors that must be mastered in a particular sequence to achieve literacy. Furthermore, the *PRI* is presented as a device that is appropriate for determining who has attained mastery and who has not for the purpose of individualizing subsequent instruction.

The *PRI* consists of six levels as follows:

Level I	Grades K.0–1.0
Level II	Grades K.5–2.0
Level A/Red	Grades 1.5–2.5
Level B/Green	Grades 2.0–3.5
Level C/Blue	Grades 3.0–4.5
Level D/Orange	Grades 4.0–6.5

The tests can be administered in a group setting and are available in either hand- or machine-scorable versions.

The Level B test consists of 153 items that purport to measure the pupil's mastery of the objectives assigned to grades 2.0–3.5 by the test authors. The *Interpretive Handbook* provided with the test indicates that forty objectives are addressed by the Level B test. To illustrate, these objectives are included: "The student will identify a correct possessive form, as used in a phrase, from among the given singular, plural, singular possessive, and plural possessive forms of the same word," and "The student will define words in isolation by matching certain words with their definitions."

With respect to the objective on possessives, six items are included in the test. Two items require the child to choose the correct form of a possessive to go into a blank in a sentence. For example:

The _____ball is round.
children   childrens
childrens'   children's

Four items are based on a simple line drawing and two short sentences related to that drawing. For example, one drawing shows two kittens playing with a ball. The first sentence says, "I have two kittens." The child's task is to choose one of three words that best fits the blank in the second sentence:

They are _____kittens.
my   your   their

The second objective is measured by four items that give the child an isolated word and four definitions. The child selects the answer that tells what the word means. For example:

follow   a young man
            go in front
            come or go after
            make someone hurry

These examples give some feel for the type of items included in the *PRI*.

There are several problems with the test content. The first has to do with some items not measuring the objectives they purport to measure. In a review of the PRI, Farr suggests that enough problems exist in this realm to cause him to rate the *PRI* relatively low on this criterion.[20] He gives an example from the Level A test (the same problem appears in Level B) in which the child is told to find the word that has the same vowel sound as the underlined word. Here knowledge of terminology is being measured, not knowledge of sound-symbol associations.

A second problem with the *PRI* relates to a lack of reliability. The examples given above clearly illustrate that relatively few items measure any one objective. Consequently, few behaviors are sampled and little confidence can be placed in the results. This is particularly troublesome when judgments are being made about whether a child has "mastered a skill." By missing more than one item the child fails an objective. Conversely, by guessing correctly on only a few items a child can pass an objective.

The *PRI* tests are quite lengthy and, although untimed, take as much time as three hours to administer on a single level. As a result these tests would probably be given at the beginning of the year only. A second set of tests, the *PRI Interim Tests*, are available for monitoring student progress throughout the school year. The *Interim Tests* are keyed to the same skill objectives as the *PRI*, of course, and provide additional information about mastery of a particular skill.

The *PRI* is subject to the same limitations that plague nearly all skills management systems. The first of these concerns the important concept of mastery that underlies criterion-referenced testing. Once a person has "mastered" something, it would seem that further growth in that skill or ability is unnecessary (even impossible). Yet it is obvious that the reading act requires the application of skills mastered in materials that grow progressively more difficult. Thus a comprehension "skill" (if such a thing exists) apparently mastered when reading easy material may not generalize to harder material. Ability to "draw conclusions" while reading a simple narrative, for example, does not lend itself to absolute mastery. The same "skill" may not be performed successfully in a Michener novel where the ideas and language are much more complex. Mastery is a notion that might apply to knowing the multiplication tables or even the letters of the alphabet, but does not apply to the thinking and problem solving skills basic to reading with understanding.

Even more basic than the above, however, is the lack of evidence that one must "master" the skills identified in the *PRI* (or other SMS) in order to read successfully. The fact that good readers do better on certain test items does not establish the content validity of that "skill." It does not follow that readers will perform better by learning the skill or knowledge measured by those test items.

Nearly all criterion-referenced tests have built into them certain assumptions regarding an optimal sequence for skill acquisition. In most cases this sequence is hierarchical in nature—that is, the skills tested build one upon another with one apparently serving as a prerequisite for the next. No evidence exists to indicate that these assumptions are applicable to reading. Yet teachers who use and believe skills management systems are led to accept the structure built into them.

There are serious reservations about any skills management system and we urge that teachers not use them if they have a choice in the matter.

As noted in Chapter 12, most basal reader programs now include a skills management system. The free standing system reviewed here is more representative of all such systems than one tied to a particular instructional program.

SUMMARY

This chapter provided detailed information about several types of reading tests: a survey test, two group and five individually administered diagnostic tests, an informal reading inventory, and a skills management system. The primary purpose was to examine these tests as examples of commercially prepared tests that can be purchased for use in the classroom and clinic. The contents of each test were described and cautions and concerns that need to be considered in their administration and interpretation were raised. Daily instruction can be planned and evaluated more effectively with the use of informal measures than with formal tests like the ones reviewed in this chapter. However, the informed teacher needs to be aware of formal tests and how to use them wisely. In certain situations, commercial tests are useful, but only if they are understood as samples of reading behavior gathered under controlled conditions.

SUGGESTED ACTIVITIES

1. Borrow a standardized reading test from your professor or curriculum lab. Read through the administrator's manual for the test noting in particular:

How to give the test

How to score the test

How to interpret the results of the test

Validity and reliability of the test

Take the test yourself. Watch for tasks that are ambiguous or confusing. Ask yourself how well performance on the items in this test match with your own conception of what is important in reading.

2. Locate a review of the test you examined in task 1 (above) in the Mental Measurements Yearbook or other collection of test reviews. Read the review and compare the reviewers' comments to your own observations.

3. Administer the test examined in tasks 1 and 2 (above) to a child, score the results, and develop a plan for incorporating the findings into the child's daily instruction. If possible, administer another reading test to the same child,

score, interpret, and compare the results. Determine whether the implications for instruction from the two tests are consistent. Discuss your conclusions with the child's classroom teacher.

NOTES

1. See Kress in Buros (1978), p. 1124.
2. See Buros (1978).
3. See Bryant in Buros (1978), p. 1124.
4. See Durrell and Catterson (1980).
5. See Fredrickson (1975); Grimes (1975).
6. See Smith (1979).
7. See Durrell and Catterson (1980).
8. See Singer (1978b), p. 1253.
9. See Singer (1978b).
10. See Buros (1978).
11. See Woodcock (1971), p. 21.
12. See Buros (1978), p. 1304.
13. See Buros (1978).
14. See Dwyer (1978); Tuinman (1978); Houck and Harris (1976).
15. See *Botel Reading Inventory Administration Manual* (1981), p. 6.
16. See Spache (1981).
17. See Stafford (1974); Schreiner (1978).
18. See Mosenthal (1981).
19. See Buros (1978).
20. See Buros (1978).

SUGGESTED READINGS

JOHNSTON, PETER H. (1984). Assessment in reading. In P. David Pearson (Ed.), *Handbook of reading research* (pp. 147–182). New York: Longman. This book reviews and summarizes investigations concerned with the assessment of reading and argues that the heavy reliance on product measures evident in the literature is largely inconsistent with the current emphasis on process in reading instruction and reading research.

JOHNSON, MARJORIE SEDDON, KRESS, ROY A., AND PIKULSKI, JOHN J. (1987). *Informal reading inventories* (2nd ed.). Newark, DE: International Reading Association. This book describes the nature of and purposes for using informal reading inventories (IRIs). It provides guidance on the administration, recording, and scoring of IRIs, and for interpreting the results in a diagnostic manner. It includes instructions for constructing IRIs and gives three case examples.

MITCHELL, JR., JAMES V. (ED.). (1985). *Ninth mental measurements yearbook.* Lincoln, NB: The University of Nebraska Press. This yearbook updates and extends the eight previous editions of this standard reference previously edited by founder Oscar K. Buros on educational tests and testing. It provides comprehensive information on stand-ardized tests of all types including oral reading, reading readiness, special fields of reading, reading speed, study skills, and miscellaneous reading tests. Basic information is provided about each test (title, copyright date, cost, author, publisher, and so forth) followed by a test references section listing all known references on the construction, validity, use, and limitations of the test. Several reviews written by experts are then provided for each test.

SCHELL, LEO M. (ED.). (1981). *Diagnostic and criterion-referenced reading tests: Review and evaluation.* Newark, DE: International Reading Association
Provides critical reivews of twelve of the most commonly used reading tests.

SCHREINER, ROBERT. (ED.). (1979). *Reading tests and teachers: A practical guide.* Newark, DE: International Reading Association.
Testing is described in this booklet as only one part of the total classroom evaluation process. The appropriate way to select tests, how to develop valid and reliable tests, and how to use test results in planning instruction are also discussed

Chapter 14

Special Remedial Techniques

OVERVIEW

As you read this chapter use the following list of main ideas to guide your understanding and reflection.

Specialists in a clinic setting provide some remedial reading instruction outside the regular classroom.

Most remedial instruction provided in a clinic is not unique but simply intensifies and individualizes the methods a classroom teacher uses.

Classroom teachers who know the techniques used in special remedial programs can coordinate their own instructional programs with the special programs as appropriate.

Principles and techniques used in clinic programs can sometimes be borrowed successfully by the classroom teacher for use in the regular classroom.

Some remedial strategies involve a number of senses to heighten the learner's involvement: examples include the Fernald tracing method and the Orton-Gillingham-Stillman method.

Some remedial reading programs, such as DISTAR, use intensive or synthetic phonics programs.

Effective classroom reading instruction attempts to prevent serious problems by identifying and correcting them before they require the attention of a special reading teacher.

Effective remedial programs offered outside the regular classroom complement and supplement the classroom teacher's instruction.

Successful remedial reading programs do not conform to one set pattern but are characterized by certain principles:

> They base instruction on learners' interests.

> They provide success to break the cycle of failure.

> They use actual reading.

Previous chapters of this book have demonstrated the conviction that remediation is an activity that can and should occur in the regular classroom. This book was written primarily for the classroom teacher and has taken the position throughout that within the daily instructional program there are numerous opportunities to assess reading progress and to adjust immediately to the needs of students experiencing difficulty. Many problems that, if neglected, could evolve into serious reading disabilities are thus nipped in the bud.

Despite the belief that remediation is an ongoing responsibility of the classroom teacher, it would be derelict to suggest that all reading problems can or will be handled in this fashion. Remedial instruction has been provided by reading specialists for decades, and there are no signs that this approach is about to be abandoned. (However, fewer remedial programs, especially federally funded ones such as Chapter I, will exist in the future, thus making regular classroom remediation even more important that it has been.) The intent of this comment should be clear: special remedial programs should not be abandoned. As will be indicated later in this chapter, reading clinics (the name often used to identify special remedial programs provided outside the regular classroom) often offer the best means for helping some children. However, a main theme of this text is that remediation can and should be an ongoing activity of the regular teacher. Consequently a more complete discussion of clinical reading programs has been left for other textbooks written especially for the specialist in reading.

Since there may be pupils in the classroom who participate in special reading programs, a teacher needs to have a sense of what occurs in those programs and how to build on the help that has been provided. Although most special reading programs use the same developmental methods and materials as classroom teachers, certain more individualized learning techniques are used more often by reading specialists. The reason these techniques are used less frequently by classroom teachers is because they demand more time and attention than is normally available to someone who must manage an entire class. By knowing about these approaches a teacher will be in a better position to consider how they might be adjusted for use in the classroom.

This chapter first looks at multisensory techniques as represented by the Fernald method and the Orton-Gillingham-Stillman method, then considers synthetic phonics methods and examines the *DISTAR* program as an example. A final section describes principles that should undergird any remedial program provided outside the regular classroom.

MULTISENSORY TECHNIQUES

A number of special instructional techniques are based on the principle of using multiple senses to introduce and study new words. In a typical classroom reading lesson the teacher introduces a new word by writing it on the chalkboard and asking someone to pronounce it. A sound-symbol (phonic) attack may be made as a way of teaching its pronunciation. Some teachers make it a point to discuss the meaning of the word, and some have children use the word in a sentence. Other activities might involve looking up a new word in the glossary or dictionary and writing the definition found in a notebook or examining the word for conformance to a particular spelling pattern.

Multisensory teaching techniques attempt to intensify the child's learning by involving as many senses as possible. *(Alan Carey/The Image Works)*

This by no means exhausts the possibilities, but in a normal classroom situation few teachers go beyond this in introducing a word, and many stop well short of using all these means. Most children can learn new words using these activities, particularly if a story to be read uses the words a number of times in varied contexts and if follow-up activities involve further practice with the words. As indicated, however, not all children succeed with this approach. One explanation offered suggests that some children need more sensory input than this in order to learn and, consequently, teachers should develop a repertoire of multisensory learning activities.

The scenario described earlier involves only two of the child's senses—visual and auditory. The child *sees* the word and *hears* the word. When children also pronounce or write the word, motor involvement occurs as well. Normally, two or at most three senses are involved. Kirk, Kliebhan, and Lerner (1978) state, "The theory underlying the . . . multisensory approach is that the more avenues of sensory input that are activated and combined in a single learning experience, the greater the probability of success."

Two highly structured approaches to remediation springing from the multisenses notion are those described by Fernald (1943) and Gillingham and Stillman (1966).

The Fernald Method

The Fernald method is a label applied to an approach developed and first used successfully at the clinic school of UCLA in the 1920s. Grace Fernald, a professor of pyschology at UCLA, described her approach in great detail in a book titled *Remedial Techniques in Basic School Subjects* (1943) that has become a classic in the fields of reading, reading disability, and learning disability. In addition to a full description of her tracing technique and how it can be used with total and partial reading-disabled students, Fernald provides numerous case studies in her book that document the effectiveness of her approach. Although a summary of her method will be presented here, one must read the original to gain a full sense of how the Fernald method works.

The child, Alex, is first asked to select any word he wants to learn, regardless of length or difficulty. Of course, the principle at work here is that the meaning of the word will be known to the child and interest will be high. The word selected might be a name or a topic of personal interest, such as *motorcycle*.

The teacher writes the word on a large (4" x 10") strip of paper with crayon or felt-tipped pen. Manuscript or cursive writing is used depending on which seems best for the age of the child (whatever is used in the classroom is a factor in this determination). Alex then traces the word with a finger that is in contact with the paper saying the word slowly but without exaggeration as he traces it. He repeats this tracing and recitation process until he can write the word on a separate piece of paper *without looking at the original*. This is not to be a task of copying, so the original word card is covered while he writes from memory. If he cannot write the word successfully from memory, he goes back to the original and traces and recites the word again until he knows it. When he is again ready to try writing the word from memory, he starts with a fresh piece of paper. A new piece of paper is also used if an error is made and he wants to start again—no erasures are permitted.

This process of tracing and saying the original word and then writing the word from memory on a separate piece of paper continues until Alex gets the word correct. Once he gets the word correct, he writes it on a piece of scrap paper and uses it in a story. The story would be comprised of words Alex knows or learns with his tracing technique. The story is typed for him and he reads it in print within a twenty-four-hour period. After the story is finished, Alex alphabetically files the original word cards written by the teacher in his word file. Fernald emphasizes that the child should know the meaning of the words learned in this manner and that they should always be used in context.

This first stage, called the Tracing Stage, is one Alex may be ready to leave in two to eight months. Stage II is the same as Stage I except that tracing is no longer necessary. Fernald indicates that a child will eventually discover that he or she no longer needs to trace a word in order to learn it. As fewer and fewer tracings become necessary, Alex gradually develops the ability to learn any new word by looking at it, saying it to himself, and then writing it down without copying while continuing to say the word to himself. The steps of getting the story typed, reading it, and filing the word cards continue in Stage II. In her book Fernald makes the point that while writing the word, the child must continue saying it either aloud or silently. She also states that Stages I and II overlap considerably in that some words will need to be traced while others will not.

Alex enters Stage III when he is able to learn a printed word by merely looking at it and saying it to himself before he writes it. Notice that in this stage Alex is not dependent upon the teacher to write a word down for him as the first step. It may be necessary for the teacher to help Alex pronounce some words initially since he is now dealing with an author's words rather than ones he has selected. According to Fernald, the child may still read poorly at this stage, not even recognizing some "easy" words. He will recognize the words he has written down, however, and will want to start reading from books. The teacher should encourage his reading and help with unknown words. After reading, those unknown words become ones that Alex writes down and files in his word file. Review of these words on a periodic basis is helpful.

Stage IV finds Alex beginning to generalize about how printed symbols represent spoken language. He recognizes words from their resemblance to other words already known. If topics of personal interest to Alex are selected, he will tackle books and other reading material with enthusiasm, according to Fernald.

In contrast to other approaches to remediation, the Fernald method requires Alex to do his own reading (even at home) rather than being read to.

Later, when he reads fluently, he may listen to others read. Alex must also never be asked to sound out words as he is reading. The teacher can suggest that he write the word, but phonic analysis is strictly forbidden by Fernald. A clear and complete distinction is made by Fernald between reading a word and spelling it. Heavy emphasis is given to the use of context and help is given immediately by the teacher if a word is not known. As the teacher pronounces unknown words, Alex writes them down and later studies them if they are "common enough to be important."

Fenald writes of three other abilities that must be developed to bring a disabled reader through the four stages to a point of literacy. The first ability is familiarity with word forms. The child must be able to see enough similarities between new and familiar words to identify the unknown words. The second ability is having a reading vocabulary that is large enough to comprehend the material encountered. The third ability is having sufficient concept development to understand how word groups express meaning "in any new content." According to Fernald, all three abilities derive from large amounts of reading.

Although there is more to the development of these abilities than simply reading, Fernald's theoretical views and her approach are both sensible and workable. The Fernald method demands a great deal of individual attention, thus making it impractical for widescale use in a classroom. However, techniques often used in the classroom such as the language experience approach, kinesthetic and tactile involvement of the learner, building on the learner's interests, word card files, emphasis on word meaning, and the use of words in context are all compatible with the Fernald method.

The Alphabetic Method of Orton-Gillingham-Stillman

Another remedial method, properly labeled multisensory, is variously referred to as the Gillingham method, the Orton-Gillingham method, or the Gillingham-Stillman method. Based on a theory developed by a professor of psychiatry at the University of Iowa, Samuel T. Orton (1937), and translated into an instructional strategy by psychologist Anna Gillingham and remedial teacher Bessie W. Stillman (1966), the method uses a multisensory approach to teach the sounds and letters of the alphabet. In contrast to Fernald's whole-word method of learning, the *alphabetic method* of Orton-Gillingham-Stillman focuses the child's attention on individual letters. Tracing is employed in a manner not much different from that in the Fernald method, but the assumptions made about the reading process are in sharp contrast to Fernald.

Orton was a neurologist who developed a special interest in language disorders. He observed that among children with "specific language disabilities" a high percentage exhibited mixed laterality or mixed handedness. This suggested to Orton that one hemisphere of the brain had not gained dominance, as normally occurs, thus leading to confusion for those pupils in language-related activities. According to Orton, a right-handed person normally develops a dominant left brain hemisphere (and vice versa). In cases where dominance was not well established (mixed), the child would tend to reverse and confuse word symbols while reading because impressions made on the opposite brain hemisphere while learning a word could not be ignored or suppressed. In other words, a clear image could not be learned. This confusion could occur in visual, auditory, and kinesthetic fields, thus causing errors in reading, writing, listening, and even speaking. Gillingham and Stillman (1966) state: "The degree to which the language function of an individual is controlled by one hemisphere determines the degree of language or disability in that individual."[1]

The solution, in the view of Orton, Gillingham, and Stillman, is to set up *associations* in the brain by having the learner *see* a letter, *hear* the sound the letter represents, *trace* the letter, and *write* the letter. Through simultaneous use of all modalities, the child establishes an appropriate association that is not confused later. However, Orton (1937) indicates that "simply teaching the child to give the sounds for each letter of the alphabet and for the phonograms, etc., is hopelessly inadequate for his needs." What is lacking, according to Orton, is the next step of "teaching blending of the letter sounds in the exact sequence in which they occur in the word."[2]

Detailed directions for implementing the Alphabetic Method are given in a manual by Gillingham and Stillman (1966). Little more can be done here than to give the flavor of this approach. To fully grasp the technique one must read the manual and practice the steps involved with a pupil. According to the authors, any deviation from the directions is unacceptable. They also state that no other instruction in reading, writing, or spelling should be provided while using their method. Furthermore, instruction requires a minimum of two years on a daily basis in order to be effective.

The teacher first exposes a letter card to the pupil and says the name of the letter. The pupil repeats the letter aloud. This is repeated until the letter name has been mastered.

Next the teacher gives a sound for the letter. The child repeats the sound. "Correct" pronunciation of the sound is emphasized by the authors. (The pronunciation key of the *Webster's Elementary Dictionary* is the standard for judging correctness.)

The teacher then makes the sound for a letter (or phonogram) and asks the pupil to tell the name of the letter that has that sound. No card is visible to the child.

Next the teacher writes the letter according to directions given in the manual and explains each form to the pupil. The pupil then traces the letter and writes it twice from memory.

Finally, the teacher gives the sound of the letter saying, "Write the letter that has this sound."

One letter is introduced per day until ten letters have been learned (*a, b, f, h, i, j, k, m, p, t*). These letters are then blended into short words that

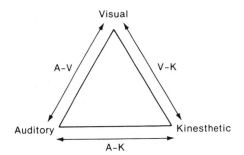

FIGURE 14.1   Language Triangle

follow a CVC pattern (for example, *pat, fat, ran, fun*). Simple sentences comprised of words using only the letters learned are read (*Fat cat ran*).

The procedure is based on associating visual, auditory, and kinesthetic elements in a language triangle, as shown in Figure 14.1.

Two aspects of the Orton-Gillingham-Stillman approach merit attention: (1) the remedial activities, and (2) the underlying theory (cerebral hemispheric dominance). The suggested remedial activities can be used regardless of whether or not Orton's ideas about dominance are accepted. Depending on how one views the reading process (especially with respect to word identification) and depending on how one believes children who are experiencing reading difficulties can best be helped, the high degree of structure and the intensity of the method may or may not be valued. In other words, one could disbelieve Orton's explanation of reading difficulties but still endorse the instructional activities spawned by that theory. The novelty of the approach, the enthusiasm of the teacher, and the intensity of the instruction may be more powerful factors than the uniqueness of the system. In any event, teachers should understand the rationale for the method and how it works.

There are reservations about the underlying theory. A thorough review of the relevant literature by Spache (1976) leaves little doubt concerning the validity of Orton's mixed dominance theory. Reversals (for example, reading *saw* for *was*), the symptom of greatest importance to Orton's theory, merely reflect normal development and decrease as a function of age and reading competence. Word images are not projected onto a screen which the brain then interprets. "Word images . . . are really neurochemical traces in the neurons of the brain. They are not received or stored in two dimensions, so a reversal is thus impossible. How would one reverse laterally the traces of catalysts and delimiting chemicals that initiate or terminate the action of a nerve cell?"[3] Lawson (1968) points out that the tendency to make reversals is psychological and something that even good readers do. While language functions do seem to center in the left hemisphere of the brain, damage to that area of the brain does not prevent the recovery of language abilities.[4]

SYNTHETIC PHONICS METHODS

Another type of remediation might properly be labeled intensive or synthetic phonics. Synthetic phonics is a label that refers to programs that emphasize the memorization of isolated elements such as the "sound of the letter b." Once the individual elements are learned, they can be applied to the identification of words through "sounding out" and "blending" the word parts. These methods emphasize the association of sounds and symbols through systematic drill and repetition. Letters of the alphabet, consonants, vowels, blending, and syllabication are typically learned, the learning sequence depending on which breed of synthetic phonics one examines. Some synthetic phonics programs come in commercially prepared packages. Examples include *DISTAR* published by SRA, and *Book A* of the Lippincott basal series. Other programs are described in books and articles, but employ primarily teacher-made materials. Examples include *Phonovisual*,[5] the *Carden Method*,[6] *Remedial Reading Drills*,[7] and the *Alphabetic Method*.[8] The fact that the Gillingham-Stillman system was described previously as a multisensory approach illustrates the inevitable overlap that exists among remedial methods. The Alphabetic Method is a synthetic phonics method as well as a multisensory method.

The synthetic approach contrasts with analytic phonics where whole words are learned initially through visual memory then analyzed for sound-symbol regularities. To illustrate, using an analytic approach, the words *boy*, *big*, and *ball* would first be learned as sight words, then compared to arrive at a generalization about the "sound of the letter b." Greater detail is given about analytic phonics in Chapter 6. This chapter will look carefully at the *DISTAR* program as an example of a commercial synthetic phonics program.

The DISTAR Program

The name *DISTAR* is a copyrighted acronym standing for "Direct Instruction Systems for Teaching Arithmetic and Reading." The *DISTAR* designation is applied to a number of programs published by Science Research Associates (SRA). *DISTAR Reading* is described as a basal reading series for preschool through third grade and is organized into *Reading I*, *Reading II*, and *Reading III* (*Reading III* was recently replaced by *Reading Mastery, Level III*). It is important to make several points about *DISTAR* before describing the program.

First, although *DISTAR Reading* is discussed in the context of a chapter on remedial approaches, the publisher and authors of the program intend it for developmental purposes. Nevertheless, *DISTAR* is often used by school systems for remedial instruction, thus prompting its inclusion here. Second, *DISTAR* is both a synthetic phonic program and a "direct instructional" program. The two elements are closely interwoven in *DISTAR*, but are not inseparable. In other words, one can implement a synthetic phonics program using other approaches to teaching and one could teach different content using the direct instruction system developed by Carl Bereiter and Siegfried

Synthetic phonics programs place heavy emphasis on memorization and "sounding out" words. *(Peter Vadnai)*

Englemann. The two elements should be kept separate since this best serves our purposes, but the uniqueness of *DISTAR* lies in its combination of content and method. It might be easier to describe *Phonovisual, Play n' Talk Phonics,* or the *Phonetic Keys to Reading* as examples of synthetic phonics programs, but it appears that these programs are not widely used in schools today, and consequently, do not merit the analysis required. The fact that a review of *DISTAR* is included should not be construed as an endorsement of the program.

Content of the DISTAR Program The philosophy underlying *DISTAR Reading I* is summarized in this statement from the teacher's guide: "The children must learn to identify and reproduce the sounds automatically if they are to decode words successfully. They need a great deal of practice in order to learn these sound symbols."[9]

Level I of *DISTAR Reading* introduces children to symbol identification as the first step in learning to read. This is essentially a matter of first learning to associate a sound with each of eight letters (*a, m, s, e, r, d, f,* and *i*). The sounds are learned in isolation without key words or picture clues through repetitive drill involving modeling by the teacher, imitation by the children, testing, and immediate feedback. All these elements are included in each lesson which is carefully directed step by step by the teacher. The sample from the *Teacher's Guide* in Figure 14.2 gives a more specific idea of how *DISTAR* lessons operate.

FIGURE 14.2   Sample from the DISTAR Teacher's Guide

Lesson 27

Sounds

TASK 1 Teaching **d** as in **dad**
---

a. Point to **d**. Here's a new sound.
   It's a quick sound.
b. My turn. (Pause.) Touch **d** for an
   instant, saying: d. Do not say
   duuh or **diih** or **dee**.
c. Again. Touch **d** and say: d.
d. Point to **d**. Your turn. When I
   touch it, you say it. (Pause.)
   Get ready. Touch **d**. *d*.
e. Again. Touch **d**. *d*.
f. Repeat *e* until firm.

SOURCE: From DISTAR® READING I, Teacher's Guide, by Siegfried Engelman. © 1974, 1969, Science Research Associates, Inc. Reprinted by permission of the publisher.

All forty sounds taught in the program are introduced in the first 158 lessons. Figure 14.3 shows the order of presentation and the day of introduction of each sound (one sound about every four days).

Once several sounds have been learned, sequencing (the order in which to read symbols), blending, and rhyming are introduced systematically over a series of thirty-six lessons. Beginning with Lesson 37, "children put all the skills together and begin to decode their first regularly spelled words." Decoding involves identifying the sounds in the words, sounding out the letters without stopping between sounds, "saying the word fast," then telling the teacher what word they have read.

By Lesson 96 sounding is no longer necessary, according to the manual, and children call whole words "reading the fast way." Sounding out is used only when a word has been misidentified. Story reading begins with Lesson 40. Most words in the lessons and stories are regular ones that conform to the sounding patterns the children have been taught. (The exceptions are handled by introducing joined letters for blends, and macrons to make "long" vowels where they would ordinarily be "short." Silent letters are printed in smaller type.)

The lessons in *DISTAR Reading* are sequenced with the assumption that one lesson serves as a prerequisite for the next. Only after mastery of a lesson has been reached by the slowest member of a group does the group move forward. Subsequent lessons present new facts (skills) and review facts (skills) learned in previous lessons.

Comprehension is given relatively little attention in *Reading, Level I*. Pictures are used to test understanding beginning with Lesson 40. Beginning with Lesson 75 the teacher asks questions about the stories for purposes of evaluation. Beginning at Lesson 151 an activity called *Read the Items* tests the

FIGURE 14.3   Sounds in Order of Presentation with Day of Introduction

a	m	s	ē	r	d
1 and 13	6 and 11	16	19	23	27

f	i	th	t	n	c	o
31	34	38	41	44	48	51

ā	h	u	g	l	w
58	61	64	68	72	76

sh	I	k	ō	v	p
80	88	92	98	102	108

ch	e	b	ing	ī
113	118	121	124	127

y	er	x	oo	J
131	135	139	142	145

ȳ	wh	qu	z	ū
149	152	154	156	158

SOURCE: From DISTAR® READING I, Teacher's Guide, by Siegfried Engelman. © 1974, 1969, Science Research Associates, Inc. Reprinted by permission of the publisher.

ability to follow directions and carry out instructions. Discussion of what is read is generally discouraged beyond assuring that the questions asked can be answered.

DISTAR Reading founders on the same rock that imperils all synthetic phonic programs: irregular words. The *Teacher's Guide* indicates that irregular words, that is, words that do not conform to predictable sound-symbol rules, are *not* taught as sight words. Rather they are sounded out by the children then pronounced by the teacher, who first says, "That's the way we sound it out, but here's the way we say it . . . ". After several days of first sounding then saying the word, the children learn to discriminate between the way it is sounded and the way it is pronounced. The goal is to show that some correspondence exists between the way a word is sounded and the way it is said.

The manual is careful to say that irregular words are not taught as sight words. They must be sounded first and they must never be "said the fast way"[10] (*Teacher's Guide*, p. 34). (It is evident why *said*, *was*, and *boy*, used in the examples, are not said the fast way since their phonetic pronunciation would be quite foreign to their normal pronunciation.) Yet the manual also says the goal of the program "is that children ultimately be able to read words without first sounding them out. In this program this kind of reading is called reading the fast way." As we interpret this, the child is to *read* irregular words the fast way, yet these are *not* sight words. The problem, of course, is that proponents of synthetic phonics reject the recognition of words at sight but find no alternative when highly irregular words are at issue. Pupils are in a particularly difficult spot once they are reading independently, of course, since no one is handy to say which words are regular and which are irregular. Thus, a "sounding strategy" as a first method of attack can cause some readers a considerable amount of confusion. The problem is compounded in the *DISTAR* program by the instructions "not to guess" at unknown words. The *Teacher's Guide* insists that the teacher have the pupil resort to sounding because "the symbols in the word determine what the word is." Not once is the child directed to ask what makes sense based on language clues or prior knowledge. This seems to be a serious flaw. Children should always read for meaning and should approach word identification flexibly using several tactics that result in a sensible interpretation.

The Direct Instruction System   The instructional methods underlying *DISTAR* are built on the belief that "all children can learn *if we teach them carefully*" [emphasis ours]. Further, instruction is effective "only if the teacher does what is required to ensure that the children master each skill."[11] Accordingly, "What the teacher does and says is specified. The teacher is not given general instruction; rather, he or she is provided with the exact words to use when presenting each of the tasks. Other behaviors—pointing, signaling the group to respond, and the like—are specified precisely. The program indicates where the children are likely to make mistakes and precisely what the teacher should do to correct each mistake."[12]

Obviously *DISTAR Reading* is a teacher-centered approach. The implication is strong that failure to learn is the teacher's fault. The *Teacher's Guide* states: "Well-intentioned teachers frequently confuse children, particularly low-performing children, with explanations that are beyond the children's understanding" (p. 1). To avoid teaching errors the *DISTAR Teacher's Guide* is thorough and complete even to the extent of showing and prescribing exactly what to say and how to give hand signals ("How to Point," "How to Touch," and so forth). Critical behaviors are listed for checking one's performance and common teaching errors identified for each teaching behavior. Teachers are expected to learn the *DISTAR* system first by watching an experienced teacher perform then by practicing in front of a fellow beginner who gives feedback and suggestions.

Lessons are conducted in a rapid-fire, no-nonsense manner with admonitions to the children to, "Sit tall, look at the book, and talk tall." Praise is dispensed generously for correct performance, and raisins, crackers, or points for earning a small toy are recommended as alternative rewards when necessary. Instruction on each "skill" is continued until the slowest learner in the group is "firm" or at criterion (can perform immediately with the correct response). The teacher first models what the children are to learn then says, "Do it with me." This is repeated until everyone is responding, then individuals are instructed to perform. When everyone is "firm" the lesson moves on to another task.

Teachers are also given very specific instructions in *DISTAR Reading* concerning how to form three reading groups, even to the extent of specifying the relative size of each group (for example, the highest performing group should be the largest). A placement test consisting of only five items is used for grouping. Children who miss no more than one item go into the highest group and begin at Lesson 11. All others are "ranked" and the lowest five or six become the low group. Instruction begins with Lesson 1 for groups two and three. One lesson is taught to each group every day. Provision is made for more capable groups to skip lessons so that they can complete the program in 120 days. Regrouping during the year is encouraged.

Reading lessons are scheduled on every available day as follows:

Teacher instruction of groups: 35 to 40 minutes a day for each group

Children's independent work: 20 to 30 minutes a day for each group

Work check: 20 minutes a day for all groups

Mastery tests are administered individually to each child every five days. Only a minute or two is required to give these tests, but they are *not* to be given during the reading lesson. Test results are used to regroup when necessary, to skip lessons when appropriate, to "backup" daily evaluation, and as a source of feedback on the effectiveness of the teaching being provided. This last purpose is given special emphasis in the *Teacher's Guide*, reinforcing the notion that failures to learn indicate the teacher is not performing as the program specifies.

The almost stifling thoroughness of the *DISTAR* instructional program is striking. The program is certainly noteworthy insofar as its design and execution are concerned. Much as children are controlled by the teacher in each lesson, the teacher is controlled by the program in *DISTAR Reading*. On this latter point there is considerable concern, however, because we see a teacher as a professional decision maker, not a technician working from a script. The amount of control over both teacher and child is stifling and consequently unacceptable. Although some schools report notable success with *DISTAR*, their tests may not be appropriate measures. Early gains on decoding abilities are being made by *DISTAR* at the expense of long-term growth in reading for meaning.

AN EFFECTIVE REMEDIAL READING PROGRAM

Suppose for a moment that you are the parent of a child who is having difficulty with reading. What type of remedial instruction would you like to see available in your child's school? In other words, what does an effective remedial reading program look like?

Speaking for ourselves, we would like to see an emphasis on the "preventive maintenance" principle advocated by one of the United States auto manufacturers. Preventive maintenance means routine care of important items and systematic inspection of areas where undetected problems could become serious if allowed to continue. With your automobile this means changing the oil, oil filter, air filter, spark plugs, and the like on a regular basis and checking wheel bearings, brake linings, transmission fluid, and so forth according to a schedule. With this approach one does not wait until a transmission begins to slip to have it inspected. By the time a transmission slips it may be too late to merely add transmission fluid; expensive repairs may be necessary.

In a school reading program, the regular classroom serves as a "preventive care center." Problems in reading are avoided to whatever extent possible by systematically monitoring the child's progress. Through largely informal means, the skillful teacher determines that progress is being made in important areas. Numerous opportunities are provided for reviewing and practicing new concepts and skills. When evidence of confusion or misunderstanding is found, instruction is provided immediately to overcome the problem. Some authorities call in-class attention to problems of this type *corrective instruction*[13]; others use the term *remediation*.[14] The label is less important than the idea that problems are dealt with routinely by the classroom teacher at the time they are discovered.

Furthermore, the teacher is constantly watching for evidence that remediation is needed and regards this as a normal occurrence.

Not all reading problems are ones the classroom teacher can be expected to handle, of course. Despite careful attention to regular, ongoing assessment and immediate, in-class remediation, some cases require the attention of a reading specialist. The availability of such a specialist is an important element in an effective remedial reading program. The regular classroom teacher should be able to refer pupils with severe problems or problems of a unique nature to the specialist for help.

Before describing our vision of an effective remedial reading program offered by a reading specialist, there are several additional points that should be made about the regular classroom as a preventive care center. Returning to one of our on-going themes, the teacher's conceptualization of reading is critical when seeking evidence of growth and, conversely, problems in reading. As pointed out earlier, a skillful classroom teacher regards temporary difficulties in reading as normal. Here it should be emphasized that what the teacher regards as an error and what the teacher considers to be evidence of a difficulty are critical. It is one thing to believe that occasional difficulties are normal and quite another thing to believe that some traditional "errors" are not really "errors" at all, but simply reflect the imprecise, constructive nature of the reading act. This perspective has been discussed fully at various places in this text so further elaboration seems unnecessary. It should be obvious that what the teacher regards as a reading problem is dependent on one's conceptualization of reading, which in turn has immediate implications for how remediation is approached.

The teacher who takes a strictly quantitative approach to oral reading miscues, for example, might identify a particular child's miscue level as evidence of the need for remediation and subsequent remedial instruction might focus on accuracy in word pronunciation. The result might be "better" oral reading (more accurate) but *less* comprehension. Given the teacher's view of reading, remediation has seemingly been effective. Given our view, remediation probably was not necessary.

Another aspect of the classroom as a preventive care center concerns the philosophy that early identification and treatment of reading difficulties are desirable. If remediation can be handled by the classroom teacher, early identification and treatment can be accomplished without labeling the problem and putting the child into the remedial category. This is exactly the course of action we would advocate. Conversely, if early identification and treatment involves referral to a specialist, we have serious reservations because once attention has been called to a difficulty, it can take on a life of its own. A self-fulfilling prophecy can occur. On the other hand, given time, room to work through the problem, and support from a skillful teacher, the child's problem will often resolve itself. A teacher who regards the classroom as a preventive care center will be cautious in referring children for special help that might cause them to believe they have a genuine problem.

Related to the above point is the belief that in a preventive care center the progress of a child should not be compared to that of other children. The teacher accepts individual rates of progress and uneven growth as normal. Materials are matched to the child's reading level and emphasis is placed on individual progress.

REMEDIATION PROVIDED BY A READING SPECIALIST

Returning to the automobile analogy for a moment, even the best-built car can break down. Despite careful attention to preventive maintenance, a valve can leak or a piston can crack. When this happens we need the help of a first-rate mechanic—a specialist who has had extensive training in locating and correcting problems of the sort we are experiencing. The mechanic who performs routine maintenance may not have the tools or the knowledge to repair a serious problem.

Children are not machines and teachers are not mechanics, of course, so the analogy has limits; but in some ways the regular classroom is like the local service station that performs preventive maintenance on your car. The teacher is like the service station attendant who routinely inspects your automobile. On the other hand, the remedial reading classroom (or the reading specialist coming into the classroom) is akin to the car clinic where special tools and specially trained personnel stand ready to diagnose and treat more complex problems. In a remedial reading program carried out by a reading specialist the child receives intensive instruction and more personal attention than the classroom teacher can provide. Special materials are also available and, if needed, special methods.

An effective remedial reading program does not conform to one pattern— different teachers have success with different approaches. But in our experience the best programs are characterized by the following:

1. Pupils are selected for remedial instruction on the basis of their potential to benefit from such help. Stated another way, low rank in reading achievement is not the sole basis for selection.

2. Pupil progress is documented in a number of ways and shared with the child. Emphasis is placed on showing gains that are being realized on a day-by-day basis. Comparisons with other learners are avoided in favor of self-comparisons.

3. Instructional approaches and materials are built on the child's personal interests and are adjusted to the child's reading level.

4. Remedial instruction is approached in a way that is different from what has been used before with the learner. The novelty inherent in

a change of methods is used to full advantage by giving the child a fresh start in "new" materials and with "new" techniques.

5. The learner is introduced to remedial instruction in a way that guarantees success. Tasks are pitched at a level and in such a manner as to break the cycle of failure all remedial readers experience daily. The language experience approach is an example of a method that can be employed to assure success.

6. Instruction is based on the individual strengths and needs of the learner. Lock-step programs that ignore the child's uniqueness are avoided.

7. Instruction is related to actual reading as much as possible with minimal drill on isolated skills. Predictable books of high interest are used to ensure success and keep motivation high.

8. The learner is encouraged to select appealing materials from among those the teacher believes are written at a level the child can handle easily.

9. Information about (a) the nature of the remedial instruction being provided, (b) progress being made, and (c) how regular classroom instruction can be adjusted to accommodate the child's needs are communicated regularly by the reading specialist to the classroom teacher.

10. The child is excused from the remedial program just as soon as possible. The reading specialist then follows up with the classroom teacher to determine that adjustment is progressing normally.

SUMMARY

This chapter examined several approaches to reading instruction that are often used in remedial programs. Except for the fact that instruction is individualized as much as possible in these approaches, they are not markedly different from the developmental instruction found in regular classrooms. Multisensory techniques described by Fernald and Orton-Gillingham-Stillman that make heavy use of tracing are described in some detail as is one synthetic phonics program often used in remedial programs: *DISTAR*. The chapter concludes with a statement about principles that underlie effective remedial reading programs both within and outside the regular classroom situation.

SUGGESTED ACTIVITIES

1. Locate a set of instructional materials that focus on intensive phonics instruction. A curriculum laboratory in your college or school should be a good

place to look for such materials. Examine the teacher's edition to gain an overview of the content that is included in the program. Look especially at the approach the materials take to teaching sound-symbol relations. Compare this approach to the description given in this chapter for *DISTAR*. Prepare a chart that shows which sounds are taught initially in each program and over what period of time. Share your results with someone who has analyzed another intensive phonics program.

2. Plan and conduct a reading lesson using the Fernald tracing method. You may wish to practice with a colleague before working with a child. Identify which senses are involved at each step in the lesson. Prepare a summary of the essential elements involved in the Fernald method. Indicate which elements could be used in the regular classroom reading program and how they would need to be adjusted for grouped instruction.

3. Visit a local elementary school that employs a reading specialist. Arrange to interview the special reading teacher and at least one classroom teacher who has occasion to work with the specialist. Prepare a list of questions ahead of time that probe for the ways in which the classroom teacher and the specialist coordinate and integrate the instructional activities planned for children who work with both teachers. If possible, observe the reading specialist working with a child or group of children, then observe the same child or children participating in the instructional program provided by the regular classroom teacher. Identify ways in which coordination between the teachers seems to be effective and ways in which it might be improved.

NOTES
1. See Gillingham and Stillman (1966), p. 16.
2. See Orton (1973), p. 162.
3. See Spache (1976), p. 199.
4. See Bryan and Bryan (1975).
5. See Schoolfield and Timberlake (1968).
6. See Carden (1940).
7. See Hegge, Kirk, and Kirk (1936).
8. See Gillingham and Stillman (1966).
9. See *DISTAR Teacher's Guide* (1974).
10. See *DISTAR Teacher's Guide* (1974), p. 34.
11. See *DISTAR Teacher's Guide* (1974), p. 1.
12. See *DISTAR Teacher's Guide* (1974), p. 1.
13. See Dechant (1968).
14. See Bond, Tinker, and Wasson (1984).

SUGGESTED READINGS

BRYANT, PETER, AND BRADLEY, LYNETTE (1985). *Children's reading problems.* New York: Basil Blackwell.

This book presents research concerning why children who are reading far below their expectancy level have difficulty learning to read. It includes teaching strategies for overcoming reading difficulties and discusses how problems in reading can be avoided through the use of phonemic analytic skills.

ELLIS, ANDREW W. (1984). *Reading, writing and dyslexia.* Hillsdale, NJ: Erlbaum.
This book presents a theoretical model of reading that focuses primarily on word recognition as a product of direct visual recognition, phonic mediation, and a semantic system. This model is then used to explain how impaired readers acquire dyslexia.

FERNALD, GRACE (1943). *Remedial techniques in basic school subjects.* New York: McGraw-Hill.
A classic reference describing the theoretical basis for the Fernald tracing methods. It includes detailed directions for implementing this method.

LIPSON, MARJORIE Y., AND WIXSON, KAREN K. (1986). Reading disability research: An interactionist perspective. *Review of Educational Research* 56: 111–136.
This article addresses the issue of what "causes" reading disabilities. The authors argue that current views are the result of a "search for pathology" the focuses exclusively on the learner for the causes of reading difficulty. They present an alternative view that takes into account the "interactive" nature of reading, a view that emphasizes other variables such as the materials being read, the purposes for reading, and the context in which the reading is taking place.

Part 4

Remedial Programs

The final part of this book brings together the elements that have been introduced and discussed in all of the previous parts. Specific suggestions are made for integrating the various elements into a cohesive and coherent remedial program. Instruction and assessment are described as regular classroom activities and as activities that can occur outside the regular classroom. The role of the reading specialist in providing remedial help within the classroom or in a special reading classroom or clinic is also discussed.

Chapter **15**

Helping Low-Achieving Readers in the Classroom and Clinic

OVERVIEW

As you read this chapter use the following list of main ideas to guide your understanding and reflection.

A regular classroom teacher and a reading specialist can work together to provide remedial reading instruction for low-achieving readers.

Low-achieving readers with the same need can be grouped together for remedial instruction focusing on that common need.

By pretesting students on basal reader skills, a classroom teacher can eliminate unnecessary basal work and, in the process, find time for nonbasal activities such as remedial reading instruction.

An advantage of a reading clinic as opposed to classroom environment for remedial reading instruction is that a great deal of concentrated effort can be delivered toward remediation.

The first part of this chapter discusses how a classroom teacher might implement a remediation program for low-achieving readers in his or her classroom. It also discusses what a reading specialist at the building level might do to work with the classroom teacher to assist low-achieving readers.[1] The second part of this chapter discusses what a tutor in a reading clinic might do with several students at a time in a tutoring situation.

The ideas presented in this chapter are only suggestions. Obviously, there are many ways in which the assessment procedures and instructional strategies presented can be implemented. Some of the ideas presented here may not work for some teachers. There are many differences from situation to situation that cannot be addressed in our illustrations. For example, some schools will have more assistance from reading specialists or reading tutors, such as through Chapter I funding, than in the school described here. In that case reading specialists or tutors could provide more of the remedial instruction and assessment and classroom teachers less. Some schools will have less assistance from reading specialists, where one full-time reading resource teacher works in an elementary school of 450 students. Where minimal assistance is available, teachers will still be able to conduct remedial reading instruction and assessment in their classrooms, but at a slower pace. Our hope, however, is that the following suggestions will make it easier for teachers to visualize how a remediation program for low-achieving readers might operate within their classrooms and buildings.

HELPING LOW-ACHIEVING READERS IN THE REGULAR CLASSROOM

Chapter 5 recommended that a classroom teacher ideally have no more than six or eight low-achieving readers so that maximum attention can be directed toward providing these below-average readers with remedial instruction in reading. By low-achieving readers is meant students who are reading below grade level (lowest 25 to 33 percent) and whose reading difficulties are interfering with their success in school. By remedial reading instruction is meant reading instruction that is in addition to instruction provided by the regular program and that helps low-achieving readers learn essential word recognition, comprehension, and vocabulary strategies they need in order to become skilled readers. These are strategies applied to actual reading which they have not learned through the regular program or through experience with reading as have most of their better reading peers.

No teacher at a particular grade level should be responsible for more than three reading groups and low-achieving readers should be spread evenly among teachers. Ideally, a classroom teacher will have eight low-achieving readers or fewer who are all reading at approximately the same level and who are therefore at the same level in the basal reading program.

If a teacher has more than eight low-achieving readers, the assessment and instruction procedures outlined in Part 2 should still be followed. Oral reading analysis can be conducted as students are reading aloud in reading group. Remedial instruction can be provided to subgroups of low-achieving readers experiencing the same problem, such as inability to attack one-syllable words or lack of skill in comprehension monitoring. Record keeping will be more difficult for a classroom teacher with more than eight low-achieving readers but needs to be done to whatever extent possible. Hopefully, a teacher who has a disproportionate share of low-achieving readers at a grade level for reading instruction will have more help from a reading specialist or aides than other teachers at the same grade level with better readers.

The following sections present situations reflecting how one intermediate grade teacher and one primary teacher at Pinewood Elementary School organize for reading instruction so they are able to provide special remedial reading instruction for low-achieving readers in their classrooms along with assistance from the reading specialist.

Providing Remedial Instruction

Mr. Davis teaches fifth grade. He has six low-achieving readers in his homeroom from across the fifth grade who are reading on a beginning third-grade level. He also has a second group of nineteen students who are average readers.

Mr. Davis is Billy Stone's teacher. Chapters 7, 9, and 11 considered word recognition, comprehension, and vocabulary difficulties experienced by Billy, based on data collected from actual reading tasks. Billy's reading difficulties are summarized in Figure 15.1 along with the diagnosed reading difficulties of the five other low-achieving readers in Mr. Davis' class. These lists of difficulties will change throughout the year as instruction is provided and additional assessment data are collected. However, Mr. Davis believes he has sufficient data to begin instruction in clear areas of need.

Let us consider how Mr. Davis uses the information in Figure 15.1 to plan for special remedial instruction in reading for these low-achieving readers. Mr. Davis realizes that he cannot attend to all of the areas in need of instruction at one time. He will have to make decisions about where he and Ms. Schmidt, the building reading specialist, should begin instruction. Mr. Davis and Ms. Schmidt consider the reading difficulties of all six low-achieving readers and look for what they believe are the most crucial skills that need to be learned at this time by the greatest number of students. The instructional needs of the six low-achieving readers in Mr. Davis' class are summarized in Figure 15.2.

Mr. Davis plans to provide special remedial instruction in word recognition once a week and in comprehension or vocabulary once a week. In addition, Ms. Schmidt will come to Mr. Davis' room once a week to provide remedial instruction in either word recognition, comprehension, or vocabulary.

In the area of word recognition Mr. Davis decides to provide instruction to all six low-achieving readers once a week in a general word recognition strategy with special emphasis on the analysis of multisyllabic (2+ syllable) words. Four of the six low-achieving readers in his room, including Billy Stone,

FIGURE 15.1   Instructional Needs of Low-Achieving Readers in a Fifth-Grade Classroom

The students below are fifth-grade students reading on a beginning third-grade level. Their remedial needs in terms of instruction in word recognition, comprehension, and vocabulary are listed below.

Billy Stone
  Word Recognition
    Using a general word recognition strategy
    Knowing CVCe pattern
    Knowing sounds for *i, ea*
    Analyzing 1 syllable and 2+ syllable words
    Self-correcting nonsemantic errors
  Comprehension
    Comprehension monitoring
    Using fix-up strategies
    Reading and answering questions based on expository text
    Answering inference questions
    Reading for main ideas of paragraphs
  Vocabulary
    Using context clues
    Learning specific words

Marcia Alexander
  Word Recognition
    Using a general word recognition strategy
    Analyzing 2+ syllable words
  Comprehension
    Comprehension monitoring
    Using fix-up strategies
    Reading and answering questions based on narrative and expository text
    Answering fact and inference questions
    Reading for main ideas of paragraphs

Mike Hopson
  Word Recognition
    Using a general word recognition strategy
    Knowing the CVCe pattern
    Knowing sounds for *ow, ou*
    Analyzing 2+ syllable words
  Comprehension
    Using fix-up strategies
    Understanding and answering questions based on expository text
    Answering inference questions
    Reading for main ideas of paragraphs
  Vocabulary
    Using the dictionary

FIGURE 15.1   Instructional Needs of Low-Achieving Readers in a Fifth-Grade Classroom (*Cont.*)

Amanda Winger
  Word Recognition
    Analyzing 2 + syllable words
    Self-correcting nonsemantic errors
  Comprehension
    Comprehension monitoring
    Using fix-up strategies
    Understanding and answering questions based on narrative and expository
      text
    Answering fact and inference questions
    Understanding anaphoric relationships
    Reading for main ideas of paragraphs
  Vocabulary
    Using context clues to determine meanings for unfamiliar words
    Using the dictionary

Terry Phillipson
  Word Recognition
    Recognizing *every/very, was/saw*
    Using a general word recognition strategy
    Knowing the CVCe pattern
    Knowing sounds for *ea, oo, ou, ow*
    Analyzing 1 syllable and 2 + syllable words
    Self-correcting nonsemantic errors
  Comprehension
    Comprehension monitoring
    Using fix-up strategies
    Understanding and answering questions based on expository text
    Answering inference questions
    Reading for main ideas of paragraphs
  Vocabulary
    Using context clues to determine meanings of unfamiliar words
    Learning specific words

Wayne Woods
  Word Recognition
    Knowing the CVCe pattern
    Analyzing 2 + syllable words
    Self-correcting nonsemantic errors
  Comprehension
    Comprehension monitoring
    Using fix-up strategies
    Understanding and answering questions based on expository text
    Reading for main ideas of paragraphs
  Vocabulary
    Using context clues to determine meanings for unfamiliar words
    Learning specific words

FIGURE 15.2 Summary of Six Low-Achieving Readers' Remedial Reading Needs (listed in Figure 15.1)

Word Recognition

Using a general word recognition strategy: 4 students
Knowing the CVCe pattern: 4 students
Knowing sounds for *ea:* 2 students
Knowing sounds for *ow:* 2 students
Knowing sounds for *ou:* 2 students
Knowing sounds for *i:* 1 student
Knowing sounds for *oo:* 1 student
Analyzing 1 syllable words: 2 students
Analyzing 2+ syllable words: 6 students
Self-correcting nonsemantic errors: 4 students

Comprehension

Comprehension monitoring: 5 students
Using fix-up strategies: 6 students
Understanding and answering questions based on narrative text: 2 students
Understanding and answering questions based on expository text: 6 students
Answering inference questions: 6 students
Answering fact questions: 2 students
Understanding anaphoric relationships: 1 student
Reading for main ideas of paragraphs: 6 students

Vocabulary

Using context clues to determine meanings for unfamiliar words: 4 students
Using the dictionary: 2 students
Learning specific words: 4 students

need to learn a general word recognition strategy and all six need help in analyzing 2+ syllable words. In Mr. Davis' judgment, after the students have received sufficient instruction in the general word recognition strategy and in the analysis of 2+ syllable words, as evidenced by their performance during oral reading analysis sessions, he will provide symbol-sound correspondence instruction once a week to students based on need (for example, four students, including Billy, need help with the CVCe pattern; two, again including Billy, with sounds for *ea*, and so forth). For the four students, including Billy, needing help with correcting nonsemantic errors, Mr. Davis will use the oral reading for meaning procedure. He plans to conduct this with one student while the other students in the group are silently reading from their basal. He will conduct oral reading for meaning with two students once or twice a week for approximately a month and then with the other two students for a month.

In the area of comprehension, Mr. Davis decides to provide instruction once a week for all six students in the comprehension rating procedure. Five of the six students, including Billy, need help with comprehension monitoring, and all six need help with fix-up strategies. Ms. Schmidt will provide instruction once a week for all six students in the reciprocal teaching procedure because all six students have difficulty with expository text, and the reciprocal teaching procedure is designed to help students better understand expository text. Later, Ms. Schmidt will provide instruction in the question-answer relationship procedure for five of the six students, including Billy, who are having difficulty with inference questions. Either Mr. Davis or Ms. Schmidt at a later point will instruct all six students in reading for main ideas of paragraphs. However, Mr. Davis and Ms. Schmidt have decided it will be more beneficial to focus initially on general comprehension-fostering strategies such as the comprehension rating, reciprocal teaching, and question-answer relationship procedures than to focus on the specific skill of reading for main ideas.

In the area of vocabulary, Mr. Davis plans to focus on helping students use context clues to determine meanings of unfamiliar words when the students are reading from the basal. Four of the six students, including Billy, need remediation in this strategy. Mr. Davis will provide special remedial instruction in using context clues to determine word meanings if he feels that the emphasis he has placed on this strategy with the vocabulary words in the basal stories has been insufficient. Mr. Davis will also spend more time helping the six students learn specific words introduced in the basal. To do this he plans to spend more time with semantic mapping of unfamiliar words.

Not all, but many of the needs of the low-achieving readers in Mr. Davis' reading class will be met by the plan presented above. Actually, at some time during the school year, all of Billy Stone's remedial reading needs, at least as far as those listed in Figure 15.1 are concerned, will be addressed by Mr. Davis' plan for remedial reading instruction. The next section will examine how Mr. Davis intends to implement this remedial program in his classroom.

Organizing for Remedial Instruction in a Fifth Grade Classroom   Mr. Davis teaches reading for sixty minutes each day. On Days 1 and 3 he works on the basal with his low-achieving readers for thirty-five minutes and with his group of average readers for twenty-five minutes. On Days 2 and 4 he works with his average group for thirty minutes on the basal and provides special remedial reading instruction and assessment to subsets of students in his low-achieving reading group for thirty minutes. On Day 5 he spends thirty minutes on the basal with his low-achieving group. The reading resource teacher also works with all or some of the low-achieving readers for thirty minutes on Day 5.

When students in the class are not working with Mr. Davis in reading group, they are engaged in independent activities. Students spend approximately twenty-five to thirty minutes two or three times per week in independent reading and independent activities not related to the basal, such as the following: preparing book-sharing projects in which students tell about their independent reading books in creative ways; meeting in book-sharing groups to share their book projects and to talk about the books they are currently reading; working on reports in interest groups on topics like dinosaurs, horses,

Independent reading is an excellent seatwork activity. *(Peter Vadnai)*

etc.; browsing in the media center for new books to read during independent reading time and at home. Students also spend approximately twenty-five to thirty-five minutes two or three times a week in independent activities related to the basal, such as the following: reading their basal story on their own after it has been introduced by the teacher; answering written comprehension questions on the story; writing a story or essay as a follow-up activity to a particular basal selection which was read and discussed; completing skill practice activities following instruction. Further suggestions for independent reading activities can be found in Harris and Smith (1986). Mr. Davis' schedule for reading instruction is presented in Table 15.1.

Mr. Davis spends somewhat less time on the basal than other teachers. He manages this by pretesting students on specific skills. Based on students' performance, he may be able to eliminate a particular skill altogether or may spend less time on a skill known relatively well by students than he might if he had not pretested.[2]

Mr. Davis spends thirty minutes twice a week during the first month of school administering individual tests, such as IRIs and informal phonics inventories, and paper and pencil assessment tasks, such as the antecedent matching task, to the six students in his low-achieving reading group.

After the first month of school, Mr. Davis usually provides instruction in a word recognition skill once a week and a comprehension or vocabulary skill once a week, as mentioned above, during the thirty-minute periods set aside for remedial instruction in reading. A student who does not need instruction in a specific skill, however, can engage in independent reading or an independent activity not related to the basal.

TABLE 15.1   Schedule for Reading Instruction in a Fifth-Grade Classroom

	Minutes	Group A*	Group B
Day 1	35	Basal**	IR/IA
	25	Basal IA	Basal
Day 2	30	Remedial Instruction	Basal IA
	30	IR/IA	Basal
Day 3	35	Basal	IR/IA
	25	Basal IA	Basal
Day 4	30	Remedial Instruction	IR/IA
	30	IR/IA	Basal
Day 5	30	Basal	Basal IA
	30	Reading Specialist	IR/IA

*Students in Group A are low-achieving readers; students in Group B are average readers
**Basal = time spent with the teacher on the basal program
 Basal IA = independent activity related to the basal
 Reading Specialist = remedial instruction with the reading specialist
 Remedial Instruction = remedial instruction with the classroom teacher
 IR = independent reading
 IA = independent activity not related to the basal

Sometimes Mr. Davis spends the time set aside for special help for his low-achieving readers on assessment activities. For instance, he may spend ten minutes introducing an assessment activity, such as the comprehension rating task or a written activity on using context to determine word meanings, which his six low-achieving readers can complete independently while he spends twenty-five minutes questioning some of these students individually about their comprehension monitoring skills.

Once a week for about twenty-five minutes during the time set aside for the basal program, Mr. Davis conducts oral reading analysis with six students in his low-achieving reading group. He spends ten minutes with the students on oral reading of their latest basal story and then spends ten minutes completing the oral reading analysis sheets while the students answer in writing comprehension questions on the basal story. Mr. Davis has the students take turns reading the questions aloud and individuals write answers to the questions on their papers.

Mr. Davis may also have the students write answers to questions on instructional level material at some other time during the week. After Mr. Davis has discussed the answers to written comprehension questions with his low-achieving readers in the reading group, he takes a few minutes to record students' comprehension scores on the reading difficulties record sheets. While he does this the students work together on a skill they have recently received instruction in, such as using context to determine word meanings, based on their latest basal story.

On day 5, rotating among his six low-achieving readers, Mr. Davis completes the reading difficulties record sheets for thirty minutes during the reading hour while the low-achieving readers work with the reading resource teacher and the average readers engage in independent reading or other independent activities. Mr. Davis also spends thirty minutes after lunch once a week completing the reading difficulties record sheets while the students in his class are engaged in independent reading.

As has already been pointed out, in addition to the special help the six low-achieving readers receive from Mr. Davis, Ms. Schmidt comes to Mr. Davis' room once a week for thirty minutes to assist Mr. Davis with both initial assessment at the beginning of the school year and ongoing assessment during the year. She also provides additional special remedial instruction for subsets of the six low-achieving readers based on diagnosed needs.

Mr. Davis has devised a plan that allows him, along with assistance from Ms. Schmidt, to provide his low-achieving readers with remedial instruction in reading. This instruction is not part of the regular basal program. It focuses on essential word recognition, comprehension, and vocabulary strategies which his low-achieving readers have not learned to use when actually reading. Many of these strategies, such as a general word recognition strategy or comprehension monitoring, have been learned by better readers with minimal explicit instruction. However, explicit instruction, based on diagnosed need, in the strategies presented in Chapters 6, 8, and 10 is needed to help low-achieving readers overcome their reading difficulties.

Organization in a Second-Grade Classroom   This section will describe a plan for remedial reading instruction in a primary classroom. Mrs. Parker teaches second grade. She has eight students in her homeroom who are reading on a first-grade level at the beginning of the school year. She has eighteen other students in her class who are in two additional reading groups.

During the first month of school, Mrs. Parker spends fifteen minutes per day administering informal tests, such as IRIs, informal phonics inventories, and other informal assessments, to her low-achieving readers. At this time the rest of the students in the class are engaged in independent reading or are read to by an aide. Ms. Schmidt, the building reading specialist, comes to Mrs. Parker's classroom for thirty minutes twice a week to help with this initial assessment.

Mrs. Parker teaches reading for ninety minutes per day. On days 1, 3, and 5 she meets with each reading group for thirty minutes and provides instruction from the basal reader. On days 2 and 4 she spends only twenty minutes with each group on the basal program and spends an additional thirty minutes providing special instruction to subsets of her eight low-achieving readers based on similar diagnosed needs.

Whenever students are not working directly with the teacher in reading group, they are engaged in independent activities. All students in the classroom spend fifteen to twenty minutes per day in independent reading or looking at books, twenty to thirty minutes per day in independent activities related to the basal, and fifteen to twenty minutes per day in other independent activities such as the following: listening to stories on the tape recorder, playing reading games, browsing in the media center, doing artwork and writing related to independent reading, and retelling favorite stories with puppets and flannelboard figures. Mrs. Parker's schedule for reading instruction is presented in Table 15.2.

Because Mrs. Parker spends somewhat less time on the basal and more time on other independent activities than other teachers, she, like Mr. Davis, pretests all her students on the skills covered in the basal. In this way she

TABLE 15.2   Schedule for Reading Instruction in a Second-Grade Classroom

	Minutes	Group A*	Group B	Group C
Day 1	30	Basal**	IR/IA	Basal IA
	30	Basal IA	Basal	IR/IA
	30	Reading Specialist	Basal IA	Basal
Day 2	20	Basal	IA	Basal IA
	20	Basal IA	Basal	IA
	30	Remedial Instruction	Basal IA	IR
	20	IR/IA	IR	Basal
Day 3	30	Basal	IR/IA	Basal IA
	30	Basal IA	Basal	IR/IA
	30	Reading Specialist	Basal IA	Basal
Day 4	20	Basal	IA	Basal IA
	20	Basal IA	Basal	IA
	30	Remedial Instruction	Basal IA	IR
	20	IR/IA	IR	Basal
Day 5	30	Basal	IR/IA	Basal IA
	30	Basal IA	Basal	IR
	30	IR/IA	Basal IA	Basal

*Students in Group A are low-achieving readers; students in Group B are average readers; students in Group C are above average readers
**Basal = time spent with the teacher on the basal program
  Basal IA = independent activity related to the basal
  Reading Specialist = remedial instruction with the reading specialist
  Remedial Instruction = remedial instruction with the classroom teacher
  IR = independent reading
  IA = independent activity not related to the basal

eliminates or spends less time on skills sufficiently well-known by students prior to instruction.

Once or twice a week for about twenty minutes during the time set aside for the basal program, Mrs. Parker conducts oral reading analysis with the eight students in her low-achieving reading group. As the students are reading from the basal, Mrs. Parker takes notes on as many of the low-achieving readers as possible during ten minutes of oral reading and then spends ten minutes completing the oral reading analysis sheets while the students reread the basal story with partners.

Once a week Mrs. Parker has her eight low-achieving readers answer comprehension questions in writing as an independent activity. She spends a few minutes before school putting the questions on chart paper and goes over the questions with the students before they work on their own at writing answers. Often, an aide is available to help them with this task. Mrs. Parker also spends a few minutes once a week recording students' scores on the reading difficulties record sheets in terms of number of narrative and expository questions correct and number of fact and inference questions correct. She does this immediately after the answers to written questions have been discussed and checked with the students in the reading group while they read silently for a few minutes from their library books.

During the thirty minutes set aside twice a week for special remedial instruction, Mrs. Parker works with one or more of the low-achieving readers at any one time. She may work with six of her low-achieving readers who need help with segmenting and blending 1 syllable words while the other two low-achieving readers work on an independent activity. Or, she may spend twenty minutes helping all eight of her low-achieving readers with comprehension monitoring skills and ten minutes conducting oral reading for meaning with one student.

On some days during the thirty minutes set aside for special help for low-achieving readers, Mrs. Parker conducts additional assessment. Some of this assessment, such as assessing students' basic sight word knowledge or questioning them about comprehension monitoring or their use of a general word recognition strategy, has to be done individually. But, for a great deal of the assessment that needs to be done, such as assessing students' comprehension rating skills, their ability to answer different types of questions, or their understanding of anaphoric relationships, a written assessment activity can be introduced to a group of students and completed as an independent activity. The building reading specialist helps Mrs. Parker prepare these written assessment tasks.

Twice a week for thirty minutes after lunch, rotating among the eight low-achieving readers, Mrs. Parker completes the reading difficulties record sheets and makes decisions about the most appropriate instruction for subsets of the group based on similar diagnosed needs. While she is doing this, an aide or parent/senior citizen volunteer reads aloud to her students and supervises the class as they engage in independent reading.

In addition to the thirty minutes twice a week which Mrs. Parker sets aside for specific remedial instruction for her low-achieving readers, Ms. Schmidt comes to the classroom twice a week for thirty minutes. She assists Mrs. Parker with initial and ongoing assessment and provides additional remedial instruction to subsets of the eight low-achieving readers in Mrs. Parker's class based on similar diagnosed needs.

The Role of the Building Reading Specialist Ms. Schmidt is the reading specialist for Pinewood Elementary School. The school has 450 students in first through sixth grade. There are three classrooms at each grade level in first through sixth grade; consequently, there are eighteen classrooms in the school. Ms. Schmidt works with from one to eight low-achieving readers in each of the primary grade classrooms twice a week for thirty minutes a session and in each of the intermediate classrooms once a week for thirty minutes a session. Because Ms. Schmidt does not work with all of the low-achieving readers in the school at one time, but rotates among them by instructing students with similar needs, she usually works with about sixty to seventy students across the week at any one time.

Her instructional time is from 9:00 A.M. to 12:10 P.M. Monday, Wednesday, and Friday and from 9:00 A.M. to 12:10 P.M. and 12:40 P.M. to 1:10 P.M. Tuesday and Thursday. For the remainder of each school day Ms. Schmidt has conferences with classroom teachers during nonclassroom time (for example, when students are at P.E. or music, or after school), prepares instructional materials, prepares lessons for instruction, and does necessary record keeping. In addition to preparing for and providing instruction, Ms. Schmidt spends time preparing informal assessment materials which she or the classroom teachers can use. She also helps some teachers complete reading difficulties record sheets. Ms. Schmidt's schedule is presented in Table 15.3.

Ms. Schmidt meets with all classroom teachers by grade level once a week for thirty minutes. She discusses with the teachers the goals and progress of their low-achieving readers as well as the things she can do to best help subsets of the low-achieving readers in the teachers' classrooms during her thirty-minute visits the upcoming week. Often she and the teachers decide upon an area of instruction which the teachers find difficult to cover, such as instruction in the comprehension rating procedure, instruction in basic sight words using predictable books and children's literature, or instruction in summarizing.

Ms. Schmidt does not work with all low-achieving readers in a classroom on every visit. She works with subsets of these students on particular skills and strategies based on diagnosed needs. That is, if she and a classroom teacher have determined that four of six students in a sixth-grade classroom need to work on attacking multisyllabic words, she will work with only those four students on that particular skill over a number of sessions.

As was mentioned at the beginning of this chapter, it is possible that some schools will have more assistance from special reading teachers, such as

TABLE 15.3 Schedule for a Building Reading Specialist

Time	Mon	Tues	Weds	Thurs	Fri
9:00–9:30	2A*	1A	2A	1A	5A
9:40–10:10	2B	1B	2B	1B	5B
10:20–10:50	2C	1C	2C	1C	5C
11:00–11:30	4A	3A	4C	3A	6A
11:40–12:10	4B	3B	6C	3B	6B
12:10–12:40	lunch				
12:40–1:10	prep	3C	prep	3C	prep
1:10–2:30	prep				
2:30–3:00	gr1**	gr2	prep	prep	prep
3:00–3:30	gr3	gr4	prep	gr5	gr6

*2A = 2nd grade, room A; 2B = 2nd grade, room B, etc.
**gr1 = 1st-grade teachers, gr2 = 2nd-grade teachers, etc.

assistance from one or more building reading specialists and several Chapter I reading tutors, than in the scenario just presented. In such situations some low-achieving readers may be receiving most, if not all, of their remedial reading instruction from reading teachers other than the regular classroom teacher. When this occurs, the reading specialist should follow the suggestions

This teacher is completing a reading difficulties record sheet while her students are out of the classroom. *(Peter Vadnai)*

The building reading specialist is conferring with the third grade teachers about low-achieving readers in their classes. *(Peter Vadnai)*

for remedial instruction and assessment in word recognition, comprehension, and vocabulary described in Part 2 of the book. We have made the point repeatedly throughout the book that the instructional strategies and assessment techniques recommended are not limited to use by classroom teachers but are the instructional strategies and assessment techniques recommended for all teachers or tutors working with low-achieving readers.

Helping Exceptional Students with Reading

The focus of this book is on initial and ongoing instruction and assessment for students experiencing reading difficulties. A number of the students at any grade level who are experiencing difficulty in reading will be exceptional students, students who have qualified for special education services. Students designated as learning-disabled, in particular, have often been found to have reading difficulties.[3]

In general, the strategies for instruction and assessment in word recognition, comprehension, and vocabulary that were presented in Part 2 of this book should be used with exceptional students who are experiencing difficulty with reading as well as with other low-achieving readers who are not receiving special education assistance. Special remedial techniques, discussed in Chapter 14, may also be found to be particularly beneficial with some exceptional students. Certain instructional strategies and assessment procedures will not be appropriate for some exceptional students, such as a number of the strategies recommended for instruction and assessment in comprehension will be beyond the level of many MMD (mildly mentally disabled) students. Special education teachers trained in working with various types of exceptional students will need to use their judgment and guide classroom teachers regarding the choice of appropriate instructional strategies and assessment techniques for exceptional students. The instructional strategies and assessment techniques presented in Part 2 of this book apply equally as well to learning disability students as to low-achieving readers not classified as learning-disabled.

Teachers may find that the instructional strategies and assessment techniques presented have to be modified to some extent for use with certain exceptional students. Again, special education teachers should provide guidance to classroom teachers in terms of needed modifications. Also, it is possible that special generic teaching techniques should be used with certain types of exceptional students when teachers are providing remedial instruction in reading. For example, it is often recommended that instruction for learning-disabled students focus on a structured environment and that small amounts of learning material be covered at any one time.[4] Texts on teaching exceptional children, such as those by Mercer (1983) and by Cartwright, Cartwright, and Ward (1981), are good sources of information on teaching techniques that have been found to be effective with certain types of exceptional students.

Students classified as exceptional will be receiving individualized help from special education teachers. Depending on what has been determined to be most beneficial for an individual student, it may be the case that an exceptional student is in the regular classroom for reading instruction or is working with a special education teacher for reading instruction. If an exceptional student experiencing difficulty in reading is receiving reading instruction from the regular classroom teacher, the special education teacher should operate in a manner similar to the building reading specialist described in the previous section. That is, the special education teacher should work with the teacher to plan the most beneficial remedial reading program possible for an exceptional student who is having difficulty in reading. As part of this program, the special education teacher should come to the classroom to provide the exceptional student with individualized remedial reading instruction.

If an exceptional student experiencing difficulty with reading is receiving remedial reading instruction primarily from the special education teacher instead of the classroom teacher, the special education teacher should follow the suggestions for instruction and assessment presented in Part 2 and in Chapter 14 to the extent that these suggestions are appropriate for an individual exceptional student, or the special education teacher should make modifications where needed.

HELPING LOW-ACHIEVING READERS IN THE READING CLINIC

This section describes the hypothetical operation of an independent reading clinic that operates in the summer. This program could be expanded to meet the needs of a year-round clinic.

Dr. Brown operates a summer reading clinic at Rutledge University. (The clinic does not need to be affiliated with a university.) Students from the greater Rutledge area in first through sixth grade who are low-achieving readers enroll in the clinic. Students attend one-hour tutoring sessions, Monday through Thursday, for ten weeks.

One efficient and effective approach in tutoring students in a reading clinic is for a tutor to work with two students at once during a one-hour tutoring session. A tutor can work one-on-one with each student while the other student is engaged in necessary independent practice or silent reading that is followed by some form of interaction with the teacher.

Tutors are employed half time. They work with two students per hour, with a total of six students, between 8:30 A.M. and 11:45 A.M. Students are paired so they are similar in age and reading level. The tutors also spend one hour a day in preparation and record keeping activities. On Fridays the tutors attend a staff meeting, have individual meetings with the director of the clinic to discuss students enrolled in the clinic, and spend the remainder of the morning in preparation and record keeping activities.

During the first few days of the clinic, students are involved in individual testing and independent reading. Tutors administer informal tests like the IRI and informal phonics inventory as well as other assessment procedures, as outlined in Chapters 7, 9, and 11. In addition to this initial assessment, ongoing assessment, used to inform the tutor of aspects of word recognition, comprehension, and vocabulary in need of instruction and to monitor progress, is a regular part of the tutoring program. A great deal is done with charting student performance on various skills or strategies pertaining to word recognition, comprehension, and vocabulary.

Tutors work with each student individually. The schedule for Student A on Days 1 and 3 is as follows: fifteen minutes of instruction in a skill or strategy based on a diagnosed need; fifteen minutes of independent practice on a skill or strategy following instruction; fifteen minutes of oral reading for meaning if the student is experiencing difficulty with word recognition or fifteen minutes of instruction on a second diagnosed need; and ten minutes spent on a pleasurable reading activity with the tutor and other student, such as reading a play together, being read to by the tutor, or playing a reading game. The schedule for Student B on Days 1 and 3 is as follows: fifteen minutes of silent reading followed by a comprehension activity; fifteen minutes of instruction in a skill or strategy based on a diagnosed need; fifteen minutes of independent practice on a skill or strategy following instruction; and ten minutes spent on a pleasurable reading activity with the tutor and other student. On Days 2 and 4 the schedules of Students A and B are reversed. Occasionally, instruction can be conducted with the two students at once, when both have the same diagnosed need. Often, however, the students will have different instructional needs and different priorities in terms of instruction. The schedule for two students who meet together during a tutoring hour is presented in Table 15.4.

If a student has difficulty with word recognition, the tutor conducts oral reading analysis during time scheduled for oral reading for meaning. The tutor

TABLE 15.4   Schedule for Two Students Paired to Work with a Tutor During the Same Hour

		Student A	Student B
Days 1 and 3	8:30–8:45	instruction with tutor	silent reading and follow-up comprehension activity
	8:45–9:00	independent practice	instruction with tutor
	9:00–9:15	oral reading for meaning or other instruction	independent practice
	9:15–9:25	pleasurable reading activity	
Days 2 and 4	8:30–8:45	silent reading and follow-up comprehension activity	instruction with tutor
	8:45–9:00	instruction with tutor	independent practice
	9:00–9:15	independent practice	oral reading for meaning or other instruction
	9:15–9:25	pleasurable reading activity	

carries out some of the needed comprehension assessment based on a student's ability to answer questions on narrative and expository text and questions involving fact and inference during the time scheduled for silent reading and a follow-up comprehension activity. During the first few weeks of the clinic other necessary assessment is carried out on some days instead of the silent reading and comprehension follow-up activity. Ongoing assessment is based on a student's performance on independent practice activities following instruction and on their oral reading performance.

Tutors prepare for the next day's lessons and complete oral reading analysis record sheets on a daily basis from 11:45 A.M. to 12:45 P.M. They update reading difficulties record sheets every Friday. A tutor's schedule is presented in Table 15.5.

Although the focus of this book has been on remedial reading instruction in the classroom, there are a number of distinct advantages to remedial reading instruction provided through a reading clinic. One obvious advantage of a tutoring program such as the one just described in that sixty minutes a day per student is devoted to remedial reading instruction. Consequently, a great deal in terms of assessment and instruction can be accomplished in a relatively

TABLE 15.5   Tutor's Schedule in a Reading Clinic

Days	Time	Activity
Mon–Thurs	8:30– 9:30	tutor students A and B
	9:35–10:35	tutor students C and D
	10:40–11:40	tutor students E and F
	11:45–12:45	preparation, record keeping
Fri	8:30– 9:30	staff meeting
	9:30–10:00	meeting with director
	10:00–12:30	preparation, record keeping

short time. A second obvious advantage is that the program is highly individualized. In addition to working with a low-achieving reader every day in a tailor-made program, a tutor is able to work with the student on an individual basis. The tutor is able to give the student a considerable amount of encouragement and feedback. Such a level of instruction (one-on-one) is not possible in most school settings. A third advantage of such a program is that remedial reading instruction does not have to compete for time with basal reading instruction as is usually the case in the regular classroom. Consequently, a great deal of concentrated effort can be directed toward remediation of specific reading difficulties.

In sum, a considerable amount of time can be directed toward working with a low-achieving reader individually in a reading clinic situation. The tutor can assess an individual on as many of the aspects of word recognition, comprehension, and vocabulary described in Chapters 7, 9, and 11 as the tutor deems necessary. The tutor can plan an instructional program, accordingly, that is based on the instructional strategies described in Chapters 6, 8, and 10. These strategies can be used with basal reader selections but are by no means limited to the basal. Actually, an effective instructional program as outlined in Part 2 of this book can be based almost entirely on trade books.

SUMMARY

This chapter provided examples of how classroom teachers might implement remedial reading programs in their classrooms for their low-achieving readers. It explained how building reading specialists might work with classroom teachers to help low-achieving readers improve their reading. It discussed how special education teachers might work with classroom teachers to help exceptional students experiencing reading difficulties improve their reading. Finally, this chapter explained how a tutor might work with low-achieving readers in a reading clinic environment.

Regardless of which type of teacher is working with low-achieving readers, the instructional strategies and assessment techniques which were presented in Part 2 of this book are sound procedures to follow. Generally, the instructional strategies recommended are word recognition, comprehension, and vocabulary strategies that low-achieving readers are taught to use as they are reading actual text. These strategies may enhance student's comprehension as they are reading, may help them monitor their ongoing comprehension, or may help them overcome a difficulty they are having in word recognition, comprehension, or vocabulary.

In general, the assessment techniques recommended involve the frequent sampling or measuring of student performance in aspects of word recognition, comprehension, and vocabulary based on students' reading of connected text. Through such assessment the teacher can best determine what a low-achieving reader is having difficulty with when the student is actually reading.

Classroom teachers must attempt to help low-achieving readers in their classrooms overcome their reading difficulties because in many instances, low-achieving readers will receive most of their reading instruction from their classroom teachers. Reading specialists and special education teachers should work with classroom teachers, to the extent that such assistance is available, to help low-achieving readers overcome their reading difficulties. Finally, teachers and parents should consider the possibility of low-achieving readers receiving one-on-one tutoring in a reading clinic environment if such assistance is economically and logistically feasible and if it seems that individuals will likely benefit from an individual tutoring program.

Most low-achieving readers can make significant improvements in reading if they are given the appropriate instruction. This book was written to provide teachers with suggestions for instruction and assessment that involve low-achieving readers in actual reading and will be most beneficial in helping them make significant improvements in reading.

SUGGESTED ACTIVITIES

1. Look at data provided by your instructor on a group of low-achieving readers, such as the data presented in Figure 15.1. Based on these data, decide what you would do and when in terms of remediation in word recognition, comprehension, and vocabulary. Your instructor will need to inform you about the grade level of the students and the number of other readers in the classroom.

2. If you are currently teaching, prepare a schedule for reading instruction which makes provisions for remedial reading instruction, such as the ones presented in Tables 15.1 and 15.2. Base your schedule on your current teaching situation.

NOTES

1. See Allington (1986) for a discussion in support of this position.
2. See Taylor and Frye (1987), which provides research support for pretesting.

3. See Gaskins (1982).
4. See Burns, Roe, and Ross (1984).

ALLINGTON, R. L. (1986). Policy constraints and effective compensatory reading instruction: A review. In J. Hoffman (Ed.), *Effective teaching of reading: Research and practice*. Newark, DE: International Reading Association.
This book discusses problems with pull-out compensatory programs and provides support for coordination between the classroom teacher and reading specialist.

CARTWRIGHT, G. P., CARTWRIGHT, C. A., AND WARD, M. E. (1981). *Educating special learners*. Belmont, CA: Wadsworth.
General techniques to use when instructing different types of special education students are presented.

HARRIS L. A., AND SMITH, C. A. (1986). *Reading instruction: Diagnostic teaching in the classroom* (4th ed.). New York: Macmillan.
The authors present numerous suggestions for independent seatwork activities. They also provide good suggestions for classroom organization for reading instruction.

MERCER, C. (1983). *Students with learning disabilities* (2nd ed.). Columbus, OH: C. E. Merrill.
Techniques for working with learning-disabled students and for teaching them to read are discussed.

References

Ackerly, S. S., and Benton A. L. (1947). Report of a case of bilateral frontal lobe defect. *Proceedings, Association for Research on Nervous and Mental Disease, 27,* 479–504.

Adams, A., Carnine D., and Gersten R. (1982). Instructional strategies for studying content area texts in the intermediate grades. *Reading Research Quarterly, 18,* 27–55.

Alexander, J. E., and Filler, R. C. (1976). *Attitudes and reading.* Newark, DE: International Reading Association.

Arlington, R. L. (1986). Policy constraints and effective compensatory reading instruction: A review. In J. Hoffman (Ed.), *Effective teaching of reading: Research and practice.* Newark, DE: International Reading Association.

Anderson, R. (1977). The notion of schemata and the educational enterprise. In R. C. Anderson, R. J. Spiro, and W. E. Montague (Eds.), *Schooling and the acquisition of knowledge.* Hillsdale, NJ: Lawrence Erlbaum.

Anderson, R. C., Armbruster, B. B., and Kantor, R. N. (1980). *How clearly written are children's textbooks? Or, of bladderworts and alfa.* (ERIC No. ED 192 275).

Anderson, R. C., and Biddle W. B. (1975). On asking people questions about what they are reading. In G. Bower (Ed.), *The psychology of learning and motivation: Vol. 9* (pp. 90–129). New York: Academic Press.

Anderson, R. C., and Freebody, P. (1981). Vocabulary knowledge. In J. Guthrie (Ed.), *Comprehension and teaching: Research reviews* (pp. 77–117). Newark, DE: International Reading Association.

Anderson, R. C., Hiebert, E. H., Scott, J. A., and Wilkinson, I. A. (1985). *Becoming a nation of readers. The report of the Commission on Reading.* Washington, DC: National Institute of Education.

Anderson, R. C., Mason, J., and Shirey L. (1984). The reading group: An experimental investigation of a labyrinth. *Reading Research Quarterly, 20,* 6–38.

Anderson, R. C., and Pearson, P. D. (1984). A schema-theoretic view of basic processes in reading comprehension. In P. D. Pearson (Ed.), *Handbook of reading research* (pp. 255–292). New York: Longman.

Anderson, R. C., Reynolds, R. E., Schallert, D. L., and Goetz, E. T. (1977). Frameworks for comprehending discourse. *American Educational Research Journal, 14,* 367–382.

Anderson, R. C., Spiro, R. J., and Anderson, M. C. (1978). Schemata as scaffolding for the representation of information in connected discourse. *American Educational Research Journal, 15*(3), 433–440.

Andre, M.E.D.A., and Anderson, T. H. (1978–1979). The development and evaluation of a self-questioning study technique. *Reading Research Quarterly, 14,* 605–623.

Annett, M. (1972). Handedness, cerebral dominance and the growth of intelligence. In D. Bakker and D. Laty (Eds.)., *Specific reading disability.* Rotterdam: Rotterdam University Press.

Arlin, M., and Roth, G. (1978). Pupils' use of time while reading comics and books. *American Educational Research Journal, 15,* 201–216.

Arlin, M., Scott, M., and Webster J. (1978–1979). The effects of pictures on rate of learning of sight words. *Reading Research Quarterly, 14,* 645–660.

Askov, E. N. (1973). *Primary pupil reading attitude inventory.* Kendal Hunt.

Au, K. H. (1979). Using the experience-text-relationship method with minority children. *The Reading Teacher, 32,* 677–679.

Au, K. H. (1981). Comprehension-oriented reading lessons *Educational Perspectives, 20,* 13–15.

Au, K., and Mason, J. (1982). Social organizational factors in learning to read: The balance of rights hypothesis. *Reading Research Quarterly, 17,* 115–152.

Bailey, M. H. (1967). The utility of phonics generalizations in grades one through six. *The Reading Teacher, 20,* 413–418.

Baker, L., and Brown, A. L. (1984). Metacognitive skills and reading. In P. D. Pearson (Ed.), *Handbook of reading research* (pp. 353–394). New York: Longman.

Balow, B. (1965). The long term effect of remedial reading. *The Reading Teacher, 18,* 581–586.

Balow, B. (1971). Perceptual-motor activities in the treatment of severe reading disability. *The Reading Teacher, 24,* 513–525.

Balow, I. H. (1963). Lateral dominance characteristics and reading achievement in the first grade. *Journal of Psychology, 55,* 323–328.

Balow, I. H., and Balow, B. (1964). Lateral dominance and reading achievement. *American Educational Research Journal, 1,* 139–143.

Baratz, J. C., and Shuy, R. W. (1969). *Teaching black children read.* Washington, DC: Center for Applied Lingustics.

Barbe, W. B., and Abbott, J. L. (1975). *Personalized reading instruction: New techniques that increase reading skill and comprehension.* West Nyack, NY: Parker.

Barnitz, J. G. (1980). Syntactic effect of the reading comprehension of pronoun-referent structures by children in grades two, four and six. *Reading Research Quarterly, 15,* 268–289.

Barrett, J. (1970). *Animals should definitely not wear clothing.* New York: Atheneum.

Bartlett, B. J. (1978). *Top-level structure as an organizational strategy for recall of classroom text.* Unpublished doctoral dissertation, Arizona State University.

Bateman, B. (1964). Learning disabilities: Yesterday, today, and tomorrow. *Exceptional Children, 31,* 167–177.

Bateman, B. (1968). The efficacy of an auditory and a visual method of first grade reading instruction with auditory and visual learners. In H. K. Smith (Ed.), *Perception and reading.* Newark, DE: International Reading Association.

Baumann, J. F. (1984). The effectiveness of a direct instructional paradigm for teaching main idea comprehension. *Reading Research Quarterly, 20,* 93–115.

Baumann, J. F., and Schmitt, M. B. (1986). The what, why, how, and when of comprehension instruction. *The Reading Teacher, 39,* 640–647.

Baumann, J. F., and Stevenson, J. A. (1982). Understanding standardized reading achievement test scores. *The Reading Teacher, 35,* 648–655.

Beck, I. L., McKeown, M. G., and McCaslin, E. S. (1983). Vocabulary development: All contexts are not created equal. *Elementary School Journal, 83,* 177–181.

Beck, I., McKeown, M., McCaslin, E., and Burkes, A. (1979). *Instructional dimensions that may affect reading comprehension: Examples from two commercial reading programs* (LRDC Publication 1979/20). Pittsburgh, PA: University of Pittsburgh, Learning Research and Development Center.

Beck, I. L., Perfetti, C. A., and McKeown, M. G. (1982). The effects of long-term vocabulary instruction on lexical access and reading comprehension. *Journal of Educational Psychology, 74,* 506–521.

Becker, W. C., and Carnine, D. W. (1976). *Direct instruction—A behavior theory model for comprehensive educational intervention with the disadvantaged.* Paper presented at the 8th Symposium on Behavior Modification, Carascas, Venezuela, February, 1978.

Becker, W. C., Engelmann, S., and Carnine, D. W. (in press). The direct instruction model. In R. Rhine (Ed.), *Encouraging change in America's school: A decade of experimentation.* New York: Academic Press.

Beebe, M. J. (1980). The effect of different types of substitution miscues on reading. *Reading Research Quarterly, 15,* 324–336.

Belmont, L., and Birch H. G. (1965). Lateral dominance, lateral awareness, and reading disability. *Child Development, 36,* 57–71.

Betts, E. A. (1946). *Foundations of reading instruction.* New York: American Book Company.

Biemiller. A. (1979). Changes in the use of graphic and contextual information as a function of passage difficulty and reading achievement level. *Journal of Reading Behavior, 11,* 307–318.

Blachowicz, C. (1985). Vocabulary development and reading: From research to instruction. *The Reading Teacher, 38,* 876–881.

Blanton, W. E., Farr, R., and Tuinman, J. J. (Eds.). (1972). *Reading tests for secondary grades: A review and evaluation.* Newark, DE: International Reading Association.

Blanton, W. E., Farr, R., and Tuinman, J. J. (1974). *Measuring reading performance.* Newark, DE: International Reading Association.

Bond, G. L., and Dykstra, R. (1967). The cooperative research program in first grade reading instruction. *Reading Research Quarterly, 2,* complete volume.

Bond, G. L., Tinker, M. A., and Wasson, B. B. (1984). *Reading difficulties: Their diagnosis and correction* (5th ed.). Englewood Cliffs, NJ: Prentice-Hall.

Bormuth, J. R., Manning, J. C., Carr, J. W., and Pearson, P. D. (1970). Chldren's comprehension of between- and within-sentence syntactic structures. *Journal of Educational Psychology, 61,* 349–357.

Bransford, J. D., Stein, B. S., Vye, N. J., Franks, J. J., Auble, P. M., Mezynski, K. J., and Perfetto, G. A. (1982). Differences in approaches to learning: An overview. *Journal of Experimental Psychology: General, 111,* 390–398.

Bridge, C. A., and Tierney, R. J. (1981). The inferential operations of children across text with narrative and expository tendencies. *Journal of Reading Behavior, 13,* 201–214.

Bridge, C. A., Winograd, P. N., and Haley, D. (1983). Using predictable materials vs. preprimers to teach beginning sight words. *The Reading Teacher, 36,* 884–891.

Bristow, P. S. (1985). Are poor readers passive readers? Some evidence, possible explanations, and potential solutions. *The Reading Teacher, 39,* 318–325.

Bristow, P. S., Pikulski, J. J., and Pelosi, P. L. (1983). A comparison of five estimates of reading instructional level. *The Reading Teacher, 37,* 273–279.

Brogan, P., and Fox, L. K. (1961). *Helping children read: A practical approach to individualized reading.* New York: Holt, Rinehart and Winston.

Brown, A. L., and Day, J. D. (1983). Macrorules for summarizing texts: The development of expertise. *Journal of Verbal Learning and Verbal Behavior, 22,* 1–14.

Brozo, W. G., Schmelze, R. V., and Spires, H. A. (1983). The beneficial effect of chunking on good readers' comprehension of expository prose. *Journal of Reading, 26,* 442–449.

Bryan, T., and Bryan, J. (1975). *Understanding learning diabilities.* Port Washington, NY: Alfred.

Bryant, N. D. (1972). Silent reading diagnostic tests. In O. K. Buros (Ed.), *Seventh mental measurements yearbook* (pp. 1122–1124). Highland Park, NJ: Gryphon Press.

Burmeister, L. E. (1968). Usefulness of phonics generalizations. *The Reading Teacher, 21,* 349–356.

Burns, P., Roe, B., and Ross. (1983). *Teaching reading in today's elementary schools.* Boston: Houghton-Mifflin.

Buros, O. K. (1969). *Reading tests and reviews.* Highland Park, NJ: Gryphon Press.

Buros, O. K. (1972). *Seventh mental measurements yearbook.* Highland Park, NJ: Gryphon Press.

Buros, O. K. (1975). *Reading tests and reviews II.* Highland Park, NJ: Gryphon Press.

Buros, O. K. (1978). *Eighth mental measurements yearbook.* Highland Park, NJ: Gryphon Press.

Buros, O. K. Suggestions to MMY reviewers. Mimeographed, no date.

Butkowsky, I. S., and Willows, D. M. (1980). Cognitive motivational characteristics of children varying in reading ability: Evidence for learned helplessness in poor readers. *Journal of Educational Psychology, 72,* 408–422.

Byers, R. K., and Lord, E. E. (1943). Late effects of lead poisoning on mental development. *American Journal of Diseases of Children, 66,* 471–493.

Calfee, R. C., Lindamood, P., and Lindamood, C. (1973). Acoustic-phonetic skills and reading: Kindergarten through twelfth grade. *Journal of Educational Psychology, 64,* 293–298.

Capobianco, R. J. (1966). Ocular-manual laterality and reading in adolescent mental retardates. *American Journal of Mental Deficiency, 70,* 781–785.

Capobianco, R. J. (1967). Ocular-manual laterality and reading in achievement in children with special learning disabilities. *American Educational Research Journal, 2,* 133–137.

Carden, M. (1936). *The Carden method, Manual I.* Glen Rock, NJ: MacCarden.

Carnine, D. W., Kameenui, E. J., and Coyle G. (1984). Utilization of contextual information in determining the meaning of unfamiliar words. *Reading Research Quarterly, 19,* 188–204.

Carnine, D., and Silbert, J. (1979). *Direct reading instruction.* Columbus, OH: Charles E. Merrill.

Carr, E. (1985). The vocabulary overview guide: A metacognitive strategy to improve vocabulary comprehension and retention. *Journal of Reading, 28,* 684–689.

Carr, E. M, Dewitz, P., and Patberg, J. P. (1983). The effect of inference training on children's comprehension of expository text. *Journal of Reading Behavior, 15,* 1–18.

Cartwright, G. P., Cartwright, C. A., and Ward, M. E. (1981). *Educating special learners.* Belmont, CA: Wadsworth.

Chall, J. S. (1983). *Learning to read: The great debate* (2nd ed.). New York: McGraw-Hill.

Chall, J. S., Roswell, F. G., and Blumenthal, S. H. (1963). Auditory blending ability: A factor in success in beginning reading. *The Reading Teacher, 17,* 113–118.

Cheek, M. C., and Cheek, E. H. Jr. (1980). *Diagnostic-prescriptive reading instruction.* Dubuque, IA: William C. Brown.

Cheyney, A. B. (1984). *Teaching reading skills through the newspaper.* Newark, DE: International Reading Association.

Chomsky, C. (1978). When you still can't read in third grade: After decoding what? In S. J. Samuels (Ed.), *What research has to say about reading instruction* (pp. 13–30). Newark, DE: International Reading Association.

Cleary, D. M. (1978). *Thinking Thursdays: Language arts in the reading lab.* Newark, DE: International Reading Association.

Clements, S. (1966). *Minimal brain dysfunction in children: Terminology and identification.* National Institute of Neurological Diseases, Monograph No. 3, Public Health Publications No. 1415. Washington, DC: Government Printing Office.

Clymer, T. (1963). The utility of phonics generalizations in the primary grades. *The Reading Teacher, 16,* 252–257.

Cohen, R. R. (1966). *Remedial training of first grade children with visual perceptual retardation.* Unpublished doctoral dissertation, University of California at Los Angeles.

Collins, A., Brown, J. S., and Larkin, K. (1980). Inference in text understanding. In R. J. Spiro, B. C. Bruce, and W. F. Brewer (Eds.), *Theoretical issues in reading comprehension.* Hillsdale, NJ: Lawrence Erlbaum.

Collins, A. M., and Quillian, M. R. (1969). Retrieval time from semantic memory. *Journal of Verbal Learning and Verbal Behavior, 8,* 240–247.

Cooper, J. D., et al. (1972). *Decision making for the diagnostic teacher* (pp. 14–16). New York: Holt, Rinehart and Winston.

Criscuolo, N. P. (1981). Creative homework with the newspaper. *Reading Teacher, 34,* 921–922.

Cruickshank, W. M. (1966). *The teacher of brain-injured children: A discussion of bases for competency.* Syracuse, NY: Syracuse University Press.

Cunningham, P. (1979). Match informal evaluation to your teaching practices. *The Reading Teacher, 31*(1), 51–56.

D'Angelo, K. (1982). Correction behavior: Implications for reading instruction. *The Reading Teacher, 35,* 395–399.

Daniels, S. (1971). *How 2 gerbils . . . and I taught them how to read.* Philadelphia: Westminster Press.

Davey, B., and Porter, S. M. (1982). Comprehension-rating: A procedure to assist poor comprehenders. *Journal of Reading, 26,* 197–202.

Davis, F. B. (1944). Fundamental factors in comprehension in reading. *Psychometrika, 9,* 185–197.

Davis, F. B. (1968). Research in comprehension in reading. *Reading Research Quarterly, 3,* 499–545.

Davis, F. B., et al. (1974). *Standards for educational and psychological tests.* Washington, DC: American Psychological Association.

Dechant, E. (1968). *Diagnosis and remediation of reading disability.* West Nyack, NY: Parker.

Delacato, C. H. (1966). *Neurological organization and reading.* Springfield, IL: Charles C. Thomas.

DiBennedetto, B., Richardson, E., and Kochnower, J. (1983). Vowe generalization in normal and learning disabled readers. *Journal of Educational Psychology, 75,* 576–582.

Doctorow, M., Wittrock, M. C., and Marks, C. (1978). Generative processes in reading comprehension. *Journal of Educational Psychology, 70,* 109–118.

Dolch, E. W. (1942). *The basic sight word test.* Champaign, IL: Garard.

Dole, J., and Pearson, P. D. (in press). Explicit comprehension instruction: A review of research and a new conceptualization of instruction. *Elementary School Journal.*

Durkin, D. (1978–1979). What classroom observations reveal about comprehension instruction. *Reading Research Quarterly, 14,* 481–533.

Durkin, D. (1981a). Reading comprehension in five basal readers series. *Reading Research Quarterly, 16,* 515–544.

Durkin, D. (1981b). *Strategies for identifying words* (2nd ed.). Boston: Allyn and Bacon.

Durkin, D. (1984a). Do basal manuals teach reading comprehension? In R. C. Anderson, J. Osborn, and R. J. Tierney (Eds.), *Learning to read in American schools: Basal readers and content texts* (pp. 29–38). Hillsdale, NJ: Lawrence Erlbaum.

Durkin, D. (1984b). Is there a match between what elementary teachers do and what basal reader manuals recommend? *The Reading Teacher, 37,* 734–745.

Durkin, D. (1984c). *The decoding ability of elementary school students* (Reading Education Report No. 49). Urbana: University of Illinois, Center for the Study of Reading.

Durrell, D., and Catterson, J. H. (1980). *Analysis of reading difficulty* (3rd ed.). New York: The Psychological Corporation.

Dwyer, C. A. (1978). Woodcock reading mastery tests. In O. K. Buros (Ed.), Eighth Mental Measurements Yearbook, Highland Park, NJ: Gryphon Press, pp. 1303–1305.

Eeds, M. (1985). Bookwords: Using a beginning word list of high frequency words from children's literature K–3. *The Reading Teacher, 38,* 418–423.

Eeds, M., and Cockrum, W. A. (1985). Teaching word meanings by expanding schemata vs. dictionary work vs. reading in context. *Journal of Reading, 28,* 492–497.

Ehri, L. C., Deffner, N. D., and Wilce, L. S. (1984). Pictorial mnemonics for phonics. *Journal of Educational Psychology, 76,* 880–893.

Ehri, L. C., and Roberts, R. T. (1979). Do beginners learn printed words better in context or in isolation? *Child Development, 50,* 675–685.

Ehri, L. C., and Wilce, L. S. (1980). Do beginners learn to read function words better in sentences or in lists? *Reading Research Quarterly, 15,* 451–476.

Ehri, L. C., and Wilce, L. S. (1983). Development of word identification speed in skilled and less skilled beginning readers. *Journal of Educational Psychology, 75,* 3–18.

Ekwall, E. T., and Shanker, J. L. (1983). *Diagnosis and remediation of the disabled reader* (2nd ed.). Boston: Allyn and Bacon.

Emans, R. (1967). The usefulness of phonics generalizations above the primary grades. *The Reading Teacher, 20,* 419–425.

Erickson, F., and Mohatt, G. (1982). Cultural organization of participation structures in two classrooms of Indian students. In G. Spindler (Ed.), *Doing the ethnography of schooling: Educational anthropology in action*. New York: Holt, Rinehart and Winston, 132–174.

Estes, T. H. (1971). A scale to measure attitudes toward reading, *Journal of Reading, 15*, 135–138.

Farr, R. (1969). *Reading: What can be measured?* Newark, DE: International Reading Association.

Farr, R. (1978). Prescriptive reading inventory. In O. K. Buros (Ed.), *Mental measurements yearbook* (pp. 1274–1277). Highland Park, NJ: Gryphon Press.

Farr, R., and Anastasiow, N. (1969). *Review of reading readiness tests*. Newark, DE: International Reading Association.

Fernald, G. (1939). *Remedial techniques in basic school subjects*. New York: McGraw-Hill.

Fernald, G. M. (1943). *Remedial techniques in basic school subjects*. New York: McGraw-Hill.

Fielding, L. G., Wilson, P. T., and Anderson, R. C. (1986). A new focus on free reading: The role of trade books in reading instruction. In T. E. Raphael (Ed.), *The Contexts of School-Based Literacy*. New York: Random House.

Fisher, C. W., Fibly, N. N., Marliave, R., Cahen, L. S., Dishaw, M. M., Moore, J. E., and Berliner, D. C. (1978). *Teaching behaviors, academic learning time, and student achievement: Final report of phase III-B, beginning teacher evaluation study*. San Francisco: Far West Educational Laboratory for Educational Research and Development.

Fox, B., and Routh, D. K. (1975). Analyzing spoken language into words, syllables, and phonemes: A developmental study. *Journal of Psycholinguistic Research, 4*, 331–342.

Frase, L. T., and Schwartz, B. J. (1975). The effect of question production and answering on prose recall. *Journal of Educational Psychology, 67*, 621–635.

Fredrickson, C. H. (1975). Representing logical and semantic structure of knowledge acquired from discourse. *Cognitive Psychology, 7*(3), 371–458.

Freebody, P., and Anderson, R. C. (1983). Effects on text comprehension of differing proportions and locations of difficult vocabulary. *Journal of Reading Behavior, 15*, 19–40.

Frostig, M., and Home, D. (1964). *The Frostig program for the development of visual perception*. Chicago: Follett.

Fuchs, L., Deno, S. L., and Mirkin, P. K. (1984). The effects of frequent curriculum-based measurement and evaluation on pedagogy, student achievement, and student awareness of learning. *American Educational Research Journal, 21*, 449–460.

Garner, R. (1980). Monitoring of understanding: An investigation of good and poor readers' awareness of induced miscomprehension of text. *Journal of Reading Behavior, 12*, 55–64.

Garner, R., Hare, V. C., Alexander, P., Haynes, J., and Winograd, P. (1984). Inducing use of a text lookback strategy among unsuccessful readers. *American Educational Research Journal, 21*, 789–798.

Garner, R., and Reis, R. (1981). Monitoring and resolving comprehension obstacles: An investigation of spontaneous text lookbacks among upper grade good and poor comprehenders. *Reading Research Quarterly, 16*, 569–582.

Garner, R., Wagoner, S., and Smith, T. (1983). Externalizing question-answering strategies of good and poor comprehenders. *Reading Research Quarterly, 18,* 439–447.

Gaskins, I. W. (1982). Let's end the reading disabilities/learning disabilities debate. *Journal of Learning Disabilities, 15,* 81–83.

Gelb, I. J. (1966). *A study of writing.* Chicago: University of Chicago Press.

Gersten, R., and Carnine, D. W. (1986). Direct instruction in reading comprehension. *Educational Leadership, 43*(7), 70–77.

Gillingham, A., and Stillman, B. (1966). *Remedial teaching for children with specific disability in reading, spelling and penmanship.* Cambridge, MA: Educator's Publishing Service.

Gipe, J. (1978–1979). Investigating techniques for teaching word meanings. *Reading Research Quarterly, 14,* 624–644.

Gitelman, H. F. (1983). Newspaper power. *The Reading Teacher, 36,* 831.

Glass, G. V., and Robbins, M. P. (1967). A critique of experiments on the role of neurological organization in reading performance. *Reading Research Quarterly, 3,* 5–52.

Golinkoff, R. (1975–1976). A comparison of reading comprehension processes in good and poor comprehenders. *Reading Research Quarterly, 11,* 623–659.

Goodman, K. S. (1969). Analysis of oral reading miscues: Applied psycholinguistics. *Reading Research Quarterly, 5,* 9–30.

Goodman, K. (1976). Reading: A psycholinguistic guessing game. In H. Singer and R. Ruddell (Eds.). *Theoretical models and processes of reading* (2nd ed.). Newark, DE: International Reading Association.

Goodman, Y. M., and Burke, C. L. (1972). *Reading miscue inventory manual: Procedures for diagnosis and evaluation.* New York: Macmillan.

Gordon, C. J. (1980). *The effects of instruction in metacomprehension and inferencing on children's comprehension abilities.* Unpublished doctoral dissertation, University of Minnesota.

Gordon, C. J. (1985). Modeling inference awareness across the curriculum. *Journal of Reading, 28,* 444–447.

Graham, S. (1984). Teacher feelings and student thoughts: An attributional approach to affect in the classroom. *The Elementary School Journal, 85,* 91–104.

Graves, M. (1987). The roles of vocabulary instruction in fostering vocabulary development. In M. G. McKeown and M. E. Curtis (Eds.), *The nature of vocabulary acquisition.* Hillsdale; NJ: Lawrence Erlbaum.

Greenberg, J. W., et al. (1965). Achievement of children from a deprived environment toward achievement related concepts. *Journal of Educational Research, 59,* 57–61.

Grimes, J. E. (1975). *The thread of discourse.* The Hague, Netherlands: Mouton.

Groden, G. (1969). Lateral preterance in normal children. *Perceptual and Motor Skills, 28,* 213–214.

Haddock, M. (1976). The effects of an auditory and auditory-visual method of blending instruction on the ability of prereaders to decode synthetic words. *Journal of Educational Psychology, 68,* 825–831.

Hagen, J. (1979). *Semantically oriented approaches to prereading vocabulary instruction.* Unpublished doctoral dissertation, University of Wisconsin.

Hall, M. (1981). *Teaching reading as a language experience.* Columbus, OH: Charles E. Merrill.

Hanf, M. B. (1971). Mapping: A technique for translating reading into thinking. *Journal of Reading, 14*(4), 225–230, 270.

Hansen, J. (1981). The effects of inference training and practice on young children's comprehension. *Reading Research Quarterly, 16,* 391–417.

Hansen J., and Pearson P. D. (1982). *An instructional study: Improving the inferential comprehension of fourth grade good and poor readers.* Urbana-Champaign: University of Illinois, Center for the Study of Reading.

Hansen, J., and Pearson, P. D. (1983). An instructional study: Improving the inferential comprehension of fourth grade good and poor readers. *Journal of Educational Psychology, 75,* 821–829.

Harris, A. J. (Ed.). 1970a). *Casebook on reading disability.* New York: David McKay.

Harris, A. J. (1970b). *How to increase reading ability* (5th ed.). New York: David McKay.

Harris, A. J., and Sipay, E. R. (1980). *How to increase reading ability: A guide to developmental and remedial methods* (7th ed.). New York: Longman.

Harris, A. J., and Sipay, E. R. (1985). *How to increase reading ability: A guide to developmental and remedial methods* (8th ed.). New York: Longman.

Harris, L. A., and Niles, J. A. (1982). An analysis of published informal reading inventories. *Reading Horizons. 22,* 159–174.

Harris, L. A., and Smith, C. B. (1986). *Reading instruction: Diagnostic teaching in the classroom* (4th ed.). New York: MacMillan.

Harris, T. L., and Hodges, R. E. (Eds.) (1981). *A dictionary of reading and related terms.* Newark, DE: International Reading Association.

Hartlage, L. C. (1976). Vision deficits and reading impairment. In G. Leisman (Ed.), *Basic visual processes and learning disability* (pp. 151–162). Springfield, IL: Charles E. Thomas.

Hayes, D., and Tierney, R. (1982). Developing readers' knowledge through analogy. *Reading Research Quarterly, 17,* 256–280.

Hegge, T., Kirk, S. A., and Kirk W. (1965). *Remedial reading drills.* Ann Arbor, MI: George Wahr.

Helfeldt, J. P., and Lalik R. (1976). Reciprocal student-teacher questioning. *The Reading Teacher, 30,* 283–287.

Helfgott, J. (1976). Phonemic segmentation and blending skills of kindergarten children: Implications for beginning reading acquisition. *Contemporary Educational Psychology, 1,* 157–169.

Herber, H. H. (1970). *Teaching reading in content areas.* Englewood Cliffs, NJ: Prentice-Hall.

Hogan, T. P. (1974). Reading tests and performance contracting. In W. Blanton, R. Farr, and J. Tuinman (Eds.), *Measuring reading performance* (pp. 51–65). Newark, DE: International Reading Association.

Holmes, B. C. (1983). The effect of prior knowledge on the question answering of good and poor readers. *Journal of Reading Behavior, 15,* 1–18.

Houck, C., and Harris, L. A. (1976). Woodcock reading mastery tests, *Journal of School Psychology, 14,* 77–79.

Hull, C. L. (1952). *A behavior system.* New Haven: Yale University.

Irwin, J. (1980). The effects of explicitness and clause order on the comprehension of reversible causal relationships. *Reading Research Quarterly, 15*(4).

Jacobs, J. N. (1968). Visual perceptual training program. *Educational Leadership Research Supplement.*

Jenkins, J. L., and Dixon R. (1983). Vocabulary learning. *Contemporary Educational Psychology, 8,* 237–260.

Jenkins, J. R., Pany D., and Schreck, J. (1978). *Vocabulary and reading comprehension: Instructional effects* (Tech. Rep. No. 100). Champaign, IL: University of Illinois, Center for the Study of Reading.

Jenkins, J., Stein, M., and Wysocki, K. (1984). Learning vocabulary through reading. *American Educational Research Journal, 21,* 767–788.

Johnson, D. D. (1976). *Johnson basic sight vocabulary test manual.* Lexington, MA: Ginn.

Johnson, D. D., and Pearson, P. (1975). Skills management systems: A critique. *The Reading Teacher, 28,* 757–764.

Johnson, D. D., and Pearson, P. D. (1978). *Teaching reading vocabulary.* New York: Holt, Rinehart and Winston.

Johnson, D. D., and Pearson, P. D. (1984). *Teaching reading vocabulary* (2nd ed.). New York: Holt, Rinehart & Winston.

Johnson, D., Toms-Bronowski, S., and Pittleman, S. (1982). *An investigation of the effectiveness of semantic mapping and semantic feature analysis with intermediate grade level children* (Program Report No. 83–3). Madison, WI: Wisconsin Center for Education Research.

Johnson, M. S., and Kress, R. A. (1965). *Informal reading inventories.* Newark, DE: International Reading Association.

Johnston, P. (1981). *Background knowledge, reading comprehension and test bias.* Unpublished doctoral dissertation, University of Illinois.

Johnston, P. (1985). Understanding reading failure: A case study approach. *Harvard Educational Review, 55,* 153–177.

Johnston, P., and Pearson, P. D. (1982). *Prior knowledge, connectivity, and the assessment of reading comprehension.* Urbana-Champaign: University of Illinois, Center for the Study of Reading.

Johnston, P. H. (1983). *Reading comprehension assessment: A cognitive basis.* Newark, DE: International Reading Association.

Johnston, P. H. (1948a). Prior knowledge and reading comprehension test bias. *Reading Research Quarterly, 19,* 219–239.

Johnston, P. H. (1984b). Assessment in reading. In P. D. Pearson (Ed.), *Handbook of reading research.* New York: Longman.

Johnston, P. H., and Winograd, P. N. (1985). Passive failure in reading. *Journal of Reading Behavior, 17,* 279–301.

Jongsma, K. S., and Jongsma, E. A. (1981) Test review: Commercial informal reading inventories. *The Reading Teacher, 34,* 697–705.

Journal of Reading. (1981). Misuse of grade equivalents, *25,* p. 112.

Juel, C. (1980). Comparison of word identification strategies with varying context, word type, and reading skill. *Reading Research Quarterly, 15,* 358–376.

Juel, C. (1983). The development and use of mediated word identification. *Reading Research Quarterly, 18,* 306–327.

Juel, C., and Holmes, B. (1981). Oral and silent reading of sentences. *Reading Research Quarterly, 16,* 545–568.

Juel, C., and Roper-Schneider, D. (1985). The influence of basal readers on first grade reading. *Reading Research Quarterly, 20,* 134–152.

Kameenui, E. J., Carnine, D. W., and Freschi, R. (1982). Effects of text instruction and instructional procedures for teaching word meanings on comprehension and recall. *Reading Research Quarterly, 17,* 367–388.

Kennedy, L. D., and Halinski, R. S. (1975). Measuring attitudes: An extra dimension. *Journal of Reading, 18,* 518–522.

Kephart, N. (1960). *The slow learner in the classroom.* Columbus, OH: Charles E. Merrill.

Kershner, J. R. (1983). Laterality and learning disabilities: Cerebral dominance as a cognitive process. *Topics in Learning and Learning Disabilities, 3,* 66–74.

Kibby, M. W. (1979). Passage readability affects the oral reading strategies of disabled readers. *Reading Teacher, 32,* 390–396.

Kirk, S. A., Kliebhan, J. M., and Lerner, J. W. (1978). *Teaching reading to slow and disabled learners.* Boston: Houghton-Mifflin.

Kirschenbaum, H., Simon, S., and Napier, R. W. (1971). *Wad-Ja-Get? The grading game in American education.* New York: Hart.

Klare, G. (1984). Readability. In P. D. Pearson (Ed.), *Handbook of reading research* (pp. 681–644). New York: Longman.

Klausmeier, H., and Ripple, R. (1971). *Learning and human abilities* (3rd ed.). New York: Harper and Row.

Kress, R. A. (1972). Silent reading diagnostic tests. In O. K. Buros (Ed.), *Seventh mental measurements yearbook* (pp. 1124–1125). Highland park, NJ: Gryphon Press.

Kuhn, T. S. (1962). *The structure of scientific revolutions.* Chicago: University of Chicago Press.

LaBerge, D., and Samuels, S. J. (1974). Toward a theory of automatic information processing in reading. *Cognitive Psychology, 6,* 294–323.

Lambert, W. E. (1978). Cognitive and socio-cultural consequences of bilingualism. *The Canadian Modern Language Review, 34,* 537–547.

Lambert, W. E. and Tucker, G. R. (1972). *Bilingual education of children.* Rowley, MA: Newbury House.

Langer, J. (1980). Relation between levels of prior knowledge and the organization of recall. In M. L. Kamil and A. J. Moe (Eds.), *Perspectives on reading and instruction.* Washington, DC: National Reading Conference.

Langer, J. A. (1984). Examining background knowledge and text comprehension. *Reading Research Quarterly, 19,* 468–481.

Langer, J. A. (1981). From theory to practice: A prereading plan. *Journal of Reading, 25,* 152–156.

Lapp, D., and Flood, J. (1978). *Teaching reading to every child.* New York: Macmillan.

Lauritzen, (1982). A modification of repeated readings for group instruction. *The Reading Teacher, 35,* 456–459.

Lawson, L. J. (1968). Ophthalmological factors in learning disabilities. In H. R. Myklebust (Ed.), *Progress in learning disabilities,* vol. I (pp. 147–181). New York: Grune and Stratton.

Lesgold, A. M. (1974). Variability in children's comprehension of syntactic structures. *Journal of Educational Psychology, 66,* 333–338.

Lesgold, A. M., and Perfetti, C. A. (1978). Interactive processes in reading comprehension. *Discourse Processes, 1,* 323–336.

Leslie, L. (1980). The use of graphic and contextual information by average and below-average readers. *Journal of Reading Behavior, 12,* 139–150.

Leslie, L., and Osol, P. (1978). Changes in oral reading strategies as a function of quantities of measures. *Journal of Reading Behavior, 10,* 442–444.

Leu, D. J. (1982). Oral reading error analysis: A critical review of research and application. *Reading Research Quarterly, 17,* 420–437.

Levin, J. R. (1981). The mnemonic '80s: Keywords in the classroom. *Educational Psychologist, 16,* 65–82.

Levin, J. R., Johnson, D. D., Pittleman, S., Levin, K., Shriberg, L., Toms-Bronowski, S., and Hayes, B. (1984). A comparison of semantic- and mnemonic-based vocabulary-learning strategies. *Reading psychology, 5,* 1–15.

Levin, J. R., McCormick, C. B., Miller, G. E., Berry, J. K., and Pressley, M. (1982). Mnemonic versus nonmnemonic vocabulary-learning strategies for children. *American Educational Research Journal, 19,* 121–136.

Lewkowicz, N. K. (1980). Phonemic awareness training: What to teach and how to teach it. *Journal of Educational Psychology, 72,* 686–700.

Liberman, I. Y. (1970). Segmentation of the spoken word and reading acquisition. *Bulletin of the Orton Society, 23,* 65–77.

Lindsay, P., and Norman, D. (1972). *Human information processing.* New York: Academic Press.

MacGinitie, W. H. (Ed.). (1973). *Assessment problems in reading.* Newark, DE: International Reading Association.

MacMillan, D. L. (1973). *Behavior modification in education.* New York: Macmillan.

Manis, F. R. (1985). Acquisition of word identification skills in normal and disabled readers. *Journal of Educational Psychology, 77,* 79–80.

Manzo, A. V. (1969). The request procedure. *Journal of Reading, 13,* 123–126.

Margosein, C. M., Pascarella, E. T., and Pflaum, S. W. (1982). The effects of instruction using semantic mapping on vocabulary and comprehension. *Journal of Early Adolescence, 2,* 185–194.

Marsh, G., and Desberg, P. (1978). Mnemonics for phonics. *Contemporary Educational Psychology, 3,* 57–61.

Marshall, N., and Glock, M. D. (1978–1979). Comprehension of connected discourse: A study into the relationships between the structure of text and information recalled. *Reading Research Quarterly, 14*(1), 20–56.

Martin, B. (1967). *Brown bear, brown bear, what do you see?* New York: Holt, Rinehart and Winston.

Marzano, R. J., Greenlaw, J., Tish, G., and Vodehnal, S. (1978). The graded word list is not a shortcut to an IRI. *The Reading Teacher, 31,* 647–651.

Maslow, A. (1970). *Motivation and personality.* New York: Harper and Row.

Mason, J. M. (1976). Overgeneralization in learning to read. *Journal of Reading Behavior, 8,* 173–182.

Mason, J. M. (1983). An examination of reading instruction in third and fourth grade. *The Reading Teacher, 36,* 906–913.

Mason, J. M., and Kendall, J. R. (1979). Facilitating reading comprehension through text structure manipulation. *The Alberta Journal of Educational Research, 25,* 68–76.

Mason, J. M., Kniseley, G., and Kendall, J. (1979). Effects of polysemous words on sentence comprehension. *Reading Research Quarterly, 15,* 49–65.

Mathewson, G. C. (1976). The function of attitude in the reading process. In H. Singer and R. Ruddell (Eds.), *Theoretical models and processes of reading* (2nd ed.) (pp. 655–673). Newark, DE: International Reading Association, 655–673.

Mathewson, G. C. (1985). Toward a comprehensive model of affect in the reading process. In H. Singer and R. Ruddell (Eds.). *Theoretical models and processes of reading* (3rd ed.) (pp. 841–857). Newark, DE: International Reading Association.

Mazurkiewicz, (1976). *Teaching about phonics.* New York: St. Martin's Press.

McBeath, P. M. (1966). *The effectiveness of three reading preparedness programs for perceptually handicapped kindergartners.* Unpublished doctoral dissertation, Stanford University.

McKenna, M. C. (1983). Informal reading inventories: A review of the issues. *The Reading Teacher, 36,* 670–679.

McKeown, M. G., Beck, I. L., Omanson, R. C., and Perfetti, C. A. (1983). The effects of long-term vocabulary instruction on reading comprehension: A replication. *Journal of Reading Behavior, 15,* 3–18.

McNeil, J. D. (1984). *Reading comprehension: New directions for classroom practice.* Glenview, IL: Scott, Foresman.

McNinch, G. H. (1981). A method for teaching sight words to disabled readers. *The Reading Teacher, 35,* 269–272.

Melmed, P. J. (1973). Black English phonology. The question of Reading interference. In J. L. Laffey and R. Shuy (Eds.), *Language differences: Do they interfere?* Newark, DE: International Reading Association, 70–85.

Mercer, C. (1983). *Student with learning disabilities* (2nd ed.). Columbus, OH: Charles E. Merrill.

Mezynski, K. (1983). Issues concerning acquisition of knowledge: Effects of vocabulary training on reading comprehension. *Review of Educational Research, 53,* 253–279.

Miller, S. D., and Smith, D. E. (1985). Differences in literal and inferential comprehension after reading orally and silently. *Journal of Educational Psychology, 77,* 341–348.

Minsky, M. (1975). A framework for representing knowledge. In P. H. Winston (Ed.), *The psychology of computer vision.* New York: McGraw-Hill.

Mitchell, J. V., Jr. (Ed.). (1985). *Ninth Mental Measurements Yearbook,* Lincoln, NB: University of Nebraska Press.

Moe, A. J. (1973). Word lists for beginning readers. *Reading Improvement, 10,* 11–15.

Mosenthal, P. (1976–1977). Psycholinguistic properties of aural and visual comprehension as determined by children's abilities to comprehend syllogisms. *Reading Research Quarterly, 12,* 55–92.

Mosenthal, P. (1981). Diagnostic reading scales. In L. M. Schell (Ed.), *Diagnostic and criterion-referenced reading tests: Review and evaluation* (pp. 23–29). Newark, DE: International Reading Association.

Nagy, W. E., and Anderson, R. C. (1984). The number of words in printed school English. *Reading Research Quarterly, 19,* 304–330.

Nagy, W. E., and Herman, P. A. (1984). *Limitations of vocabulary instruction* (Tech. Rep. No. 326). Champaign, IL: University of Illinois, Center for the Study of Reading.

Nagy, W. E., Herman, P. A., and Anderson, R. C. (1985). Learning words from context. *Reading Research Quarterly, 20,* 233–253.

Natalicio, D. S. (1979). Reading and the bilingual child. In L. B. Resnick and P. A. Weaver (Eds.), *Theory and practice of early reading* (vol. 3). Hillsdale, NJ: Lawrence Erlbaum, 131–149.

Nemko, B. (1984). Context versus isolation: Another look at beginning readers. *Reading Research Quarterly, 19,* 461–467.

Nolte, R. Y., and Singer, H. (1985). Active comprehension. Teaching a process of reading comprehension and its effect on reading achievement. *The Reading Teacher, 39,* 24–31.

O'Donnell, P. (1970). A re-evaluation of research on lateral expression. *Journal of Learning Disabilities, 3,* 344–350.

Omanson, R. C., Beck, I. L., McKeown, M. G., and Perfetti, C. A. (1984). Comprehension of texts with unfamiliar versus recently taught words: An assessment of alternative models. *Journal of Educational Psychology, 76,* 1253–1268.

Orton, J. L. (1966). The Orton-Gillingham approach. In J. Money (Ed.), *The disabled reader.* Baltimore: Johns Hopkins Press, 119–146.

Orton, S. T. (1937). *Reading, writing and speech problems in children.* New York: W. W. Norton.

O'Shea, L. J., and Sindelar, P. T. (1983). The effects of segmenting written discourse on the reading comprehension of low- and high-performance readers. *Reading Research Quarterly, 18,* 458–465.

Otto, W., and Chester, R. (1972). Sight words for beginning readers. *Journal of Educational Research, 65,* 435–443.

Owings, R. A., Peterson, G. A., Bransford, J. D., Morris, C. D., and Stein, B. S. (1980). Spontaneous monitorings and regulation of learning: A comparison of successful and less successful fifth graders. *Journal of Educational Psychology, 72,* 250–256.

Page, E. B. (1958). Teacher comments and student performance: A seventy-four classroom experiment in school motivation. *Journal of Educational Psychology, 49,* 173–181.

Paivio, A. (1971). *Imagery and verbal processes.* New York: Holt, Rinehart and Winston.

Palincsar, A. M., and Brown, A. L. (1984). Reciprocal teaching of comprehension-fostering and comprehension-monitoring activities. *Cognition and Instruction, 1,* 117–175.

Paris, S. G., and Jacobs, J. E. (1984). The benefits of informed instruction for children's reading awareness and comprehension skills. *Child Development, 55,* 2083–2093.

Paris, S. G., and Myers, M. (1981). Comprehension monitoring, memory, and study strategies of good and poor readers. *Journal of Reading Behavior, 8,* 5–22.

Pearson, P. D., and Gallagher, M. C. (1983). The instruction of reading comprehension. *Contemporary Educational Psychology, 8,* 317–344.

Pearson, P. D., Hansen, J., and Gordon, C. (1978). The effect of background knowledge on young children's comprehension of explicit and implicit information. *Journal of Reading Behavior, 11*(3), 201–209.

Pearson, P. D., Hansen, J., and Gordon, C. (1979). The effect of background knowledge on young children's comprehension of explicit and implicit information. *Journal of Reading Behavior*, *11*, 201–209.

Pearson, P. D., and Johnson, D. D. (1978). *Teaching reading comprehension*. New York: Holt, Rinehart and Winston.

Pearson, P. D., and Spiro R. (1980). Toward a theory of comprehension instruction. *Topics in Language Disorders*, *1*, 71–88.

Perfetti, C. A. (1985). *Reading ability*. New York: Oxford University Press.

Pflaum, S. W., and Bryan, T. H. (1980). Oral reading in the learning disabled. *Journal of Educational Research*, *73*, 247–251.

Pflaum, S. W., and Pascarella, E. T. (1980). Interactive effects of prior reading achievement and training in context on the reading of learning-disabled children. *Reading Research Quarterly*, *16*, 138–158.

Pflaum, S. W., Walberg, H., Karegianes, M. L., and Rasher, S. P. (1980). Reading instruction: A quantitative analysis. *Educational Researcher*, *9*, 12–18.

Phillips, S. (1972). Participant structures and communicative competence: Warm Springs children in community and classroom. In C. Cazdeu, D. Hymes, and V. John (Eds.), *Foundations of language in the classroom*. New York: Teachers College Press.

Piaget, J. (1952). *The origins of intelligence in children* (2nd ed.). New York: International University Press.

Pikulski, J. A. (1974). A critical review: Informal reading inventories. *Reading Teacher*, *28*, 141–153.

Pikulski, J. J., and Shanahan, T. (Eds.). (1982a). *Approaches to the informal evaluation of reading*. Newark, DE: International Reading Association.

Pikulski, J. J., and Shanahan, T. (1982b). Informal reading inventories: A critical analysis. In J. J. Pikulski and T. Shanahan (Eds.), *Approaches to the informal evaluation of reading*. Newark, DE: International Reading Association.

Powell, W. R. (1971). The validity of the instructional reading level. In R. E. Leibert (Ed.), *Diagnostic viewpoints in reading*. Newark, DE: International Reading Association.

Powell, W. R. (1979). Reappraising the criteria for interpreting informal reading inventories. In D. DeBoer (Ed.), *Reading diagnosis and evaluation*. Newark, DE: International Reading Association.

Powell, W. R., and Dunkeld, C. G. (1971). Validity of the IRI reading levels. *Elementary English*, *48*, 637–642.

Prell, J. M., and Prell, P. A. (1986). Improving test scores—Teaching test-wiseness. *Research Bulletin, no. 5*. Bloomington, IN: Phi Delta Kappa.

Pressley, M., Levin, J. R., and Miller, G. E. (1981). How does the keyword method affect vocabulary comprehension and usage? *Reading Research Quarterly*, *16*, 213–226.

Quandt, I., and Selznick, R. (1984). *Self-concept and reading*. Newark, DE: International Reading Associaiton.

Rankin, E. F., and Overholser, B. M. (1969). Reaction of intermediate grade children to contextual clues. *Journal of Reading Behavior*, *1*, 50–73.

Rankin, E. F., and Tracy, R. J. (1965). Residual gain as a measure of individual differences in reading improvement. *Journal of Reading*, *8*, 224–333.

Raphael, T. E., and Pearson, P. D. (1985). Increasing students' awareness of sources of information for answering questions. *American Educational Research Journal,* *22,* 217–236.

Raphael, T. E., Winograd, P., and Pearson, P. D. (1980). Strategies children use when answering questions. In M. Kamil and A. Moe (Eds.), *Perspectives on reading research and instruction* (pp. 56–63). Washington, DC: National Reading Conference.

Raphael, T. E., and Wonnacutt, C. A. (1985). Metacognitive training in question-answering strategies: Implementation in a fourth grade developmental reading program. *Reading Research Quarterly, 20,* 282–297.

Rash, J., Johnson, T. D., and Gleadow, N. (1984). Acquisition and retention of written words by kindergarten children under varying learning conditions. *Reading Research Quarterly, 19,* 452–460.

Reder, L. M. (1980). The role of elaboration in the comprehension and retention of prose: A critical review. *Review of Educational Research, 50,* 5–33.

Richek, M. (1976–1977). Reading comprehension of anaphoric forms in varying linguistic contexts. *Reading Research Quarterly, 12,* 145–165.

Richek, M. A., List, L., and Lerner, J. (1983). *Reading problems: Diagnosis and remediation.* Englewood Cliffs, NJ: Prentice-Hall.

Ringness, T. A. (1975). *The affective domain in education.* Boston: Little, Brown.

Robbins, M. P. (1966). The Delacato interpretation of neurological organization. *Reading Research Quarterly, 1,* 57–58.

Robinson, F. P. (1941). Diagnostic and remedial techniques for effective study. New York: Harper and Brothers.

Robinson, H. (1972). Visual and auditory modalities related to methods for beginning reading. *Reading Research Quarterly, 8,* 7–39.

Roehler, L. R., and Duffy, G. G. (1984). Direct explanation of comprehension processes. In G. Duffy, L. Roehler, and J. Mason (Eds.), *Comprehension instruction: Perspectives and suggestions* (pp. 265–280). New York: Longman.

Rosado, M. V. (1982). Reluctant readers respond to the newspaper. *Journal of Reading, 26,* 173.

Rosen, C. L. (1965). Visual deficiencies and reading. *Journal of Reading, 9,* 57–61.

Rosenshine, B., and Stevens, R. (1984). Classroom instruction in reading. In P. D. Pearson (Ed.), *Handbook of reading research.* New York: Longman.

Rosenthal, R., and Jacobson, L. (1968). *Pygmalion in the classroom.* New York: Holt, Rinehart and Winston.

Rosso, B. R., and Emans, R. (1981). Children's use of phonics generalizations. *The Reading Teacher, 34,* 653–658.

Rowell, E. H. (1976). Do elementary students read better orally or silently? *The Reading Teacher, 29,* 367–370.

Rumelhart, D. E. (1979). Some problems with the notion of literal meanings. In A. Ortony (Ed.), *Metaphor and thought.* New York: Cambridge University Press.

Rumelhart, D. E. (1980). Schemata: The building blocks of cognition. In R. J. Spiro, B. C. Bruce, and W. F. Brewer (Eds.), *Theoretical issues in reading comprehension.* Hillsdale, NJ: Lawrence Erlbaum.

Rumelhart, D. E., and Ortony, A. (1977). The representation of knowledge in memory. In R. C. Anderson, R. J. Spiro, and W. F. Montague (Eds.), *Schooling and the acquisition of knowledge.* Hillsdale, NJ: Lawrence Erlbaum.

Rupley, w. H. (1979). ERIC/RCS: Using newspapers to teach reading. *Reading Teacher*, *33*, 346–349.

Ryan, E. B. (1981). Identifying and remediating failures in reading comprehension: Toward an instructional approach for poor comprehenders. In T. G. Waller and G. E. MacKinnon (Eds.), *Advances in reading research: Vol. 2* (pp. 223–261). New York: Academic Press.

Salvia, J., and Ysseldyke, J. E. (1981). *Assessment in special and remedial education* (2nd ed.). Boston: Houghton-Mifflin.

Samuels, S. J. (1979). The method of repeated readings. *The Reading Teacher, 32*, 403–408.

Sartain, H. W. (1970). *Reading attitude inventory*. In H. J. Heimberger (ERIC No. ED 045 291).

Schoolfield, L., and Timberlake, J. B. (1968). *The phonovisual method book*. Washington, DC: Phonovisual Products.

Schank, R. C. (1972). Conceptual dependency: A theory of natural language understanding. *Cognitive Psychology, 3*, 552–631.

Schell, L. M. (Ed.), (1981). *Diagnostic and criterion-referenced reading tests: Review and evaluation*. Newark, DE: International Reading Association.

Schell, L. M., and Jennings, R. E. (1981). Test review: Durrell analysis of reading difficulty (3rd ed.). *The Reading Teacher, 35*(2), 204–210.

Schreiner, R. L. (1978). Diagnostic reading scales (rev. ed.). In O. K. Buros (Ed.), *Eighth mental measurements yearbook* (pp. 1242–1243). Highland Park, NJ: Gryphon Press.

Schreiner, R. L. (Ed.) (1979). *Reading tests and teachers: A practical guide*. Newark, DE: International Reading Association.

Sherman, T. M., and Wildman, T. M. (1982). *Proven strategies for successful test taking*. Columbus, OH: Charles E. Merrill.

Shoben, E. J. (1980). Theories of semantic memory: Approach to knowledge and sentence comprehension. In R. J. Spiro, B. C. Bruce, and W. F. Brewer (Eds.), *Theoretical issues in reading comprehension*. Hillsdale, NJ: Lawrence Erlbaum.

Simon, H., and Johnson, K. Black English syntax and reading interference. *Research in the teaching of English*, 1974, *8*, 339–358.

Simons, H. D. (1979). Black dialect, reading interference, and classroom interaction. In L. B. Resnict and P. A. Weaver (Eds.), Theory and practice of early reading (vol 3). Hillsdale, NJ: Lawrence Erlbaum, 111–129.

Singer, H. (1978a). Active comprehension: From answering to asking questions. *The Reading Teacher*, 901–908.

Singer, H. (1978b). Gates-McKillop reading diagnostic tests. In O. K. Buros (Ed.), Eighth mental measurements yearbook (pp. 1252–1254). Highland Park, NJ: Gryphon Press.

Singer, H., and Donlan, D. (1982). Active comprehension: Problem solving schema with question generation for comprehension of complex short stories. *Reading Research Quarterly, 17*(2), 166–186.

Singer, H., Samuels, S. J., and Spiroff, J. (1974). Effects of pictures and contextual conditions on learning responses to printed words. *Reading Research Quarterly*, *5*, 427–451.

Skinner, B. F. (1953). *Science and human behavior*. New York: Macmillan.

Sledd, S. (1969). Bi-dialectalism: The linguistics of white supremacy. *English Journal, 58*, 176 184.

Smith, E. B., Goodman, K. S., and Meredith, R. (1970). *Language and thinking in the elementary school.* New York: Holt, Rinehart and Winston.

Smith, F. (1971). Understanding reading: A psycholinguistic analysis of reading learning to read. New York: Holt, Rinehart and Winston.

Smith, F. (1975). *Comprehension and learning.* New York: Holt, Rinehart and Winston.

Spache, G. (1981). *Diagnosing and correcting reading disabilities* (2nd ed.). Boston: Allyn and Bacon.

Stafford, J. (1973). The diagnostic reading scales. *Reading World, 14*, 5–8.

Stahl, S. (1983). Differential word knowledge and reading comprehension. *Journal of Reading Behavior, 15*, 33–50.

Stanovich, K. E. (1980). Toward an interactive-compensatory model of individual differences in the development of reading fluency. *Reading Research Quarterly, 16*, 32–71.

Stanovich, K. E., Cunningham, A. E., and Feeman, D. J. (1984a). Intelligence, cognitive skills, and early reading progress. *Reading Research Quarterly, 19*, 278–303.

Stanovich, K. E., Cunningham, A. E., and Feeman, D. J. (1984b). Relation between early reading acquisition and word decoding with and without decoding. *Journal of Educational Psychology, 76*, 668–667.

Stanovich, K. E., Cunningham, A. E., and West, R. F. (1981). A longitudinal study of the development of automatic recognition skills in first graders. *Journal of Reading Behavior, 13*, 57–74.

Stauffer, R. G. (1969). *Directing reading maturity as a cognitive process.* New York: Harper and Row.

Stauffer, R. G. (1970). *The language experience approach to reading instruction.* New York: Harper and Row.

Steinberg, R., and Powell, W. (1983). Comprehending verbal comprehension. *American Psychologist, 38*, 878–893.

Stevens, K. C. (1981). Chunking material as an aid to reading comprehension. *Journal of Reading, 25*, 126–129.

Stevens, K. C. (1982). Can we improve reading by teaching background information: *Journal of Reading, 25*, 326–329.

Suchoff, I. B. (1981). Research in the relationship between reading and vision—What does it mean? *Journal of Learning Disabilities, 14*, 573–576.

Taylor, B. M. (1982). Text structure and children's comprehension and memory for expository material. *Journal of Educational Psychology, 74*, 323–340.

Taylor, B. M. (1984). The search for a meaningful approach to assessing comprehension of expository text. In J. Niles and L. Harris (Eds.), *Changing perspectives on research in reading language processing and instruction* (pp. 257–263). Rochester, NY: National Reading Conference.

Taylor, B. M. (1985a). Improving middle-grade students' reading and writing of expository text. *Journal of Educational Research, 79*, 119–125.

Taylor, B. M. (1985b). *Teaching middle grade students to read for main ideas.* Paper presented at the annual meeting of the National Reading Conference, San Diego.

Taylor, B. M. (1985c) Toward an understanding of factors contributing to children's difficulty summarizing textbook material. In J. Niles and R. Lalik (Eds.), *Issues in literacy: A research perspective* (pp. 125–131). Rochester, NY: National Reading Conference.

Taylor, B. M. (1986). Teaching middle grade students to summarize content textbook material. In J. Baumann (Ed.), *Teaching main idea comprehension*. Newark, DE: International Reading Association.

Taylor, B. M., and Beach, R. W. (1984). The effects of text structure instruction on middle grade students' comprehension and production of expository texts. *Reading Research Quarterly, 19*, 134–146.

Taylor, B. M., and Berkowitz, S. B. (1980). Facilitating children's comprehension of content area material. In M. Kamil and A. Moe (Eds.), *Perspectives on reading research and instruction* (pp. 64–68). Washington, DC: National Reading Conference.

Taylor, B. M., and Frye, B. (1987). *Reducing time on skill instruction and practice and increasing time on independent reading in the elementary classroom*. University of Minnesota, manuscript submitted for publication.

Taylor, B. M., and Nosbush, L. (1983). Oral reading for meaning: A technique for improving word identification. *The Reading Teacher, 37*, 234–237.

Taylor, B. M., Olson, V., Prenn, M., Rybczynski, M., and Zakaluk, B. (1985). A comparison of students' ability to read for main ideas in social studies and to complete main idea worksheets. *Reading World, 24*, 10–15.

Tharp, R. G. (1982). The effective instruction of comprehension: Results and description of the Kamehameha Early Education Program. *Reading Research Quarterly, 17*, 503–527.

Thoms, S. (1982). *A comparison of different approaches to vocabulary instruction*. Unpublished doctoral dissertation. University of Wisconsin.

Thorndike, R. L. (1973). *Reading comprehension education in fifteen countries*. New York: Wiley.

Tierney, R. J., and Cunningham, J. W. (1984). Research on teaching reading comprehension. In P. D. Pearson (Ed.), *Handbook of reading research* (pp. 609–655). New York: Longman.

Tindal, G., Marston, D., and Deno, S. L. (1983). *The reliability of direct and repeated measure* (Research Report No. 109). Minneapolis, University of Minnesota, IRLD.

Tuinman, J. J. (1978). Woodcock reading mastery tests. In O. K. Buros (Ed.), *Eighth mental measurements yearbook* (pp. 1306–1308)⟩ Highland Park, NJ: Gryphon Press.

Van Allen, R. (1976). *Language experiences in communication*. Boston: Houghton-Mifflin.

van Dijk, T. A., and Kintsch, W. (1983). *Strategies of discourse comprehension*. New York: Academic Press.

Veatch, J. (1959). *Individualizing your reading program*. New York: G. P. Putnam.

Veatch, J., et al. (1979). *Key words to reading: The language experience approach begins*. Columbus, OH: Charles E. Merrill.

Venezky, R. L., and Johnson, D. (1973). Development of two letter-sound patterns in grade one through three. *Journal of Educational Psychology, 64*, 109–115.

Wagner, G., and Hosier, M. (1970). *Reading games*. New York: Macmillan.

Wagoner, S. A. (1983). Comprehension monitoring: What it is and what we know about it. *Reading Research Quarterly, 17,* 328–346.

Weiner, B. (1974). *Achievement motivation as conceptualized by an attribution theory* (pp. 3–48). Morriston, NJ: General Learning Press.

Weintraub, S. (1972). *Auditory perception and deafness.* Newark, DE: International Reading Association.

Weintraub, S., and Cowan, R. J. (1982). *Vision/visual perception: An annotated bibliography,* Newark, DE: International Reading Association.

White, R. W. (1959). Motivation reconsidered: The concept of competence. *Psychological Review, 66,* 297–333.

Williams, J. P. (1979). The ABD's of reading: A program for the learning-disabled. In L. B. Resnick and P. A. Weaver (Eds.), *Theory and practice in beginning reading, Vol. 3.* Hillsdale, NJ: Lawrence Erlbaum.

Williams, J. P. (1980). Teaching decoding with an emphasis on phoneme analysis and phoneme blending. *Journal of Educational Psychology, 72,* 1–15.

Williams, J. P. (1985). The case for explicit decoding instruction. In J. Osborn, P. T. Wilson, and R. C. Anderson (Eds.), *Reading Education: Foundations for a literate America* (pp. 205–213). Lexington, MA: Lexington Books.

Williamson, L. E., and Young, F. (1974). The IRI and RMI diagnostic concepts should be synthesized. *Journal of Reading Behavior, 6,* 183–194.

Willows, D. M., and Ryan, E. B. (1981). Differential utilization of syntactic and semantic information by skilled and less skilled readers in the itermediate grades. *Journal of Educational Psychology, 73,* 607–615.

Wilson, M. M. (1979). The processing strategies of average and below average readers answering factual and inferential questions on three equivalent passages. *Journal of Reading Behavior, 11,* 235–245.

Winograd, P. N. (1984). Strategic difficulties in summarizing texts. *Reading Research Quarterly, 19,* 404–425.

Wixson, K. (1979). Miscue analysis: A critical review. *Journal of Reading Behavior, 11,* 163–175.

Woodcock, R. W. (1973). *Woodcock reading mastery tests.* Circle Pines, MN. American Guidance Service.

Woods, M. L., and Moe, A. J. (1981). *Analytical reading inventory.* Columbus, OH: Charles E. Merrill.

Wright, G. (1979). The comic book—A forgotten medium in the classroom. *The Reading Teacher, 33* (2), 158–161.

Yacorzynsky G., and Tucker, B. (1960). What price intelligence? *American Psychologist, 15,* 201–203.

Zigmond, N., and Silverman, R. C. (1984). Informal assessment for program planning and evaluation in special education. *Educational Psychologist, 19,* 163–171.

Index

ABOUT THE AUTHORS

Barbara Taylor is associate professor of education at the University of Minnesota, where she has taught since 1978. A former elementary and high school teacher, she received her Ed.D. from Virginia Tech. In addition to this text, she is currently co-authoring a language arts text with Diane Monson and Robert Dykstra.

Larry Harris is associate dean of the graduate school at Virginia Tech, where he has taught since 1974. After receiving his Ph.D. from the University of Minnesota, he taught at the University of North Dakota and at Indiana University. He is co-author (with Carl Smith) of a highly successful elementary methods text entitled *Reading Instruction*, 4e.

P. David Pearson is professor of education and co-director of the Center for the Study of Reading at the University of Illinois. He received his Ph.D. from the University of Minnesota, where he taught for several years before moving to Illinois. His publications include *Teaching Reading Comprehension* and *Teaching Reading Vocabulary*, both with Dale Johnson at the University of Wisconsin, as well as the highly respected *Handbook of Research on Reading*, for which he is the general editor.